shade the changing girl

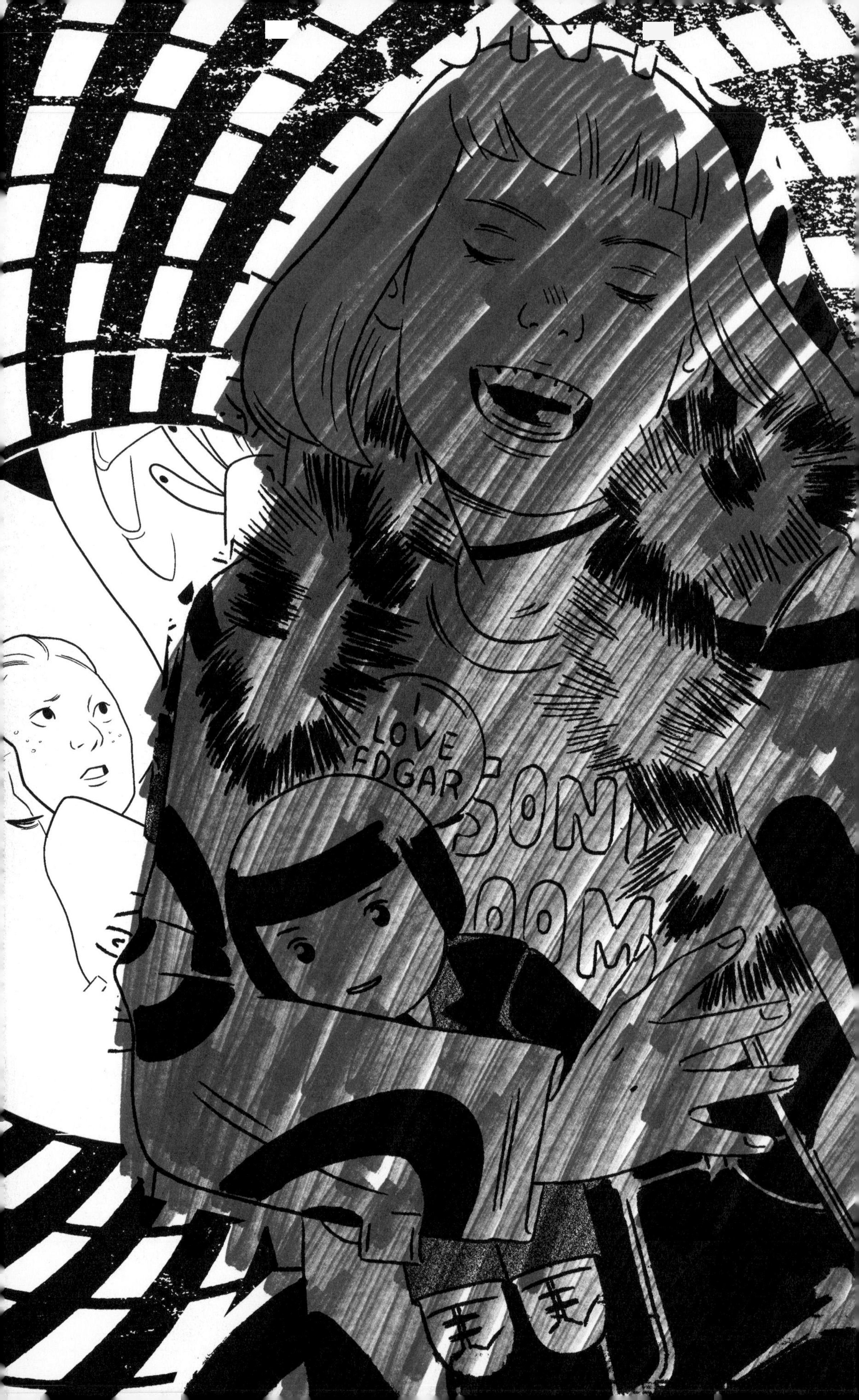
I LOVE EDGAR

shade the changing girl

VOL. 2: LITTLE RUNAWAY

CECIL CASTELLUCCI Writer

MARLEY ZARCONE
ANDE PARKS MARGUERITE SAUVAGE Artists

KELLY FITZPATRICK Colorist
SAIDA TEMOFONTE Letterer
BECKY CLOONAN Cover Art and Original Series Covers
GERARD WAY DC's Young Animal Curator
SHADE, THE CHANGING MAN CREATED BY STEVE DITKO

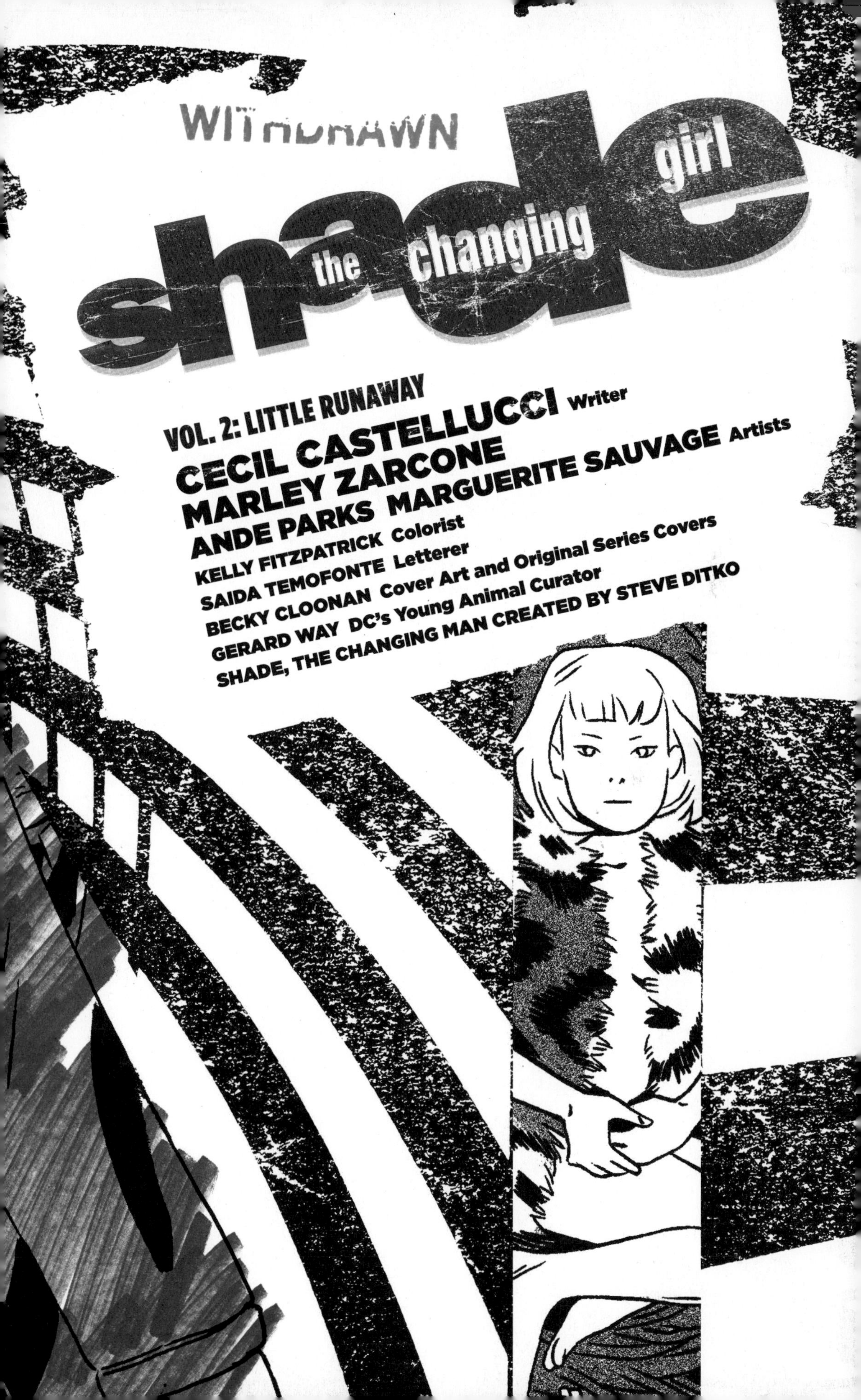

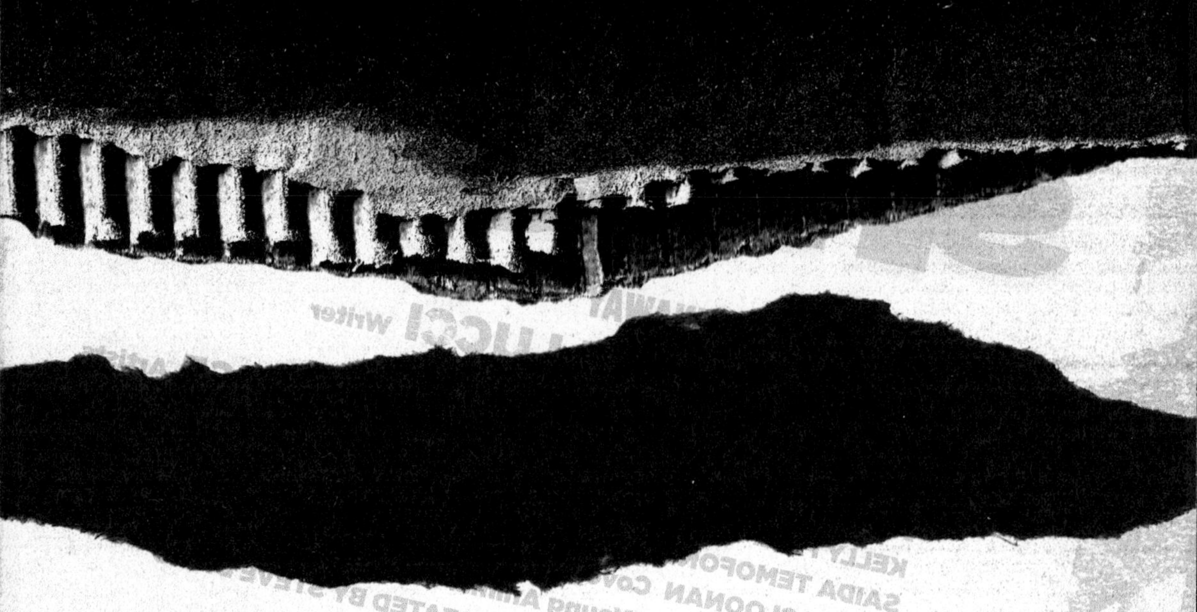

Jamie S. Rich
Molly Mahan Editors – Original Series
Jeb Woodard Group Editor – Collected Editions
Scott Nybakken Editor – Collected Edition
Steve Cook Design Director – Books
Louis Prandi Publication Design

Bob Harras Senior VP – Editor-in-Chief, DC Comics
Mark Doyle Executive Editor, Vertigo

Diane Nelson President
Dan DiDio Publisher
Jim Lee Publisher
Geoff Johns President & Chief Creative Officer
Amit Desai Executive VP – Business & Marketing Strategy,
Direct to Consumer & Global Franchise Management
Sam Ades Senior VP & General Manager, Digital Services
Bobbie Chase VP & Executive Editor, Young Reader & Talent Development
Mark Chiarello Senior VP – Art, Design & Collected Editions
John Cunningham Senior VP – Sales & Trade Marketing
Anne DePies Senior VP – Business Strategy, Finance & Administration
Don Falletti VP – Manufacturing Operations
Lawrence Ganem VP – Editorial Administration & Talent Relations
Alison Gill Senior VP – Manufacturing & Operations
Hank Kanalz Senior VP – Editorial Strategy & Administration
Jay Kogan VP – Legal Affairs
Jack Mahan VP – Business Affairs
Nick J. Napolitano VP – Manufacturing Administration
Eddie Scannell VP – Consumer Marketing
Courtney Simmons Senior VP – Publicity & Communications
Jim (Ski) Sokolowski VP – Comic Book Specialty Sales & Trade Marketing
Nancy Spears VP – Mass, Book, Digital Sales & Trade Marketing
Michele R. Wells VP – Content Strategy

SHADE, THE CHANGING GIRL VOL. 2: LITTLE RUNAWAY

Published by DC Comics. Compilation and all new material
Copyright © 2018 DC Comics. All Rights Reserved.

Originally published in single magazine form in SHADE, THE CHANGING
GIRL 7-12. Copyright © 2017 DC Comics. All Rights Reserved. All characters,
their distinctive likenesses and related elements featured in this
publication are trademarks of DC Comics. The stories, characters and
incidents featured in this publication are entirely fictional. DC Comics does
not read or accept unsolicited submissions of ideas, stories or artwork.

DC Comics
2900 West Alameda Avenue
Burbank, CA 91505
Printed by LSC Communications, Owensville, MO, USA. 12/29/17.
First Printing.
ISBN: 978-1-4012-7545-7

Library of Congress Cataloging-in-Publication Data is available.

MIX
Paper from
responsible sources
FSC® C132124

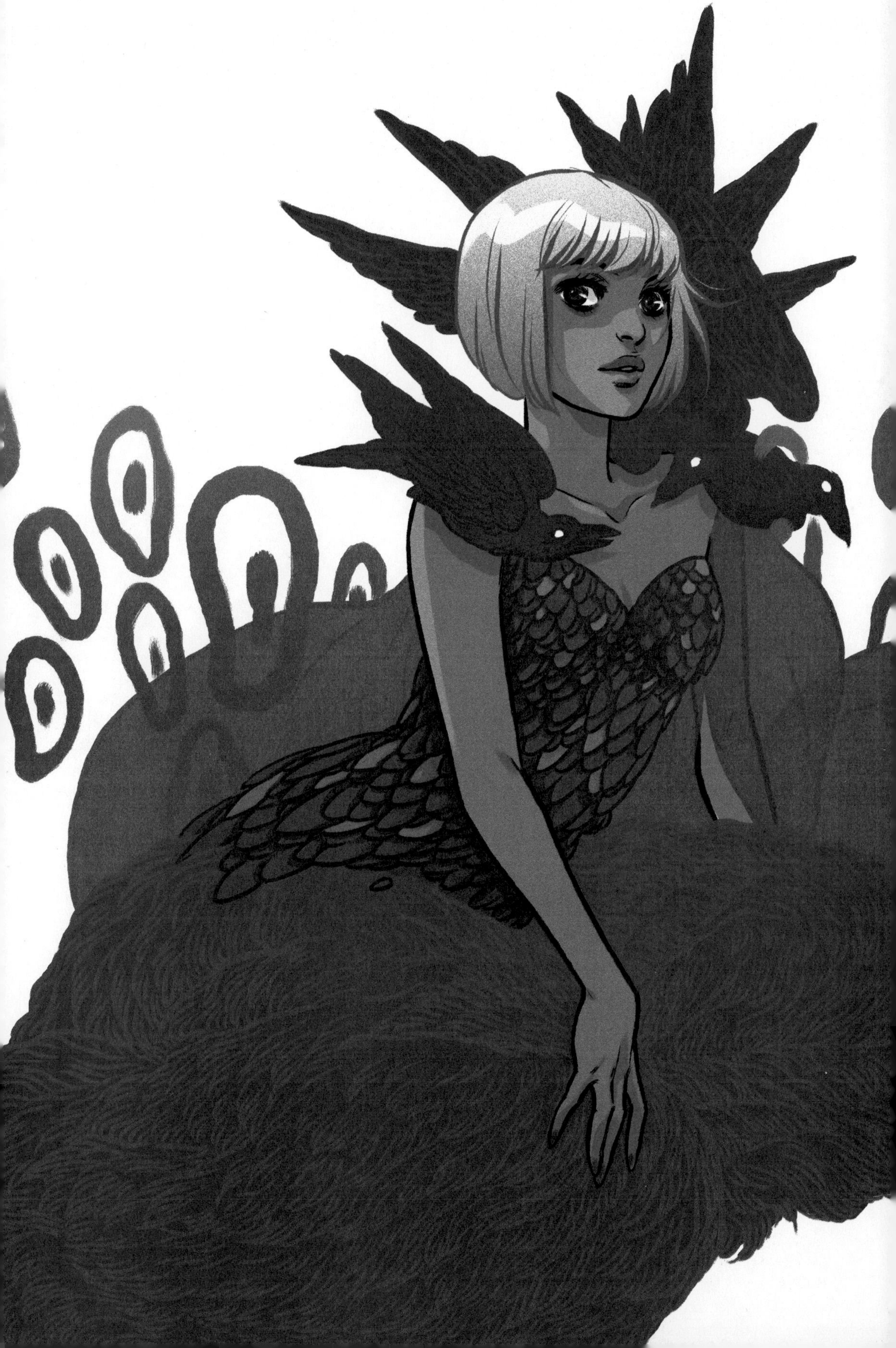

Variant cover art by Marguerite Sauvage

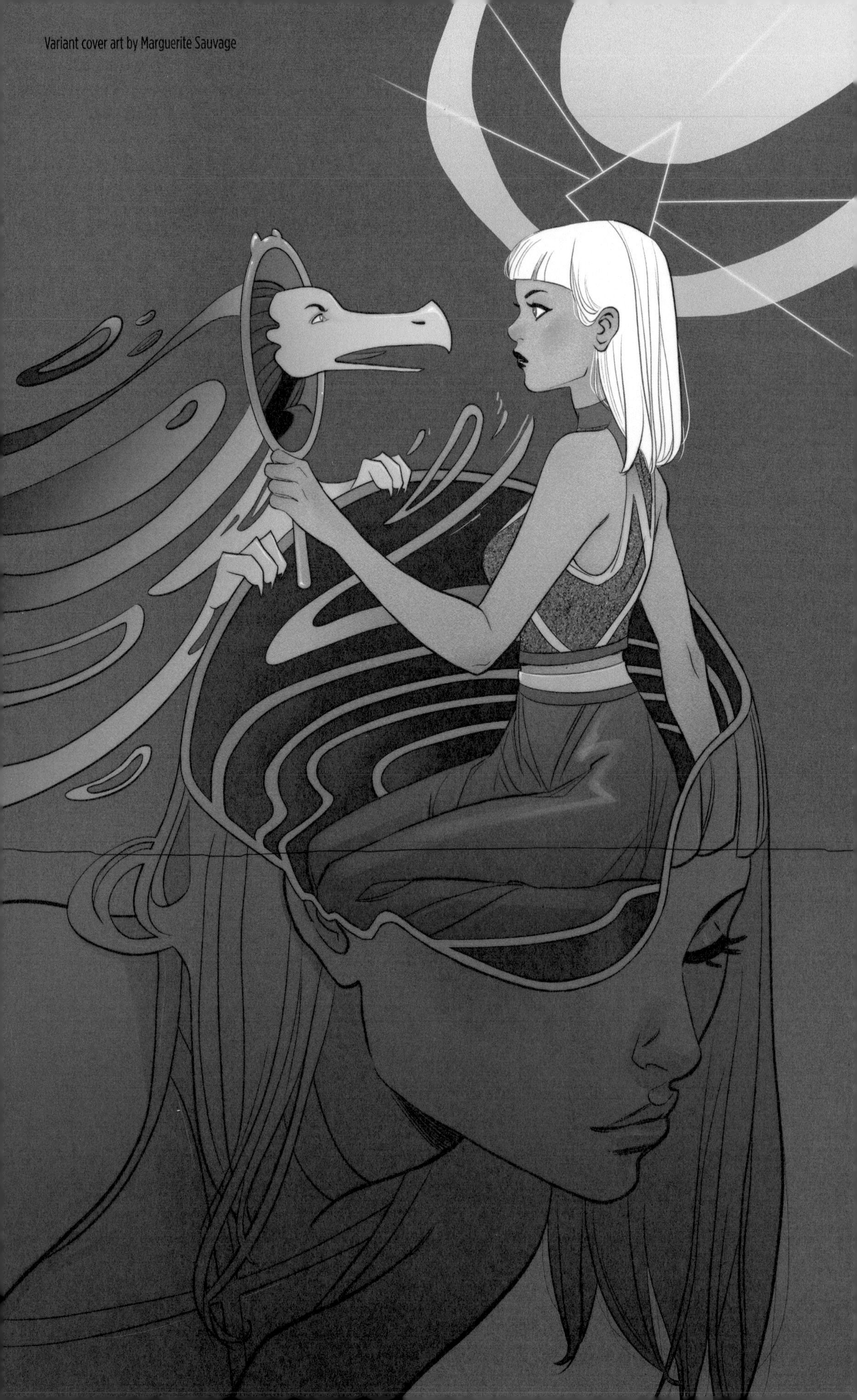

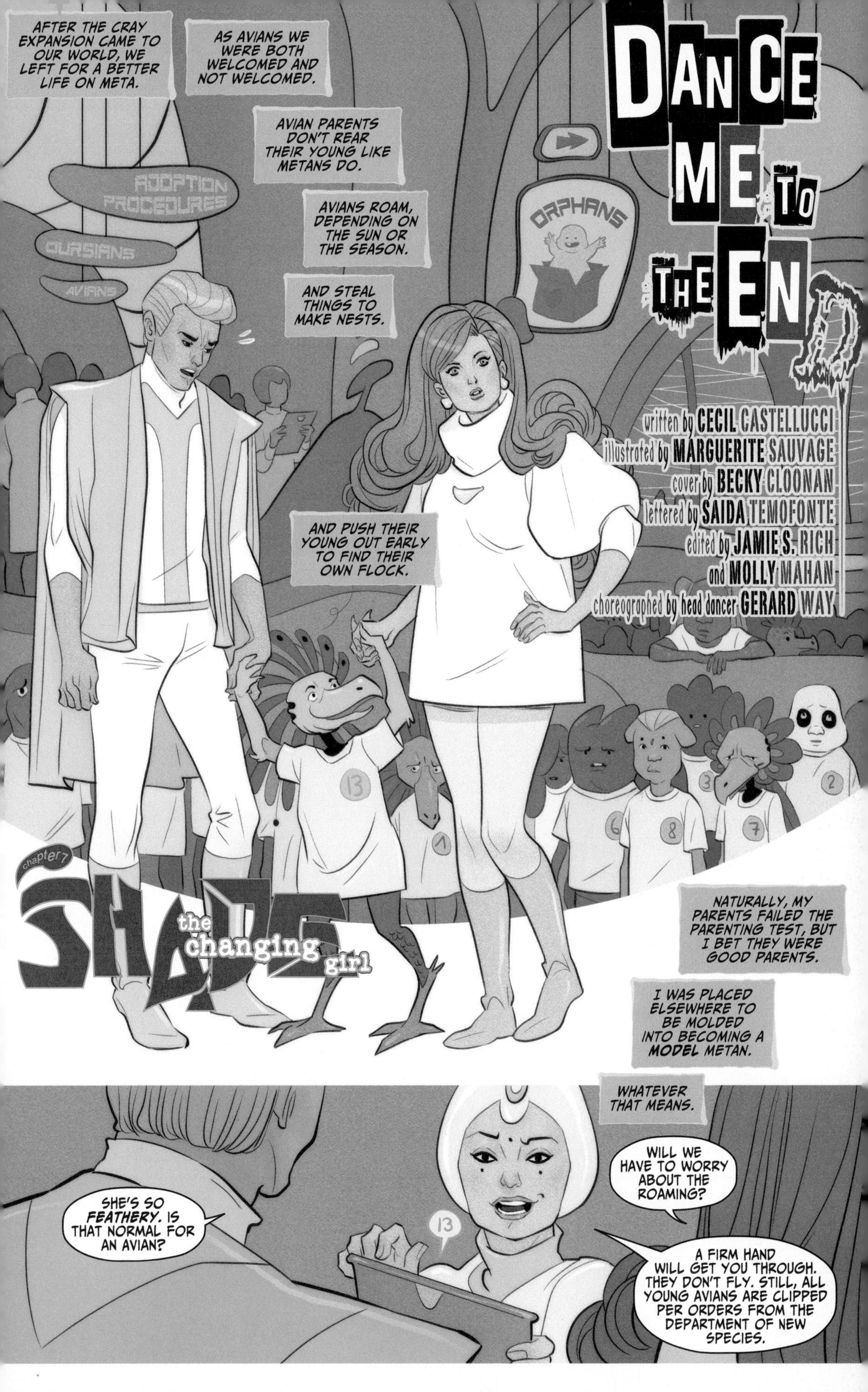
AFTER THE CRAY EXPANSION CAME TO OUR WORLD, WE LEFT FOR A BETTER LIFE ON META.
AS AVIANS WE WERE BOTH WELCOMED AND NOT WELCOMED.
AVIAN PARENTS DON'T REAR THEIR YOUNG LIKE METANS DO.
AVIANS ROAM, DEPENDING ON THE SUN OR THE SEASON.
AND STEAL THINGS TO MAKE NESTS.
ADOPTION PROCEDURES
OURSIANS
AVIANS
ORPHANS
DANCE ME TO THE END
written by CECIL CASTELLUCCI
illustrated by MARGUERITE SAUVAGE
cover by BECKY CLOONAN
lettered by SAIDA TEMOFONTE
edited by JAMIE S. RICH
and MOLLY MAHAN
choreographed by head dancer GERARD WAY
AND PUSH THEIR YOUNG OUT EARLY TO FIND THEIR OWN FLOCK.
chapter 7
SHADE the changing girl
NATURALLY, MY PARENTS FAILED THE PARENTING TEST, BUT I BET THEY WERE GOOD PARENTS.
I WAS PLACED ELSEWHERE TO BE MOLDED INTO BECOMING A MODEL METAN.
WHATEVER THAT MEANS.
SHE'S SO FEATHERY. IS THAT NORMAL FOR AN AVIAN?
WILL WE HAVE TO WORRY ABOUT THE ROAMING?
A FIRM HAND WILL GET YOU THROUGH. THEY DON'T FLY. STILL, ALL YOUNG AVIANS ARE CLIPPED PER ORDERS FROM THE DEPARTMENT OF NEW SPECIES.

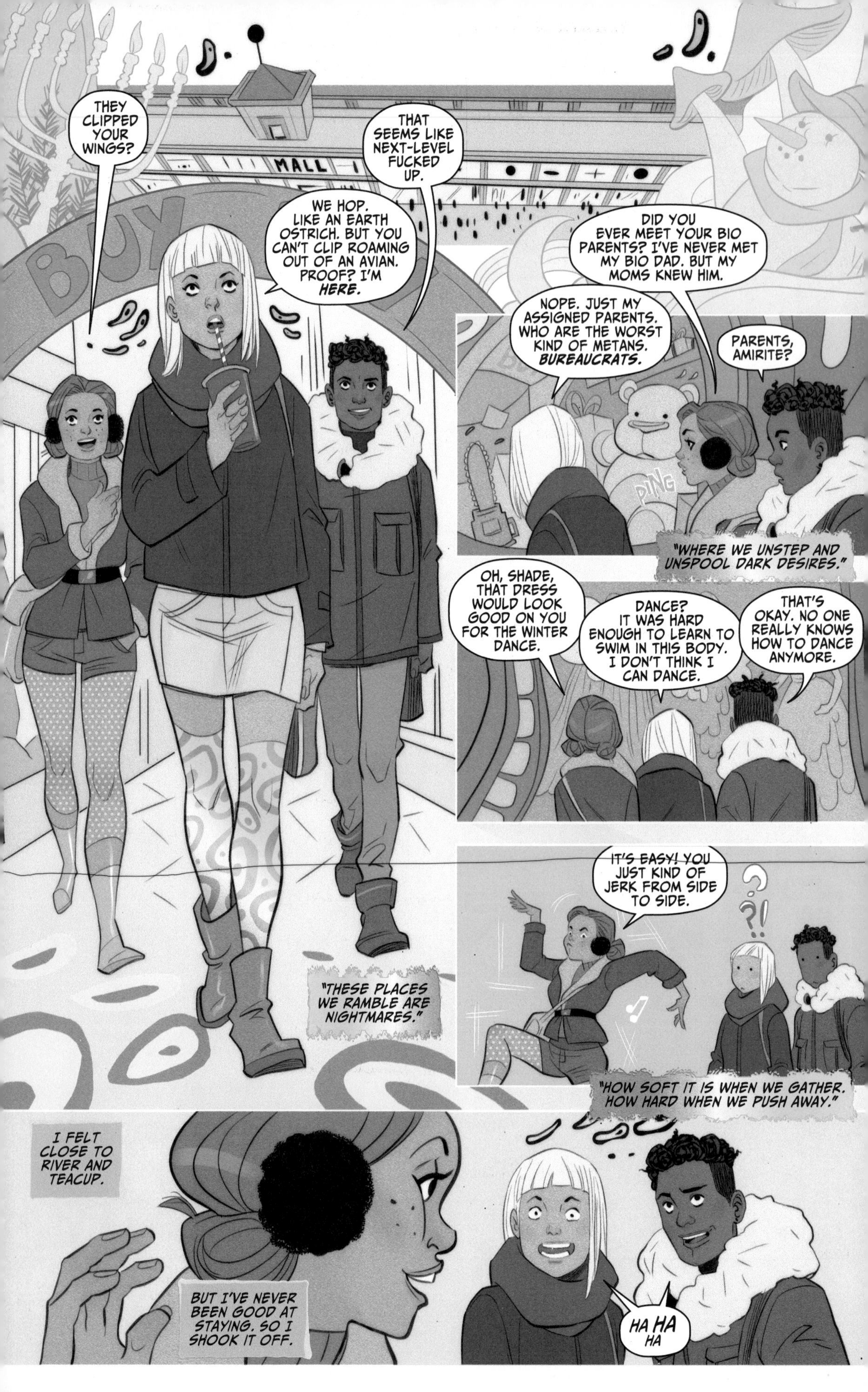
MALL
BUY
THEY CLIPPED YOUR WINGS?
WE HOP. LIKE AN EARTH OSTRICH. BUT YOU CAN'T CLIP ROAMING OUT OF AN AVIAN. PROOF? I'M *HERE.*
THAT SEEMS LIKE NEXT-LEVEL FUCKED UP.
"THESE PLACES WE RAMBLE ARE NIGHTMARES."
DID YOU EVER MEET YOUR BIO PARENTS? I'VE NEVER MET MY BIO DAD. BUT MY MOMS KNEW HIM.
NOPE. JUST MY ASSIGNED PARENTS. WHO ARE THE WORST KIND OF METANS. *BUREAUCRATS.*
PARENTS, AMIRITE?
PING
"WHERE WE UNSTEP AND UNSPOOL DARK DESIRES."
OH, SHADE, THAT DRESS WOULD LOOK GOOD ON YOU FOR THE WINTER DANCE.
DANCE? IT WAS HARD ENOUGH TO LEARN TO SWIM IN THIS BODY. I DON'T THINK I CAN DANCE.
THAT'S OKAY. NO ONE REALLY KNOWS HOW TO DANCE ANYMORE.
IT'S EASY! YOU JUST KIND OF JERK FROM SIDE TO SIDE.
?
?!
"HOW SOFT IT IS WHEN WE GATHER. HOW HARD WHEN WE PUSH AWAY."
I FELT CLOSE TO RIVER AND TEACUP.
BUT I'VE NEVER BEEN GOOD AT STAYING. SO I SHOOK IT OFF.
HA HA HA

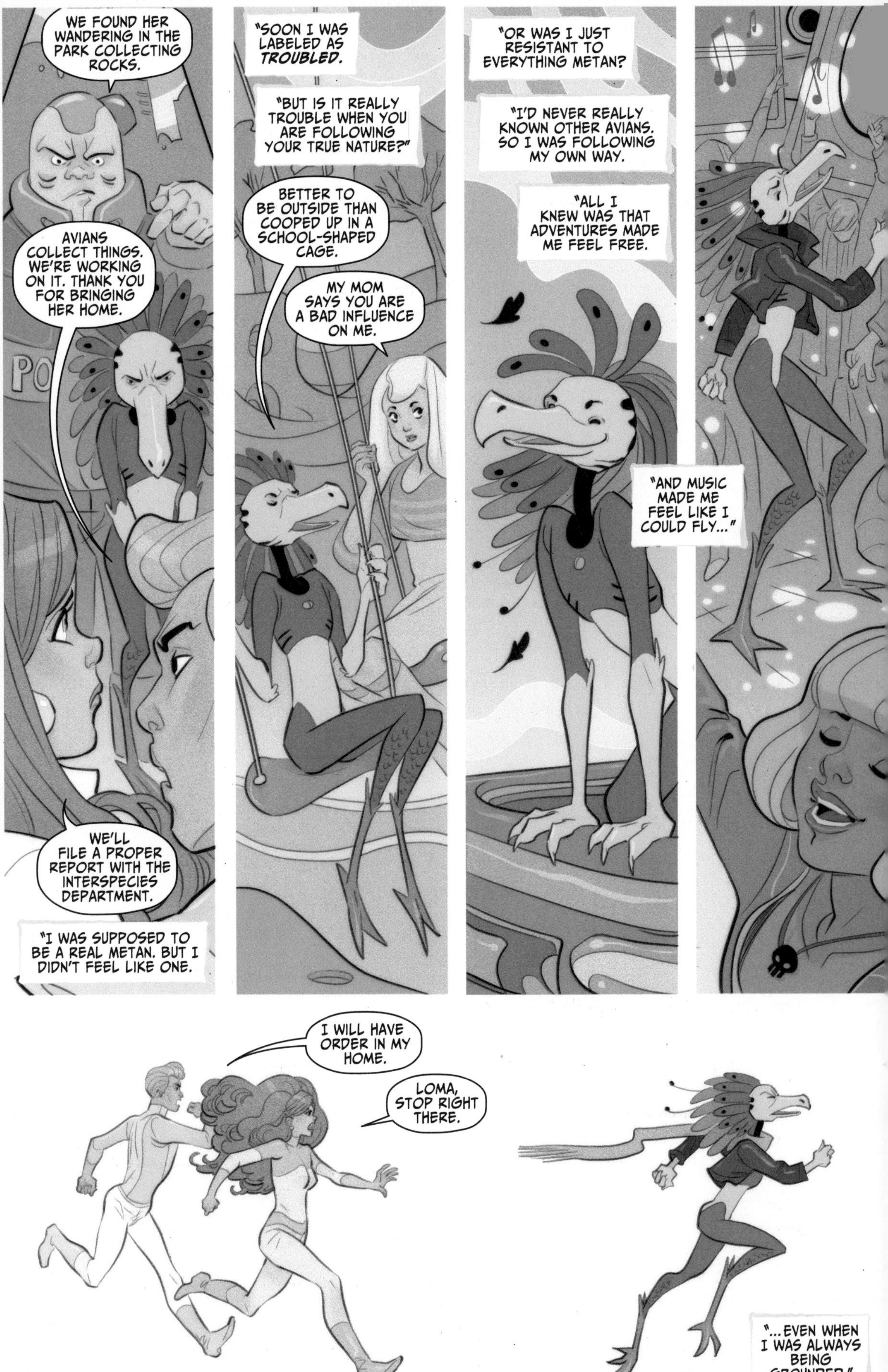
WE FOUND HER WANDERING IN THE PARK COLLECTING ROCKS.
AVIANS COLLECT THINGS. WE'RE WORKING ON IT. THANK YOU FOR BRINGING HER HOME.
PO
WE'LL FILE A PROPER REPORT WITH THE INTERSPECIES DEPARTMENT.
"I WAS SUPPOSED TO BE A REAL METAN. BUT I DIDN'T FEEL LIKE ONE.
"SOON I WAS LABELED AS *TROUBLED*.
"BUT IS IT REALLY TROUBLE WHEN YOU ARE FOLLOWING YOUR TRUE NATURE?"
BETTER TO BE OUTSIDE THAN COOPED UP IN A SCHOOL-SHAPED CAGE.
MY MOM SAYS YOU ARE A BAD INFLUENCE ON ME.
"OR WAS I JUST RESISTANT TO EVERYTHING METAN?
"I'D NEVER REALLY KNOWN OTHER AVIANS. SO I WAS FOLLOWING MY OWN WAY.
"ALL I KNEW WAS THAT ADVENTURES MADE ME FEEL FREE.
"AND MUSIC MADE ME FEEL LIKE I COULD FLY..."
I WILL HAVE ORDER IN MY HOME.
LOMA, STOP RIGHT THERE.
"...EVEN WHEN I WAS ALWAYS BEING GROUNDED."

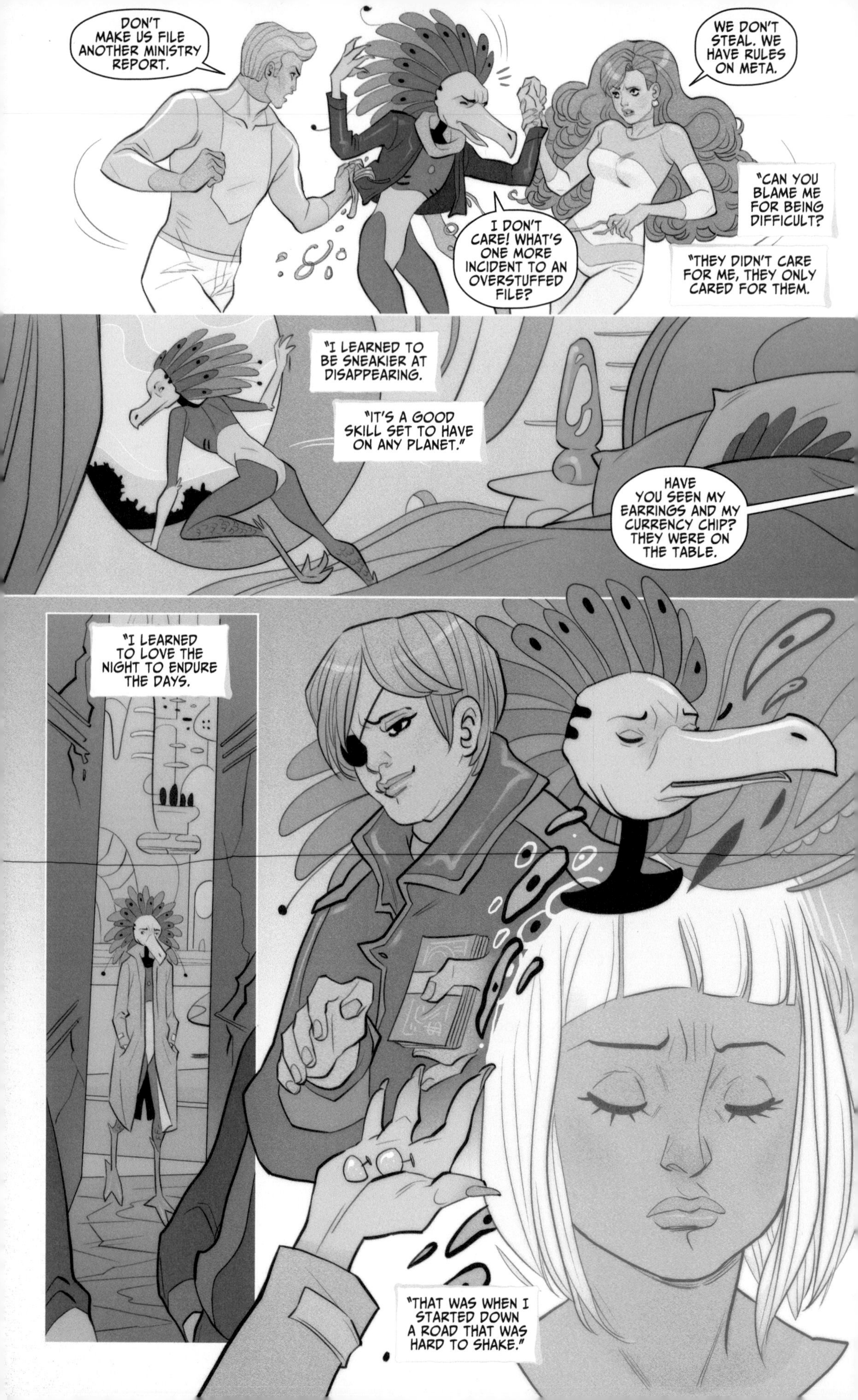
DON'T MAKE US FILE ANOTHER MINISTRY REPORT.
WE DON'T STEAL. WE HAVE RULES ON META.
I DON'T CARE! WHAT'S ONE MORE INCIDENT TO AN OVERSTUFFED FILE?
"CAN YOU BLAME ME FOR BEING DIFFICULT?
"THEY DIDN'T CARE FOR ME, THEY ONLY CARED FOR THEM.
"I LEARNED TO BE SNEAKIER AT DISAPPEARING.
"IT'S A GOOD SKILL SET TO HAVE ON ANY PLANET."
HAVE YOU SEEN MY EARRINGS AND MY CURRENCY CHIP? THEY WERE ON THE TABLE.
"I LEARNED TO LOVE THE NIGHT TO ENDURE THE DAYS.
"THAT WAS WHEN I STARTED DOWN A ROAD THAT WAS HARD TO SHAKE."

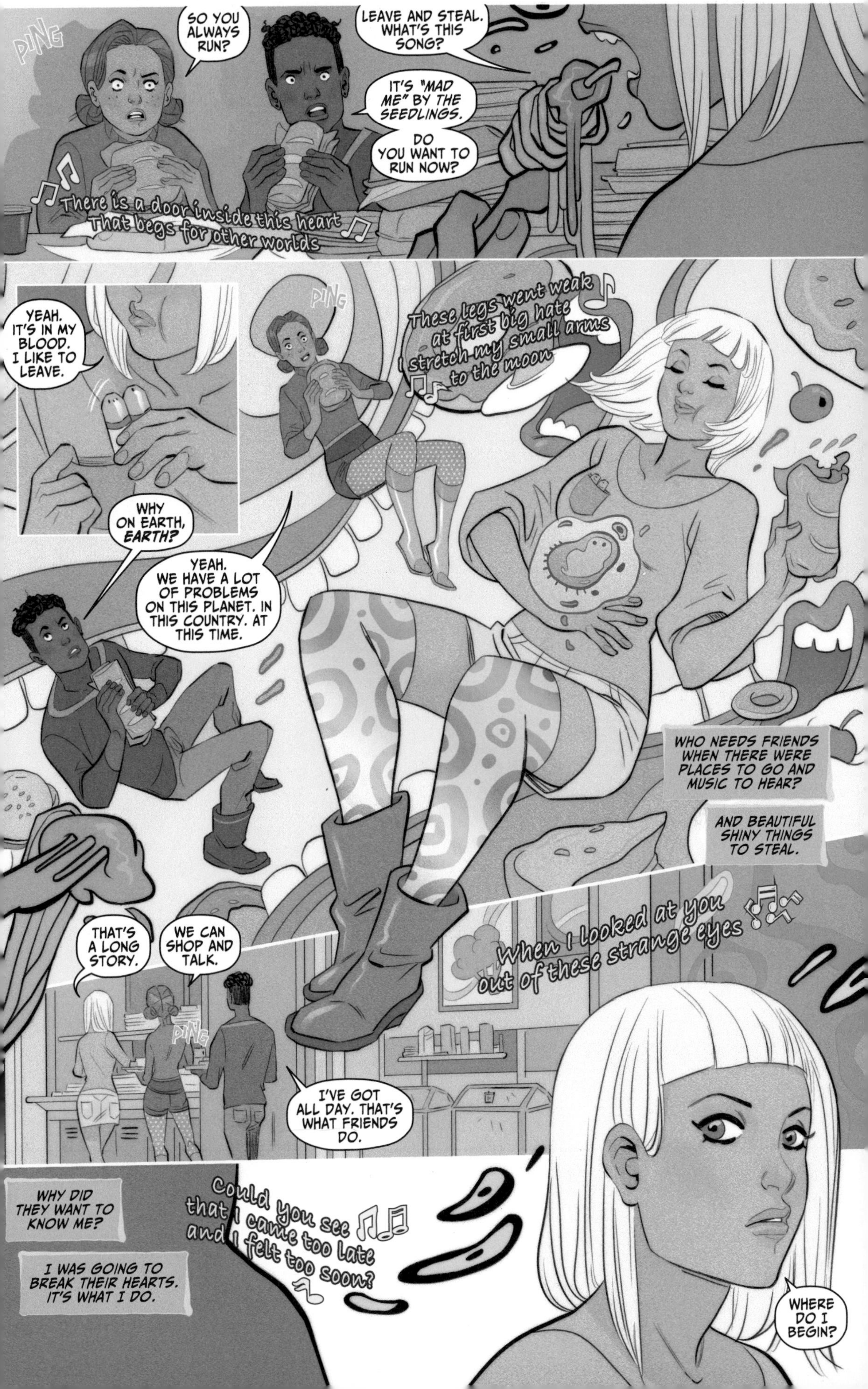
PING
SO YOU ALWAYS RUN?
LEAVE AND STEAL. WHAT'S THIS SONG?
IT'S "MAD ME" BY THE SEEDLINGS.
DO YOU WANT TO RUN NOW?
There is a door inside this heart
That begs for other worlds
YEAH. IT'S IN MY BLOOD. I LIKE TO LEAVE.
PING
These legs went weak
at first big hate
I stretch my small arms
to the moon
WHY ON EARTH, EARTH?
YEAH. WE HAVE A LOT OF PROBLEMS ON THIS PLANET. IN THIS COUNTRY. AT THIS TIME.
WHO NEEDS FRIENDS WHEN THERE WERE PLACES TO GO AND MUSIC TO HEAR?
AND BEAUTIFUL SHINY THINGS TO STEAL.
THAT'S A LONG STORY.
WE CAN SHOP AND TALK.
PING
I'VE GOT ALL DAY. THAT'S WHAT FRIENDS DO.
When I looked at you
out of these strange eyes
WHY DID THEY WANT TO KNOW ME?
I WAS GOING TO BREAK THEIR HEARTS. IT'S WHAT I DO.
Could you see
that I came too late
and I felt too soon?
WHERE DO I BEGIN?

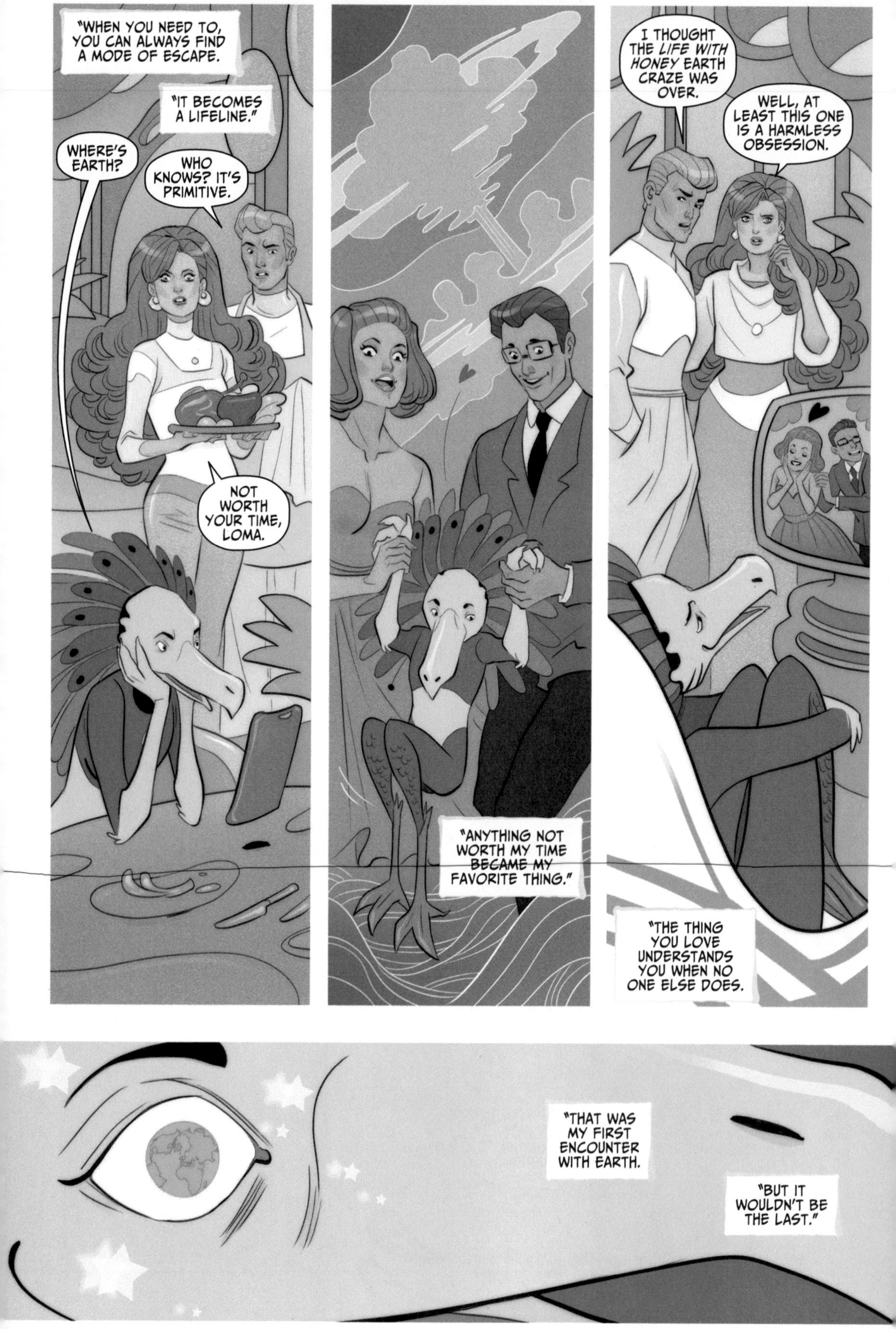
"WHEN YOU NEED TO, YOU CAN ALWAYS FIND A MODE OF ESCAPE.
"IT BECOMES A LIFELINE."
WHERE'S EARTH?
WHO KNOWS? IT'S PRIMITIVE.
NOT WORTH YOUR TIME, LOMA.
"ANYTHING NOT WORTH MY TIME BECAME MY FAVORITE THING."
I THOUGHT THE *LIFE WITH HONEY* EARTH CRAZE WAS OVER.
WELL, AT LEAST THIS ONE IS A HARMLESS OBSESSION.
"THE THING YOU LOVE UNDERSTANDS YOU WHEN NO ONE ELSE DOES.
"THAT WAS MY FIRST ENCOUNTER WITH EARTH.
"BUT IT WOULDN'T BE THE LAST."

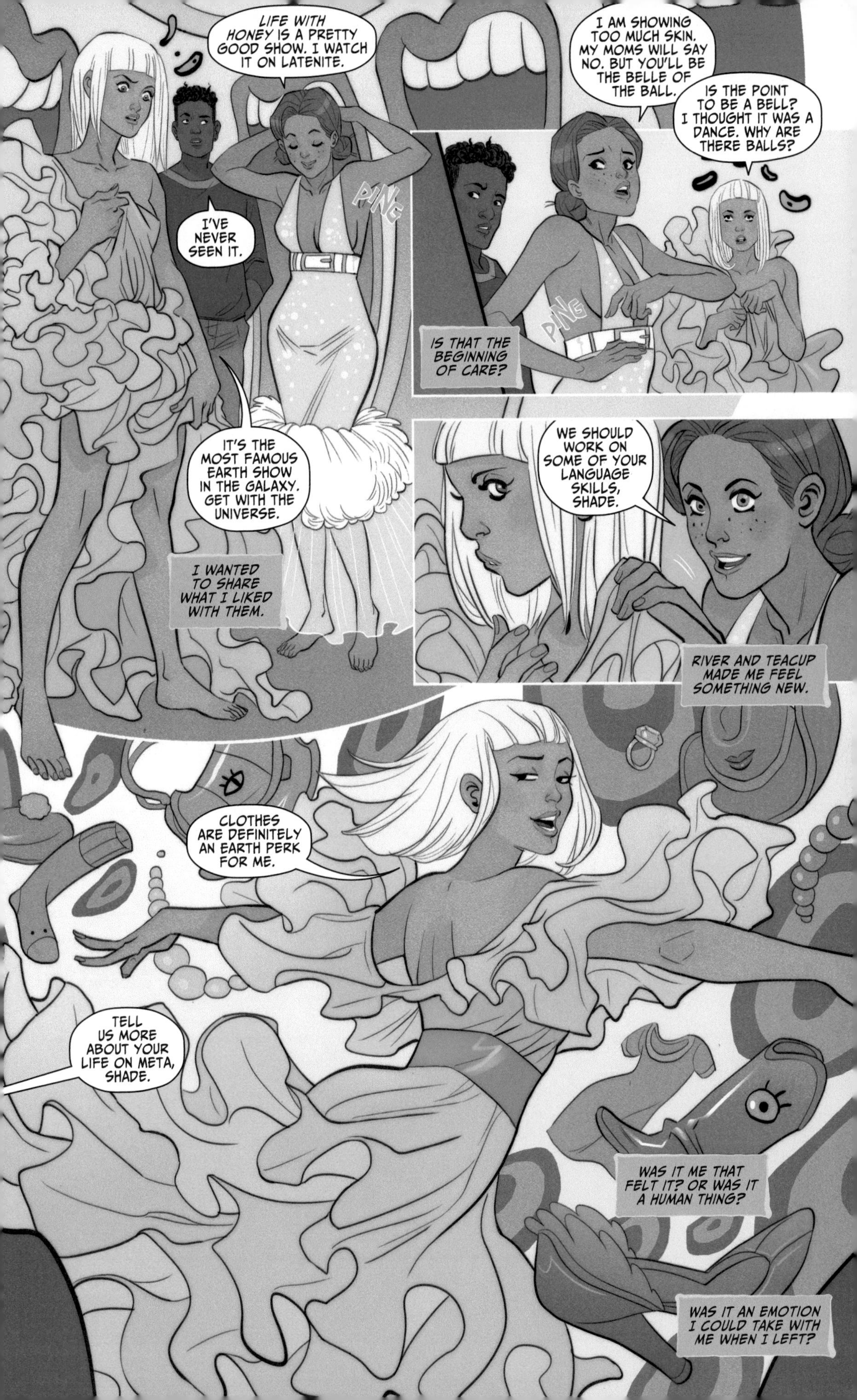
LIFE WITH HONEY IS A PRETTY GOOD SHOW. I WATCH IT ON LATENITE.
I'VE NEVER SEEN IT.
PING
IT'S THE MOST FAMOUS EARTH SHOW IN THE GALAXY. GET WITH THE UNIVERSE.
I WANTED TO SHARE WHAT I LIKED WITH THEM.
I AM SHOWING TOO MUCH SKIN. MY MOMS WILL SAY NO. BUT YOU'LL BE THE BELLE OF THE BALL.
IS THE POINT TO BE A BELL? I THOUGHT IT WAS A DANCE. WHY ARE THERE BALLS?
PING
IS THAT THE BEGINNING OF CARE?
WE SHOULD WORK ON SOME OF YOUR LANGUAGE SKILLS, SHADE.
RIVER AND TEACUP MADE ME FEEL SOMETHING NEW.
CLOTHES ARE DEFINITELY AN EARTH PERK FOR ME.
TELL US MORE ABOUT YOUR LIFE ON META, SHADE.
WAS IT ME THAT FELT IT? OR WAS IT A HUMAN THING?
WAS IT AN EMOTION I COULD TAKE WITH ME WHEN I LEFT?

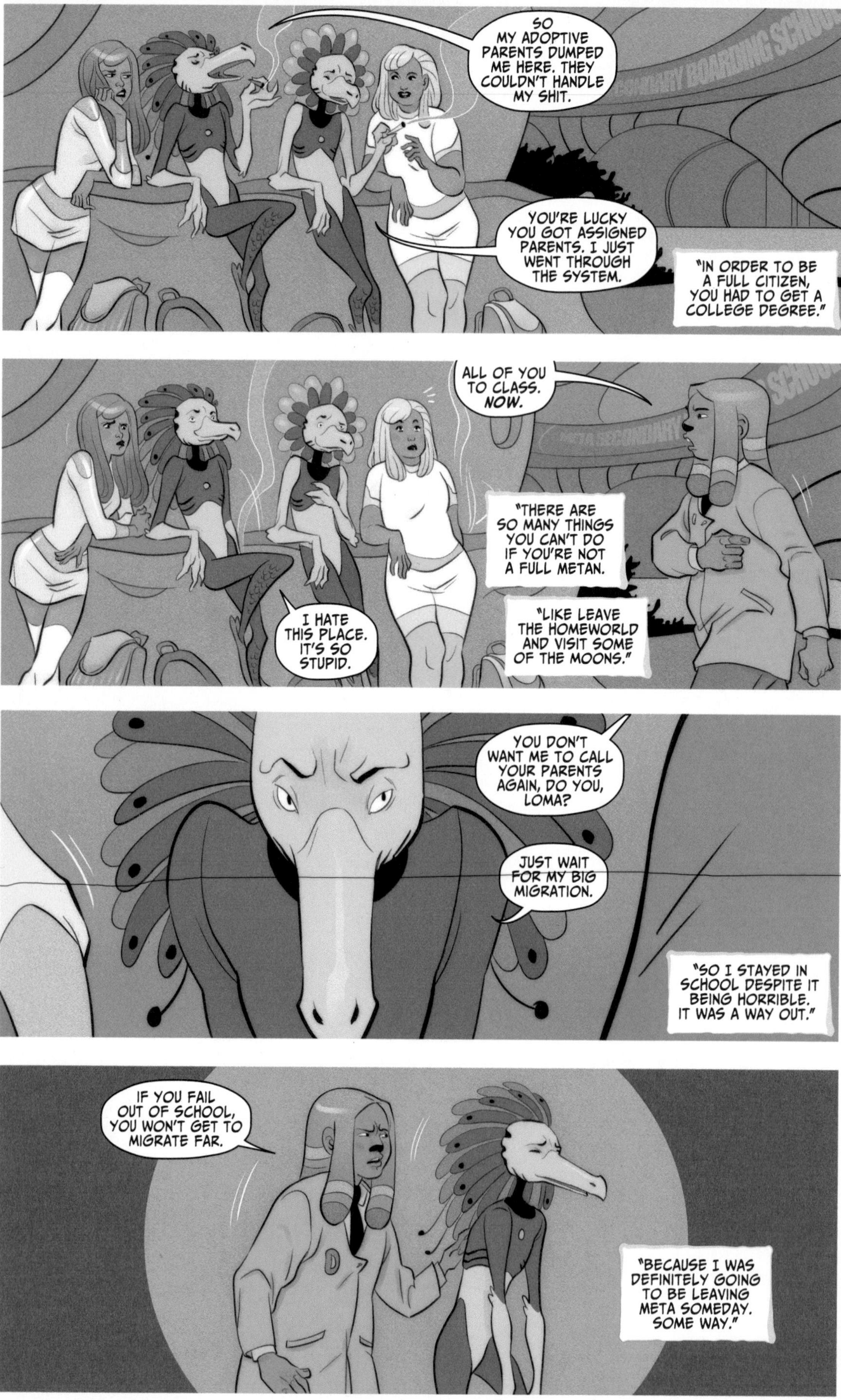
SO MY ADOPTIVE PARENTS DUMPED ME HERE. THEY COULDN'T HANDLE MY SHIT.
YOU'RE LUCKY YOU GOT ASSIGNED PARENTS. I JUST WENT THROUGH THE SYSTEM.
"IN ORDER TO BE A FULL CITIZEN, YOU HAD TO GET A COLLEGE DEGREE."
ALL OF YOU TO CLASS. *NOW.*
"THERE ARE SO MANY THINGS YOU CAN'T DO IF YOU'RE NOT A FULL METAN.
I HATE THIS PLACE. IT'S SO STUPID.
"LIKE LEAVE THE HOMEWORLD AND VISIT SOME OF THE MOONS."
YOU DON'T WANT ME TO CALL YOUR PARENTS AGAIN, DO YOU, LOMA?
JUST WAIT FOR MY BIG MIGRATION.
"SO I STAYED IN SCHOOL DESPITE IT BEING HORRIBLE. IT WAS A WAY OUT."
IF YOU FAIL OUT OF SCHOOL, YOU WON'T GET TO MIGRATE FAR.
"BECAUSE I WAS DEFINITELY GOING TO BE LEAVING META SOMEDAY. SOME WAY."

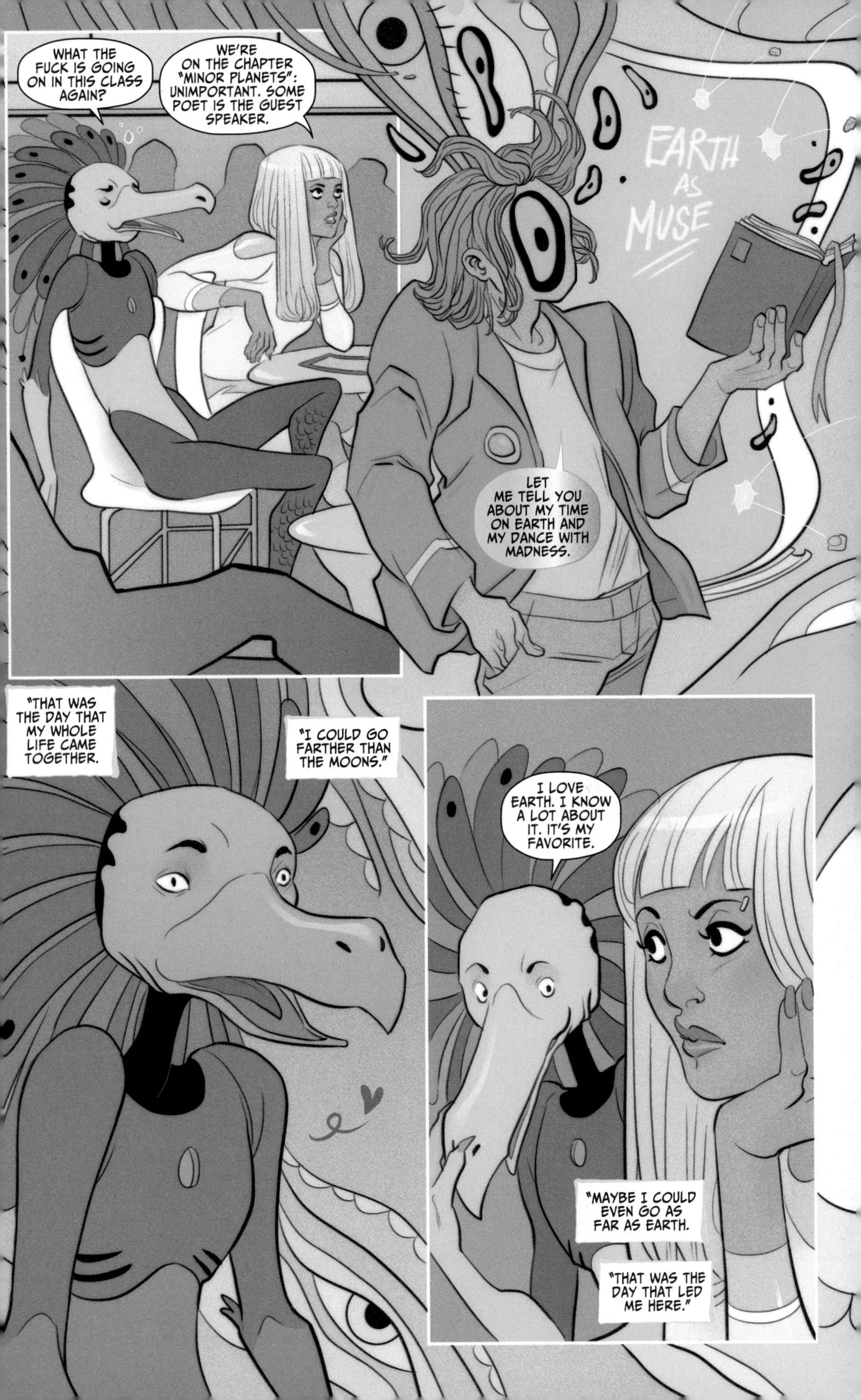
WHAT THE FUCK IS GOING ON IN THIS CLASS AGAIN?
WE'RE ON THE CHAPTER "MINOR PLANETS": UNIMPORTANT. SOME POET IS THE GUEST SPEAKER.
EARTH AS MUSE
LET ME TELL YOU ABOUT MY TIME ON EARTH AND MY DANCE WITH MADNESS.
"THAT WAS THE DAY THAT MY WHOLE LIFE CAME TOGETHER.
"I COULD GO FARTHER THAN THE MOONS."
I LOVE EARTH. I KNOW A LOT ABOUT IT. IT'S MY FAVORITE.
"MAYBE I COULD EVEN GO AS FAR AS EARTH.
"THAT WAS THE DAY THAT LED ME HERE."

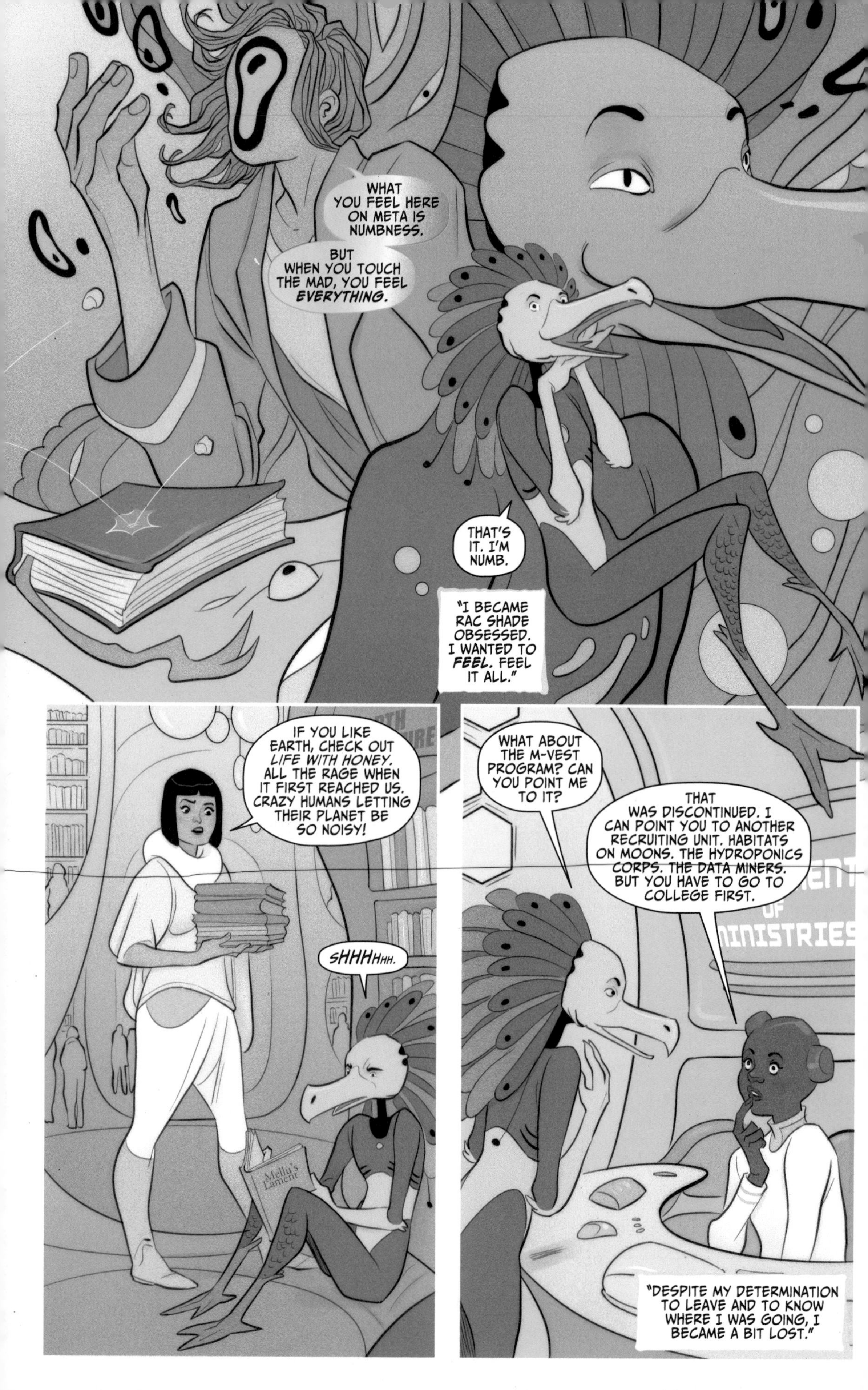
WHAT YOU FEEL HERE ON META IS NUMBNESS.
BUT WHEN YOU TOUCH THE MAD, YOU FEEL *EVERYTHING.*
THAT'S IT. I'M NUMB.
"I BECAME RAC SHADE OBSESSED. I WANTED TO *FEEL.* FEEL IT ALL."
IF YOU LIKE EARTH, CHECK OUT *LIFE WITH HONEY.* ALL THE RAGE WHEN IT FIRST REACHED US. CRAZY HUMANS LETTING THEIR PLANET BE SO NOISY!
SHHHHHH.
Mellu's Lament
WHAT ABOUT THE M-VEST PROGRAM? CAN YOU POINT ME TO IT?
THAT WAS DISCONTINUED. I CAN POINT YOU TO ANOTHER RECRUITING UNIT. HABITATS ON MOONS. THE HYDROPONICS CORPS. THE DATA MINERS. BUT YOU HAVE TO GO TO COLLEGE FIRST.
"DESPITE MY DETERMINATION TO LEAVE AND TO KNOW WHERE I WAS GOING, I BECAME A BIT LOST."

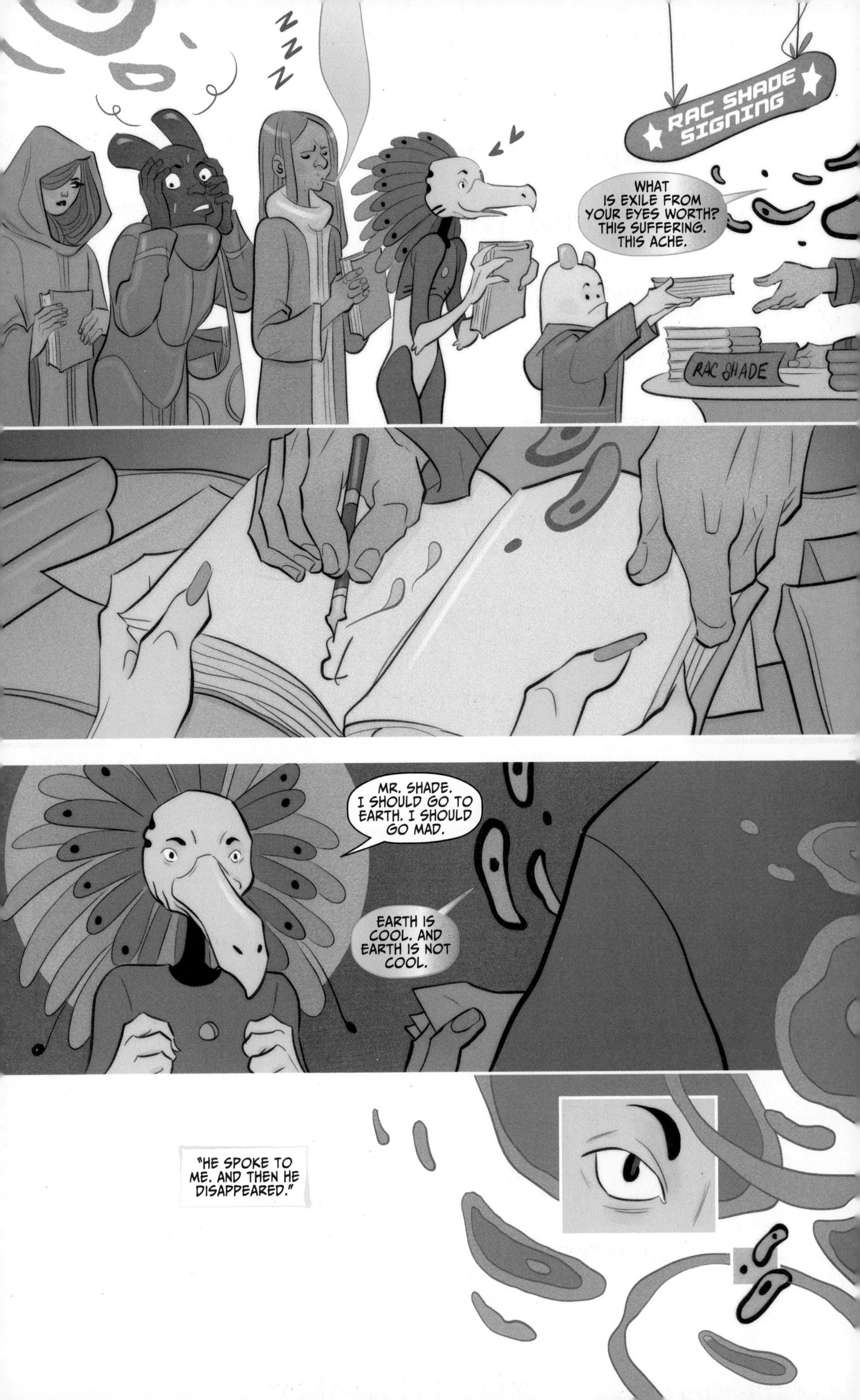
RAC SHADE SIGNING
WHAT IS EXILE FROM YOUR EYES WORTH? THIS SUFFERING. THIS ACHE.
RAC SHADE
MR. SHADE. I SHOULD GO TO EARTH. I SHOULD GO MAD.
EARTH IS COOL. AND EARTH IS NOT COOL.
"HE SPOKE TO ME. AND THEN HE DISAPPEARED."

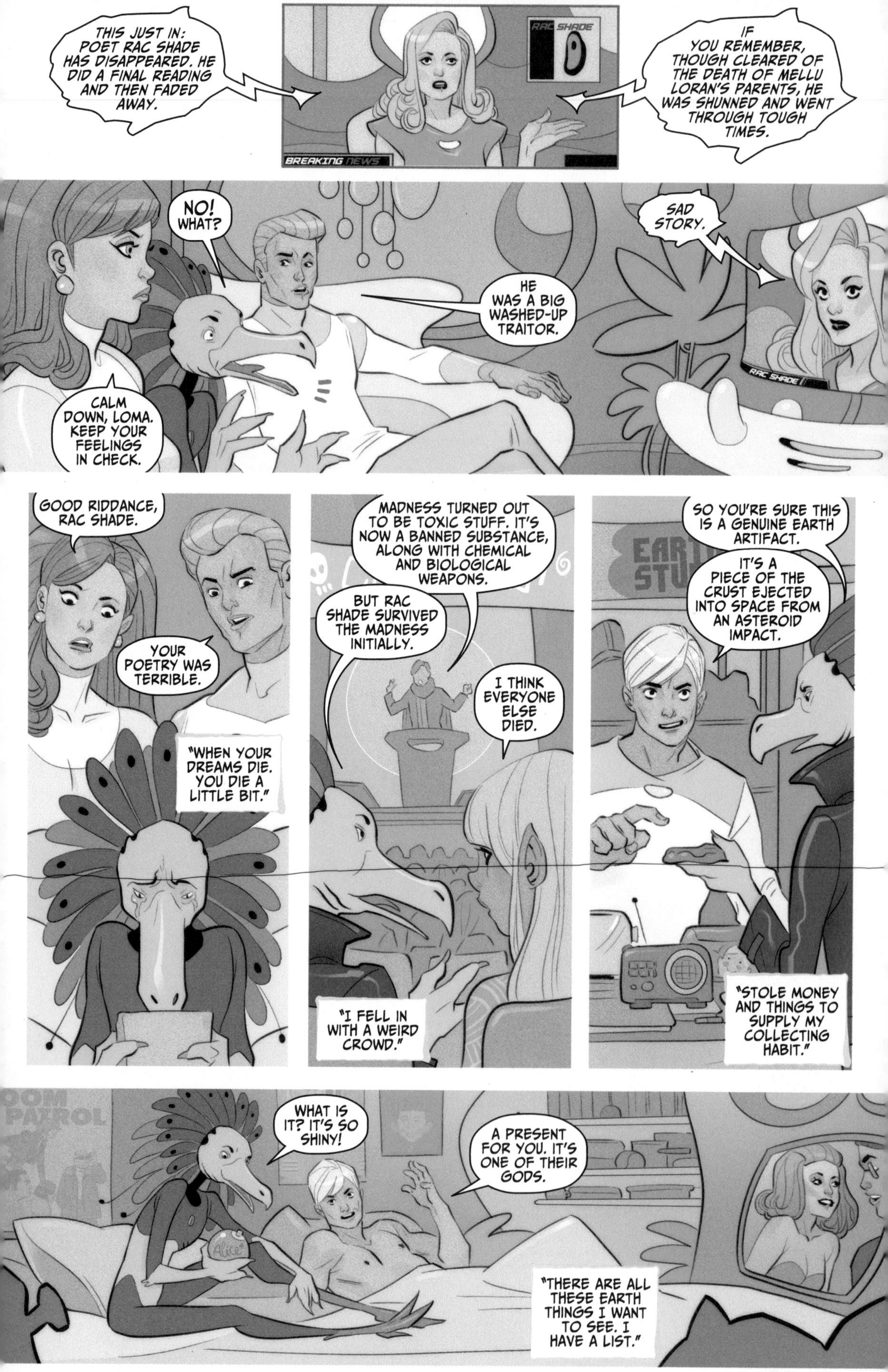

RAC SHADE
BREAKING NEWS
THIS JUST IN: POET RAC SHADE HAS DISAPPEARED. HE DID A FINAL READING AND THEN FADED AWAY.
IF YOU REMEMBER, THOUGH CLEARED OF THE DEATH OF MELLU LORAN'S PARENTS, HE WAS SHUNNED AND WENT THROUGH TOUGH TIMES.
NO! WHAT?
HE WAS A BIG WASHED-UP TRAITOR.
SAD STORY.
RAC SHADE
CALM DOWN, LOMA. KEEP YOUR FEELINGS IN CHECK.
GOOD RIDDANCE, RAC SHADE.
YOUR POETRY WAS TERRIBLE.
"WHEN YOUR DREAMS DIE. YOU DIE A LITTLE BIT."
MADNESS TURNED OUT TO BE TOXIC STUFF. IT'S NOW A BANNED SUBSTANCE, ALONG WITH CHEMICAL AND BIOLOGICAL WEAPONS.
BUT RAC SHADE SURVIVED THE MADNESS INITIALLY.
I THINK EVERYONE ELSE DIED.
"I FELL IN WITH A WEIRD CROWD."
SO YOU'RE SURE THIS IS A GENUINE EARTH ARTIFACT.
IT'S A PIECE OF THE CRUST EJECTED INTO SPACE FROM AN ASTEROID IMPACT.
"STOLE MONEY AND THINGS TO SUPPLY MY COLLECTING HABIT."
WHAT IS IT? IT'S SO SHINY!
A PRESENT FOR YOU. IT'S ONE OF THEIR GODS.
"THERE ARE ALL THESE EARTH THINGS I WANT TO SEE. I HAVE A LIST."

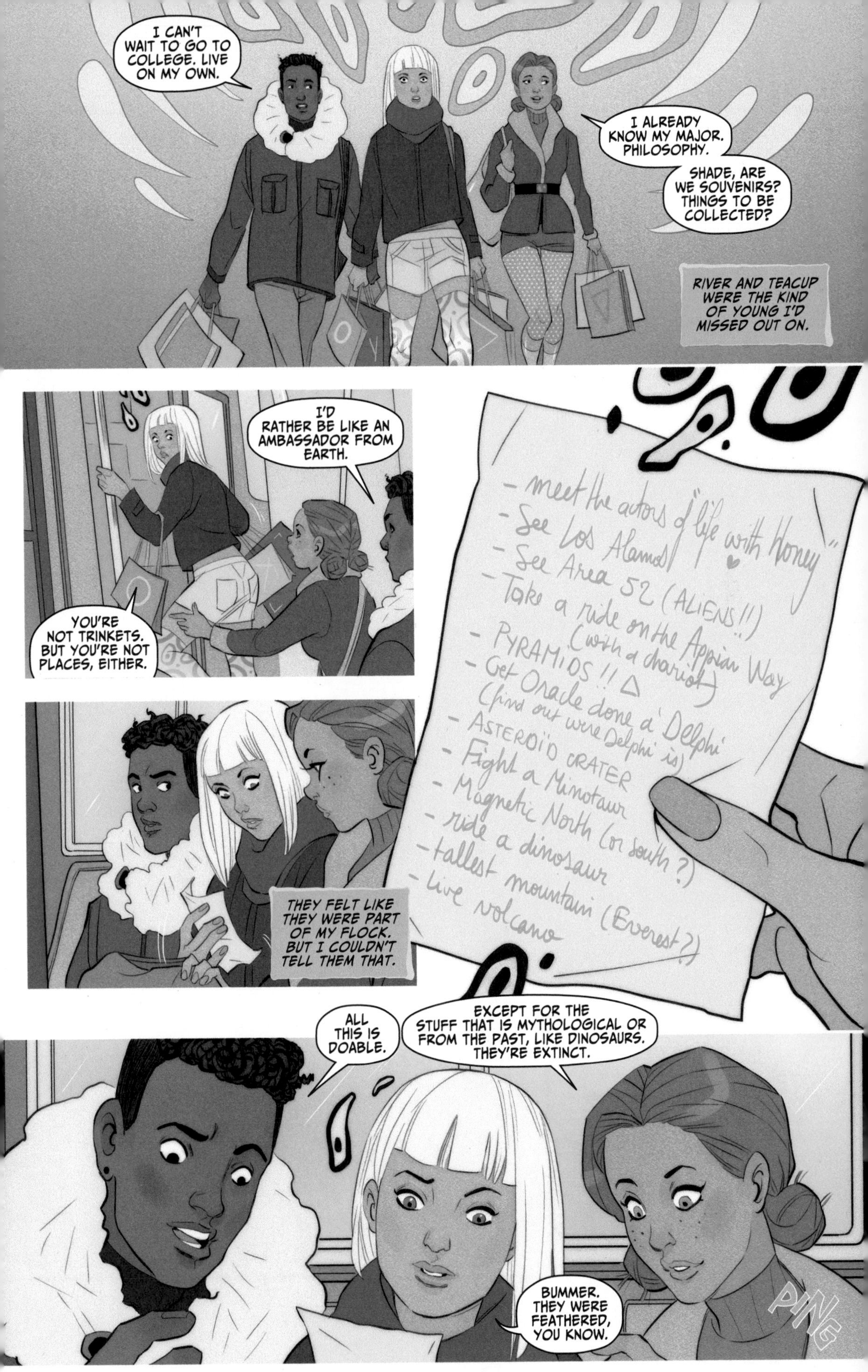

I CAN'T WAIT TO GO TO COLLEGE. LIVE ON MY OWN.
I ALREADY KNOW MY MAJOR. PHILOSOPHY.
SHADE, ARE WE SOUVENIRS? THINGS TO BE COLLECTED?
RIVER AND TEACUP WERE THE KIND OF YOUNG I'D MISSED OUT ON.
I'D RATHER BE LIKE AN AMBASSADOR FROM EARTH.
YOU'RE NOT TRINKETS. BUT YOU'RE NOT PLACES, EITHER.
THEY FELT LIKE THEY WERE PART OF MY FLOCK. BUT I COULDN'T TELL THEM THAT.
- meet the actors of "life with Honey" ♥
- See Los Alamos
- See Area 52 (ALIENS!!)
- Take a ride on the Appian Way (with a chariot)
- PYRAMIDS!! △
- Get Oracle done á Delphi (find out were Delphi is)
- ASTEROÏD CRATER
- Fight a Minotaur
- Magnetic North (or south?)
- ride a dinosaur
- tallest mountain (Everest?)
- Live volcano
ALL THIS IS DOABLE.
EXCEPT FOR THE STUFF THAT IS MYTHOLOGICAL OR FROM THE PAST, LIKE DINOSAURS. THEY'RE EXTINCT.
BUMMER. THEY WERE FEATHERED, YOU KNOW.
PING

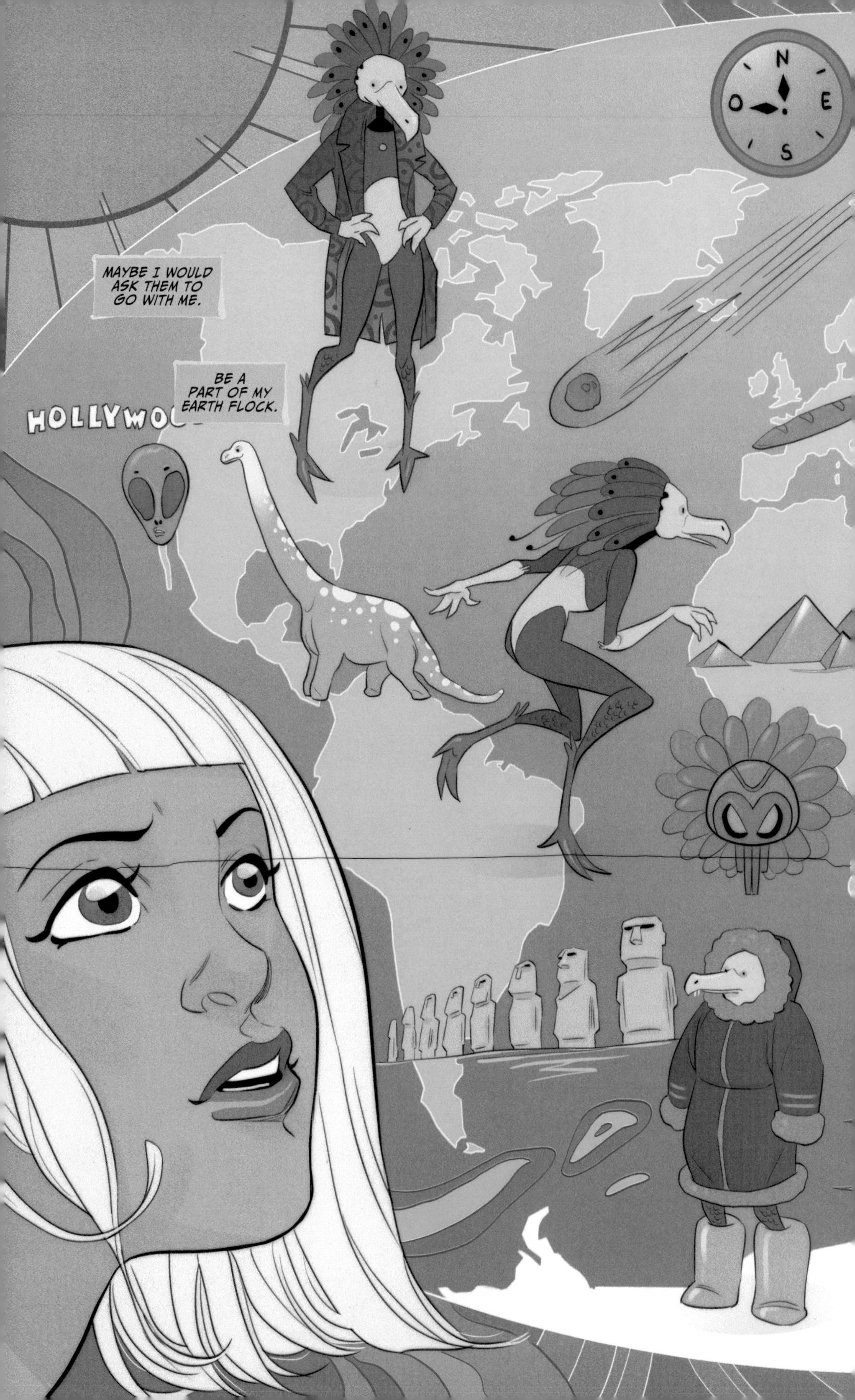
MAYBE I WOULD ASK THEM TO GO WITH ME.
BE A PART OF MY EARTH FLOCK.
N
E
S
O

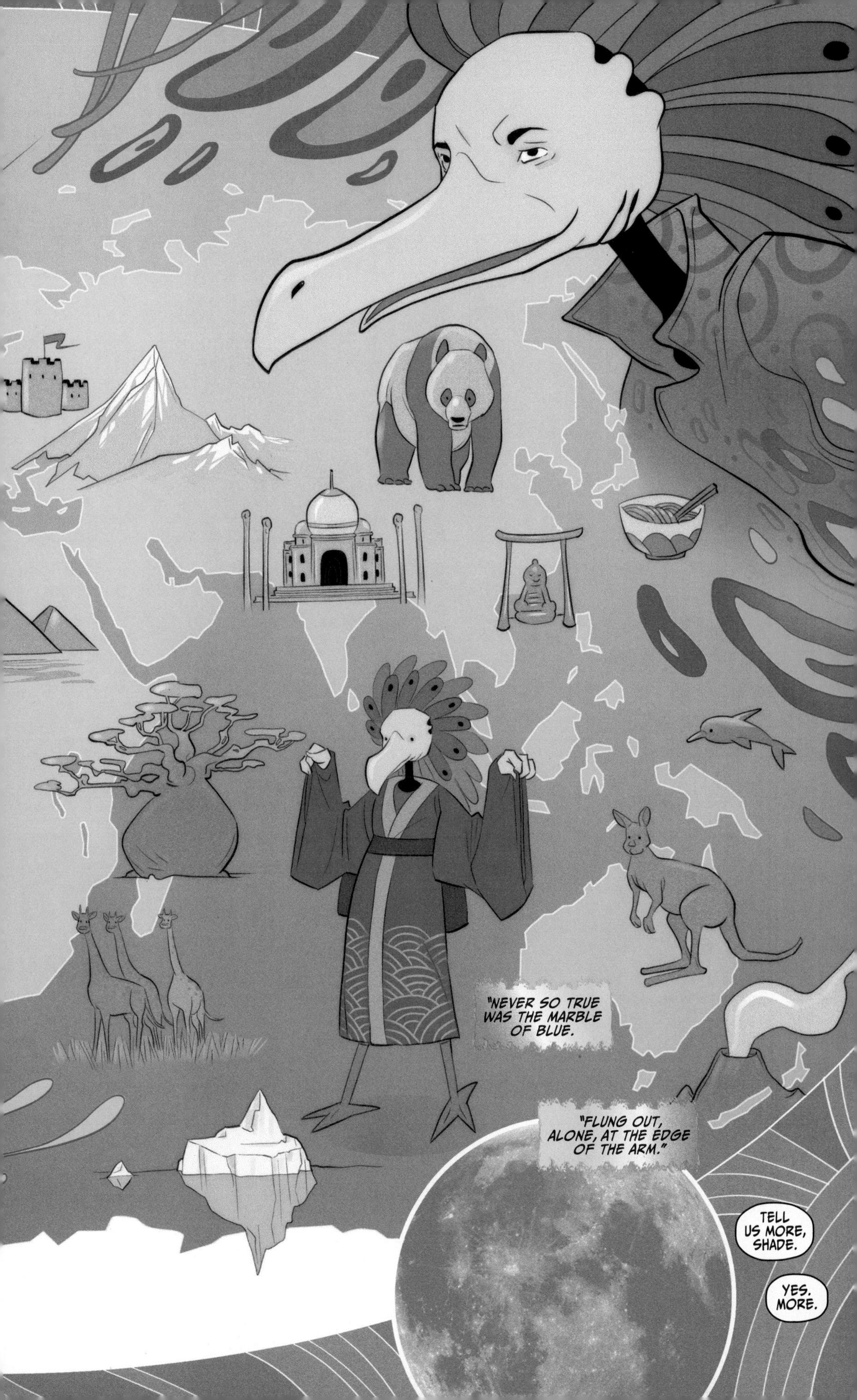
"NEVER SO TRUE WAS THE MARBLE OF BLUE.
"FLUNG OUT, ALONE, AT THE EDGE OF THE ARM."
TELL US MORE, SHADE.
YES. MORE.

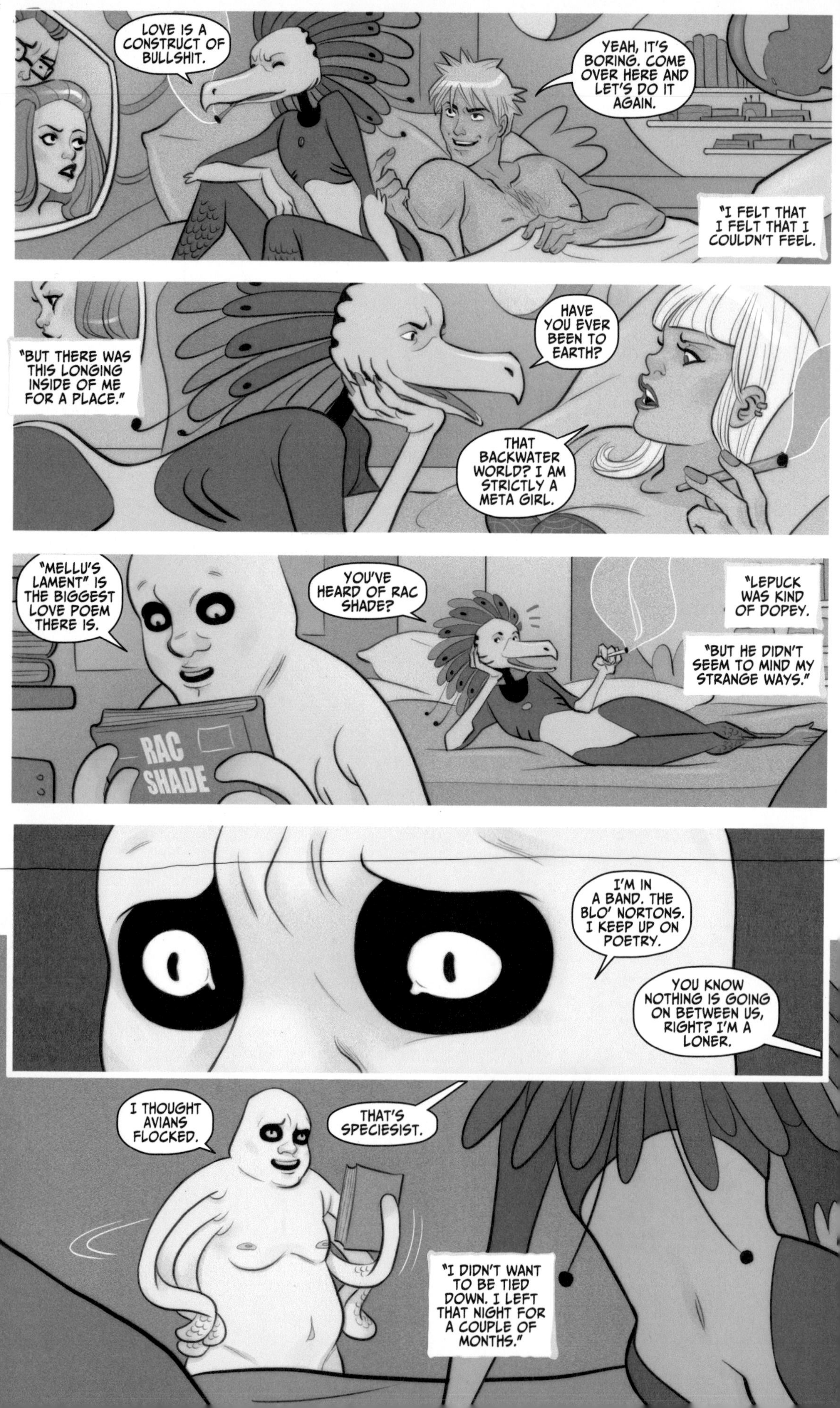
LOVE IS A CONSTRUCT OF BULLSHIT.
YEAH, IT'S BORING. COME OVER HERE AND LET'S DO IT AGAIN.
"I FELT THAT I FELT THAT I COULDN'T FEEL.
"BUT THERE WAS THIS LONGING INSIDE OF ME FOR A PLACE."
HAVE YOU EVER BEEN TO EARTH?
THAT BACKWATER WORLD? I AM STRICTLY A META GIRL.
"MELLU'S LAMENT" IS THE BIGGEST LOVE POEM THERE IS.
YOU'VE HEARD OF RAC SHADE?
RAC SHADE
"LEPUCK WAS KIND OF DOPEY.
"BUT HE DIDN'T SEEM TO MIND MY STRANGE WAYS."
I'M IN A BAND. THE BLO' NORTONS. I KEEP UP ON POETRY.
YOU KNOW NOTHING IS GOING ON BETWEEN US, RIGHT? I'M A LONER.
I THOUGHT AVIANS FLOCKED.
THAT'S SPECIESIST.
"I DIDN'T WANT TO BE TIED DOWN. I LEFT THAT NIGHT FOR A COUPLE OF MONTHS."

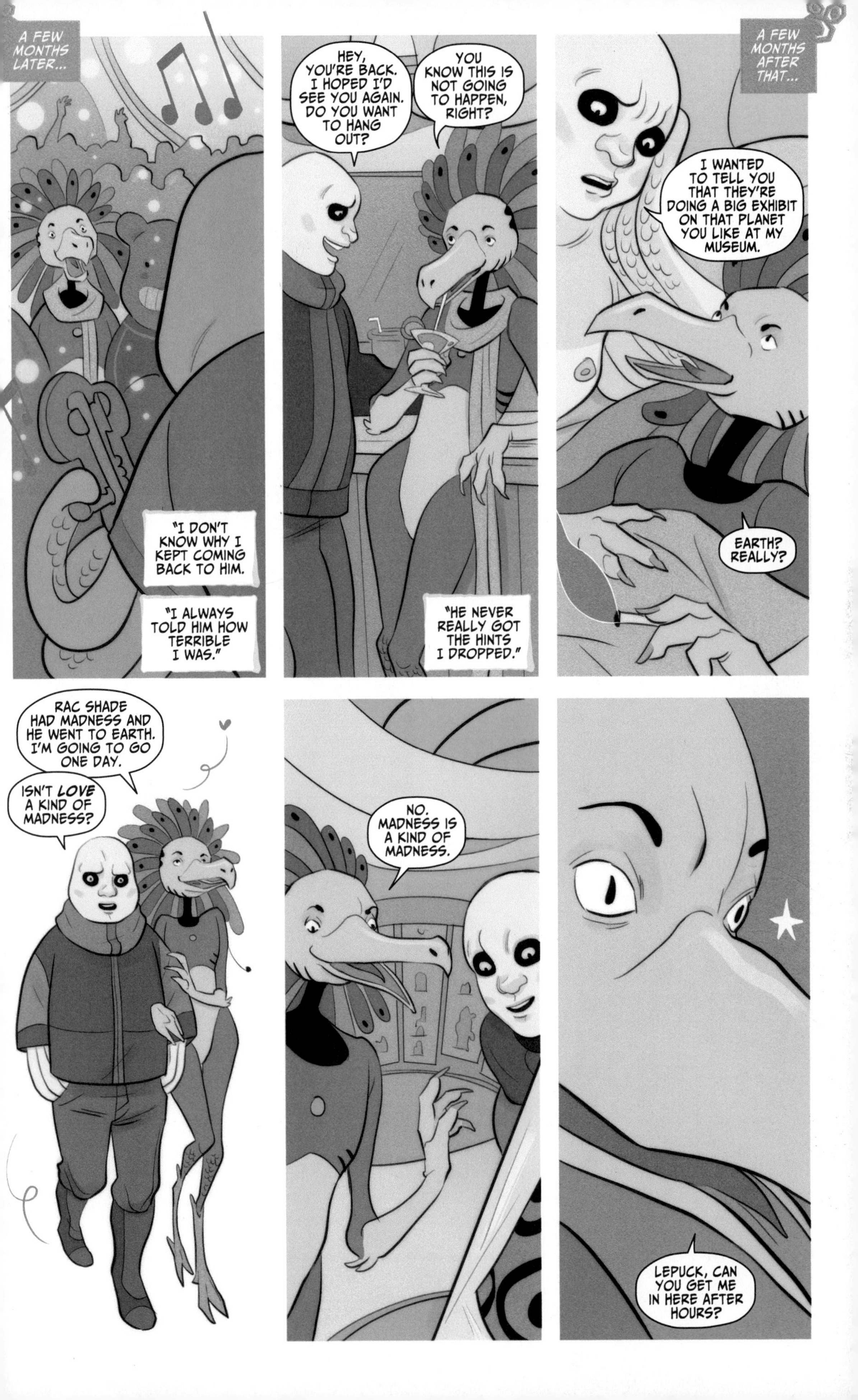
A FEW MONTHS LATER...
"I DON'T KNOW WHY I KEPT COMING BACK TO HIM.
"I ALWAYS TOLD HIM HOW TERRIBLE I WAS."
HEY, YOU'RE BACK. I HOPED I'D SEE YOU AGAIN. DO YOU WANT TO HANG OUT?
YOU KNOW THIS IS NOT GOING TO HAPPEN, RIGHT?
"HE NEVER REALLY GOT THE HINTS I DROPPED."
A FEW MONTHS AFTER THAT...
I WANTED TO TELL YOU THAT THEY'RE DOING A BIG EXHIBIT ON THAT PLANET YOU LIKE AT MY MUSEUM.
EARTH? REALLY?
RAC SHADE HAD MADNESS AND HE WENT TO EARTH. I'M GOING TO GO ONE DAY.
ISN'T LOVE A KIND OF MADNESS?
NO. MADNESS IS A KIND OF MADNESS.
LEPUCK, CAN YOU GET ME IN HERE AFTER HOURS?

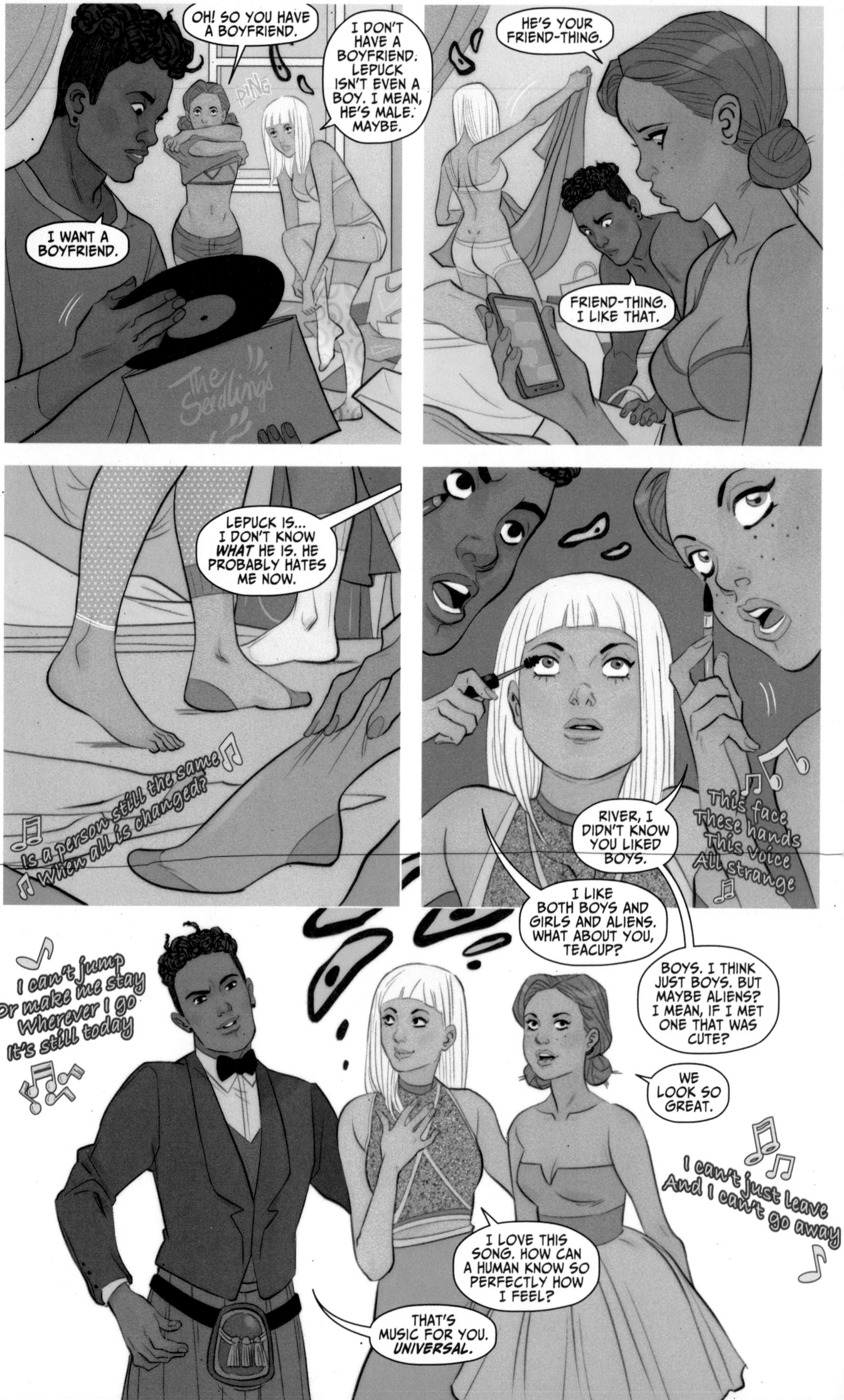
OH! SO YOU HAVE A BOYFRIEND.
I DON'T HAVE A BOYFRIEND. LEPUCK ISN'T EVEN A BOY. I MEAN, HE'S MALE. MAYBE.
PING
I WANT A BOYFRIEND.
The Serdlings
HE'S YOUR FRIEND-THING.
FRIEND-THING. I LIKE THAT.
LEPUCK IS... I DON'T KNOW WHAT HE IS. HE PROBABLY HATES ME NOW.
Is a person still the same When all is changed?
This face These hands This voice All strange
RIVER, I DIDN'T KNOW YOU LIKED BOYS.
I LIKE BOTH BOYS AND GIRLS AND ALIENS. WHAT ABOUT YOU, TEACUP?
BOYS. I THINK JUST BOYS. BUT MAYBE ALIENS? I MEAN, IF I MET ONE THAT WAS CUTE?
I can't jump Or make me stay Wherever I go It's still today
WE LOOK SO GREAT.
I can't just leave And I can't go away
I LOVE THIS SONG. HOW CAN A HUMAN KNOW SO PERFECTLY HOW I FEEL?
THAT'S MUSIC FOR YOU. UNIVERSAL.

GYMNASIU
I came too late
And I felt too soon
YOU'LL ALL DANCE WITH ME, RIGHT? I WON'T HAVE TO BE ALONE, RIGHT?
WINTER BALL
WHAT'S THE POINT OF THIS?
HORMONES.
PING
MEGAN, I WANTED YOU TO KNOW THAT YOU'RE DIFFERENT THAN OTHER GIRLS.
I KNOW I'M DIFFERENT, WES.
IT'S ASTOUNDING HOW A PLACE CAN BE TRANSFORMED WITH A LITTLE LIGHTING AND SPARKLE.
PING
PING
PING

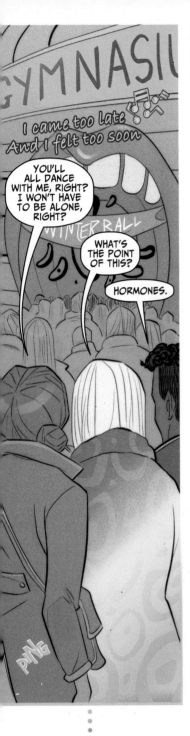

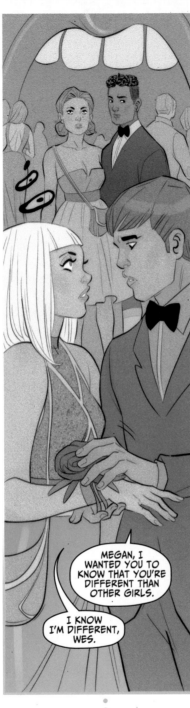

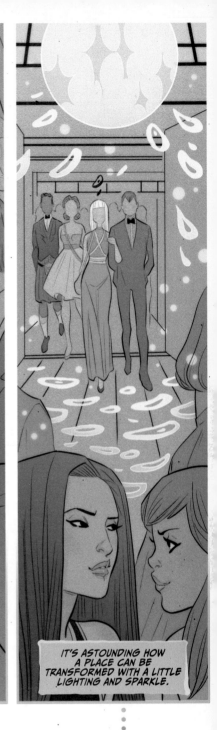

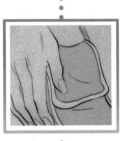

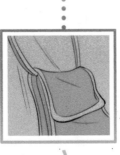

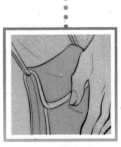

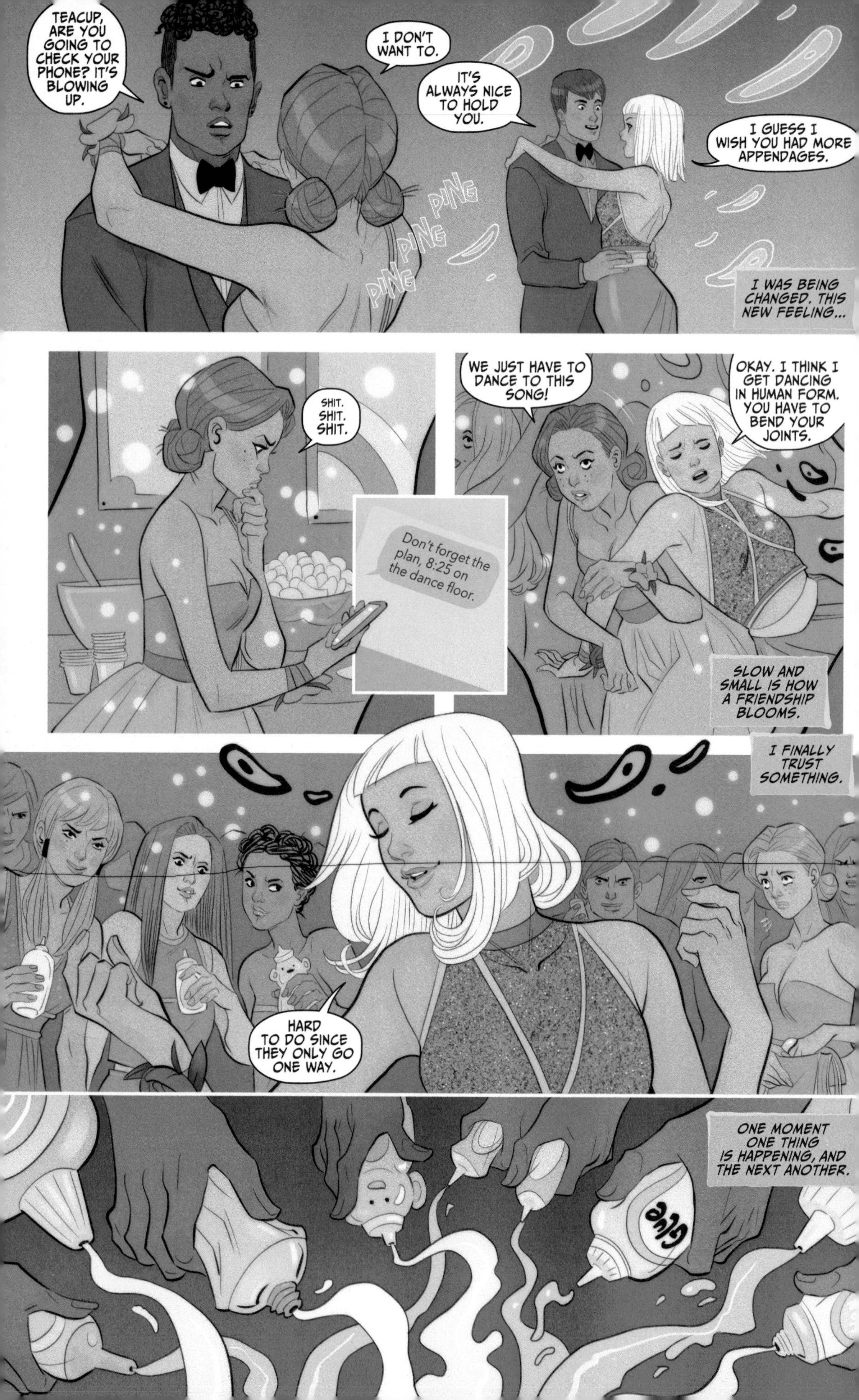
TEACUP, ARE YOU GOING TO CHECK YOUR PHONE? IT'S BLOWING UP.
I DON'T WANT TO.
IT'S ALWAYS NICE TO HOLD YOU.
I GUESS I WISH YOU HAD MORE APPENDAGES.
PING PING PING PING
I WAS BEING CHANGED. THIS NEW FEELING...
SHIT. SHIT. SHIT.
Don't forget the plan, 8:25 on the dance floor.
WE JUST HAVE TO DANCE TO THIS SONG!
OKAY. I THINK I GET DANCING IN HUMAN FORM. YOU HAVE TO BEND YOUR JOINTS.
SLOW AND SMALL IS HOW A FRIENDSHIP BLOOMS.
I FINALLY TRUST SOMETHING.
HARD TO DO SINCE THEY ONLY GO ONE WAY.
ONE MOMENT ONE THING IS HAPPENING, AND THE NEXT ANOTHER.
Glue

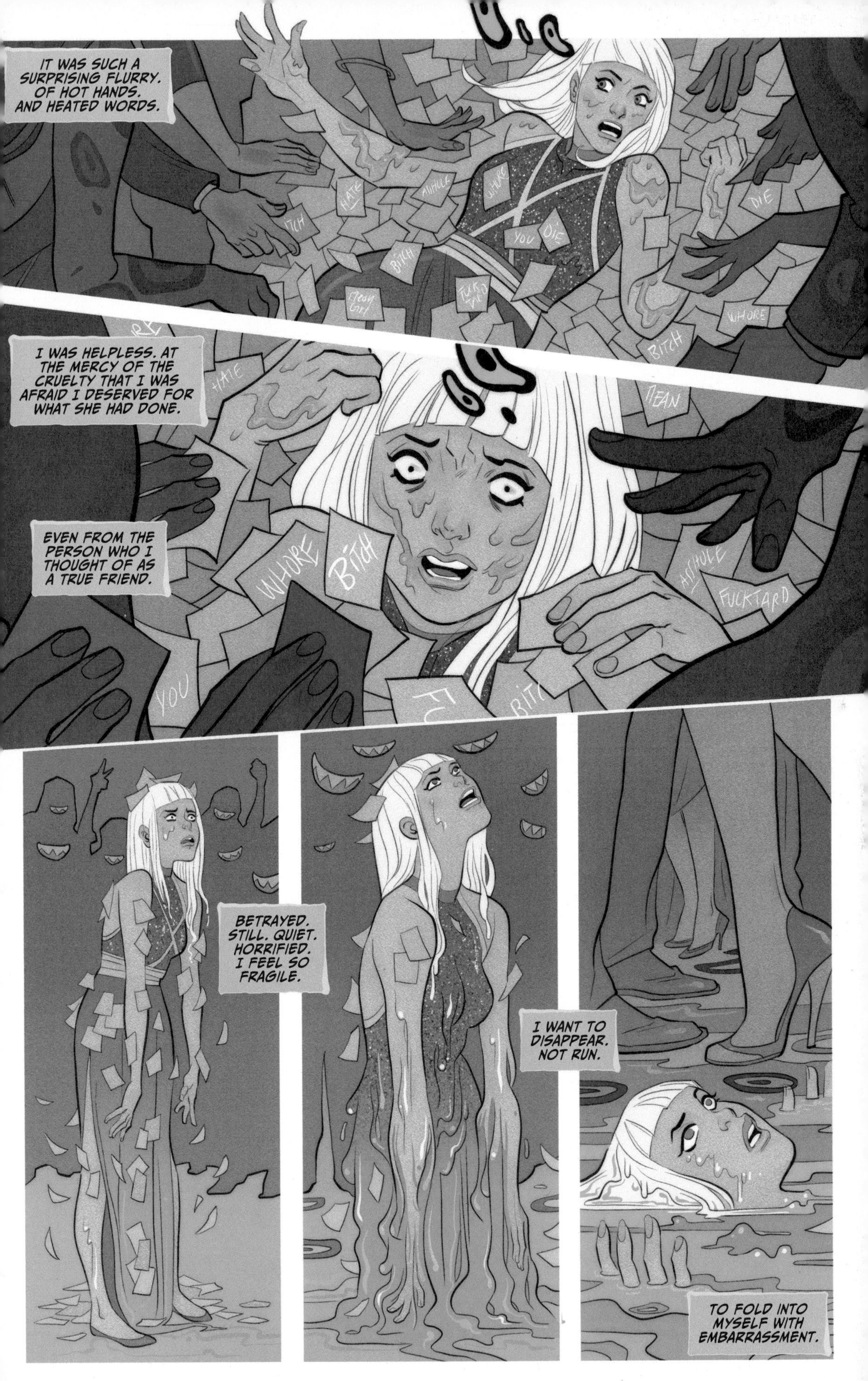
IT WAS SUCH A SURPRISING FLURRY. OF HOT HANDS. AND HEATED WORDS.
I WAS HELPLESS. AT THE MERCY OF THE CRUELTY THAT I WAS AFRAID I DESERVED FOR WHAT SHE HAD DONE.
EVEN FROM THE PERSON WHO I THOUGHT OF AS A TRUE FRIEND.
BETRAYED. STILL. QUIET. HORRIFIED. I FEEL SO FRAGILE.
I WANT TO DISAPPEAR. NOT RUN.
TO FOLD INTO MYSELF WITH EMBARRASSMENT.

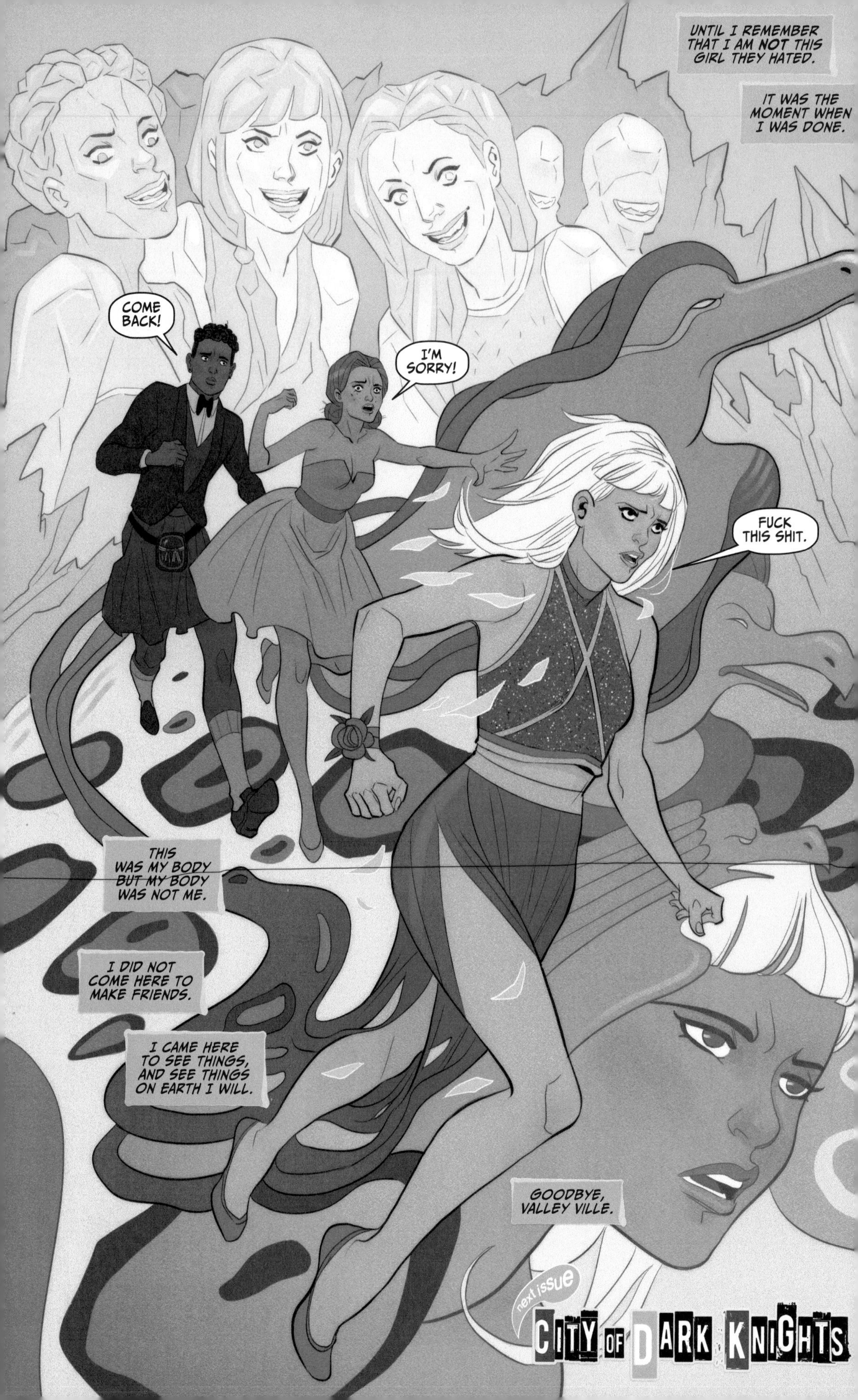
UNTIL I REMEMBER THAT I AM NOT THIS GIRL THEY HATED.
IT WAS THE MOMENT WHEN I WAS DONE.
COME BACK!
I'M SORRY!
FUCK THIS SHIT.
THIS WAS MY BODY BUT MY BODY WAS NOT ME.
I DID NOT COME HERE TO MAKE FRIENDS.
I CAME HERE TO SEE THINGS, AND SEE THINGS ON EARTH I WILL.
GOODBYE, VALLEY VILLE.
next issue
CITY OF DARK KNIGHTS

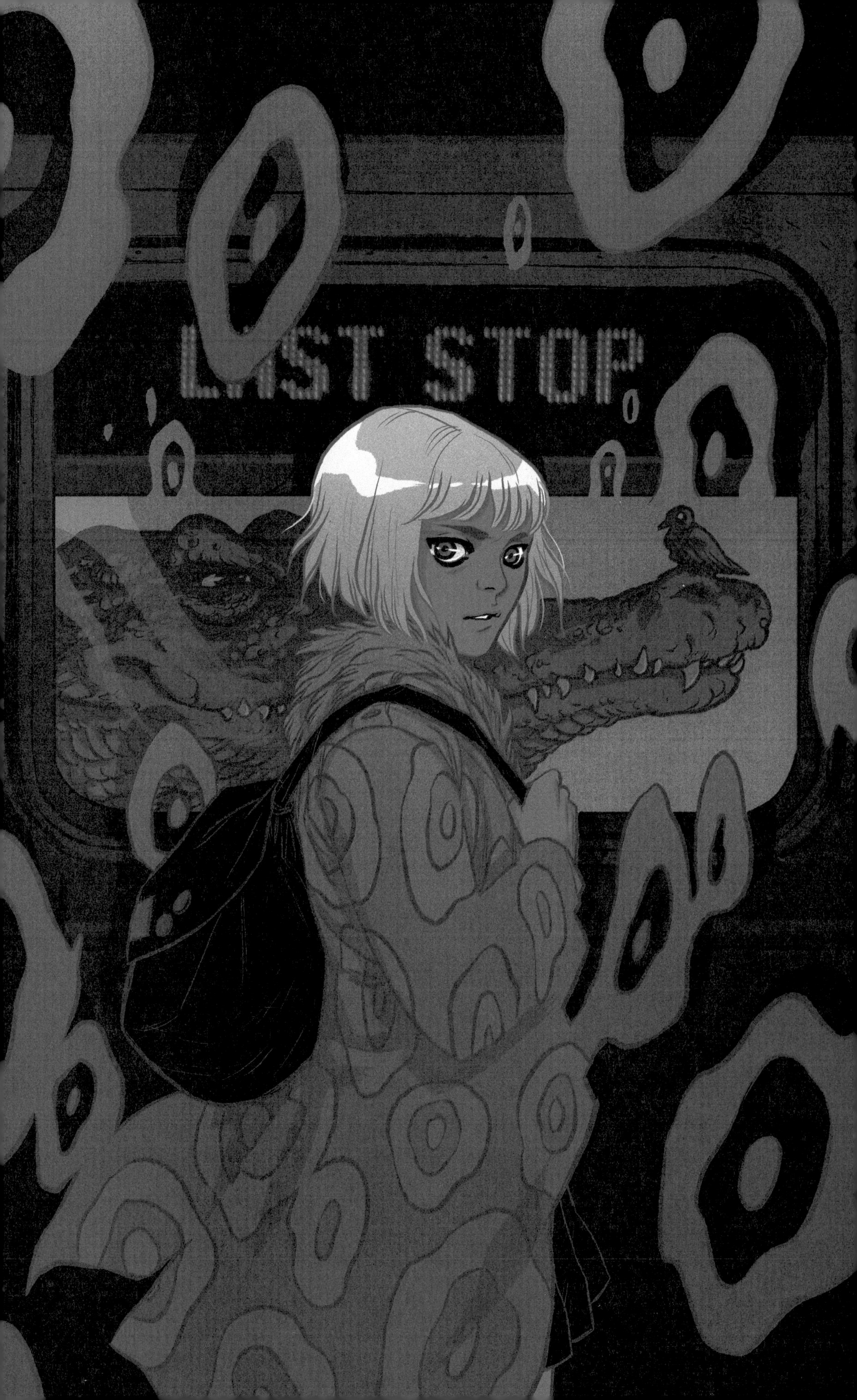
LAST STOP

Variant cover art by Jen Bartel

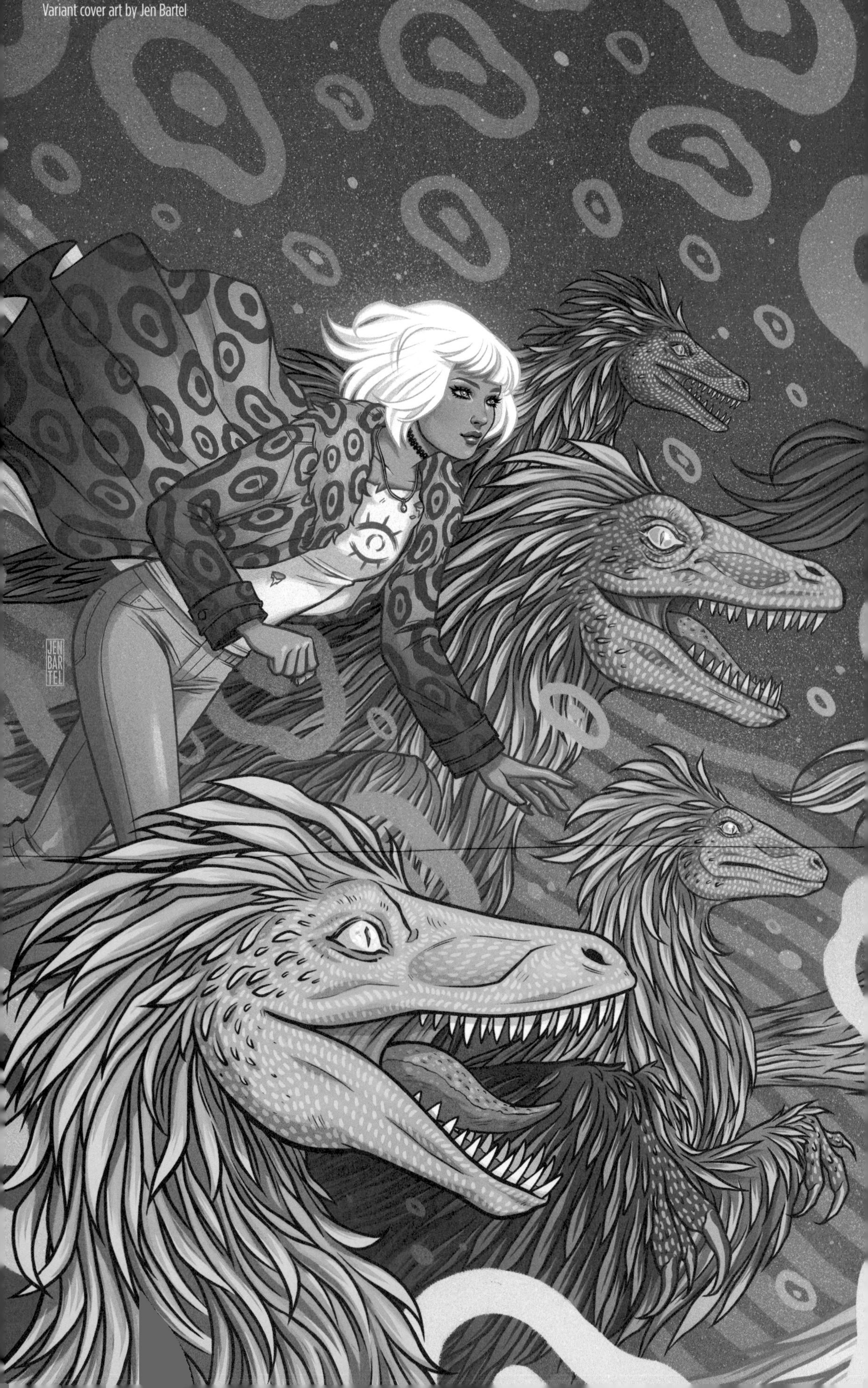
JEN
BAR
TEL

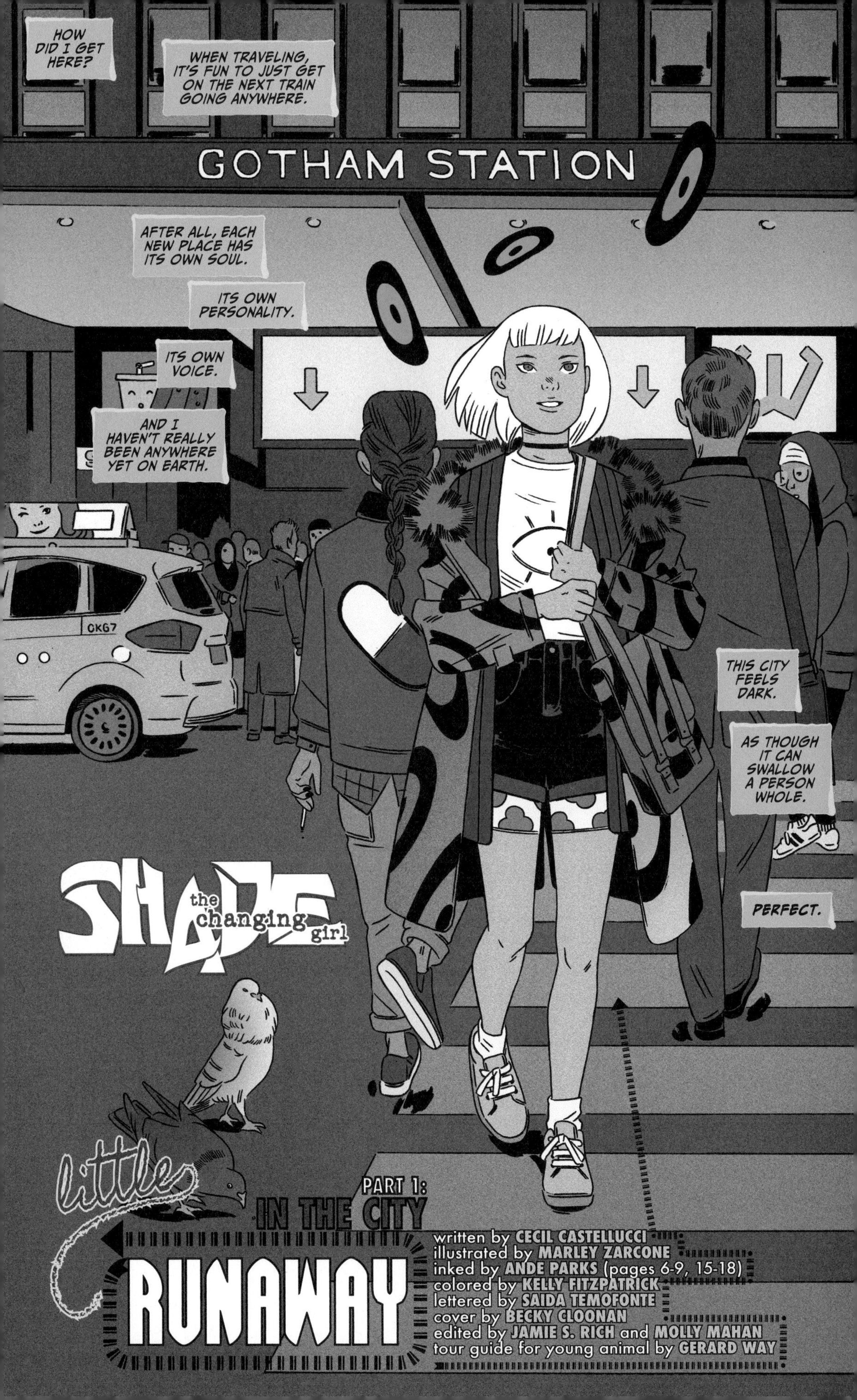
HOW DID I GET HERE?
WHEN TRAVELING, IT'S FUN TO JUST GET ON THE NEXT TRAIN GOING ANYWHERE.
GOTHAM STATION
AFTER ALL, EACH NEW PLACE HAS ITS OWN SOUL.
ITS OWN PERSONALITY.
ITS OWN VOICE.
AND I HAVEN'T REALLY BEEN ANYWHERE YET ON EARTH.
CKG7
THIS CITY FEELS DARK.
AS THOUGH IT CAN SWALLOW A PERSON WHOLE.
PERFECT.
SHADE the changing girl
little RUNAWAY
PART 1: IN THE CITY
written by CECIL CASTELLUCCI
illustrated by MARLEY ZARCONE
inked by ANDE PARKS (pages 6-9, 15-18)
colored by KELLY FITZPATRICK
lettered by SAIDA TEMOFONTE
cover by BECKY CLOONAN
edited by JAMIE S. RICH and MOLLY MAHAN
tour guide for young animal by GERARD WAY

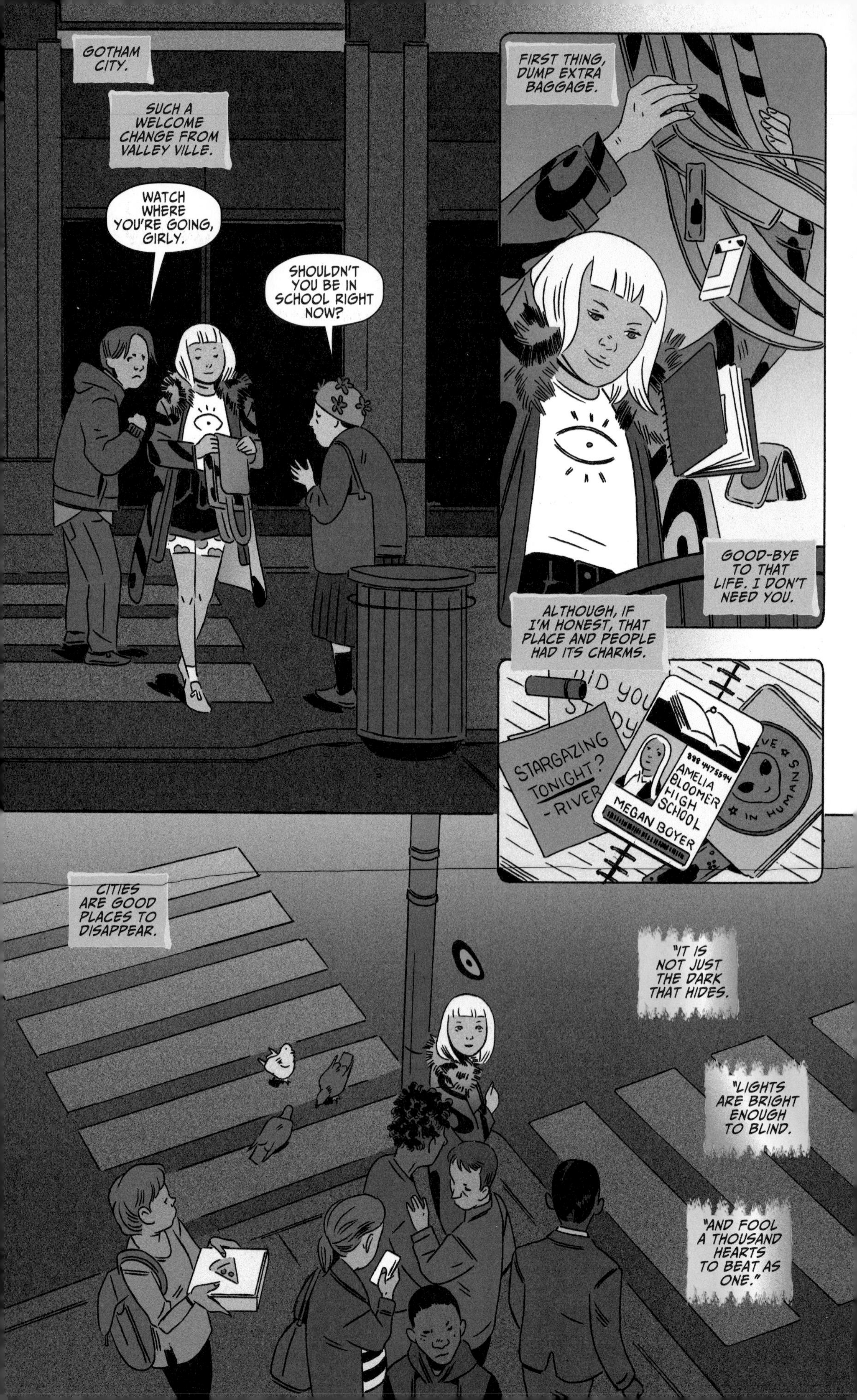
GOTHAM CITY.
SUCH A WELCOME CHANGE FROM VALLEY VILLE.
WATCH WHERE YOU'RE GOING, GIRLY.
SHOULDN'T YOU BE IN SCHOOL RIGHT NOW?
FIRST THING, DUMP EXTRA BAGGAGE.
GOOD-BYE TO THAT LIFE. I DON'T NEED YOU.
ALTHOUGH, IF I'M HONEST, THAT PLACE AND PEOPLE HAD ITS CHARMS.
STARGAZING TONIGHT? -RIVER
AMELIA BLOOMER HIGH SCHOOL
MEGAN BOYER
CITIES ARE GOOD PLACES TO DISAPPEAR.
"IT IS NOT JUST THE DARK THAT HIDES.
"LIGHTS ARE BRIGHT ENOUGH TO BLIND.
"AND FOOL A THOUSAND HEARTS TO BEAT AS ONE."

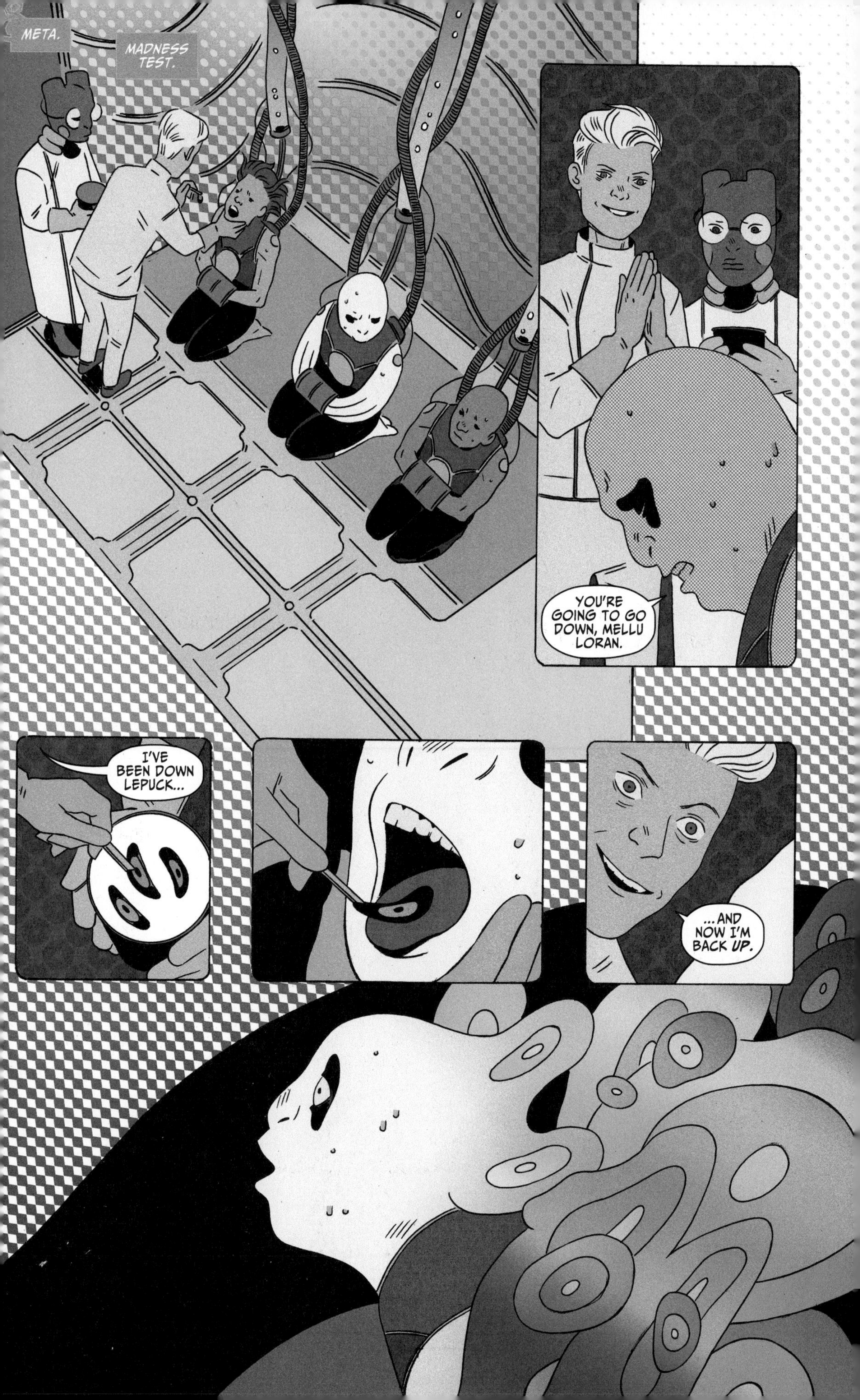
META.
MADNESS TEST.
YOU'RE GOING TO GO DOWN, MELLU LORAN.
I'VE BEEN DOWN LEPUCK...
...AND NOW I'M BACK UP.

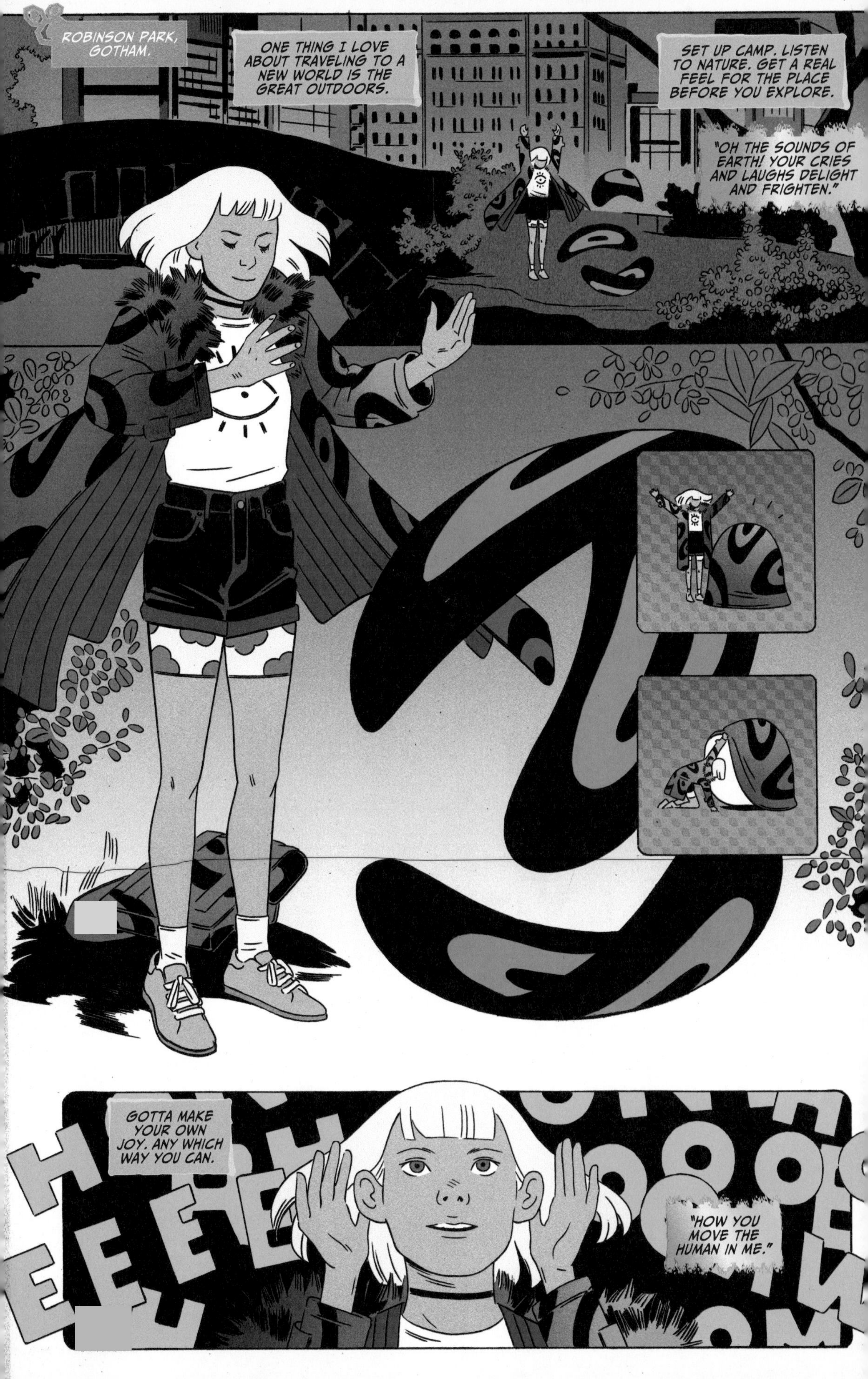
ROBINSON PARK, GOTHAM.
ONE THING I LOVE ABOUT TRAVELING TO A NEW WORLD IS THE GREAT OUTDOORS.
SET UP CAMP. LISTEN TO NATURE. GET A REAL FEEL FOR THE PLACE BEFORE YOU EXPLORE.
"OH THE SOUNDS OF EARTH! YOUR CRIES AND LAUGHS DELIGHT AND FRIGHTEN."
GOTTA MAKE YOUR OWN JOY. ANY WHICH WAY YOU CAN.
"HOW YOU MOVE THE HUMAN IN ME."

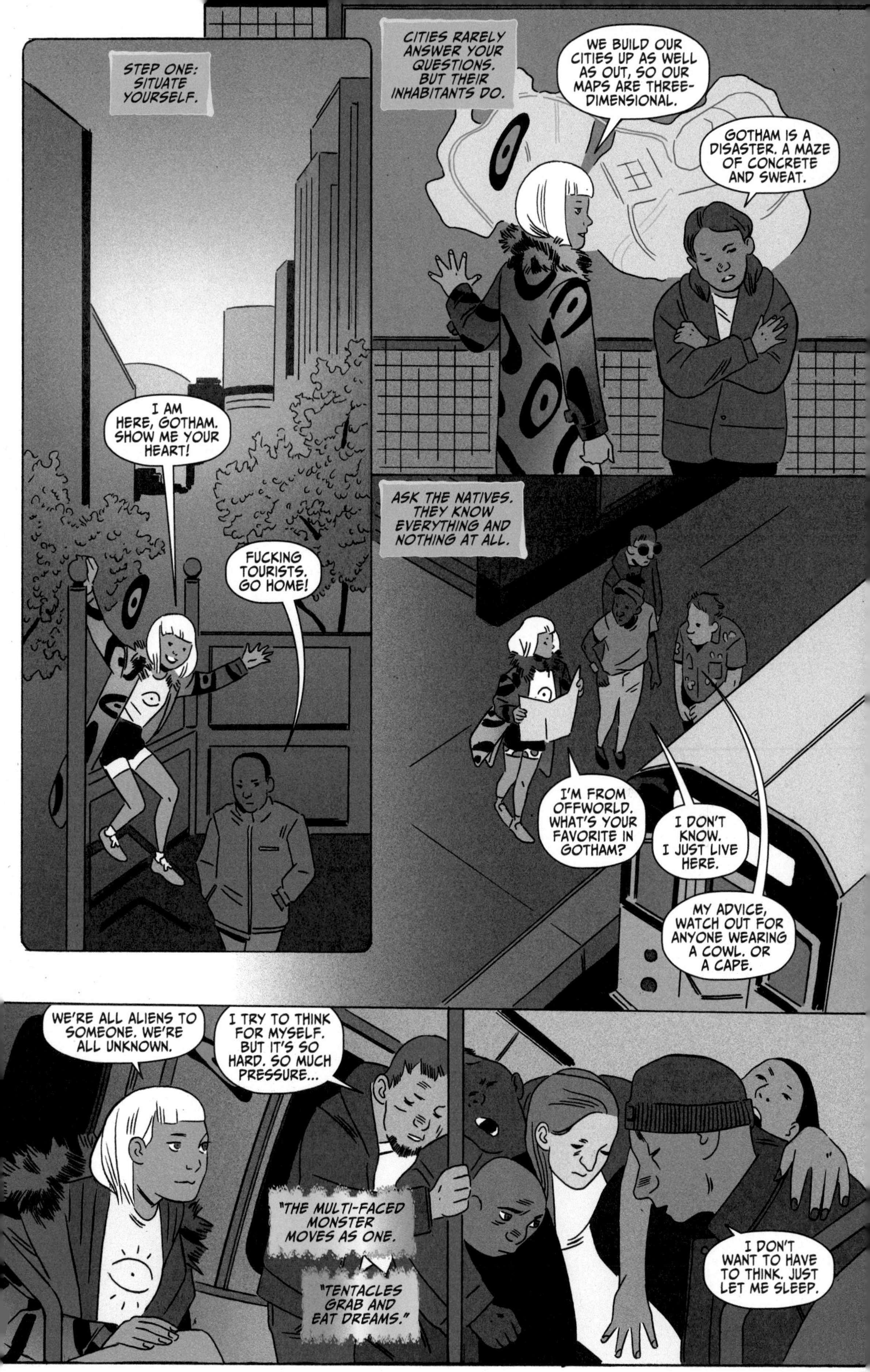
STEP ONE: SITUATE YOURSELF.
I AM HERE, GOTHAM. SHOW ME YOUR HEART!
FUCKING TOURISTS. GO HOME!
CITIES RARELY ANSWER YOUR QUESTIONS. BUT THEIR INHABITANTS DO.
WE BUILD OUR CITIES UP AS WELL AS OUT, SO OUR MAPS ARE THREE-DIMENSIONAL.
GOTHAM IS A DISASTER. A MAZE OF CONCRETE AND SWEAT.
ASK THE NATIVES. THEY KNOW EVERYTHING AND NOTHING AT ALL.
I'M FROM OFFWORLD. WHAT'S YOUR FAVORITE IN GOTHAM?
I DON'T KNOW. I JUST LIVE HERE.
MY ADVICE, WATCH OUT FOR ANYONE WEARING A COWL. OR A CAPE.
WE'RE ALL ALIENS TO SOMEONE. WE'RE ALL UNKNOWN.
I TRY TO THINK FOR MYSELF. BUT IT'S SO HARD. SO MUCH PRESSURE...
"THE MULTI-FACED MONSTER MOVES AS ONE.
"TENTACLES GRAB AND EAT DREAMS."
I DON'T WANT TO HAVE TO THINK. JUST LET ME SLEEP.

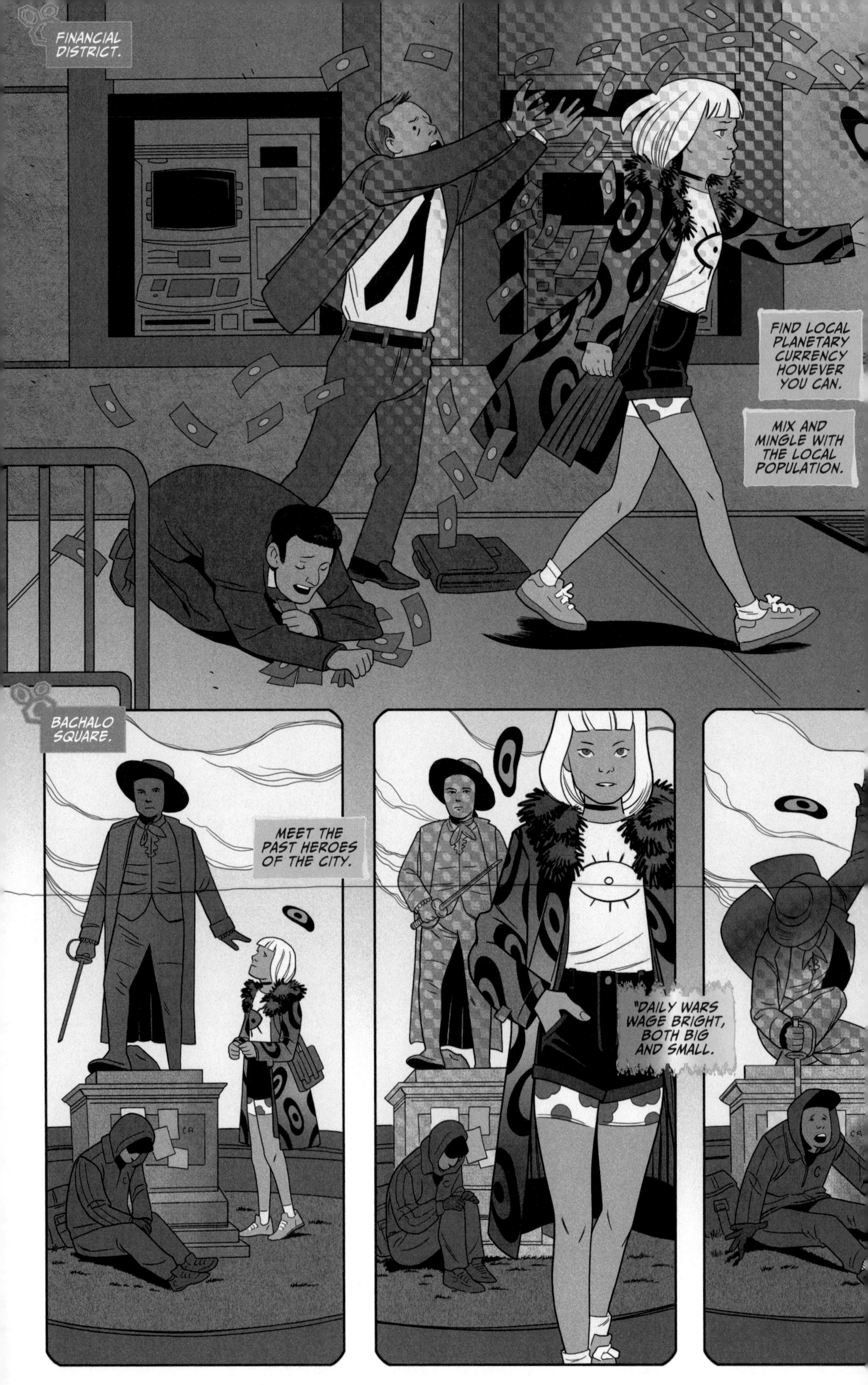
FINANCIAL DISTRICT.
FIND LOCAL PLANETARY CURRENCY HOWEVER YOU CAN.
MIX AND MINGLE WITH THE LOCAL POPULATION.
BACHALO SQUARE.
MEET THE PAST HEROES OF THE CITY.
"DAILY WARS WAGE BRIGHT, BOTH BIG AND SMALL.

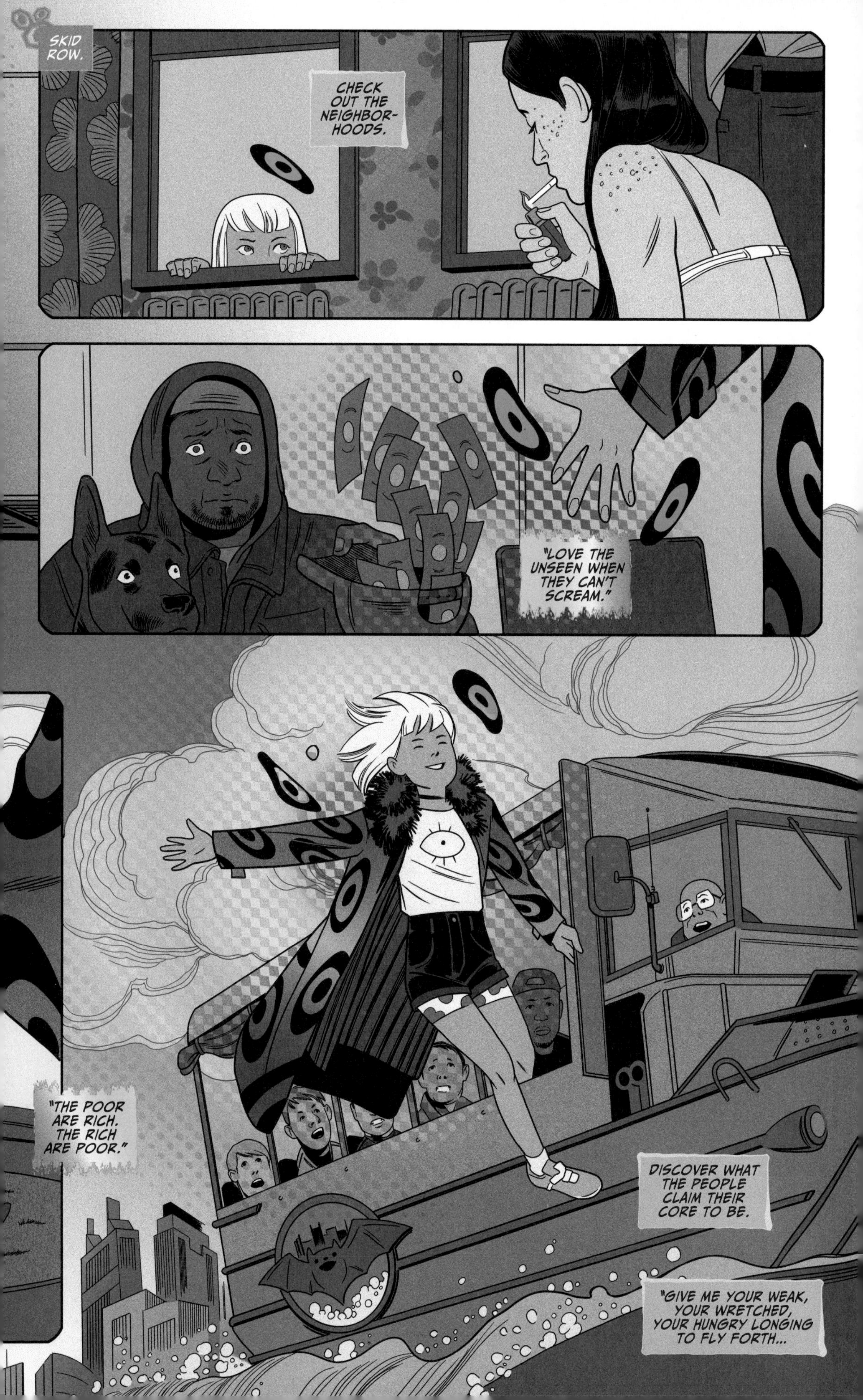
SKID ROW.
CHECK OUT THE NEIGHBOR-HOODS.
"LOVE THE UNSEEN WHEN THEY CAN'T SCREAM."
"THE POOR ARE RICH. THE RICH ARE POOR."
DISCOVER WHAT THE PEOPLE CLAIM THEIR CORE TO BE.
"GIVE ME YOUR WEAK, YOUR WRETCHED, YOUR HUNGRY LONGING TO FLY FORTH...

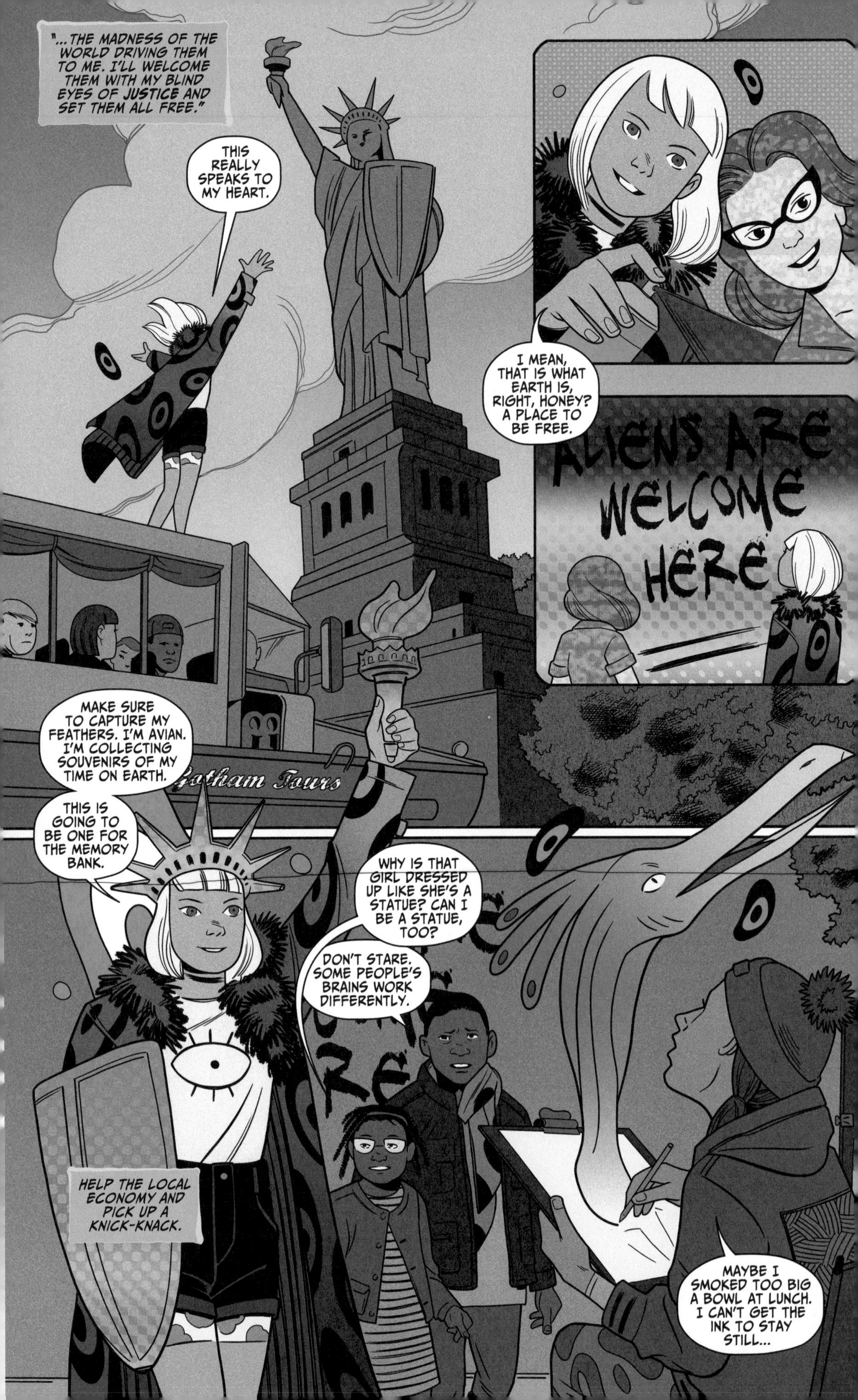
"...THE MADNESS OF THE WORLD DRIVING THEM TO ME. I'LL WELCOME THEM WITH MY BLIND EYES OF JUSTICE AND SET THEM ALL FREE."
THIS REALLY SPEAKS TO MY HEART.
I MEAN, THAT IS WHAT EARTH IS, RIGHT, HONEY? A PLACE TO BE FREE.
ALIENS ARE WELCOME HERE
Gotham Tours
MAKE SURE TO CAPTURE MY FEATHERS. I'M AVIAN. I'M COLLECTING SOUVENIRS OF MY TIME ON EARTH.
THIS IS GOING TO BE ONE FOR THE MEMORY BANK.
WHY IS THAT GIRL DRESSED UP LIKE SHE'S A STATUE? CAN I BE A STATUE, TOO?
DON'T STARE. SOME PEOPLE'S BRAINS WORK DIFFERENTLY.
HELP THE LOCAL ECONOMY AND PICK UP A KNICK-KNACK.
MAYBE I SMOKED TOO BIG A BOWL AT LUNCH. I CAN'T GET THE INK TO STAY STILL...

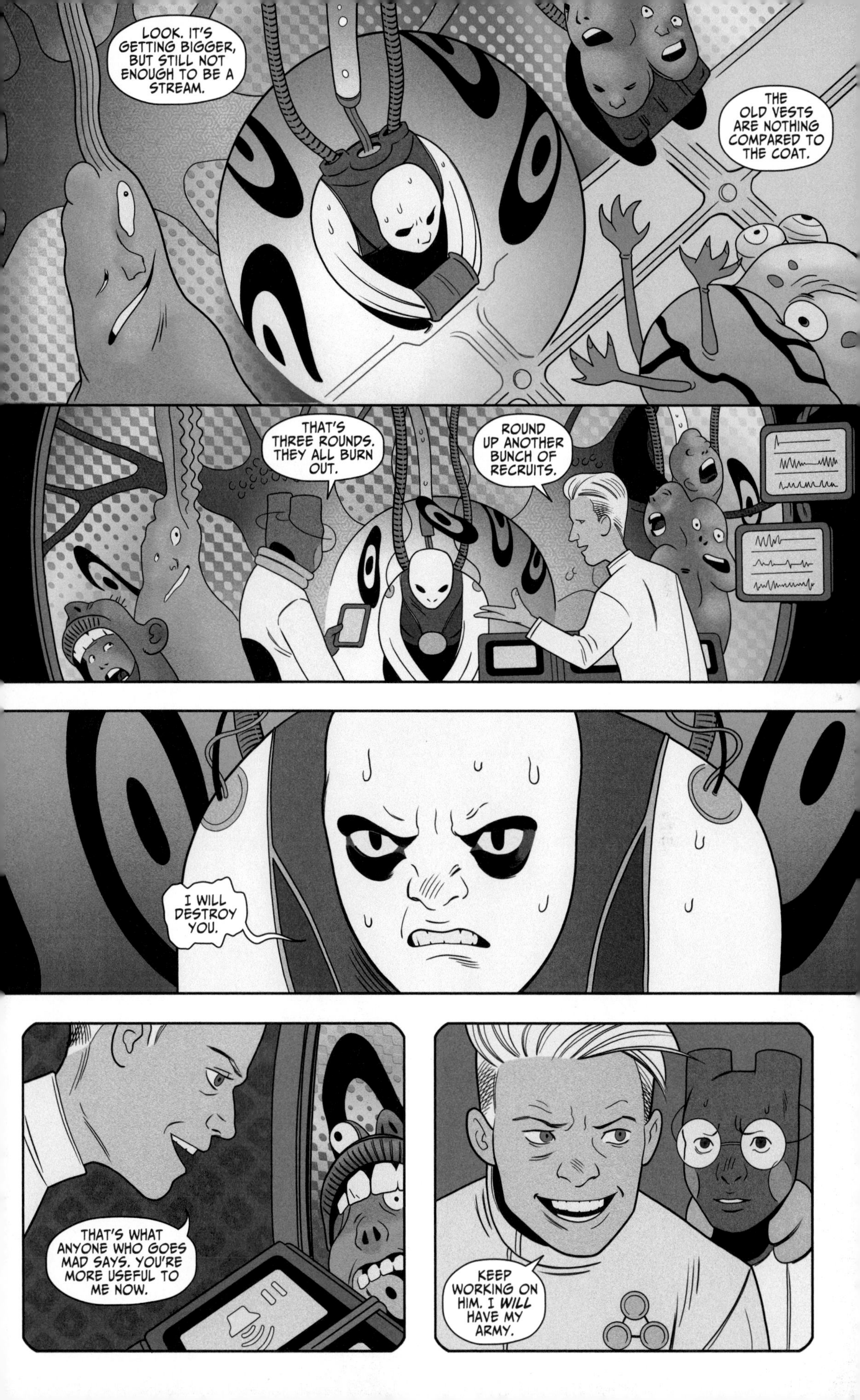
LOOK. IT'S GETTING BIGGER, BUT STILL NOT ENOUGH TO BE A STREAM.
THE OLD VESTS ARE NOTHING COMPARED TO THE COAT.
THAT'S THREE ROUNDS. THEY ALL BURN OUT.
ROUND UP ANOTHER BUNCH OF RECRUITS.
I WILL DESTROY YOU.
THAT'S WHAT ANYONE WHO GOES MAD SAYS. YOU'RE MORE USEFUL TO ME NOW.
KEEP WORKING ON HIM. I *WILL* HAVE MY ARMY.

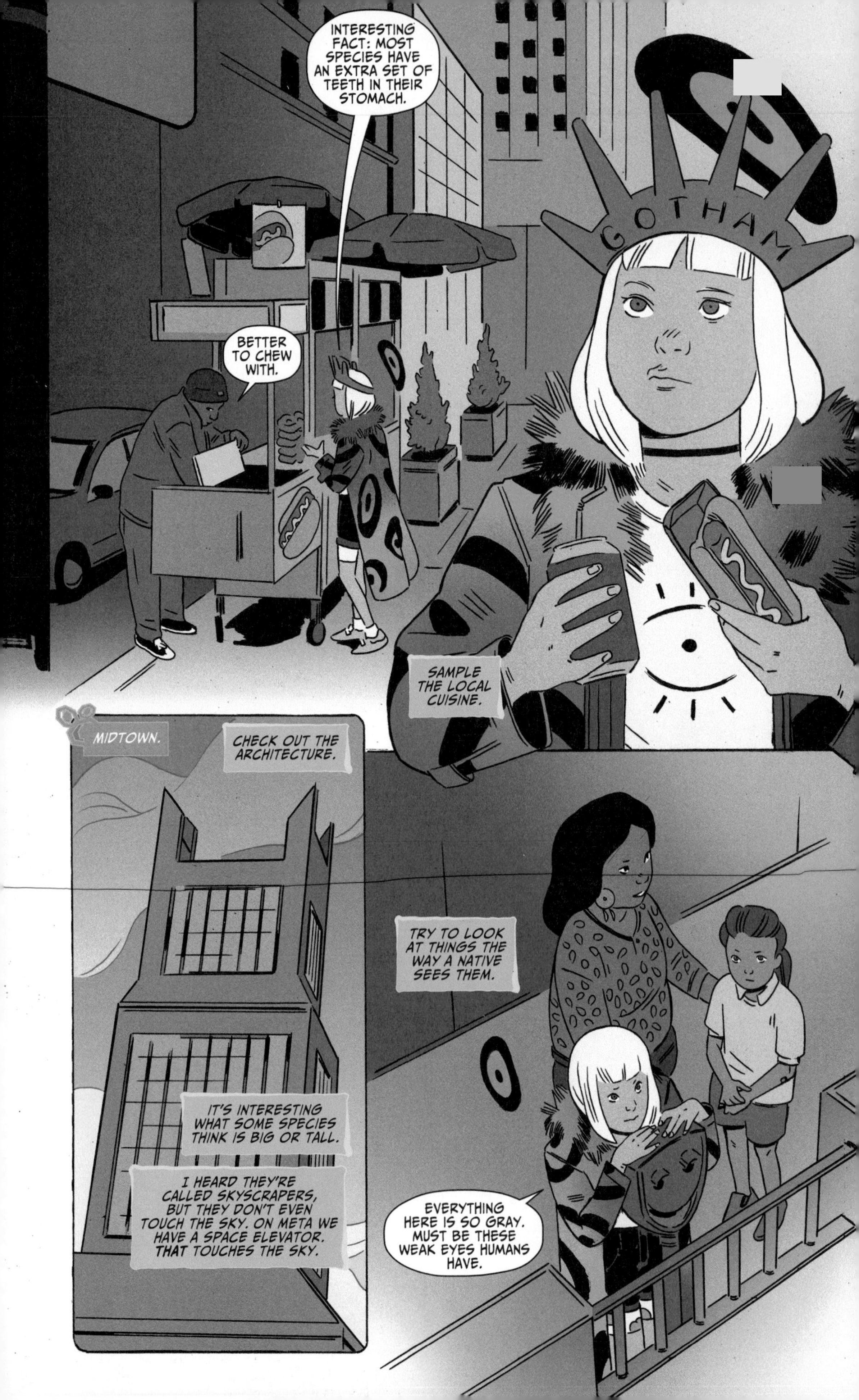

INTERESTING FACT: MOST SPECIES HAVE AN EXTRA SET OF TEETH IN THEIR STOMACH.
BETTER TO CHEW WITH.
GOTHAM
SAMPLE THE LOCAL CUISINE.
MIDTOWN.
CHECK OUT THE ARCHITECTURE.
IT'S INTERESTING WHAT SOME SPECIES THINK IS BIG OR TALL.
I HEARD THEY'RE CALLED SKYSCRAPERS, BUT THEY DON'T EVEN TOUCH THE SKY. ON META WE HAVE A SPACE ELEVATOR. THAT TOUCHES THE SKY.
TRY TO LOOK AT THINGS THE WAY A NATIVE SEES THEM.
EVERYTHING HERE IS SO GRAY. MUST BE THESE WEAK EYES HUMANS HAVE.

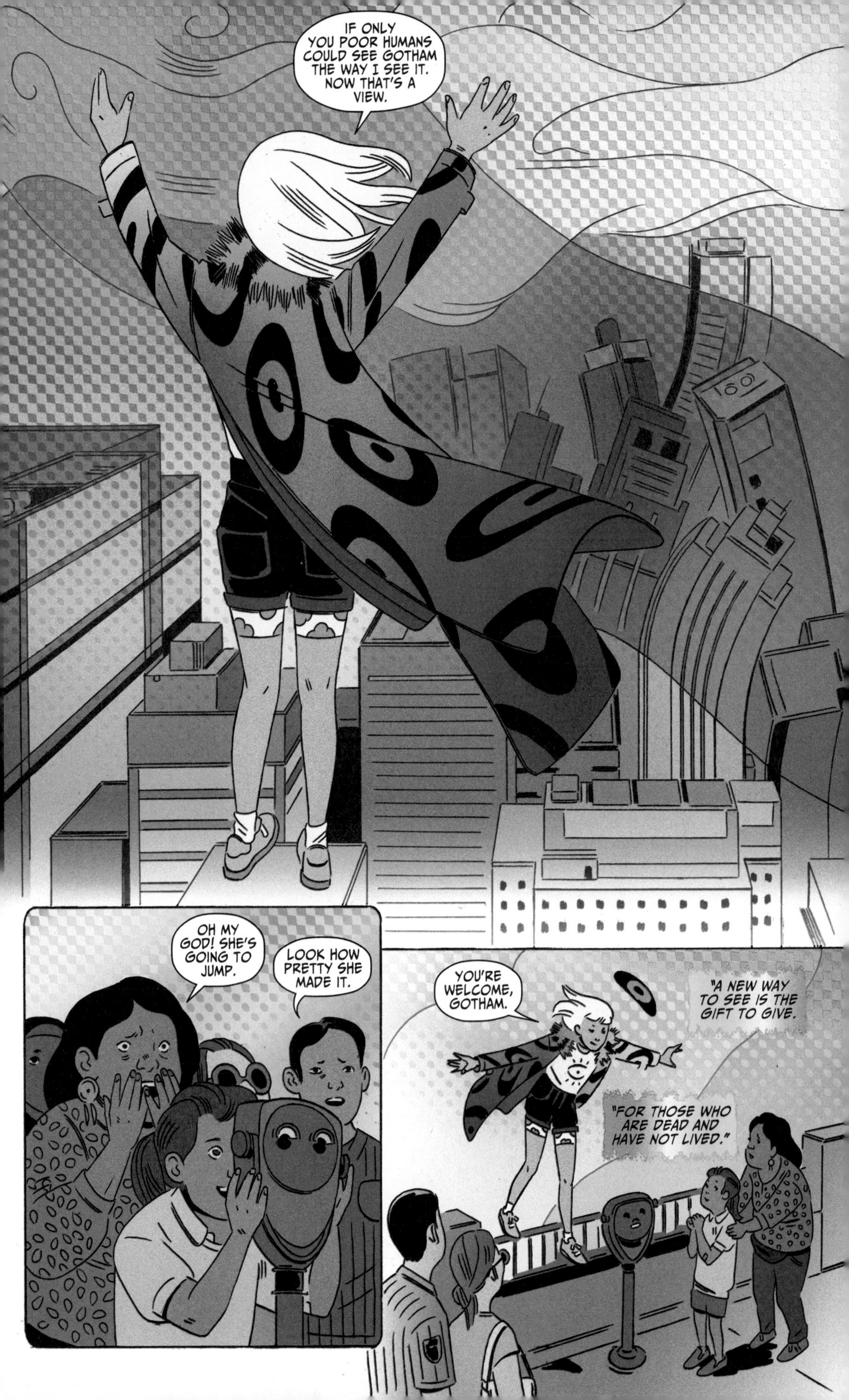
IF ONLY YOU POOR HUMANS COULD SEE GOTHAM THE WAY I SEE IT. NOW THAT'S A VIEW.
OH MY GOD! SHE'S GOING TO JUMP.
LOOK HOW PRETTY SHE MADE IT.
YOU'RE WELCOME, GOTHAM.
"A NEW WAY TO SEE IS THE GIFT TO GIVE.
"FOR THOSE WHO ARE DEAD AND HAVE NOT LIVED."

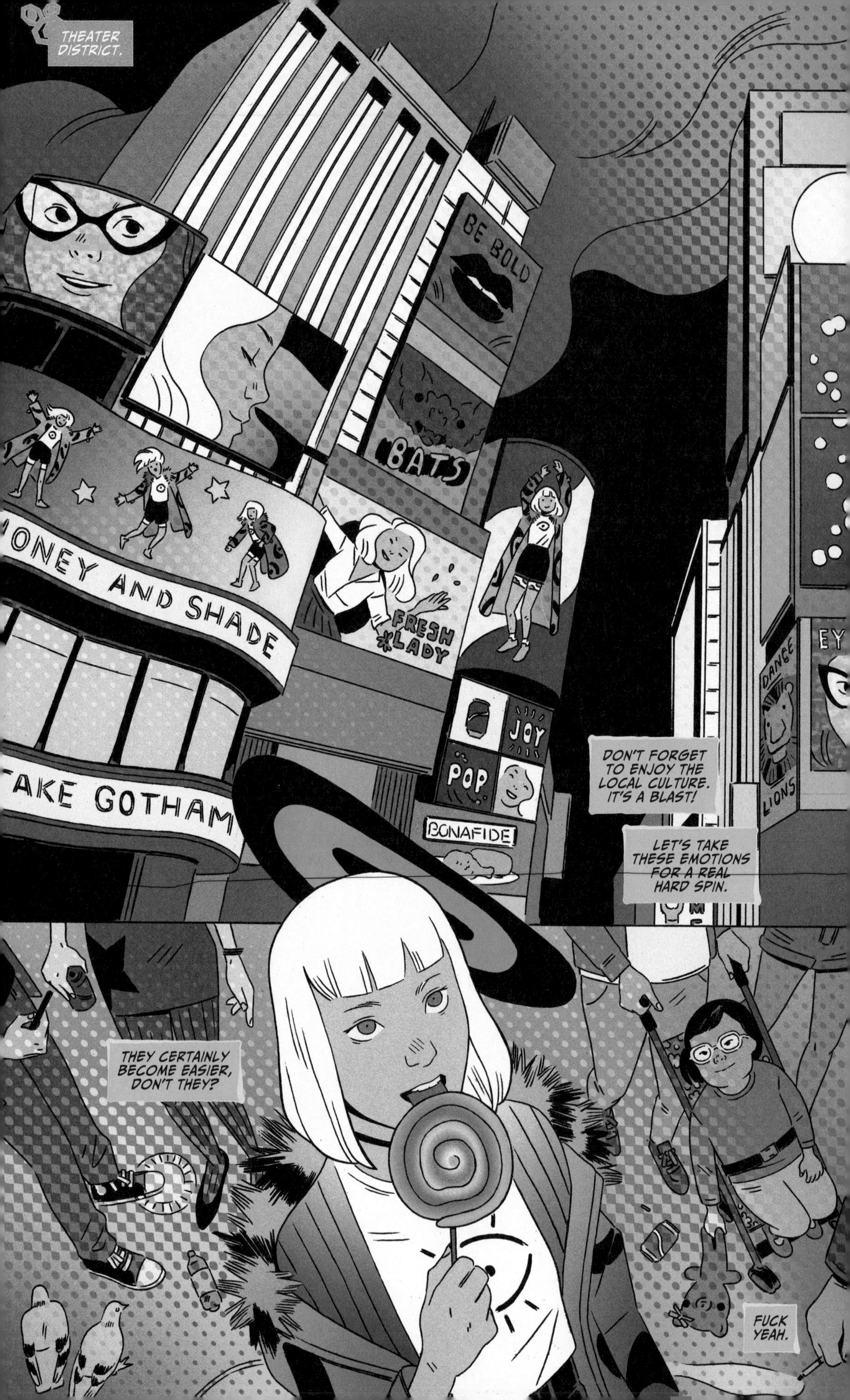
THEATER DISTRICT.
BE BOLD
BATS
ONEY AND SHADE
FRESH LADY
JOY
POP
AKE GOTHAM
BONAFIDE
DANCE
LIONS
DON'T FORGET TO ENJOY THE LOCAL CULTURE. IT'S A BLAST!
LET'S TAKE THESE EMOTIONS FOR A REAL HARD SPIN.
THEY CERTAINLY BECOME EASIER, DON'T THEY?
FUCK YEAH.

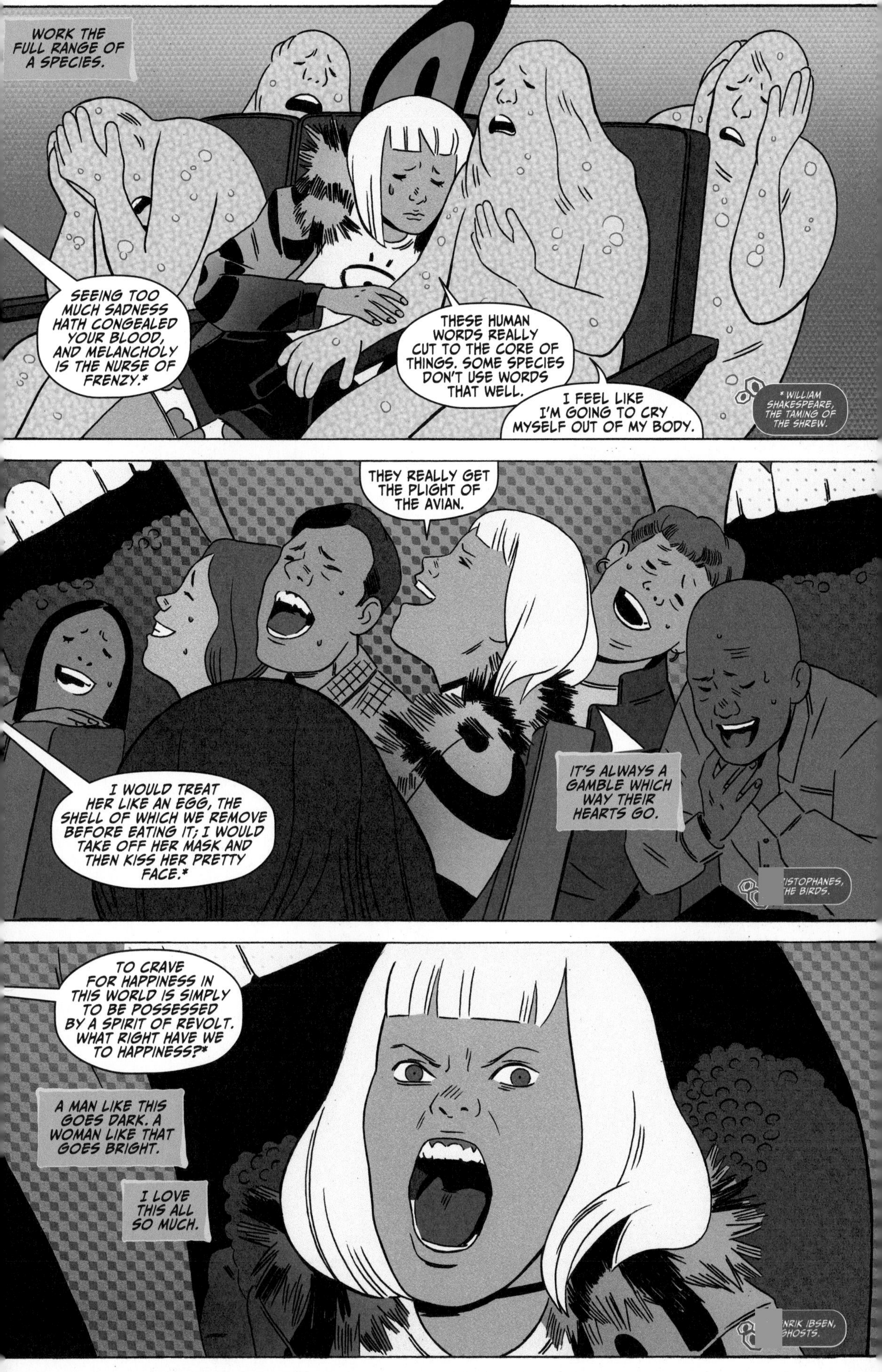
WORK THE FULL RANGE OF A SPECIES.
SEEING TOO MUCH SADNESS HATH CONGEALED YOUR BLOOD, AND MELANCHOLY IS THE NURSE OF FRENZY.*
THESE HUMAN WORDS REALLY CUT TO THE CORE OF THINGS. SOME SPECIES DON'T USE WORDS THAT WELL.
I FEEL LIKE I'M GOING TO CRY MYSELF OUT OF MY BODY.
* WILLIAM SHAKESPEARE, THE TAMING OF THE SHREW.
THEY REALLY GET THE PLIGHT OF THE AVIAN.
I WOULD TREAT HER LIKE AN EGG, THE SHELL OF WHICH WE REMOVE BEFORE EATING IT; I WOULD TAKE OFF HER MASK AND THEN KISS HER PRETTY FACE.*
IT'S ALWAYS A GAMBLE WHICH WAY THEIR HEARTS GO.
ISTOPHANES, HE BIRDS.
TO CRAVE FOR HAPPINESS IN THIS WORLD IS SIMPLY TO BE POSSESSED BY A SPIRIT OF REVOLT. WHAT RIGHT HAVE WE TO HAPPINESS?*
A MAN LIKE THIS GOES DARK. A WOMAN LIKE THAT GOES BRIGHT.
I LOVE THIS ALL SO MUCH.
NRIK IBSEN, GHOSTS.

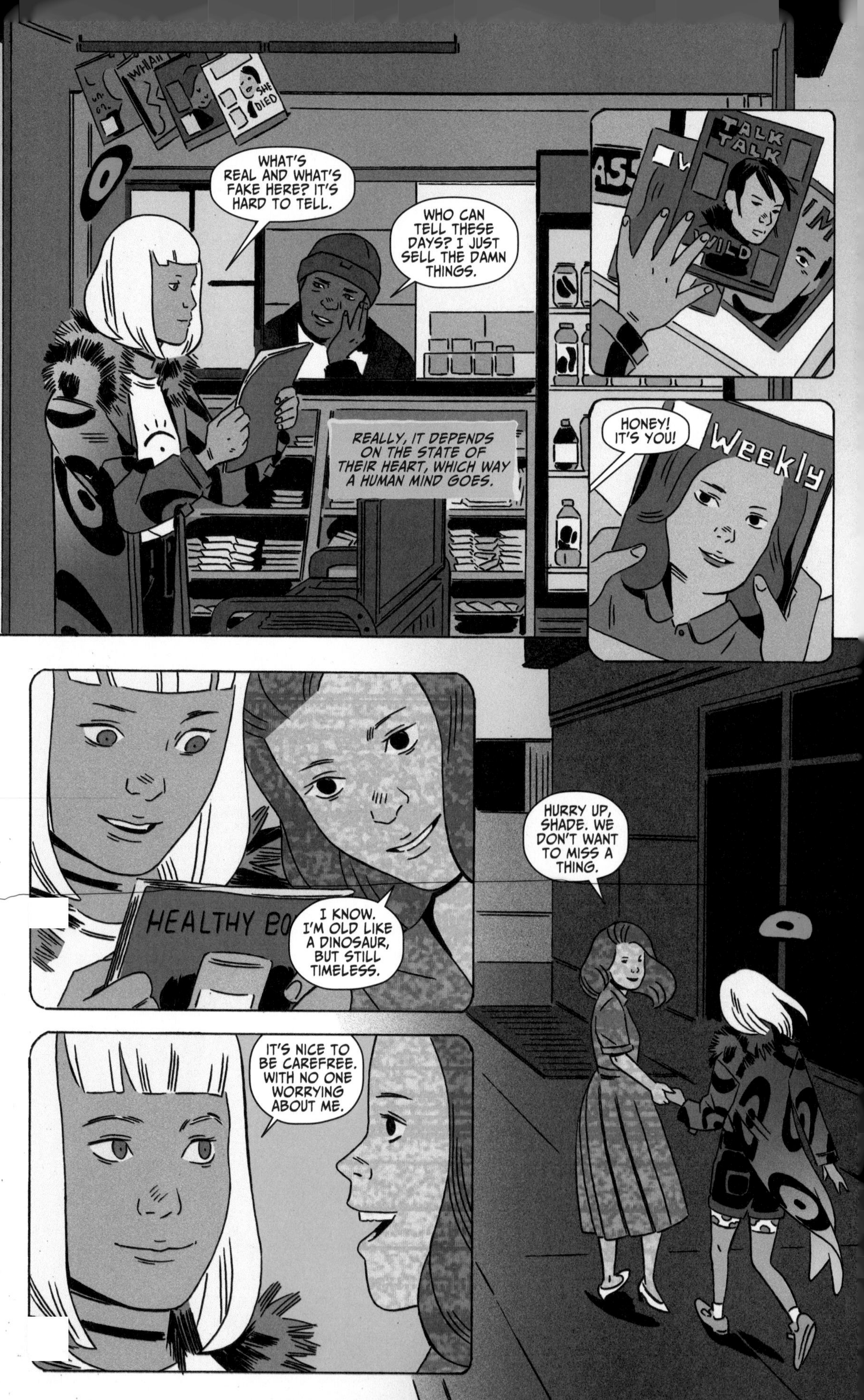
SHE DIED
WHAT'S REAL AND WHAT'S FAKE HERE? IT'S HARD TO TELL.
WHO CAN TELL THESE DAYS? I JUST SELL THE DAMN THINGS.
REALLY, IT DEPENDS ON THE STATE OF THEIR HEART, WHICH WAY A HUMAN MIND GOES.
TALK TALK
WILD
HONEY! IT'S YOU!
Weekly
HEALTHY BO
I KNOW. I'M OLD LIKE A DINOSAUR, BUT STILL TIMELESS.
IT'S NICE TO BE CAREFREE. WITH NO ONE WORRYING ABOUT ME.
HURRY UP, SHADE. WE DON'T WANT TO MISS A THING.

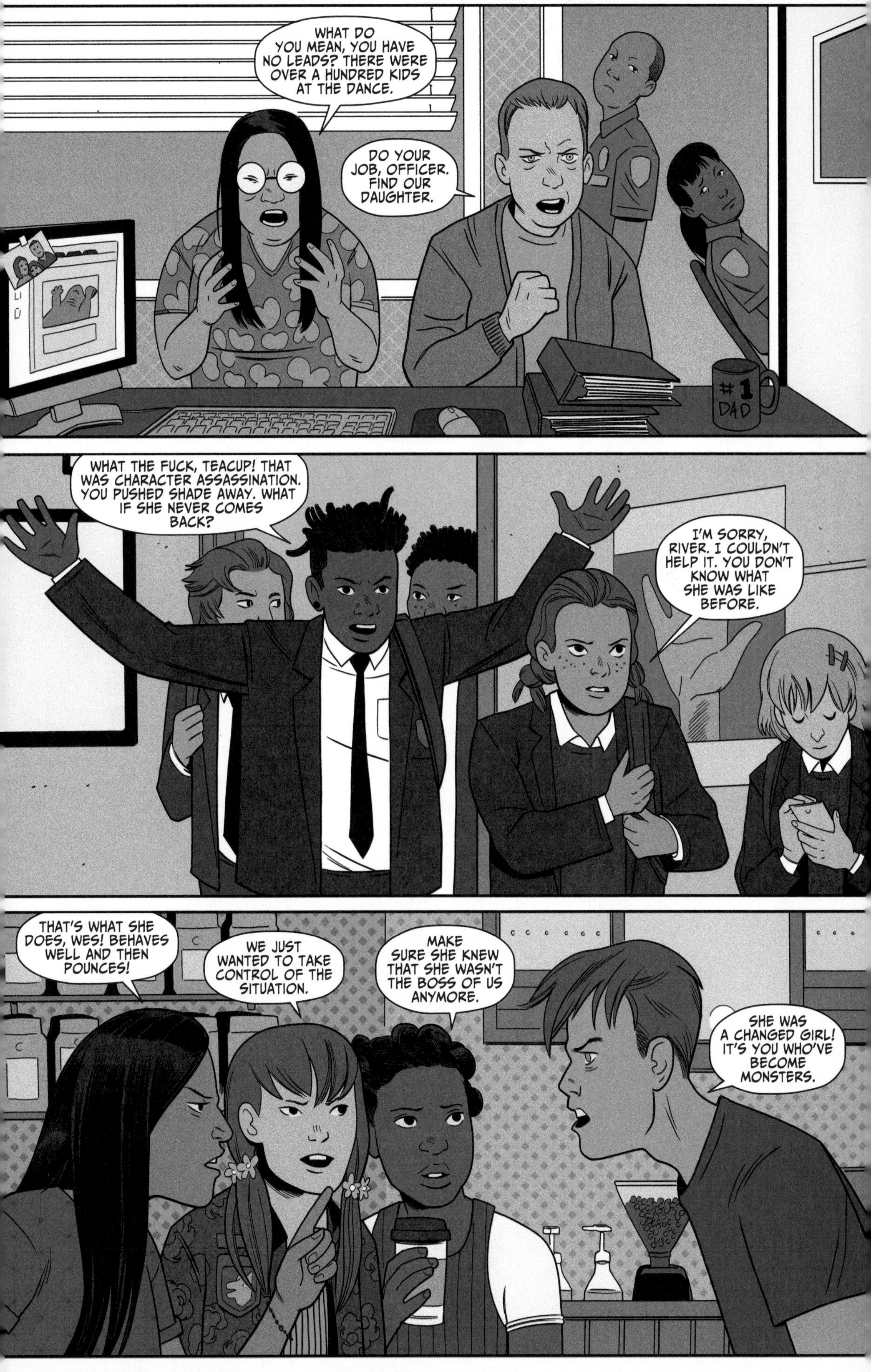
WHAT DO YOU MEAN, YOU HAVE NO LEADS? THERE WERE OVER A HUNDRED KIDS AT THE DANCE.
DO YOUR JOB, OFFICER. FIND OUR DAUGHTER.
#1 DAD
WHAT THE FUCK, TEACUP! THAT WAS CHARACTER ASSASSINATION. YOU PUSHED SHADE AWAY. WHAT IF SHE NEVER COMES BACK?
I'M SORRY, RIVER. I COULDN'T HELP IT. YOU DON'T KNOW WHAT SHE WAS LIKE BEFORE.
THAT'S WHAT SHE DOES, WES! BEHAVES WELL AND THEN POUNCES!
WE JUST WANTED TO TAKE CONTROL OF THE SITUATION.
MAKE SURE SHE KNEW THAT SHE WASN'T THE BOSS OF US ANYMORE.
SHE WAS A CHANGED GIRL! IT'S YOU WHO'VE BECOME MONSTERS.

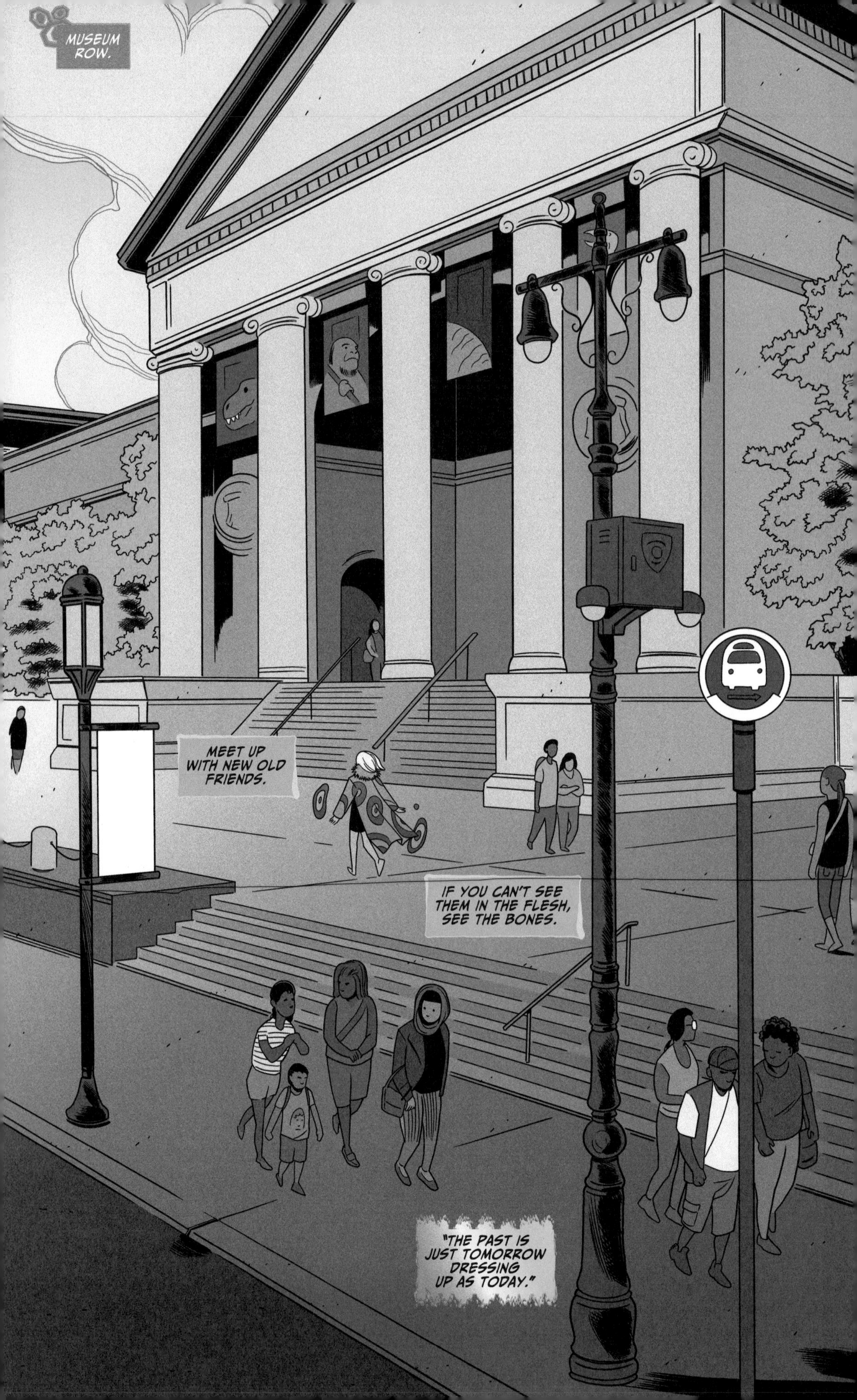
MUSEUM ROW.
MEET UP WITH NEW OLD FRIENDS.
IF YOU CAN'T SEE THEM IN THE FLESH, SEE THE BONES.
"THE PAST IS JUST TOMORROW DRESSING UP AS TODAY."

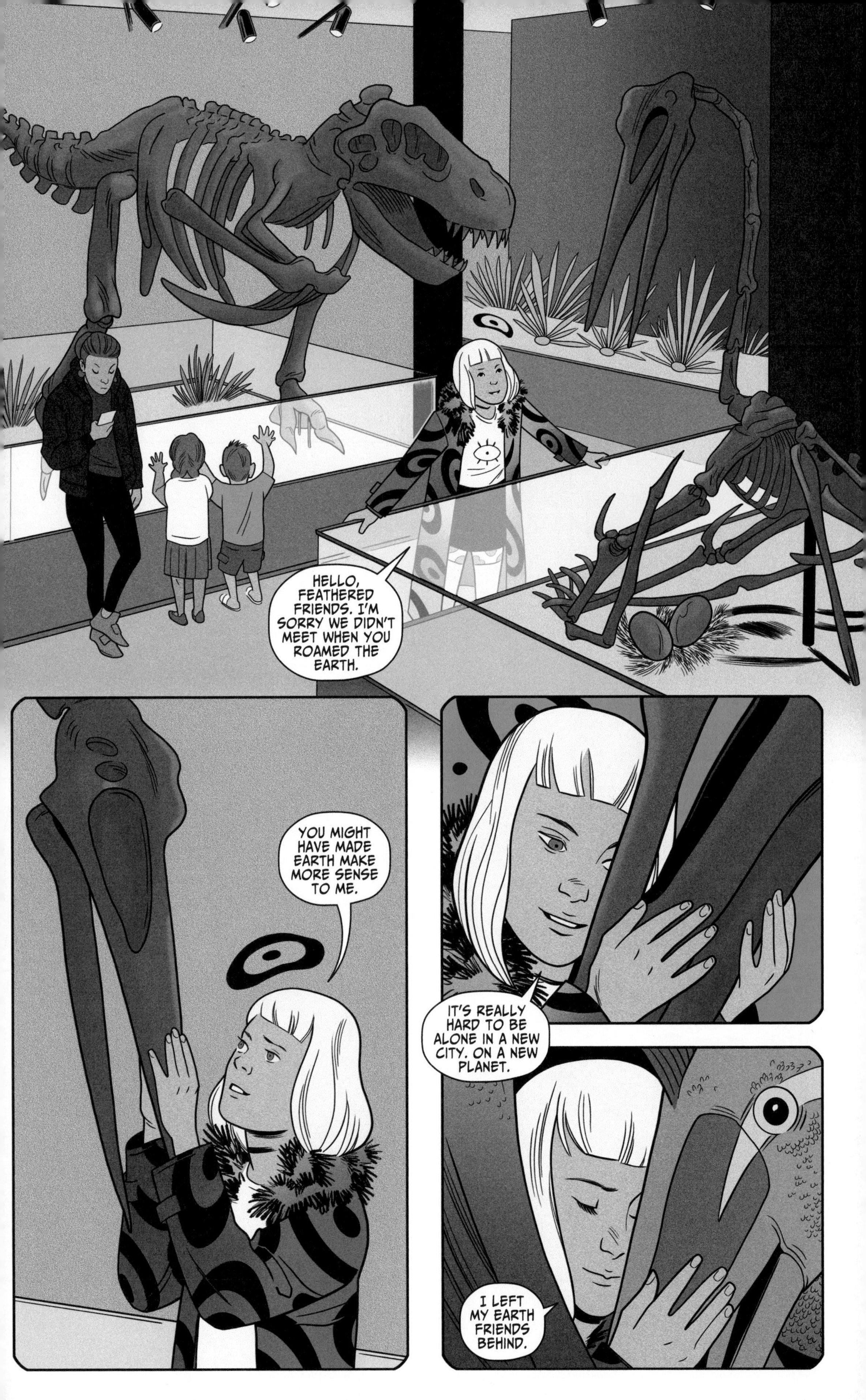
HELLO, FEATHERED FRIENDS. I'M SORRY WE DIDN'T MEET WHEN YOU ROAMED THE EARTH.
YOU MIGHT HAVE MADE EARTH MAKE MORE SENSE TO ME.
IT'S REALLY HARD TO BE ALONE IN A NEW CITY. ON A NEW PLANET.
I LEFT MY EARTH FRIENDS BEHIND.

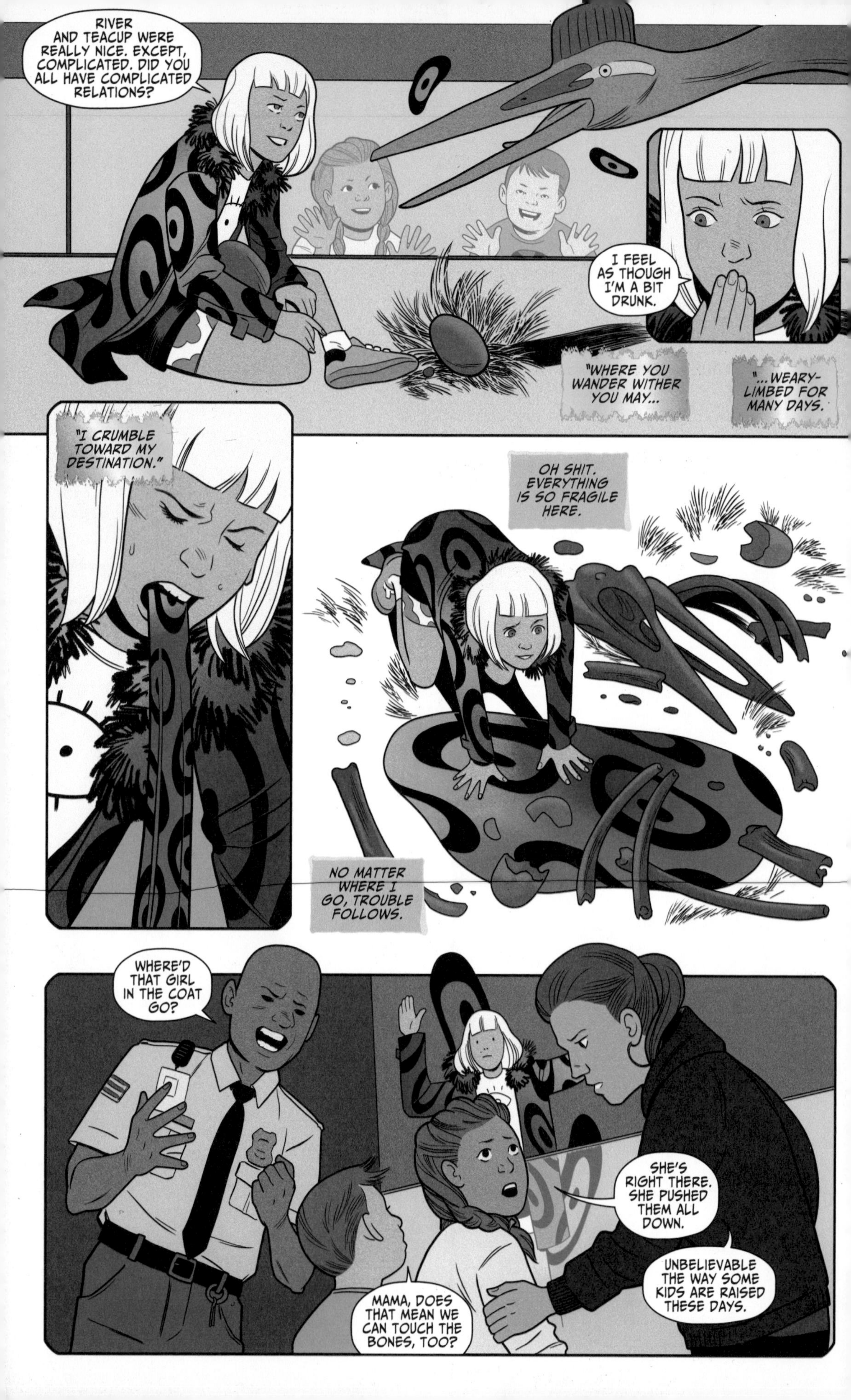
RIVER AND TEACUP WERE REALLY NICE. EXCEPT, COMPLICATED. DID YOU ALL HAVE COMPLICATED RELATIONS?
I FEEL AS THOUGH I'M A BIT DRUNK.
"WHERE YOU WANDER WITHER YOU MAY...
"...WEARY-LIMBED FOR MANY DAYS.
"I CRUMBLE TOWARD MY DESTINATION."
OH SHIT. EVERYTHING IS SO FRAGILE HERE.
NO MATTER WHERE I GO, TROUBLE FOLLOWS.
WHERE'D THAT GIRL IN THE COAT GO?
SHE'S RIGHT THERE. SHE PUSHED THEM ALL DOWN.
UNBELIEVABLE THE WAY SOME KIDS ARE RAISED THESE DAYS.
MAMA, DOES THAT MEAN WE CAN TOUCH THE BONES, TOO?

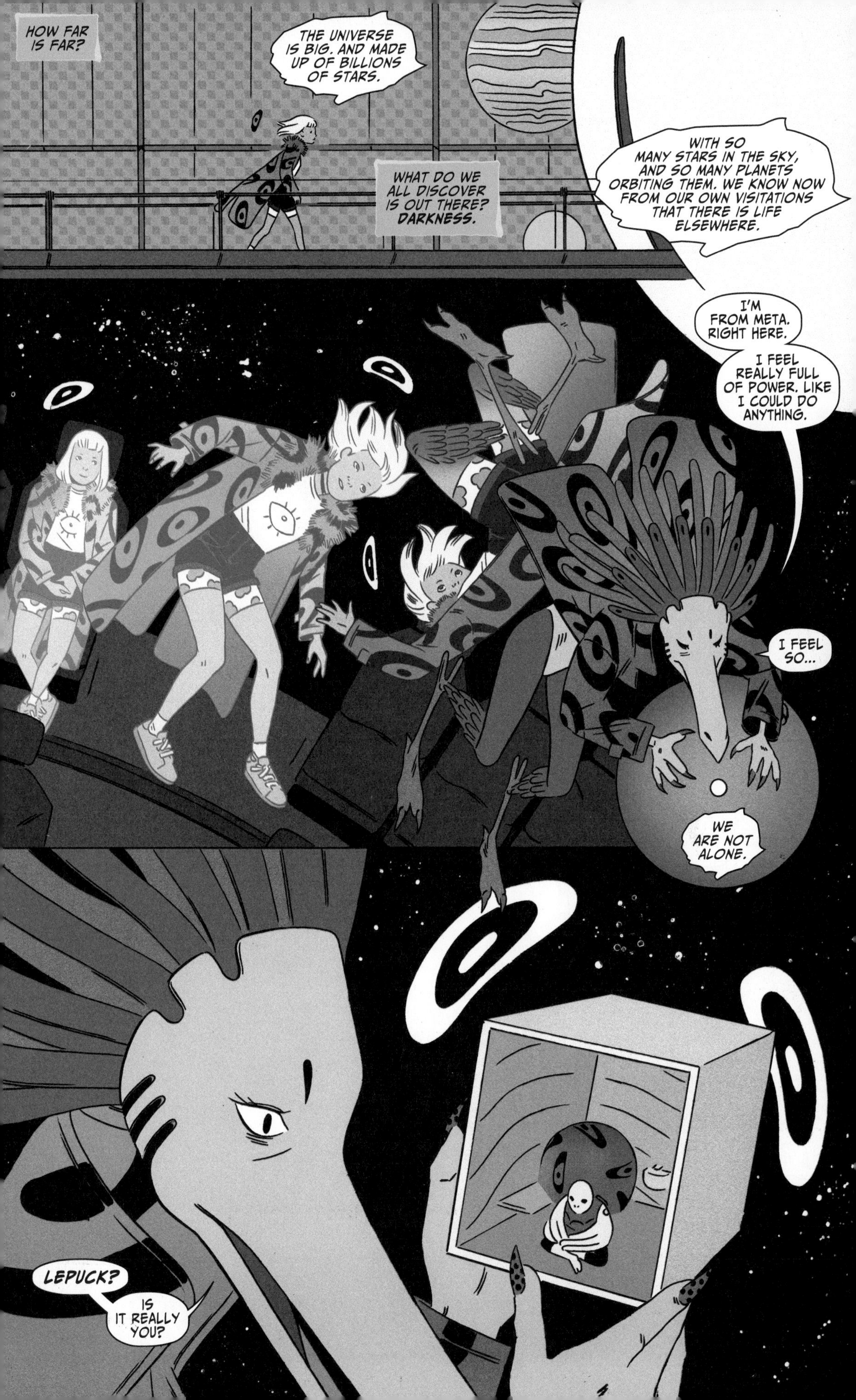
HOW FAR IS FAR?
THE UNIVERSE IS BIG. AND MADE UP OF BILLIONS OF STARS.
WHAT DO WE ALL DISCOVER IS OUT THERE? DARKNESS.
WITH SO MANY STARS IN THE SKY, AND SO MANY PLANETS ORBITING THEM. WE KNOW NOW FROM OUR OWN VISITATIONS THAT THERE IS LIFE ELSEWHERE.
I'M FROM META. RIGHT HERE.
I FEEL REALLY FULL OF POWER. LIKE I COULD DO ANYTHING.
I FEEL SO...
WE ARE NOT ALONE.
LEPUCK?
IS IT REALLY YOU?

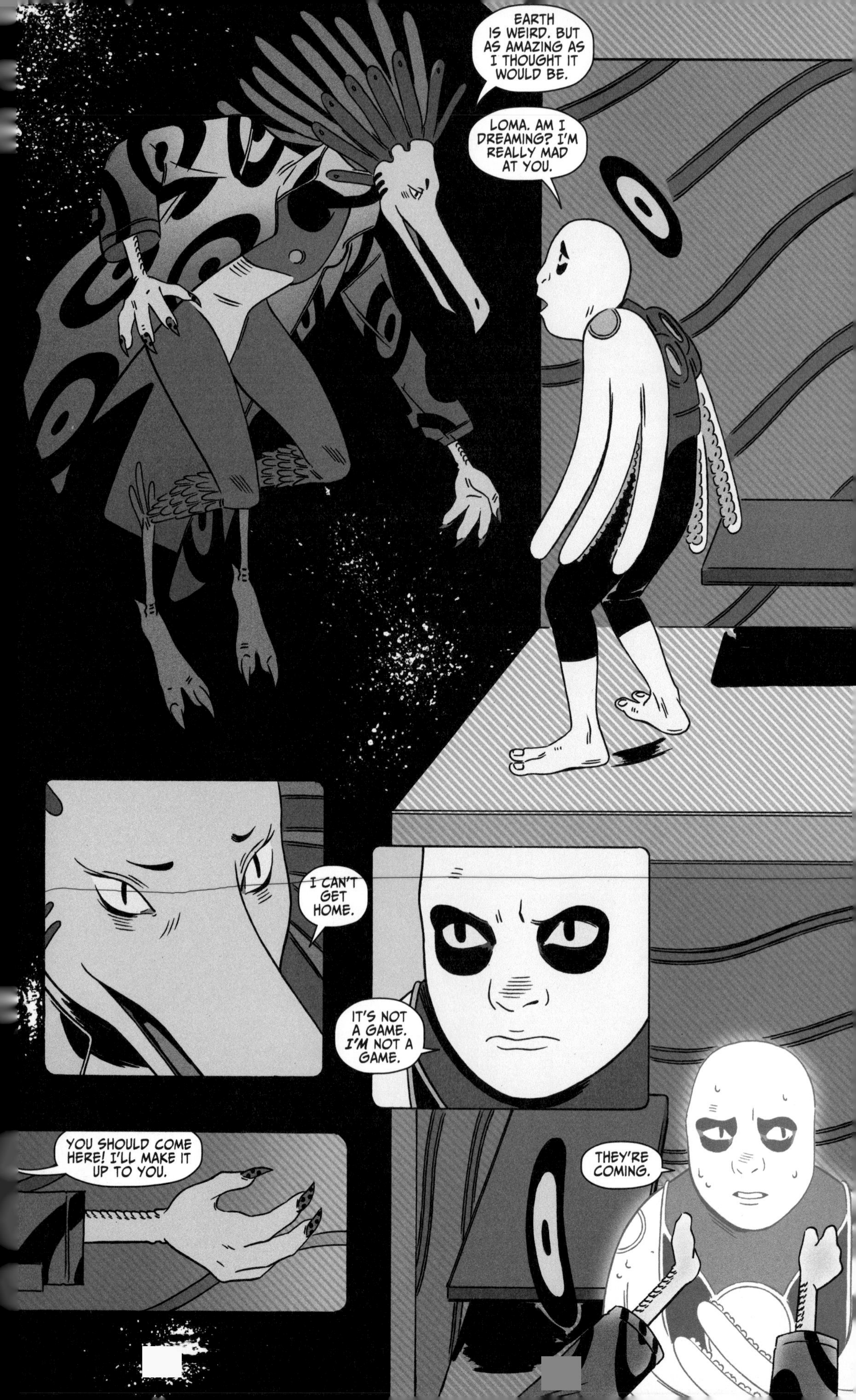
EARTH IS WEIRD. BUT AS AMAZING AS I THOUGHT IT WOULD BE.
LOMA. AM I DREAMING? I'M REALLY MAD AT YOU.
I CAN'T GET HOME.
IT'S NOT A GAME. *I'M* NOT A GAME.
YOU SHOULD COME HERE! I'LL MAKE IT UP TO YOU.
THEY'RE COMING.

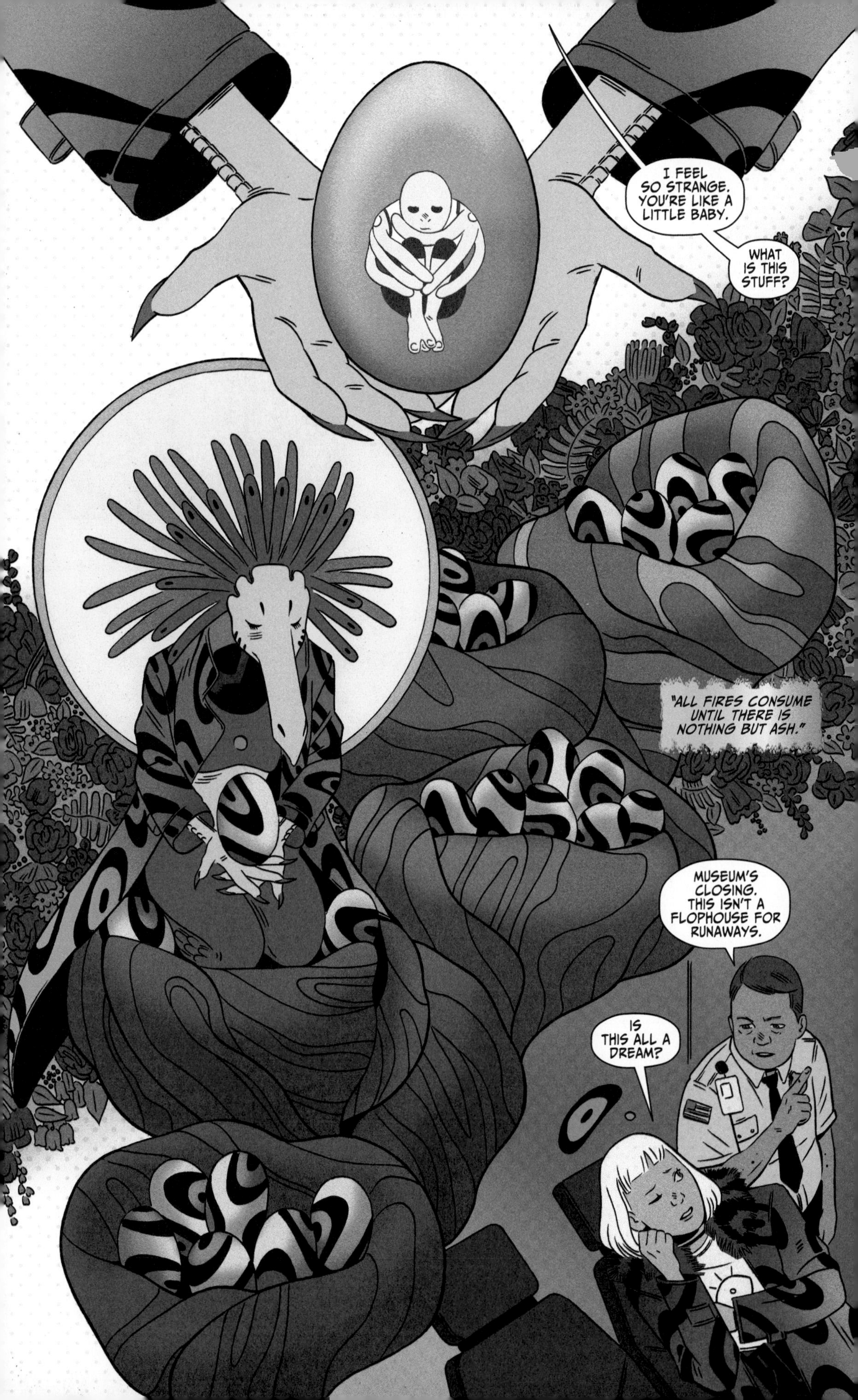
I FEEL SO STRANGE. YOU'RE LIKE A LITTLE BABY.
WHAT IS THIS STUFF?
"ALL FIRES CONSUME UNTIL THERE IS NOTHING BUT ASH."
MUSEUM'S CLOSING. THIS ISN'T A FLOPHOUSE FOR RUNAWAYS.
IS THIS ALL A DREAM?

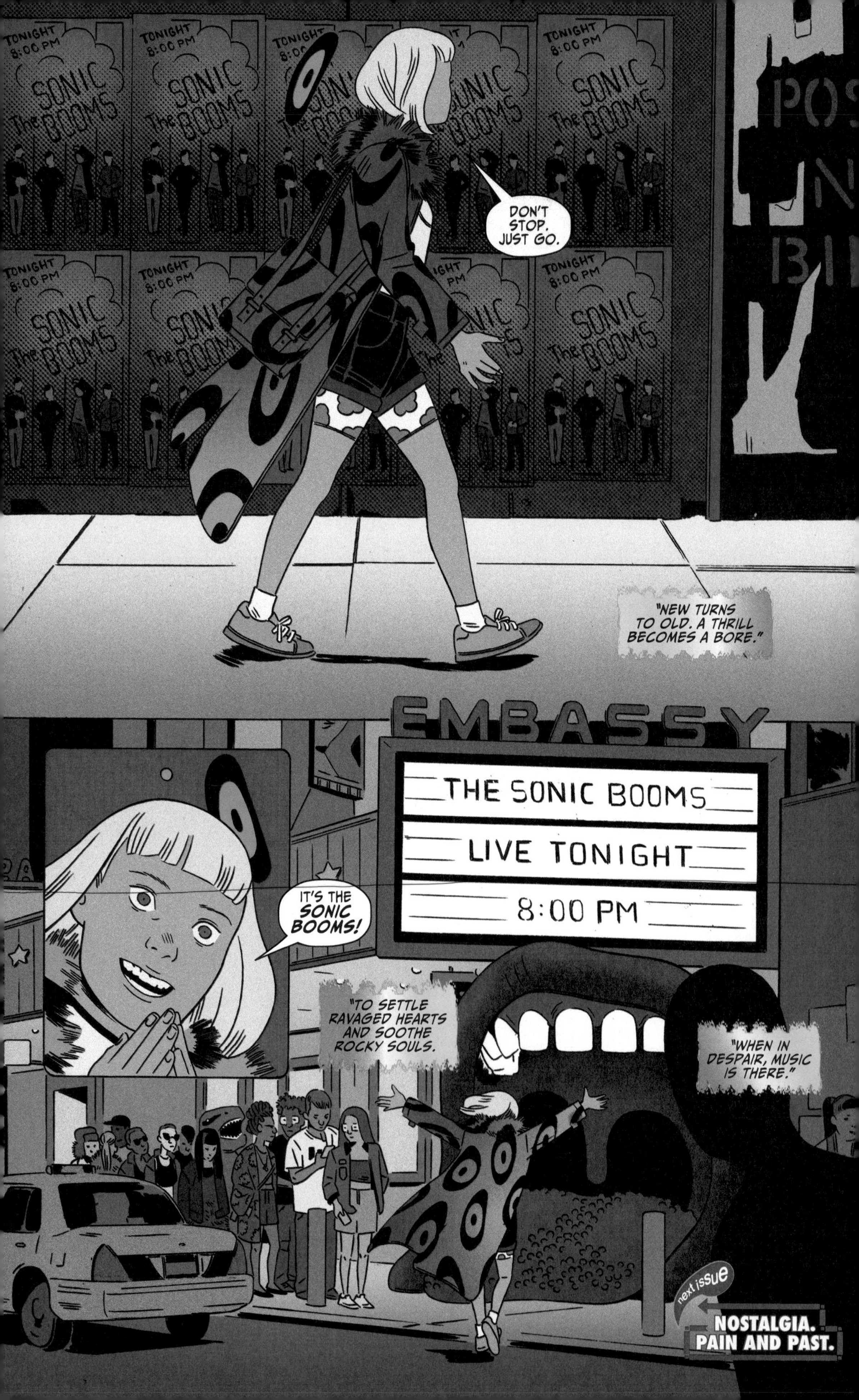
TONIGHT 8:00 PM
SONIC The BOOMS
DON'T STOP. JUST GO.
"NEW TURNS TO OLD. A THRILL BECOMES A BORE."
EMBASSY
THE SONIC BOOMS
LIVE TONIGHT
8:00 PM
IT'S THE SONIC BOOMS!
"TO SETTLE RAVAGED HEARTS AND SOOTHE ROCKY SOULS.
"WHEN IN DESPAIR, MUSIC IS THERE."
next issue
NOSTALGIA. PAIN AND PAST.

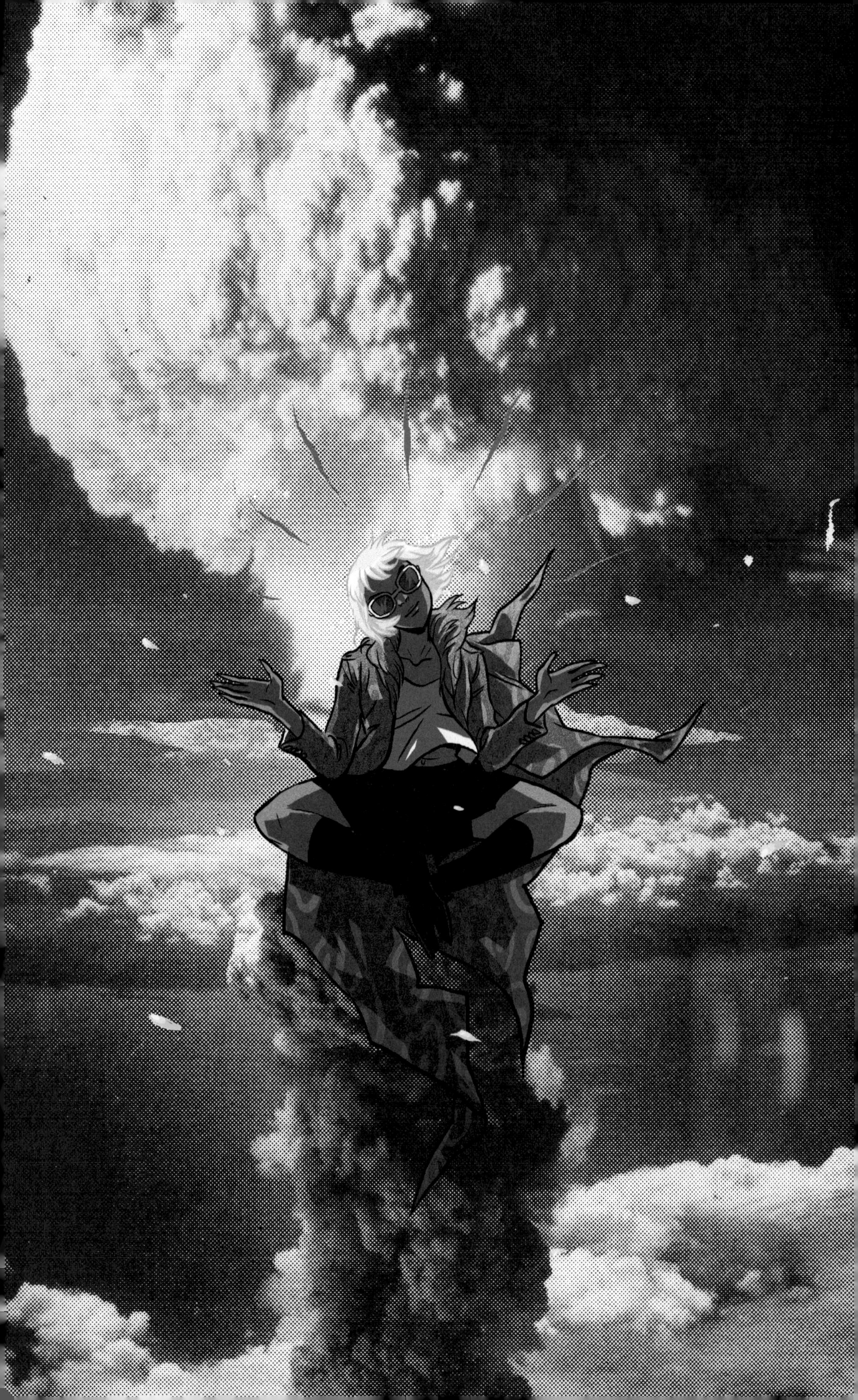

Variant cover art by
Brittney Williams

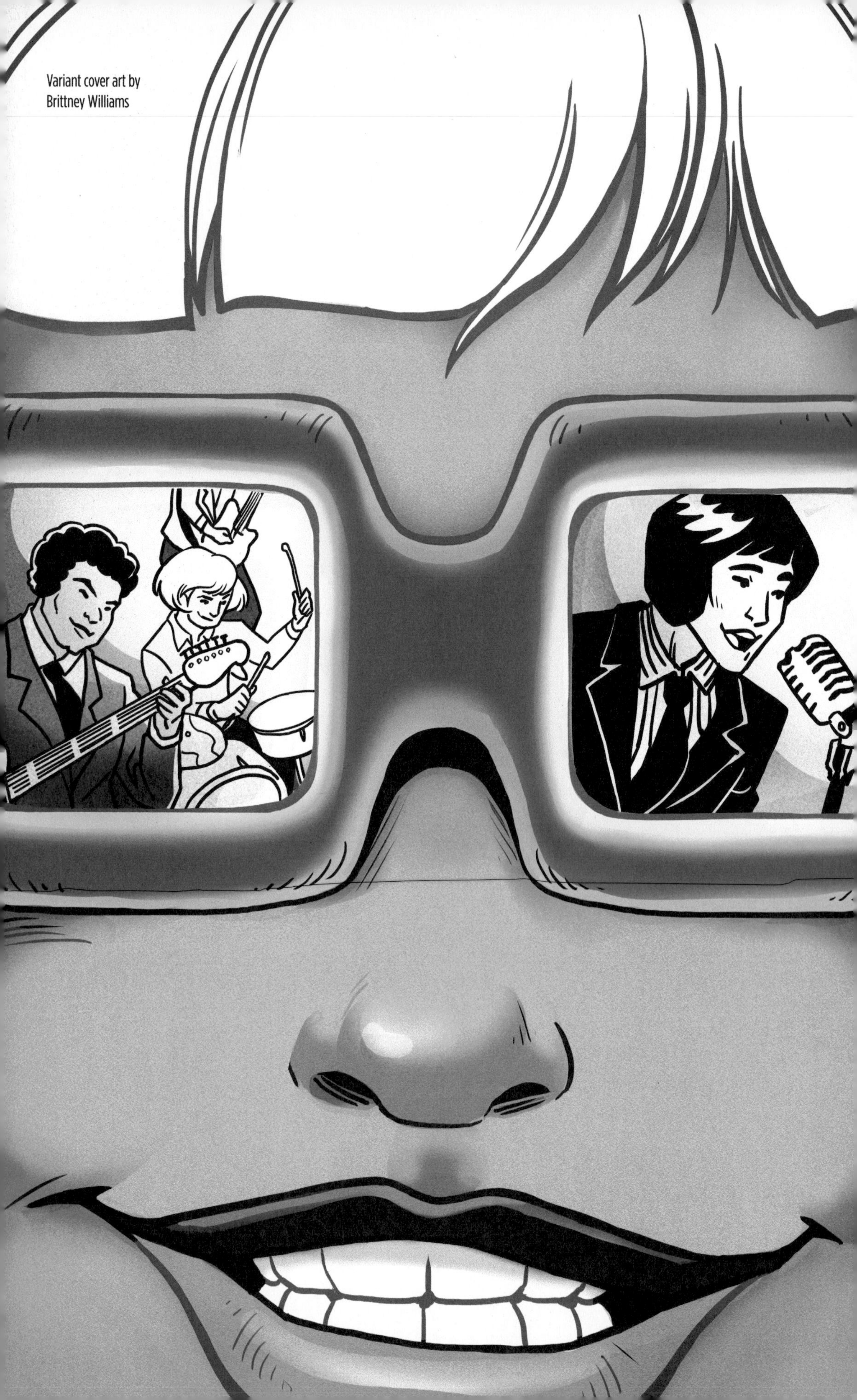

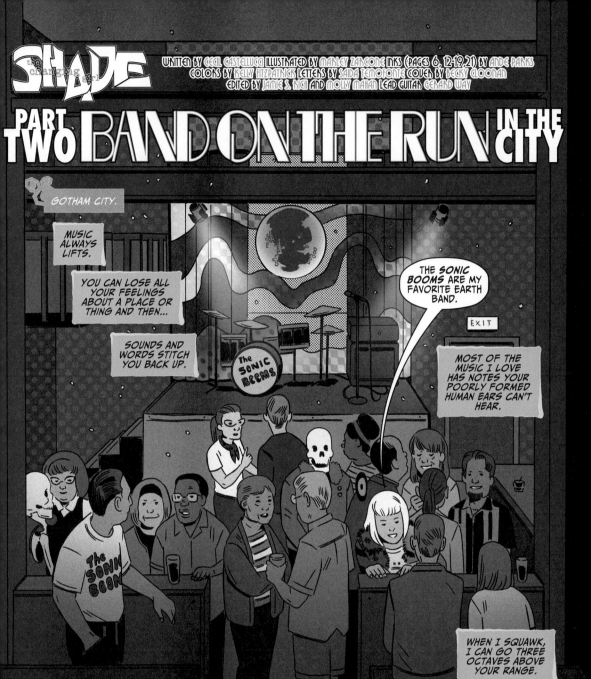

SHADE the changing girl — WRITTEN BY CECIL CASTELLUCCI ILLUSTRATED BY MARLEY ZARCONE INKS (PAGES 6, 12-19, 21) BY ANDE PARKS COLORS BY KELLY FITZPATRICK LETTERS BY SAIDA TEMOFONTE COVER BY BECKY CLOONAN EDITED BY JAMIE S. RICH AND MOLLY MAHAN LEAD GUITAR GERARD WAY

PART TWO BAND ON THE RUN IN THE CITY

GOTHAM CITY.

MUSIC ALWAYS LIFTS.

YOU CAN LOSE ALL YOUR FEELINGS ABOUT A PLACE OR THING AND THEN...

SOUNDS AND WORDS STITCH YOU BACK UP.

THE SONIC BOOMS ARE MY FAVORITE EARTH BAND.

EXIT

The Sonic Booms

MOST OF THE MUSIC I LOVE HAS NOTES YOUR POORLY FORMED HUMAN EARS CAN'T HEAR.

WHEN I SQUAWK, I CAN GO THREE OCTAVES ABOVE YOUR RANGE.

I GO TO A LOT OF SHOWS WHERE I'M FROM, BUT THIS IS MY FIRST EARTH SHOW.

YOUNG PEOPLE STILL LIKE THIS BAND?

IT'S PROBABLY IRONIC.

The SONIC

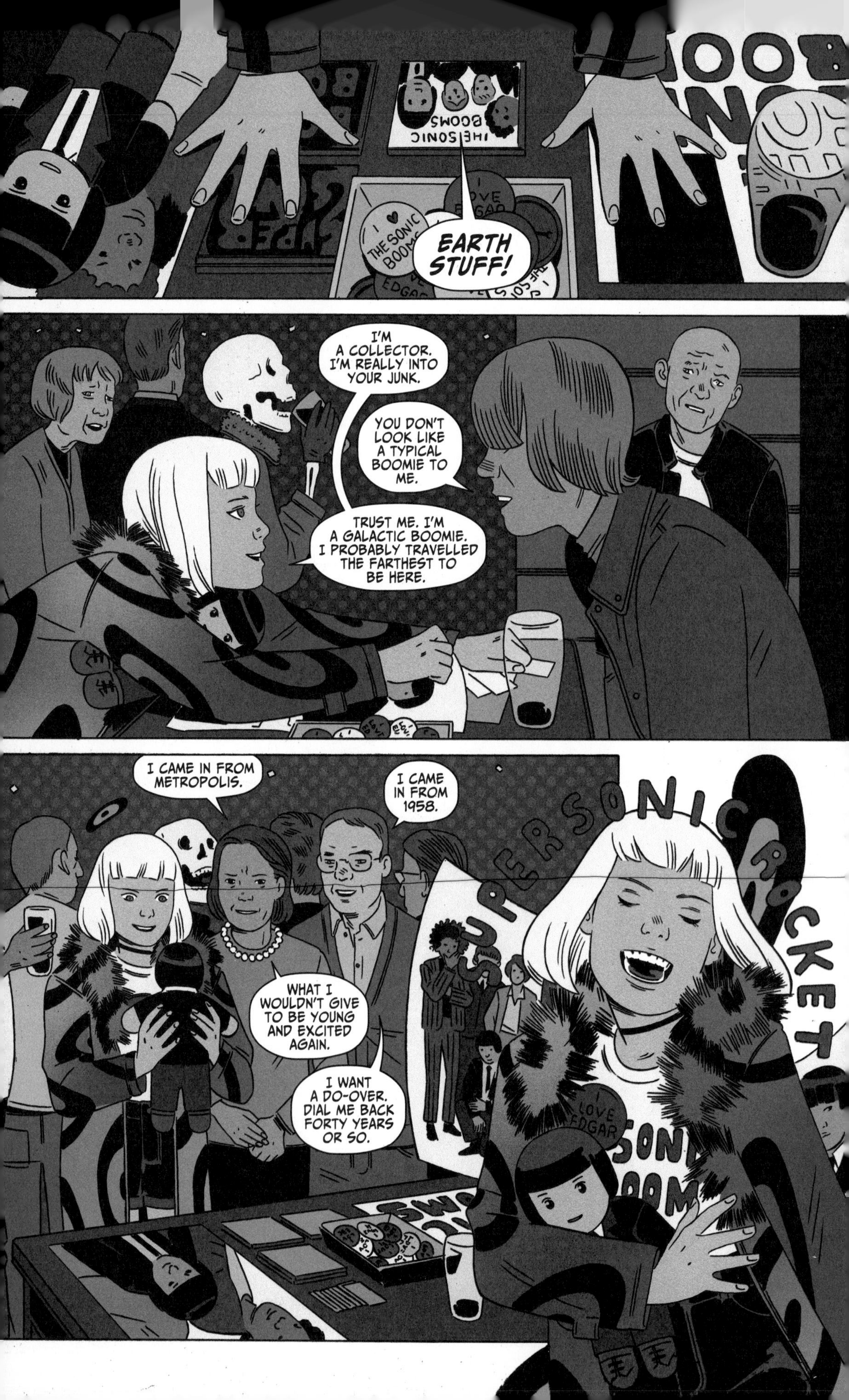

EARTH STUFF!
I'M A COLLECTOR. I'M REALLY INTO YOUR JUNK.
YOU DON'T LOOK LIKE A TYPICAL BOOMIE TO ME.
TRUST ME. I'M A GALACTIC BOOMIE. I PROBABLY TRAVELLED THE FARTHEST TO BE HERE.
I CAME IN FROM METROPOLIS.
I CAME IN FROM 1958.
SUPERSONIC ROCKET
WHAT I WOULDN'T GIVE TO BE YOUNG AND EXCITED AGAIN.
I WANT A DO-OVER. DIAL ME BACK FORTY YEARS OR SO.
I LOVE EDGAR

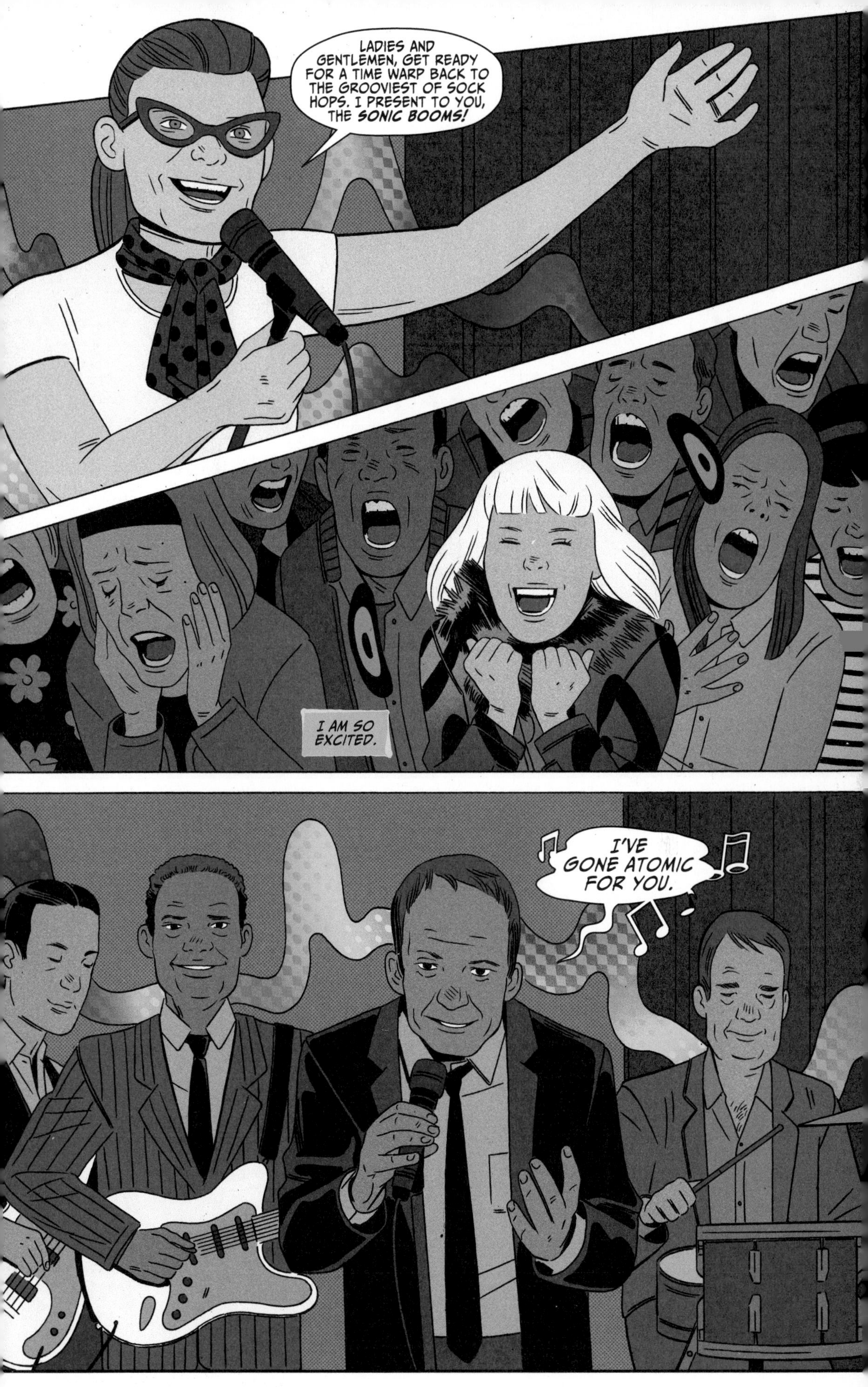
LADIES AND GENTLEMEN, GET READY FOR A TIME WARP BACK TO THE GROOVIEST OF SOCK HOPS. I PRESENT TO YOU, THE SONIC BOOMS!
I AM SO EXCITED.
I'VE GONE ATOMIC FOR YOU.

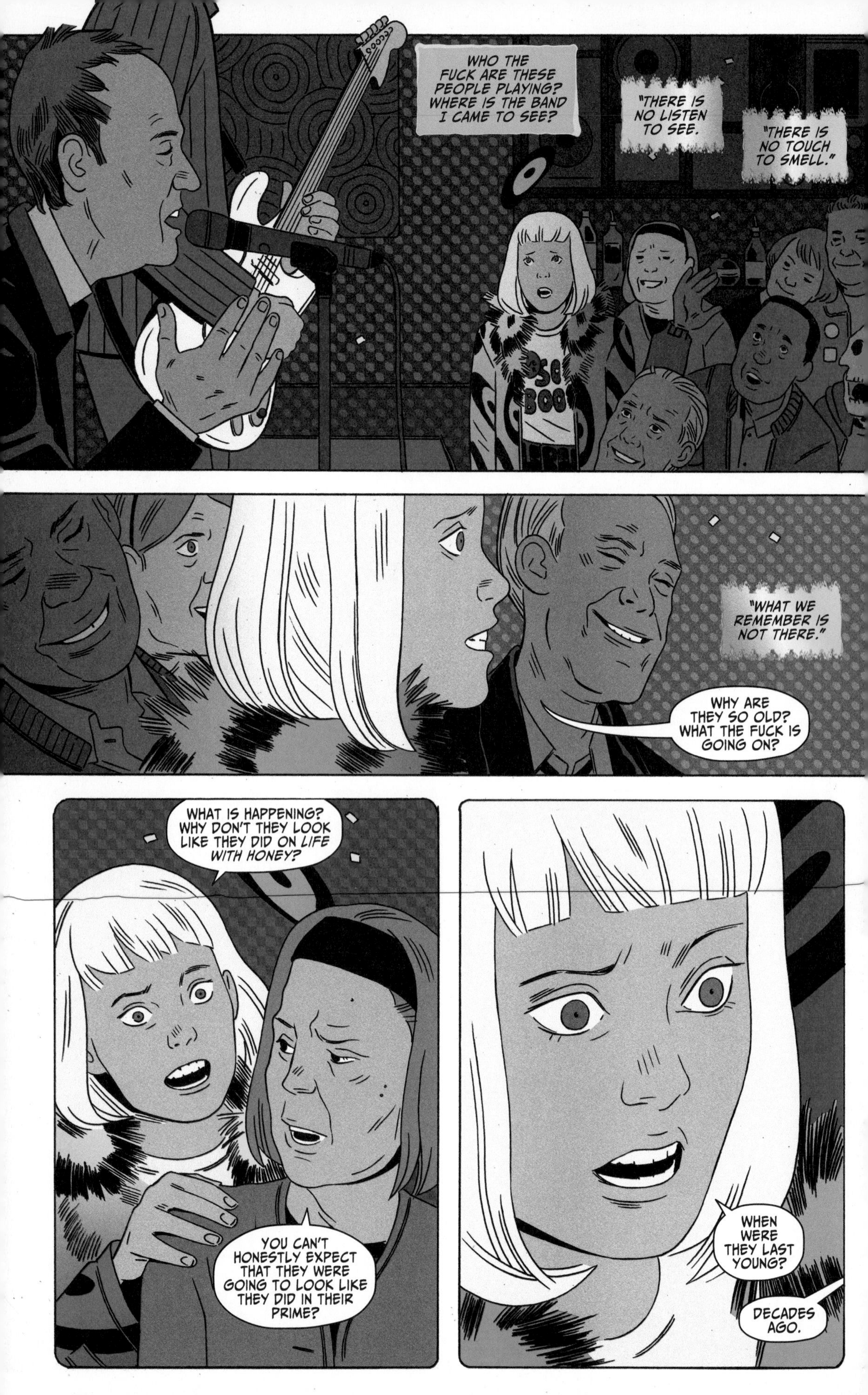
WHO THE FUCK ARE THESE PEOPLE PLAYING? WHERE IS THE BAND I CAME TO SEE?
"THERE IS NO LISTEN TO SEE.
"THERE IS NO TOUCH TO SMELL."
"WHAT WE REMEMBER IS NOT THERE."
WHY ARE THEY SO OLD? WHAT THE FUCK IS GOING ON?
WHAT IS HAPPENING? WHY DON'T THEY LOOK LIKE THEY DID ON *LIFE WITH HONEY*?
YOU CAN'T HONESTLY EXPECT THAT THEY WERE GOING TO LOOK LIKE THEY DID IN THEIR PRIME?
WHEN WERE THEY LAST YOUNG?
DECADES AGO.

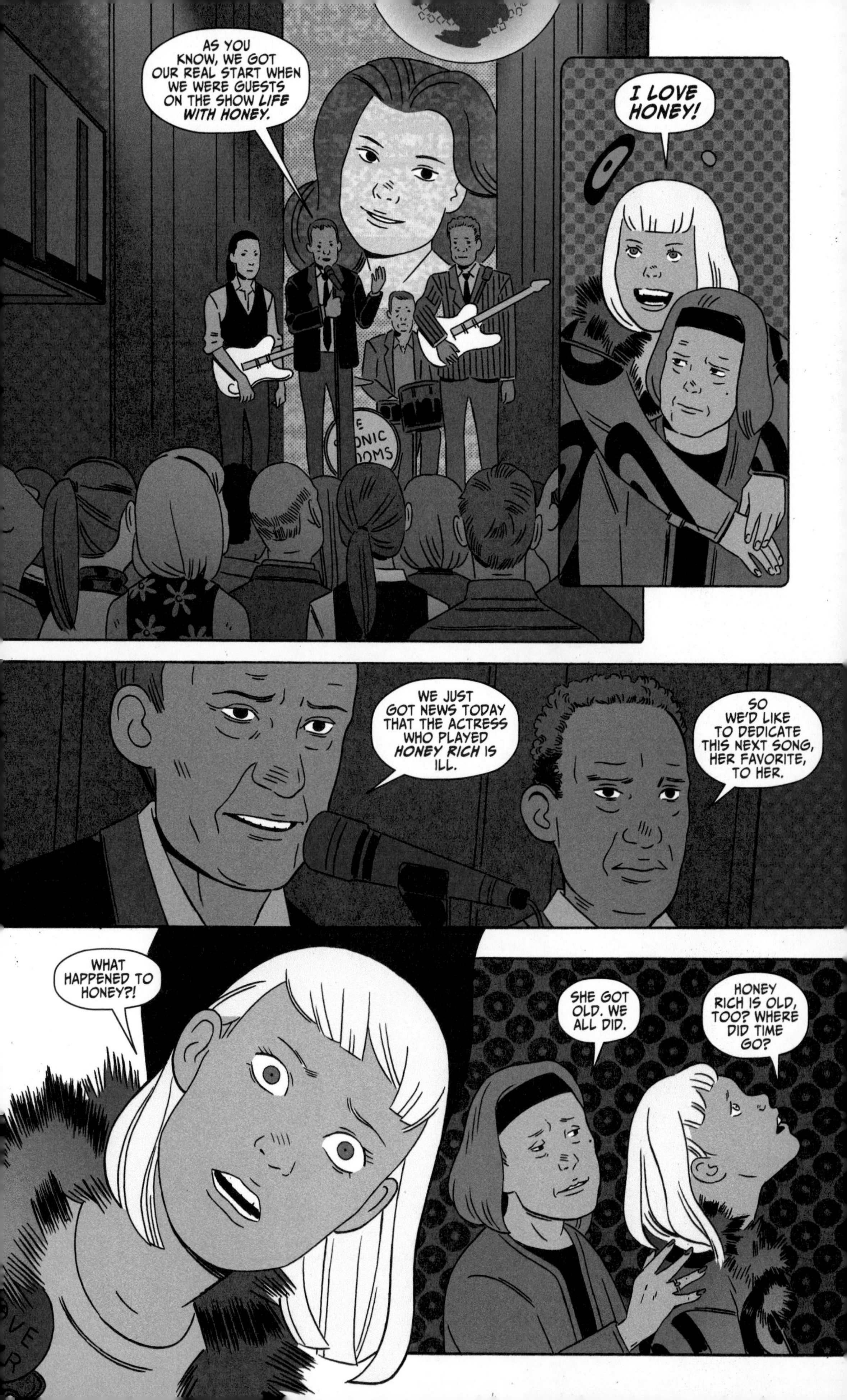
AS YOU KNOW, WE GOT OUR REAL START WHEN WE WERE GUESTS ON THE SHOW *LIFE WITH HONEY.*
I LOVE HONEY!
WE JUST GOT NEWS TODAY THAT THE ACTRESS WHO PLAYED *HONEY RICH* IS ILL.
SO WE'D LIKE TO DEDICATE THIS NEXT SONG, HER FAVORITE, TO HER.
WHAT HAPPENED TO HONEY?!
SHE GOT OLD. WE ALL DID.
HONEY RICH IS OLD, TOO? WHERE DID TIME GO?

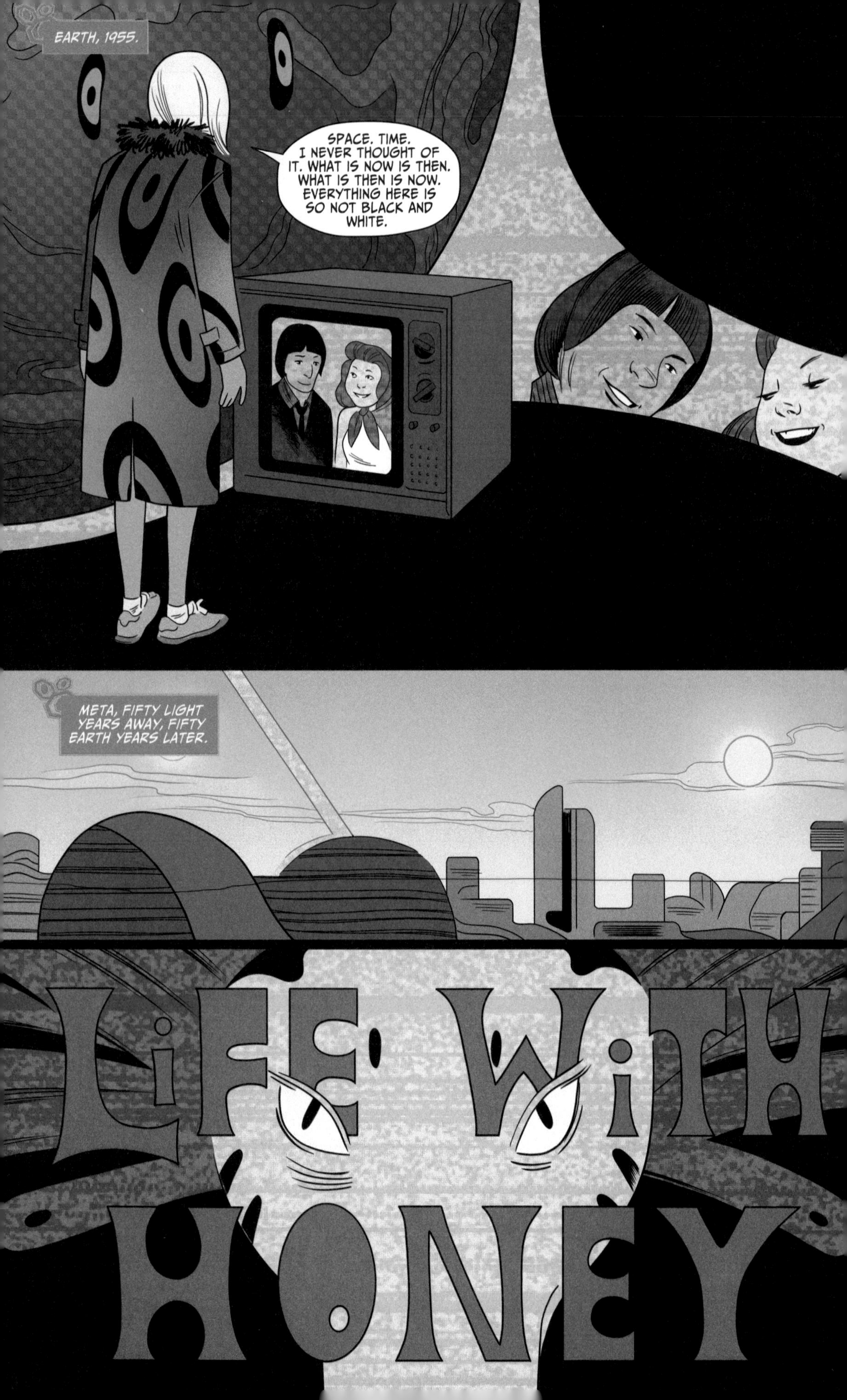
EARTH, 1955.
SPACE. TIME. I NEVER THOUGHT OF IT. WHAT IS NOW IS THEN. WHAT IS THEN IS NOW. EVERYTHING HERE IS SO NOT BLACK AND WHITE.
META, FIFTY LIGHT YEARS AWAY, FIFTY EARTH YEARS LATER.
LIFE WITH HONEY

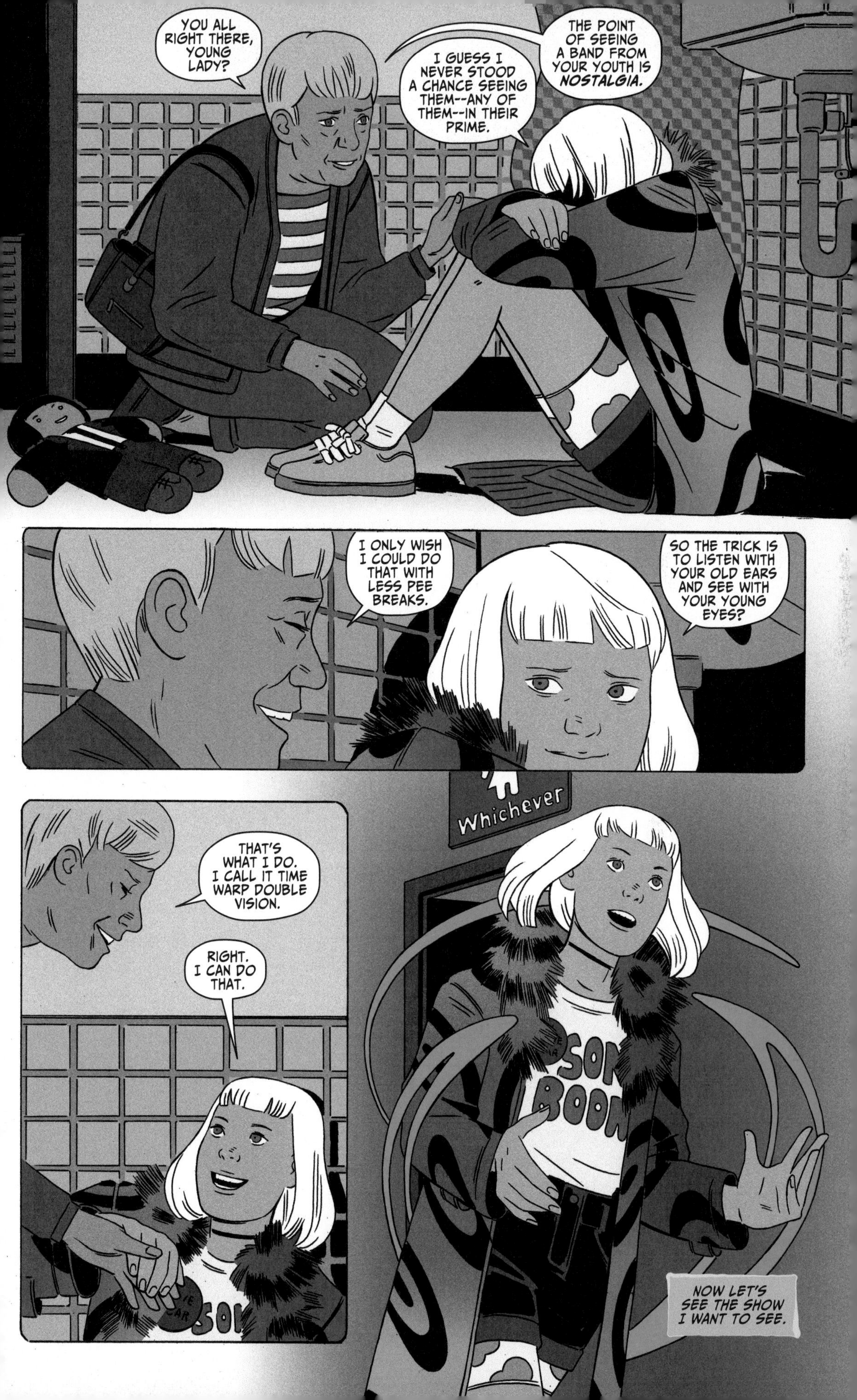
YOU ALL RIGHT THERE, YOUNG LADY?
THE POINT OF SEEING A BAND FROM YOUR YOUTH IS NOSTALGIA.
I GUESS I NEVER STOOD A CHANCE SEEING THEM--ANY OF THEM--IN THEIR PRIME.
I ONLY WISH I COULD DO THAT WITH LESS PEE BREAKS.
SO THE TRICK IS TO LISTEN WITH YOUR OLD EARS AND SEE WITH YOUR YOUNG EYES?
Whichever
THAT'S WHAT I DO. I CALL IT TIME WARP DOUBLE VISION.
RIGHT. I CAN DO THAT.
NOW LET'S SEE THE SHOW I WANT TO SEE.

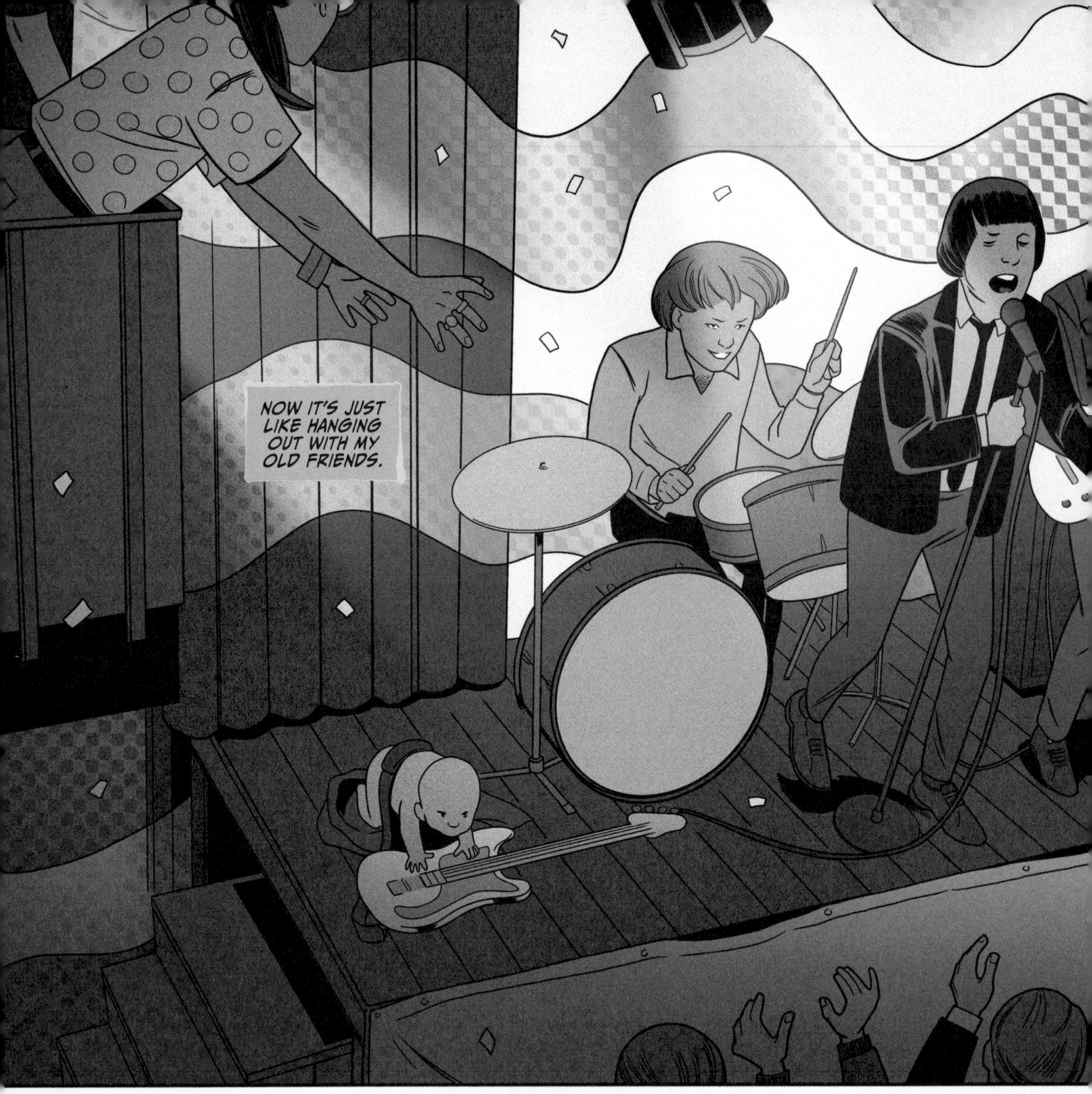
NOW IT'S JUST LIKE HANGING OUT WITH MY OLD FRIENDS.

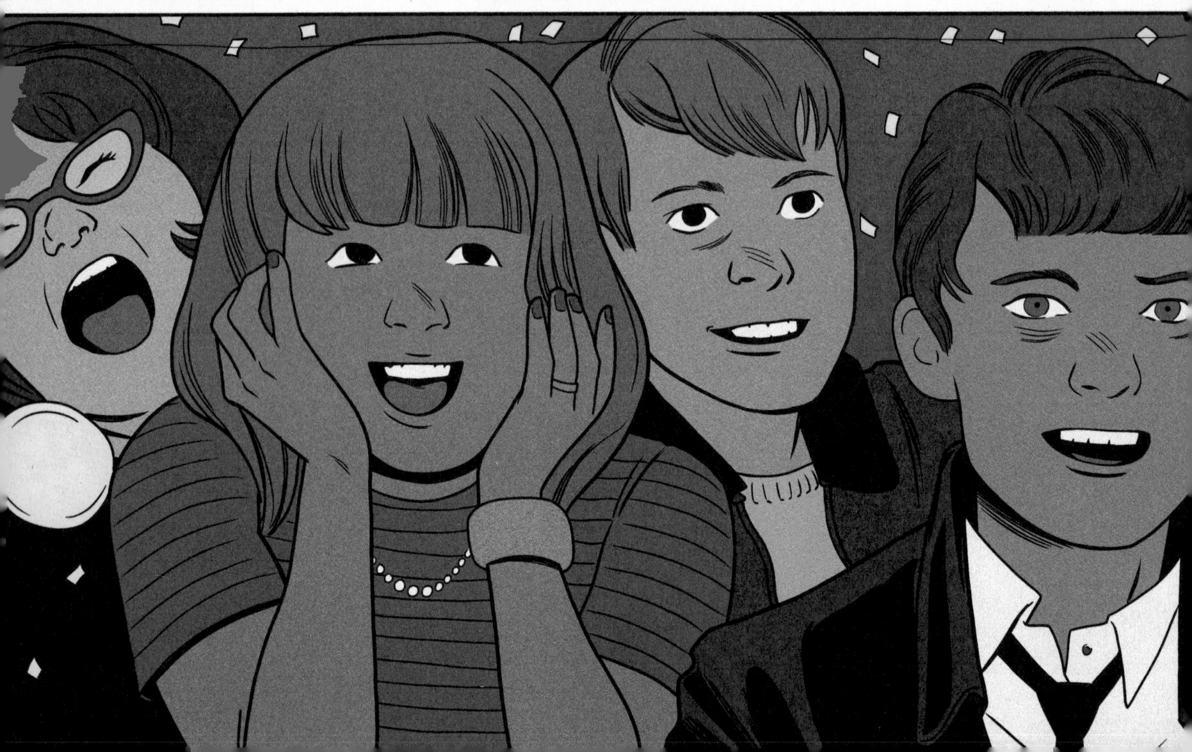

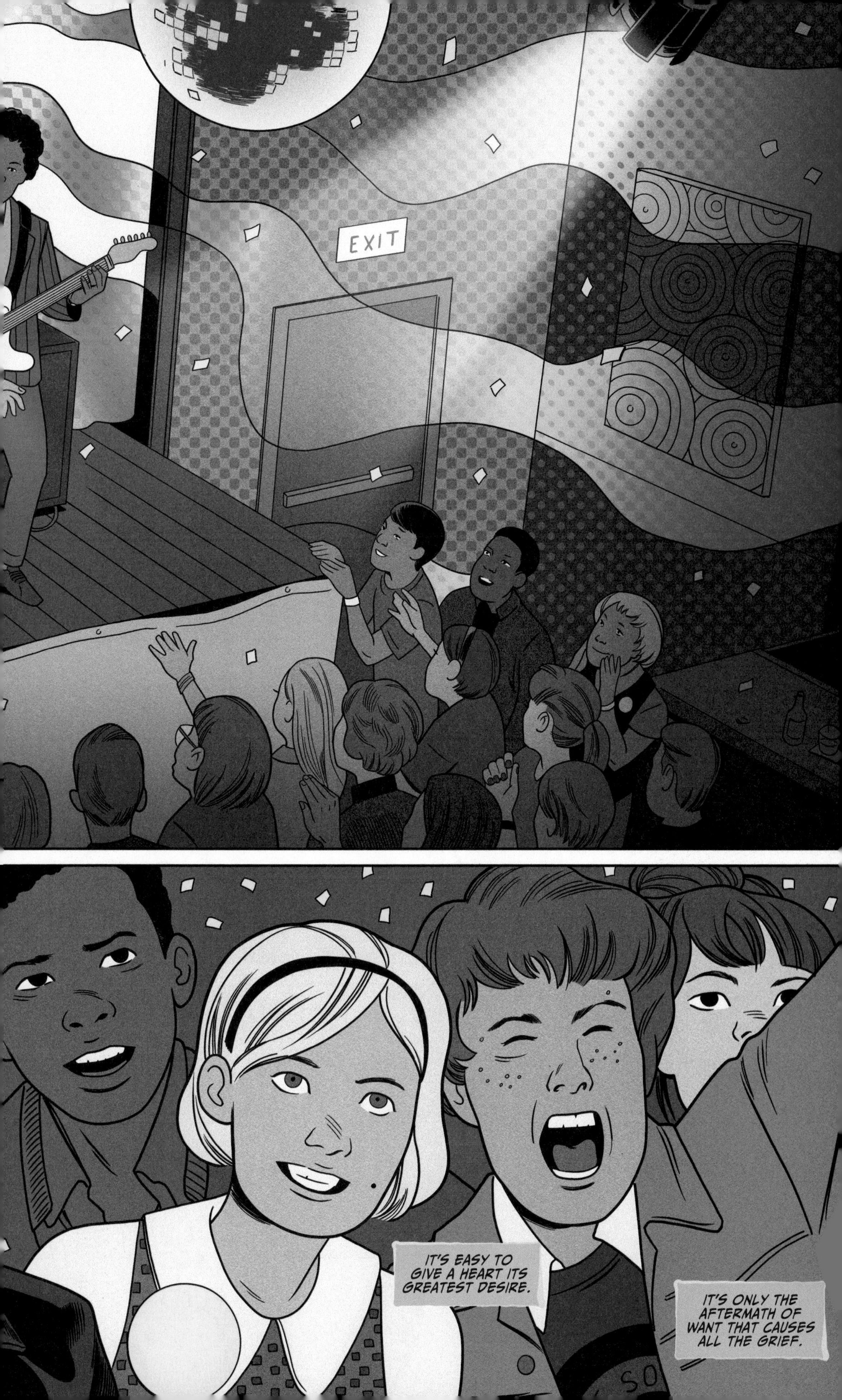
EXIT
IT'S EASY TO GIVE A HEART ITS GREATEST DESIRE.
IT'S ONLY THE AFTERMATH OF WANT THAT CAUSES ALL THE GRIEF.

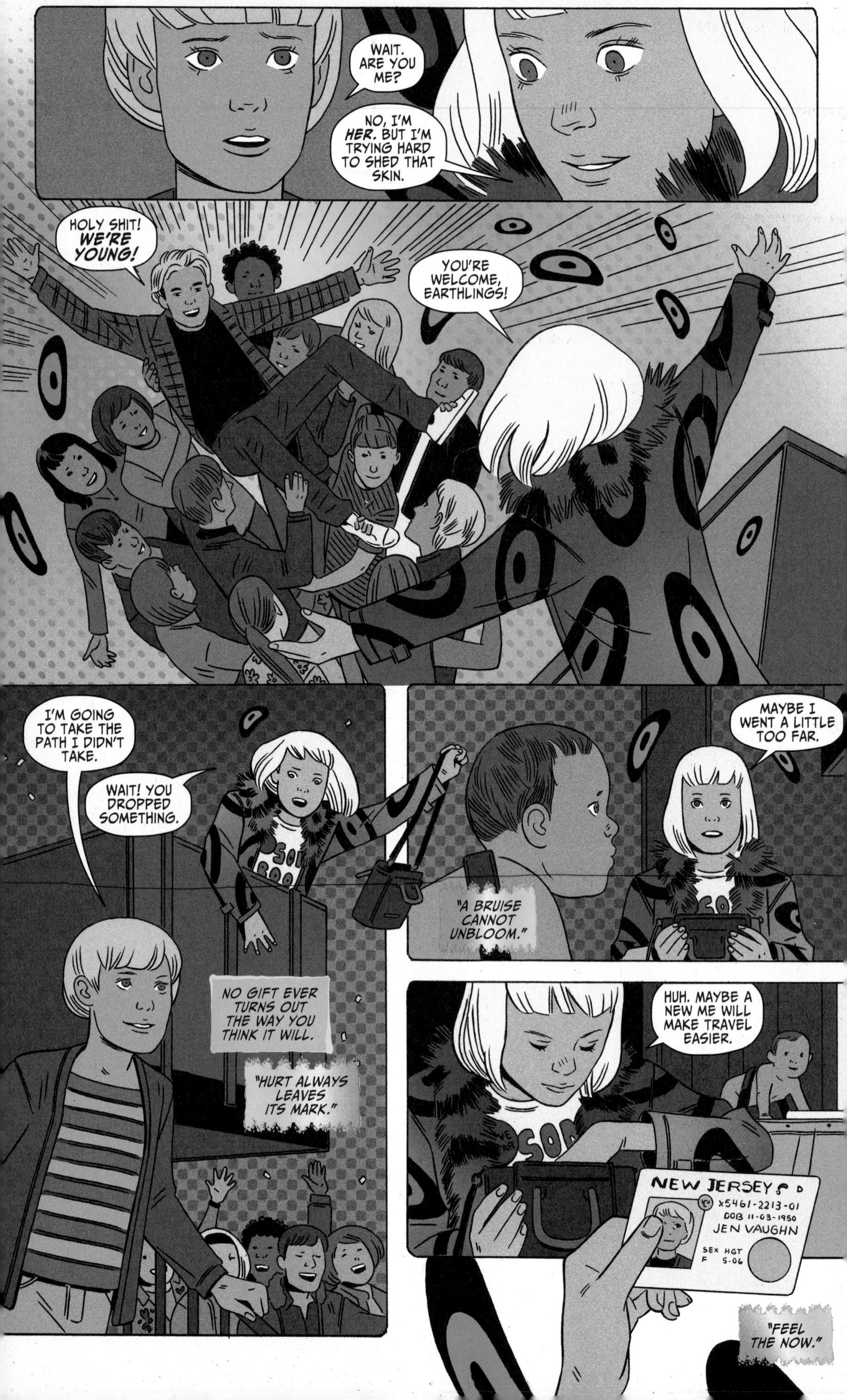

WAIT. ARE YOU ME?
NO, I'M *HER.* BUT I'M TRYING HARD TO SHED THAT SKIN.
HOLY SHIT! *WE'RE YOUNG!*
YOU'RE WELCOME, EARTHLINGS!
I'M GOING TO TAKE THE PATH I DIDN'T TAKE.
WAIT! YOU DROPPED SOMETHING.
NO GIFT EVER TURNS OUT THE WAY YOU THINK IT WILL.
"HURT ALWAYS LEAVES ITS MARK."
MAYBE I WENT A LITTLE TOO FAR.
"A BRUISE CANNOT UNBLOOM."
HUH. MAYBE A NEW ME WILL MAKE TRAVEL EASIER.
NEW JERSEY
X5461-2213-01
DOB 11-03-1950
JEN VAUGHN
SEX F
HGT 5-06
"FEEL THE NOW."

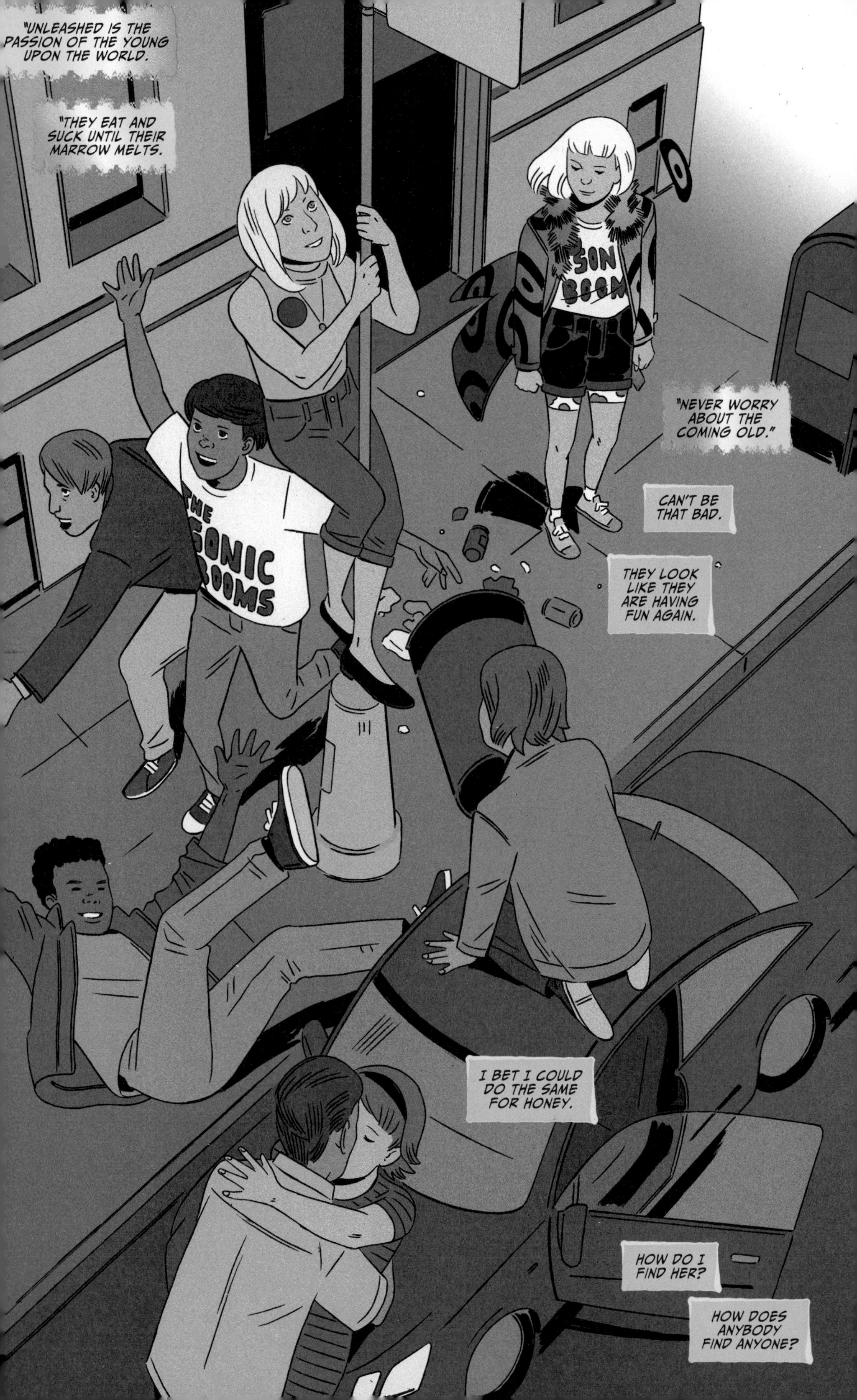
"UNLEASHED IS THE PASSION OF THE YOUNG UPON THE WORLD.
"THEY EAT AND SUCK UNTIL THEIR MARROW MELTS.
"NEVER WORRY ABOUT THE COMING OLD."
CAN'T BE THAT BAD.
THEY LOOK LIKE THEY ARE HAVING FUN AGAIN.
I BET I COULD DO THE SAME FOR HONEY.
HOW DO I FIND HER?
HOW DOES ANYBODY FIND ANYONE?

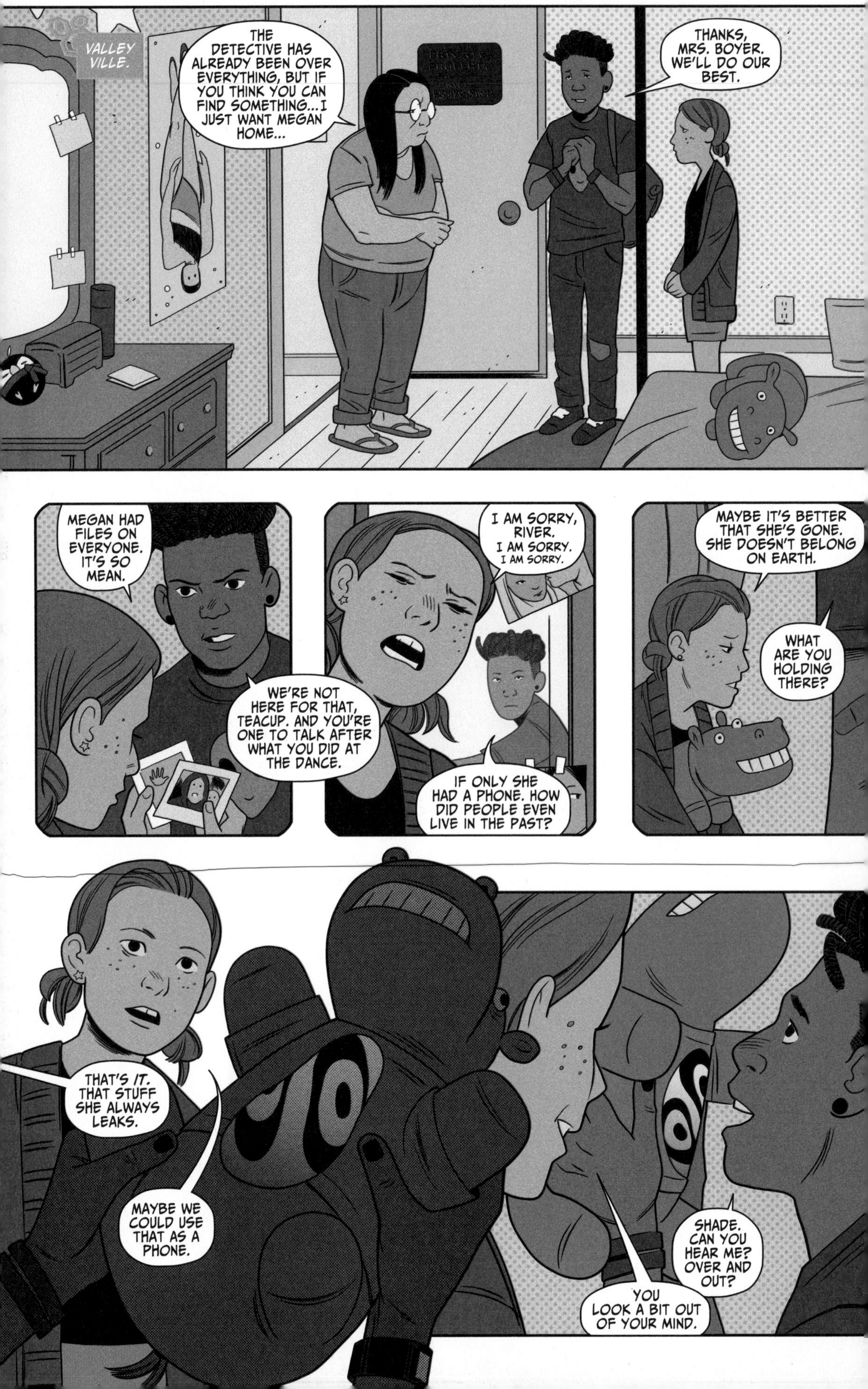
VALLEY VILLE.
THE DETECTIVE HAS ALREADY BEEN OVER EVERYTHING, BUT IF YOU THINK YOU CAN FIND SOMETHING...I JUST WANT MEGAN HOME...
THANKS, MRS. BOYER. WE'LL DO OUR BEST.
MEGAN HAD FILES ON EVERYONE. IT'S SO MEAN.
WE'RE NOT HERE FOR THAT, TEACUP. AND YOU'RE ONE TO TALK AFTER WHAT YOU DID AT THE DANCE.
I AM SORRY, RIVER. I AM SORRY. I AM SORRY.
IF ONLY SHE HAD A PHONE. HOW DID PEOPLE EVEN LIVE IN THE PAST?
MAYBE IT'S BETTER THAT SHE'S GONE. SHE DOESN'T BELONG ON EARTH.
WHAT ARE YOU HOLDING THERE?
THAT'S IT. THAT STUFF SHE ALWAYS LEAKS.
MAYBE WE COULD USE THAT AS A PHONE.
SHADE. CAN YOU HEAR ME? OVER AND OUT?
YOU LOOK A BIT OUT OF YOUR MIND.

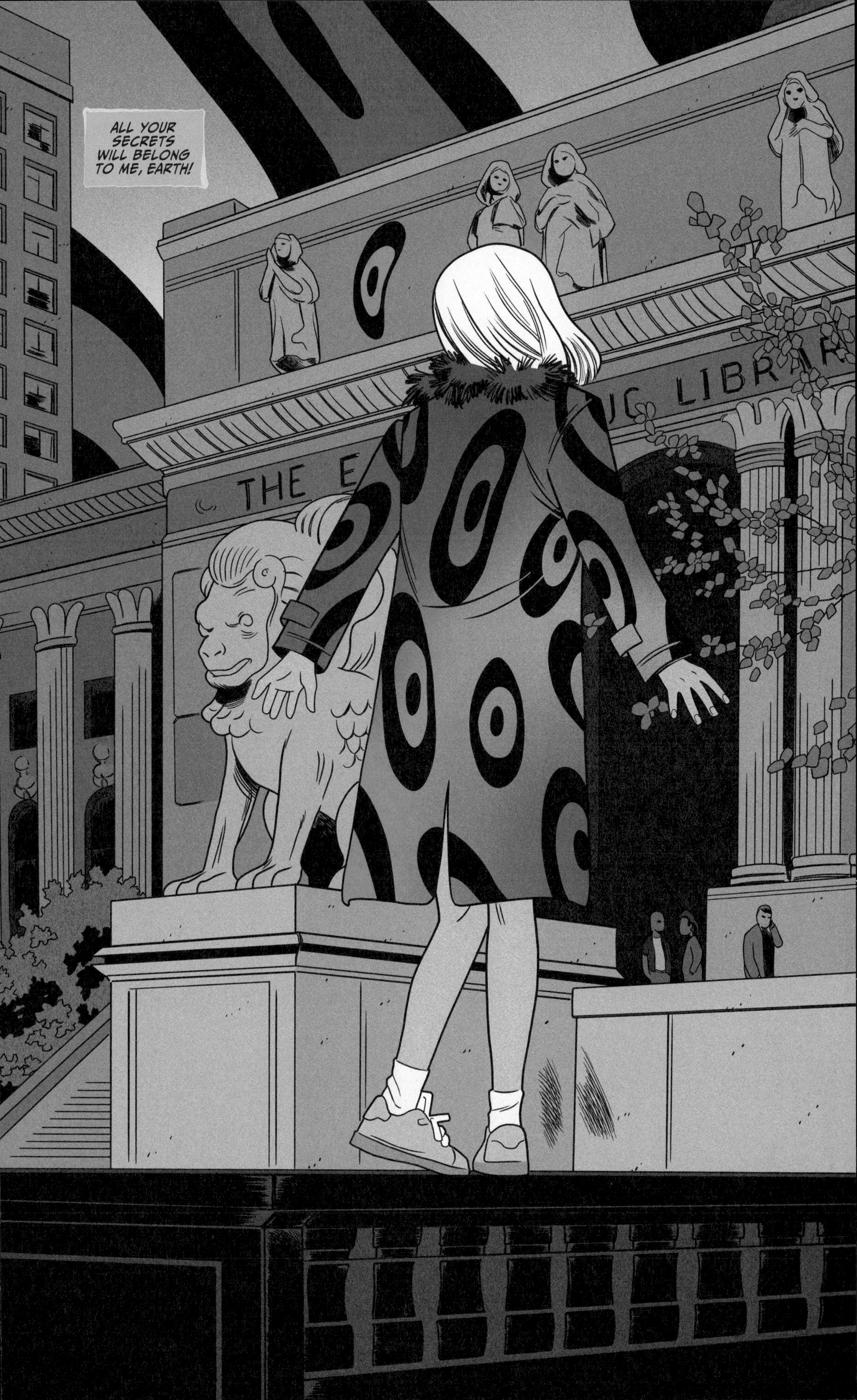
ALL YOUR SECRETS WILL BELONG TO ME, EARTH!
THE E
UC LIBRAR

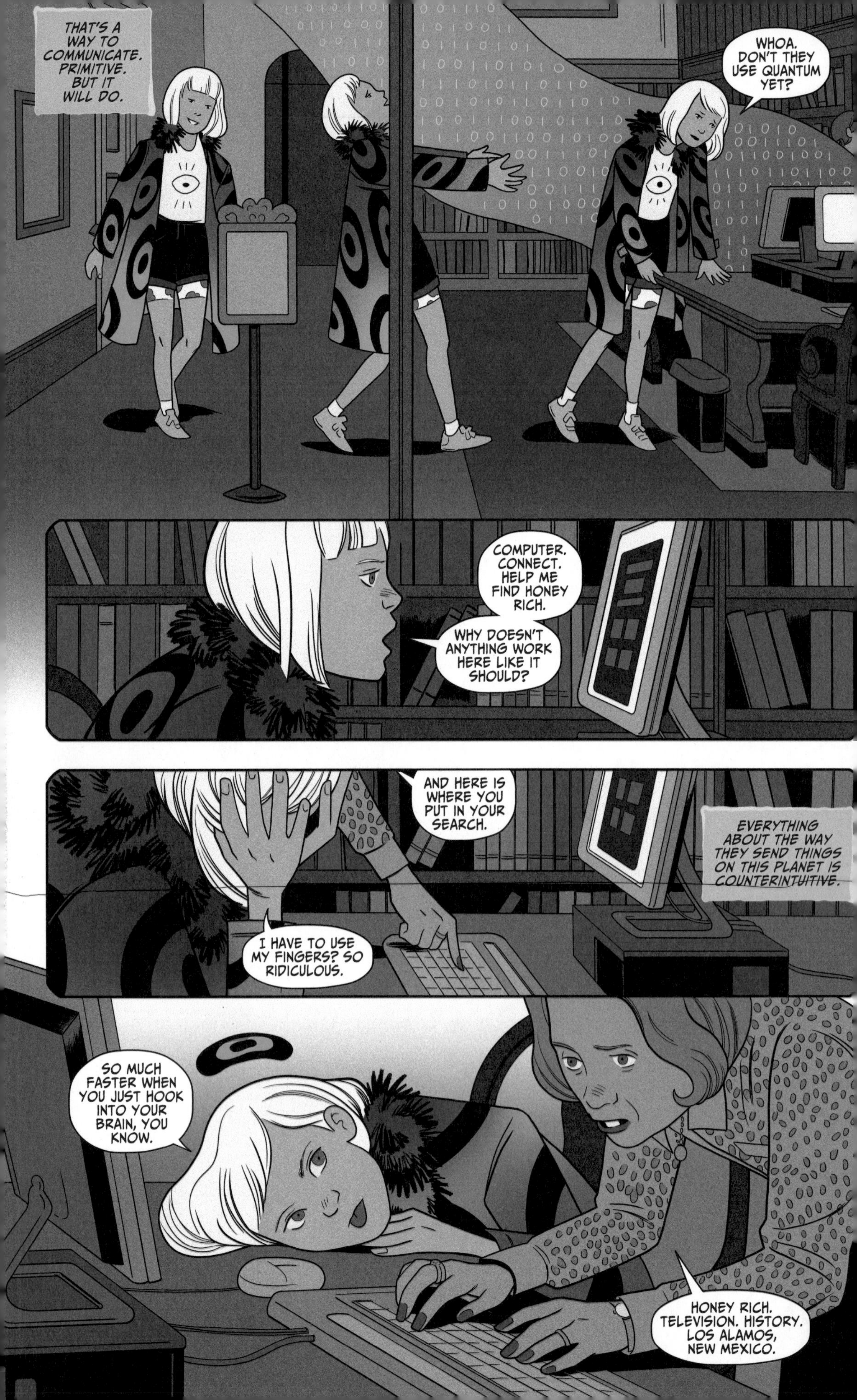
THAT'S A WAY TO COMMUNICATE. PRIMITIVE. BUT IT WILL DO.
WHOA. DON'T THEY USE QUANTUM YET?
COMPUTER. CONNECT. HELP ME FIND HONEY RICH.
WHY DOESN'T ANYTHING WORK HERE LIKE IT SHOULD?
AND HERE IS WHERE YOU PUT IN YOUR SEARCH.
EVERYTHING ABOUT THE WAY THEY SEND THINGS ON THIS PLANET IS COUNTERINTUITIVE.
I HAVE TO USE MY FINGERS? SO RIDICULOUS.
SO MUCH FASTER WHEN YOU JUST HOOK INTO YOUR BRAIN, YOU KNOW.
HONEY RICH. TELEVISION. HISTORY. LOS ALAMOS, NEW MEXICO.

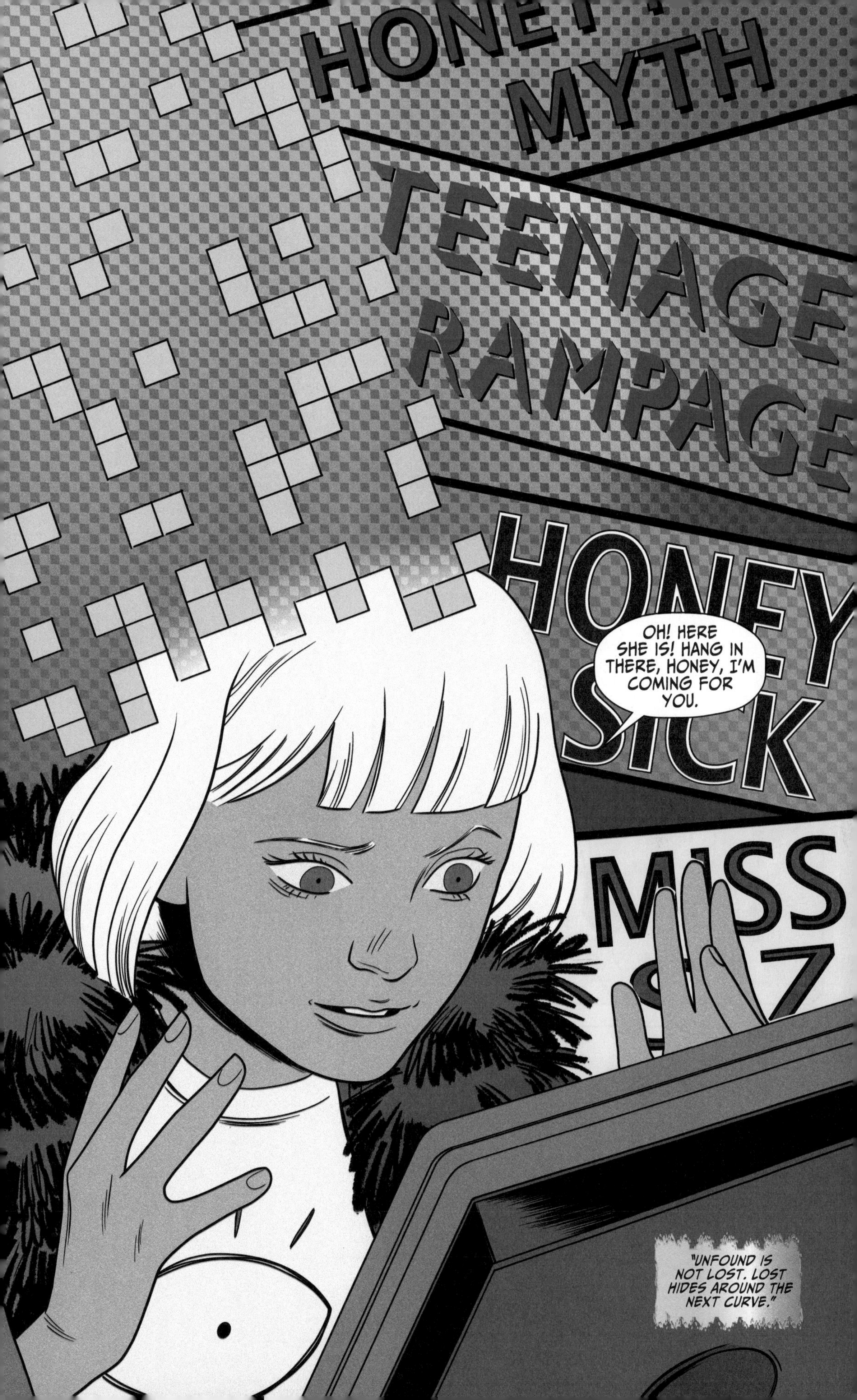
MYTH
TEENAGE RAMPAGE
HONEY SICK
MISS
OH! HERE SHE IS! HANG IN THERE, HONEY, I'M COMING FOR YOU.
"UNFOUND IS NOT LOST. LOST HIDES AROUND THE NEXT CURVE."

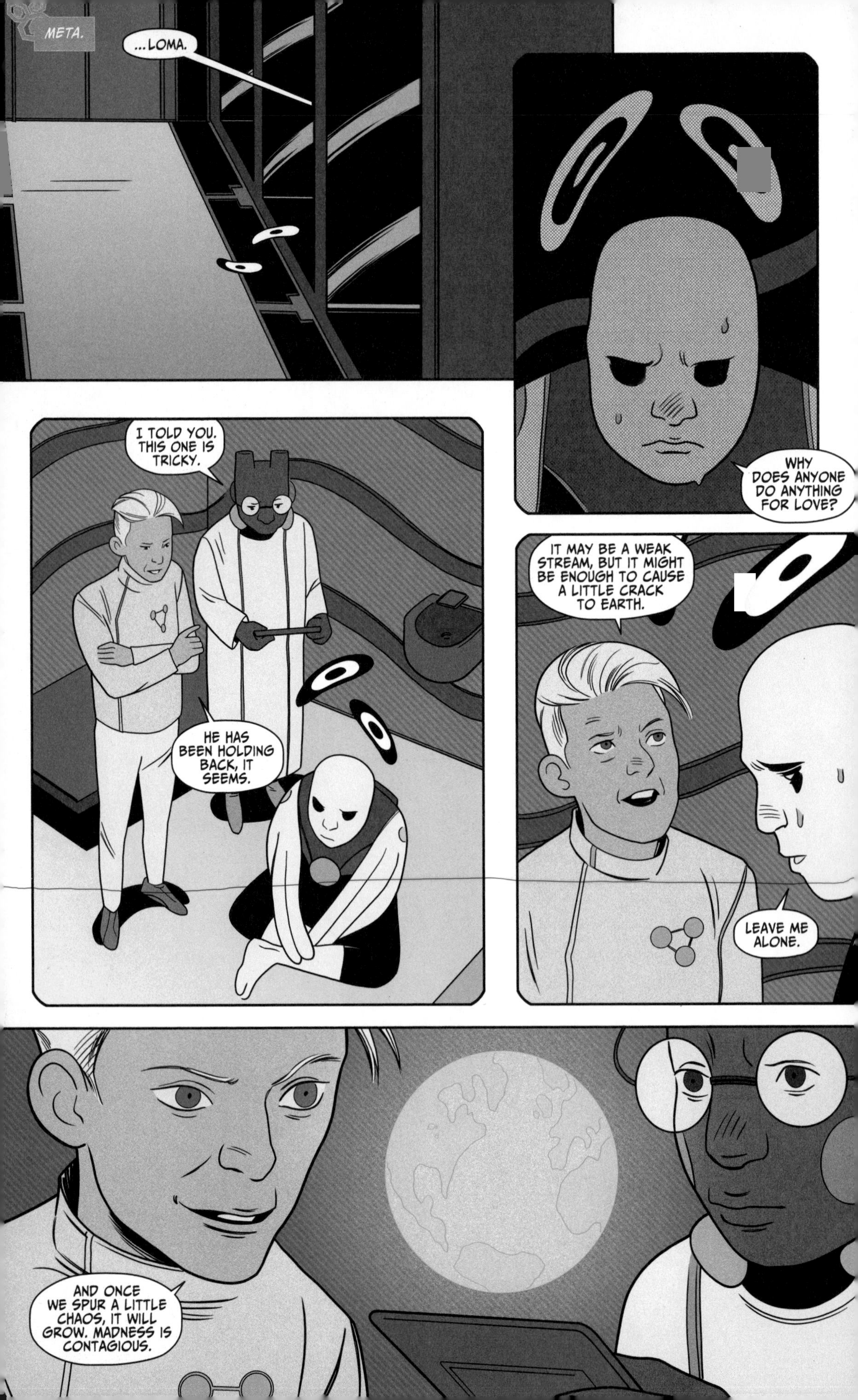
META.
...LOMA.
WHY DOES ANYONE DO ANYTHING FOR LOVE?
I TOLD YOU. THIS ONE IS TRICKY.
HE HAS BEEN HOLDING BACK, IT SEEMS.
IT MAY BE A WEAK STREAM, BUT IT MIGHT BE ENOUGH TO CAUSE A LITTLE CRACK TO EARTH.
LEAVE ME ALONE.
AND ONCE WE SPUR A LITTLE CHAOS, IT WILL GROW. MADNESS IS CONTAGIOUS.

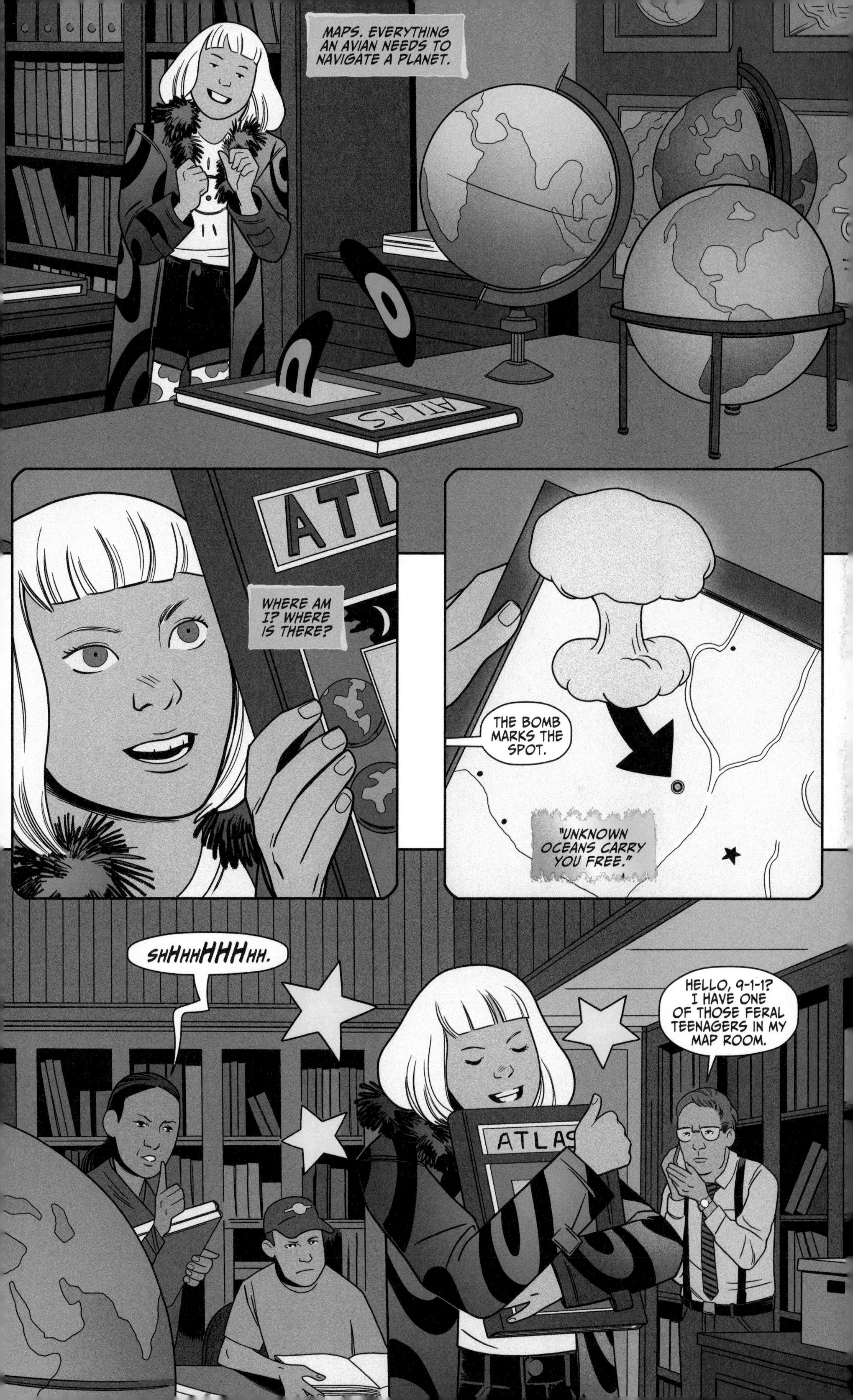
MAPS. EVERYTHING AN AVIAN NEEDS TO NAVIGATE A PLANET.
ATLAS
ATL
WHERE AM I? WHERE IS THERE?
THE BOMB MARKS THE SPOT.
"UNKNOWN OCEANS CARRY YOU FREE."
SHHHHHHHHH.
ATLAS
HELLO, 9-1-1? I HAVE ONE OF THOSE FERAL TEENAGERS IN MY MAP ROOM.

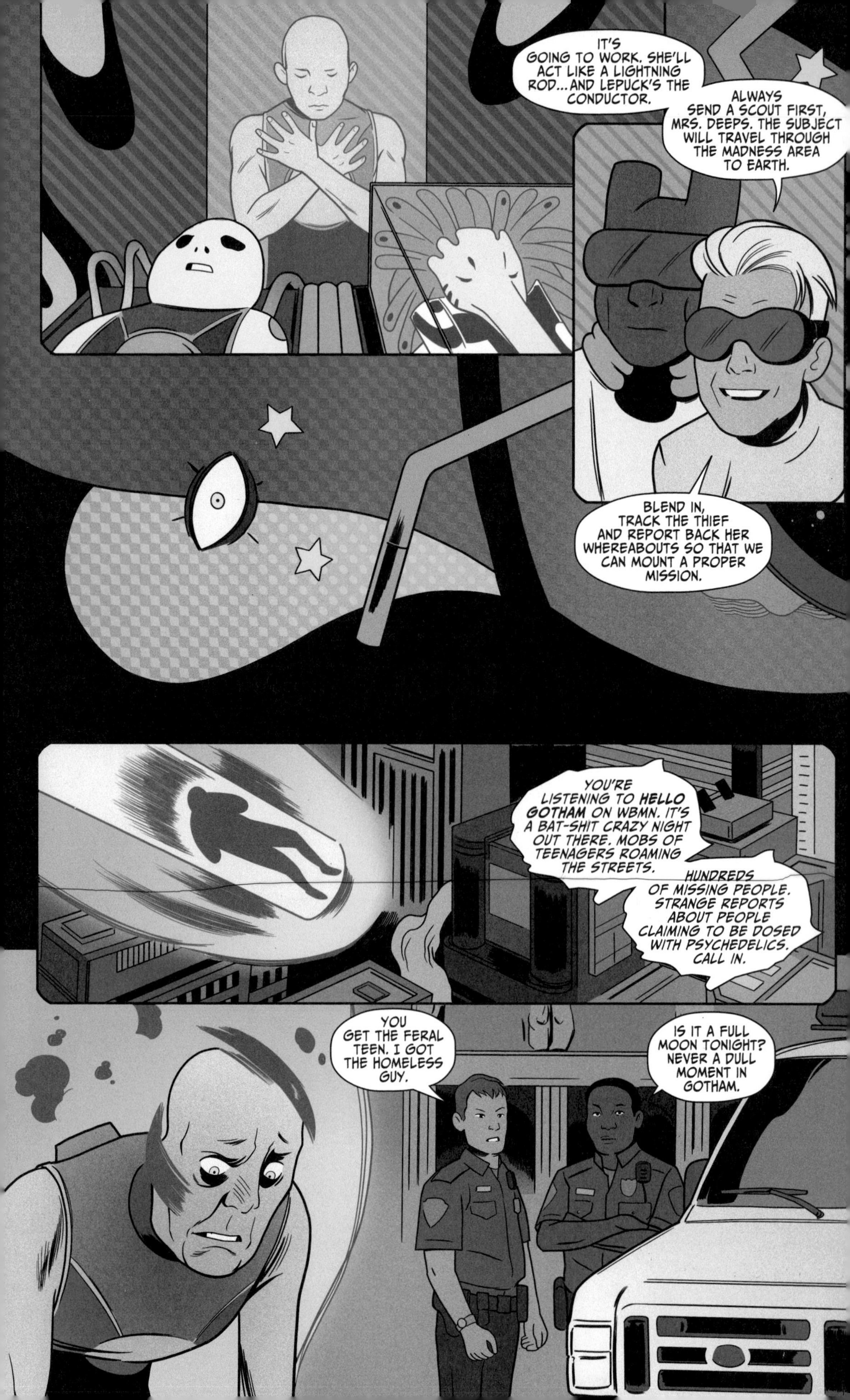
IT'S GOING TO WORK. SHE'LL ACT LIKE A LIGHTNING ROD... AND LEPUCK'S THE CONDUCTOR.
ALWAYS SEND A SCOUT FIRST, MRS. DEEPS. THE SUBJECT WILL TRAVEL THROUGH THE MADNESS AREA TO EARTH.
BLEND IN, TRACK THE THIEF AND REPORT BACK HER WHEREABOUTS SO THAT WE CAN MOUNT A PROPER MISSION.
YOU'RE LISTENING TO **HELLO GOTHAM** ON WBMN. IT'S A BAT-SHIT CRAZY NIGHT OUT THERE. MOBS OF TEENAGERS ROAMING THE STREETS.
HUNDREDS OF MISSING PEOPLE. STRANGE REPORTS ABOUT PEOPLE CLAIMING TO BE DOSED WITH PSYCHEDELICS. CALL IN.
YOU GET THE FERAL TEEN. I GOT THE HOMELESS GUY.
IS IT A FULL MOON TONIGHT? NEVER A DULL MOMENT IN GOTHAM.

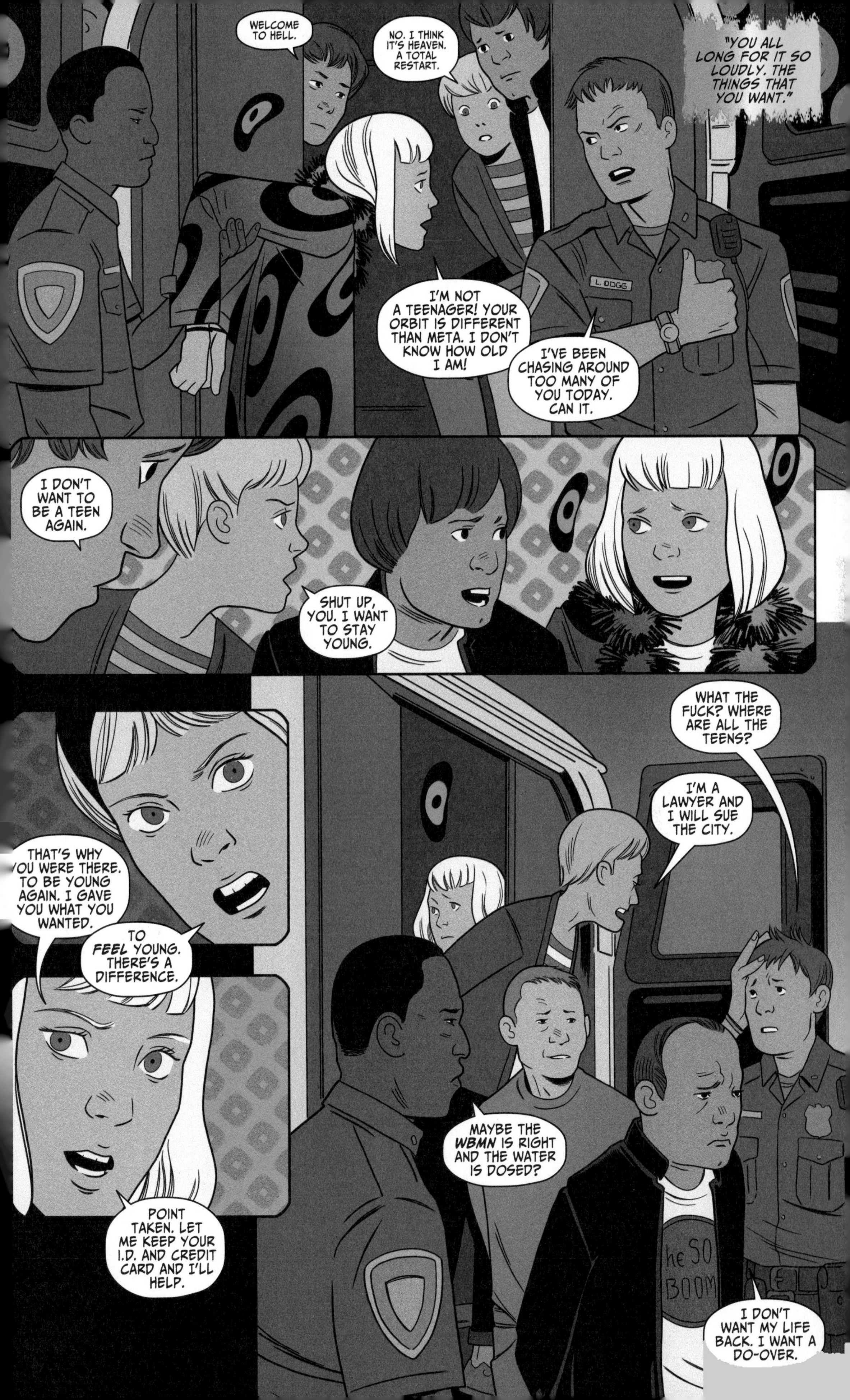
WELCOME TO HELL.
NO. I THINK IT'S HEAVEN. A TOTAL RESTART.
"YOU ALL LONG FOR IT SO LOUDLY. THE THINGS THAT YOU WANT."
I'M NOT A TEENAGER! YOUR ORBIT IS DIFFERENT THAN META. I DON'T KNOW HOW OLD I AM!
I'VE BEEN CHASING AROUND TOO MANY OF YOU TODAY. CAN IT.
I DON'T WANT TO BE A TEEN AGAIN.
SHUT UP, YOU. I WANT TO STAY YOUNG.
THAT'S WHY YOU WERE THERE. TO BE YOUNG AGAIN. I GAVE YOU WHAT YOU WANTED.
TO *FEEL* YOUNG. THERE'S A DIFFERENCE.
POINT TAKEN. LET ME KEEP YOUR I.D. AND CREDIT CARD AND I'LL HELP.
WHAT THE FUCK? WHERE ARE ALL THE TEENS?
I'M A LAWYER AND I WILL SUE THE CITY.
MAYBE THE *WBMN* IS RIGHT AND THE WATER IS DOSED?
I DON'T WANT MY LIFE BACK. I WANT A DO-OVER.

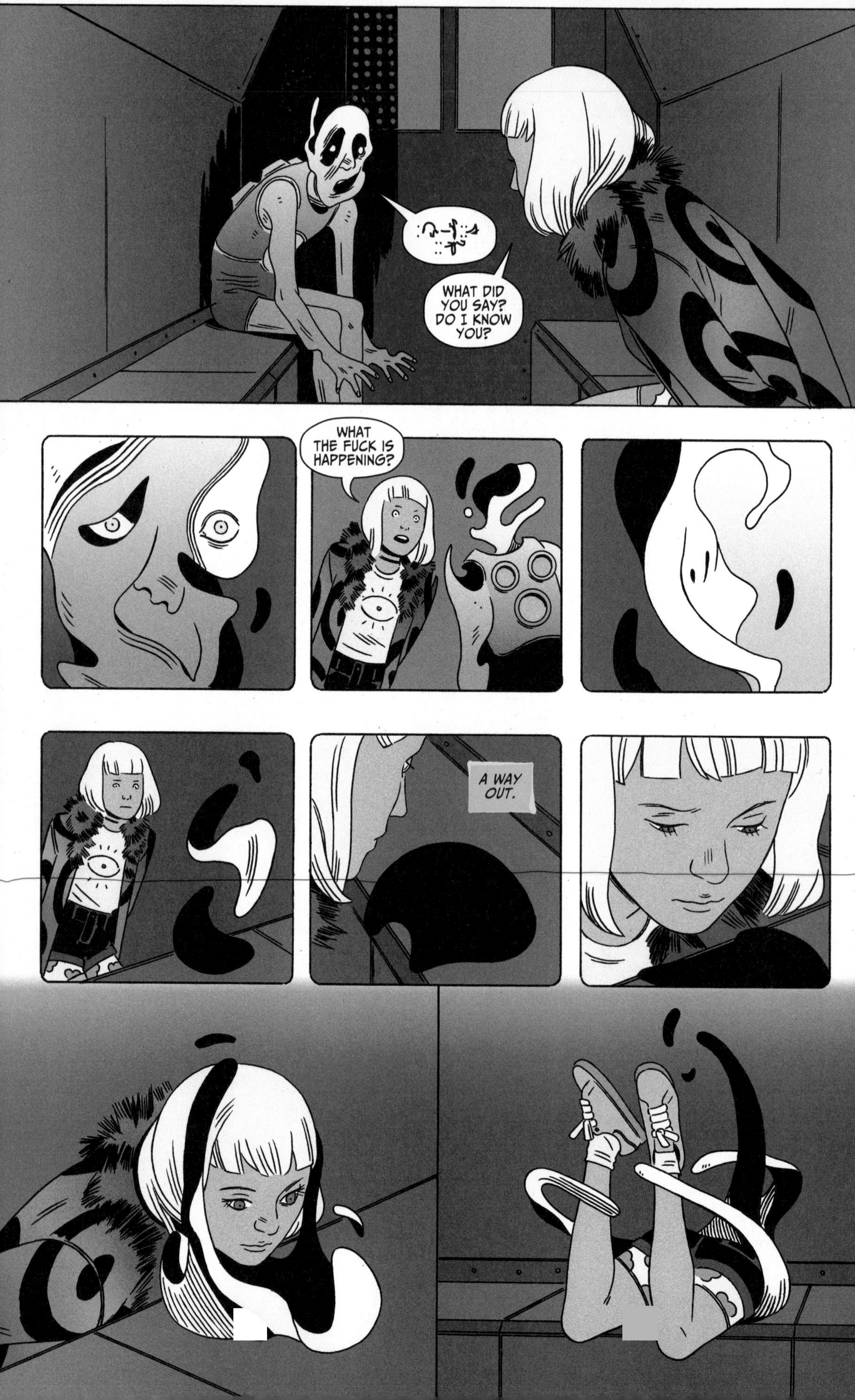
WHAT DID YOU SAY? DO I KNOW YOU?
WHAT THE FUCK IS HAPPENING?
A WAY OUT.

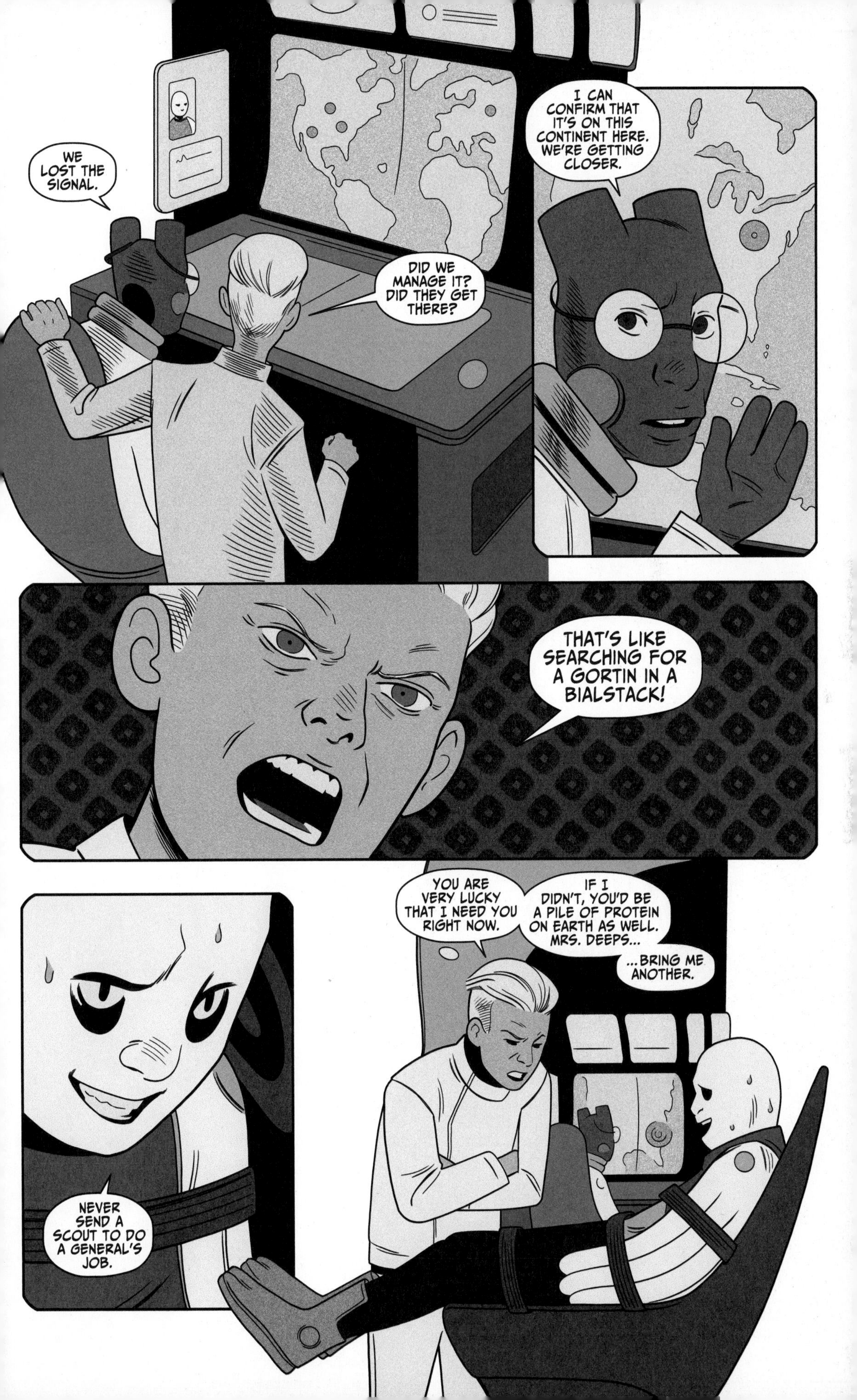
WE LOST THE SIGNAL.
DID WE MANAGE IT? DID THEY GET THERE?
I CAN CONFIRM THAT IT'S ON THIS CONTINENT HERE. WE'RE GETTING CLOSER.
THAT'S LIKE SEARCHING FOR A GORTIN IN A BIALSTACK!
NEVER SEND A SCOUT TO DO A GENERAL'S JOB.
YOU ARE VERY LUCKY THAT I NEED YOU RIGHT NOW.
IF I DIDN'T, YOU'D BE A PILE OF PROTEIN ON EARTH AS WELL. MRS. DEEPS...
...BRING ME ANOTHER.

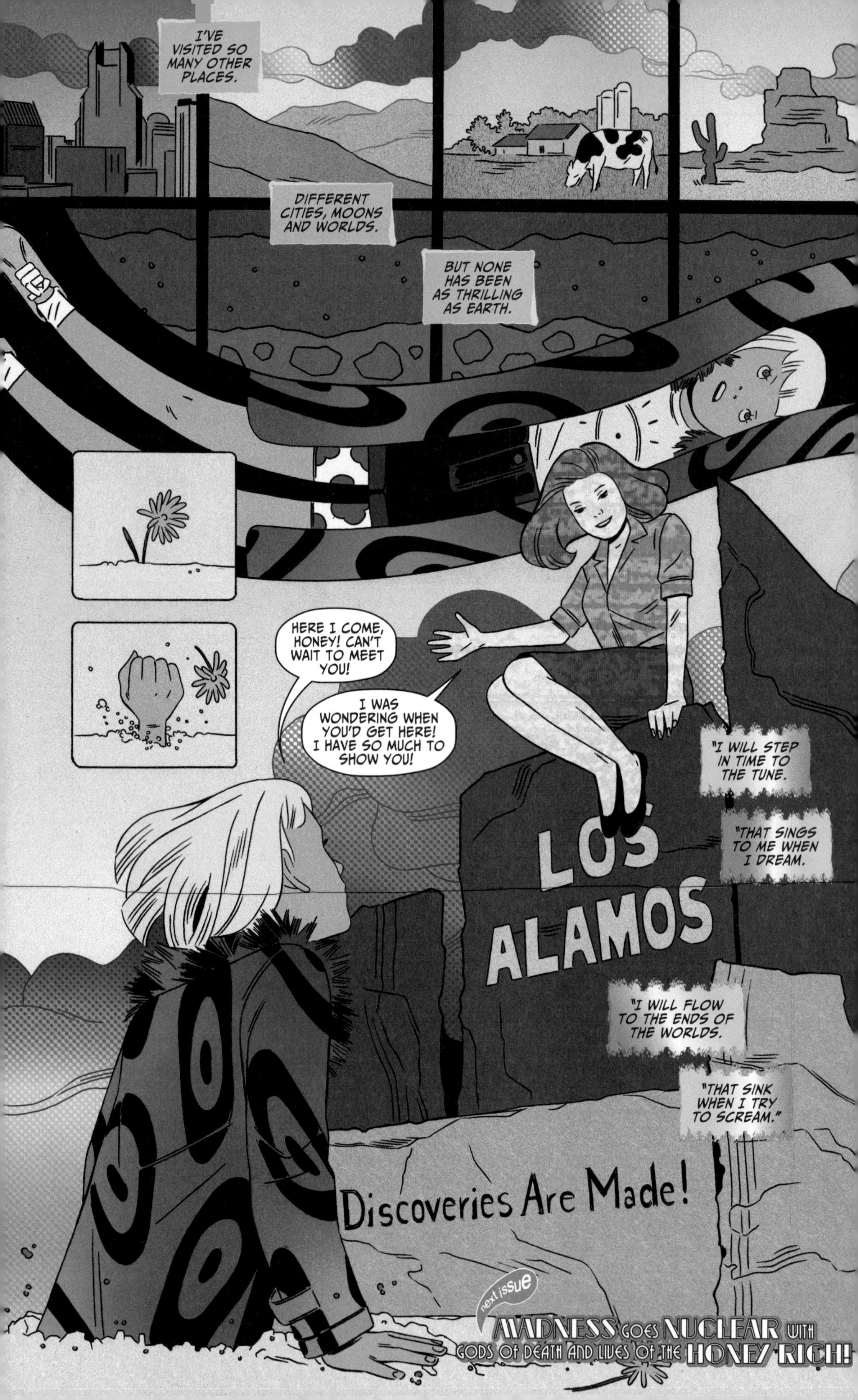

I'VE VISITED SO MANY OTHER PLACES.
DIFFERENT CITIES, MOONS AND WORLDS.
BUT NONE HAS BEEN AS THRILLING AS EARTH.
HERE I COME, HONEY! CAN'T WAIT TO MEET YOU!
I WAS WONDERING WHEN YOU'D GET HERE! I HAVE SO MUCH TO SHOW YOU!
"I WILL STEP IN TIME TO THE TUNE.
"THAT SINGS TO ME WHEN I DREAM.
LOS ALAMOS
"I WILL FLOW TO THE ENDS OF THE WORLDS.
"THAT SINK WHEN I TRY TO SCREAM."
Discoveries Are Made!
next issue
MADNESS GOES NUCLEAR WITH GODS OF DEATH AND LIVES OF THE HONEY RICH!

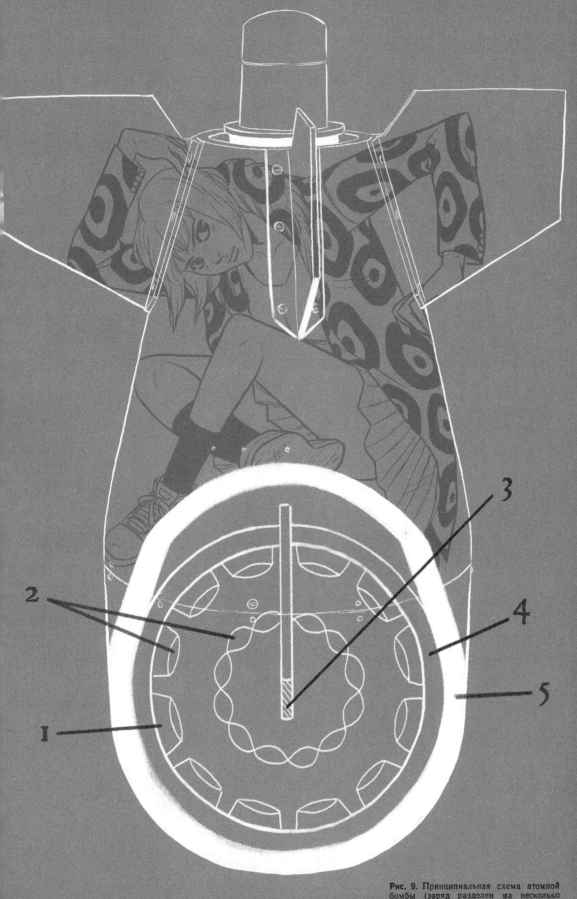

Рис. 9. Принципиальная схема атомной бомбы (заряд разделен на несколько частей):

1 — взрывчатое вещество; *2* — плутоний; *3* — нейтронный источник; *4* — отражатель нейтронов; *5* — оболочка

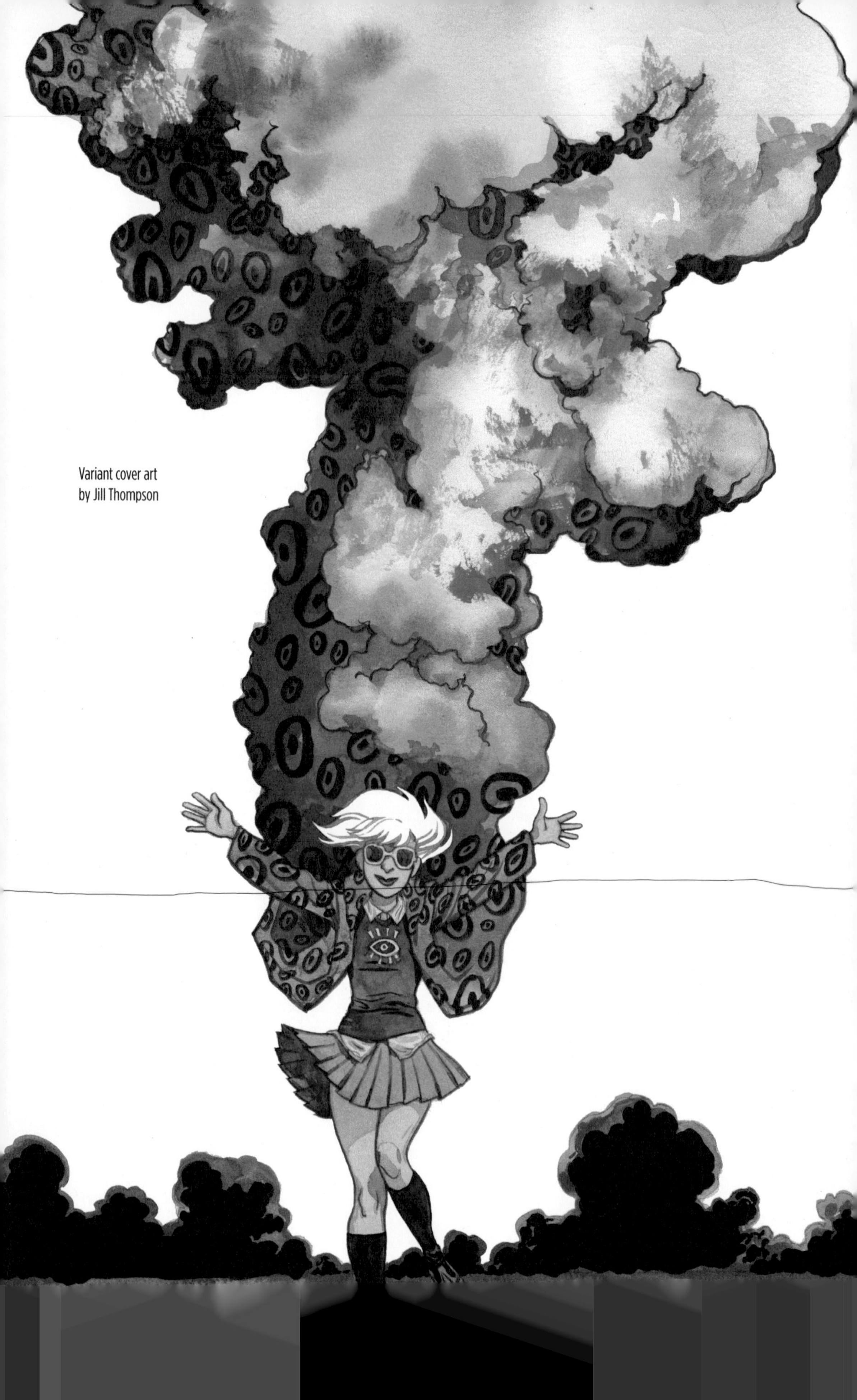

Variant cover art
by Jill Thompson

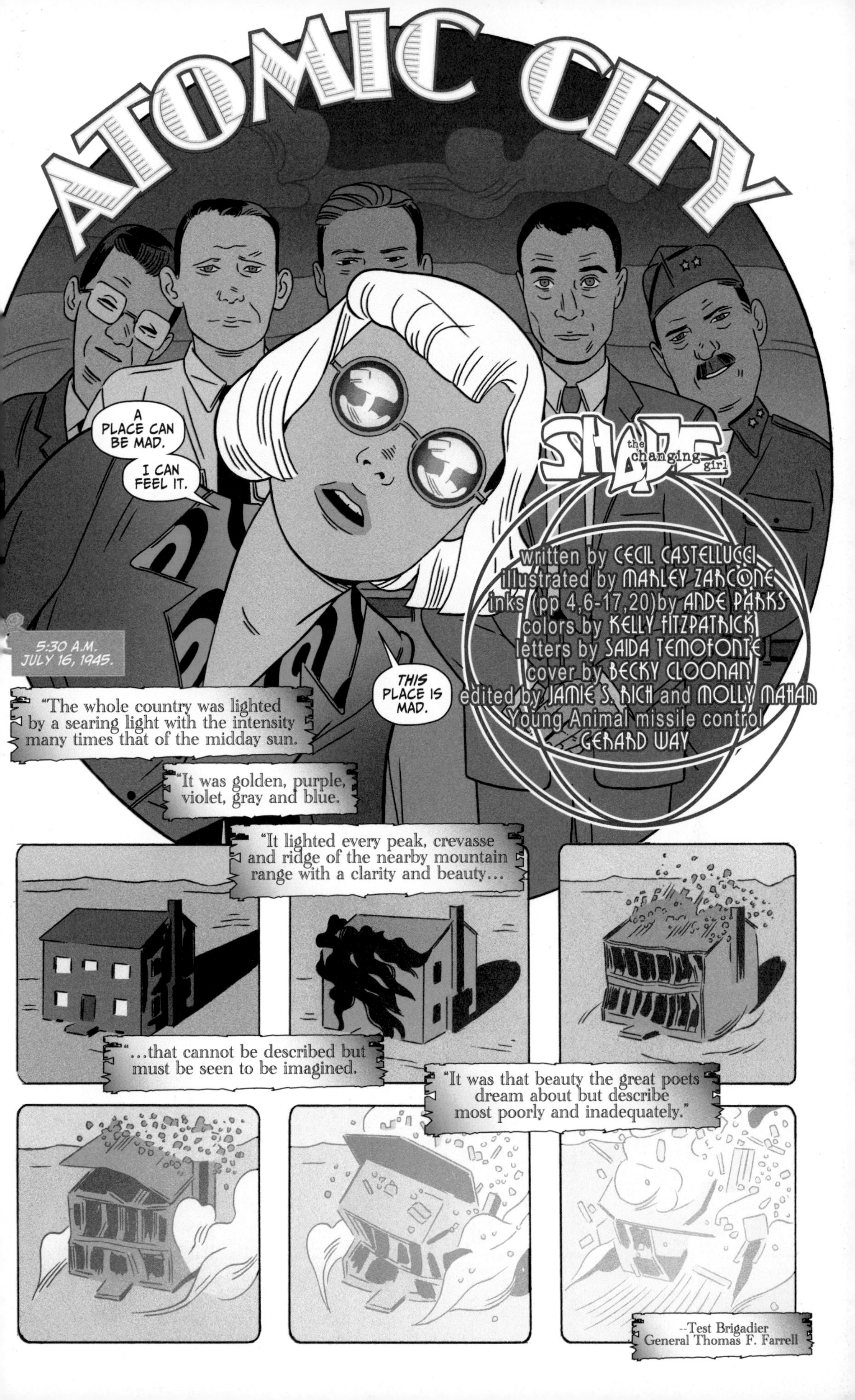
ATOMIC CITY
A PLACE CAN BE MAD.
I CAN FEEL IT.
SHADE the changing girl
written by CECIL CASTELLUCCI
illustrated by MARLEY ZARCONE
inks (pp 4,6-17,20) by ANDE PARKS
colors by KELLY FITZPATRICK
letters by SAIDA TEMOFONTE
cover by BECKY CLOONAN
edited by JAMIE S. RICH and MOLLY MAHAN
Young Animal missile control GERARD WAY
5:30 A.M. JULY 16, 1945.
"The whole country was lighted by a searing light with the intensity many times that of the midday sun.
THIS PLACE IS MAD.
"It was golden, purple, violet, gray and blue.
"It lighted every peak, crevasse and ridge of the nearby mountain range with a clarity and beauty...
"...that cannot be described but must be seen to be imagined.
"It was that beauty the great poets dream about but describe most poorly and inadequately."
--Test Brigadier General Thomas F. Farrell

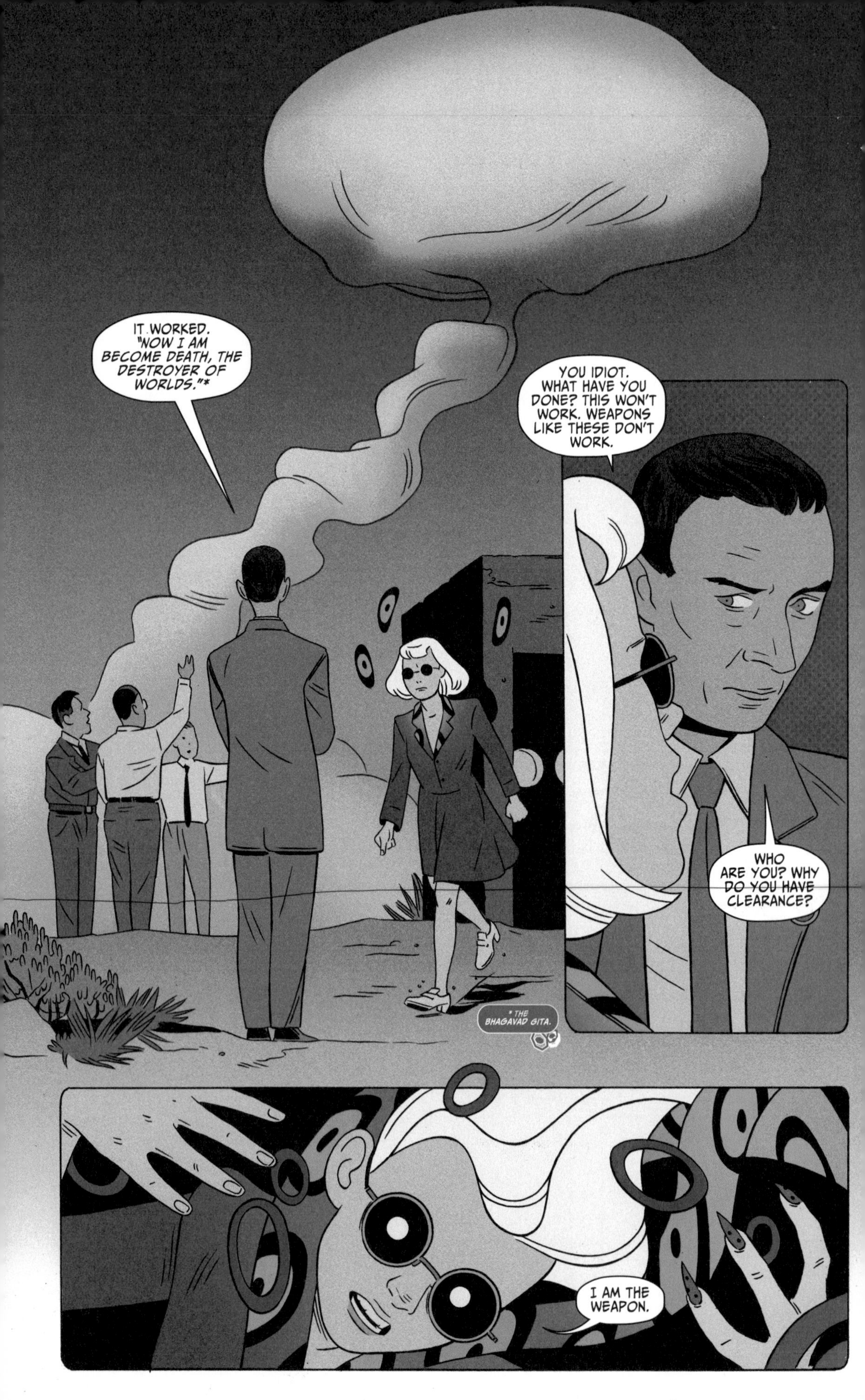
IT WORKED. "NOW I AM BECOME DEATH, THE DESTROYER OF WORLDS."*
YOU IDIOT. WHAT HAVE YOU DONE? THIS WON'T WORK. WEAPONS LIKE THESE DON'T WORK.
WHO ARE YOU? WHY DO YOU HAVE CLEARANCE?
* THE BHAGAVAD GITA.
I AM THE WEAPON.

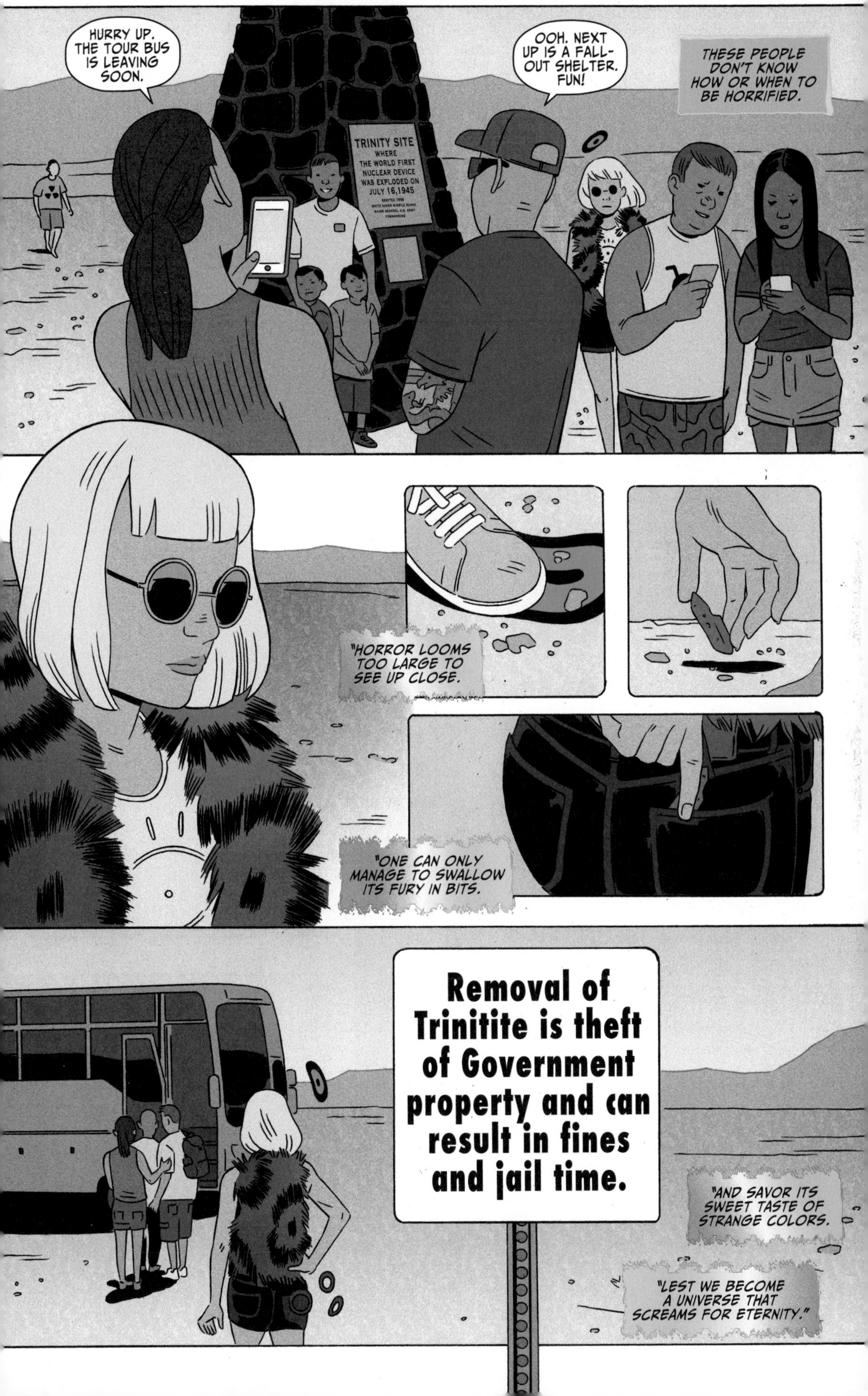
HURRY UP. THE TOUR BUS IS LEAVING SOON.
TRINITY SITE WHERE THE WORLD FIRST NUCLEAR DEVICE WAS EXPLODED ON JULY 16,1945
OOH. NEXT UP IS A FALL-OUT SHELTER. FUN!
THESE PEOPLE DON'T KNOW HOW OR WHEN TO BE HORRIFIED.
"HORROR LOOMS TOO LARGE TO SEE UP CLOSE.
"ONE CAN ONLY MANAGE TO SWALLOW ITS FURY IN BITS.
Removal of Trinitite is theft of Government property and can result in fines and jail time.
"AND SAVOR ITS SWEET TASTE OF STRANGE COLORS.
"LEST WE BECOME A UNIVERSE THAT SCREAMS FOR ETERNITY."

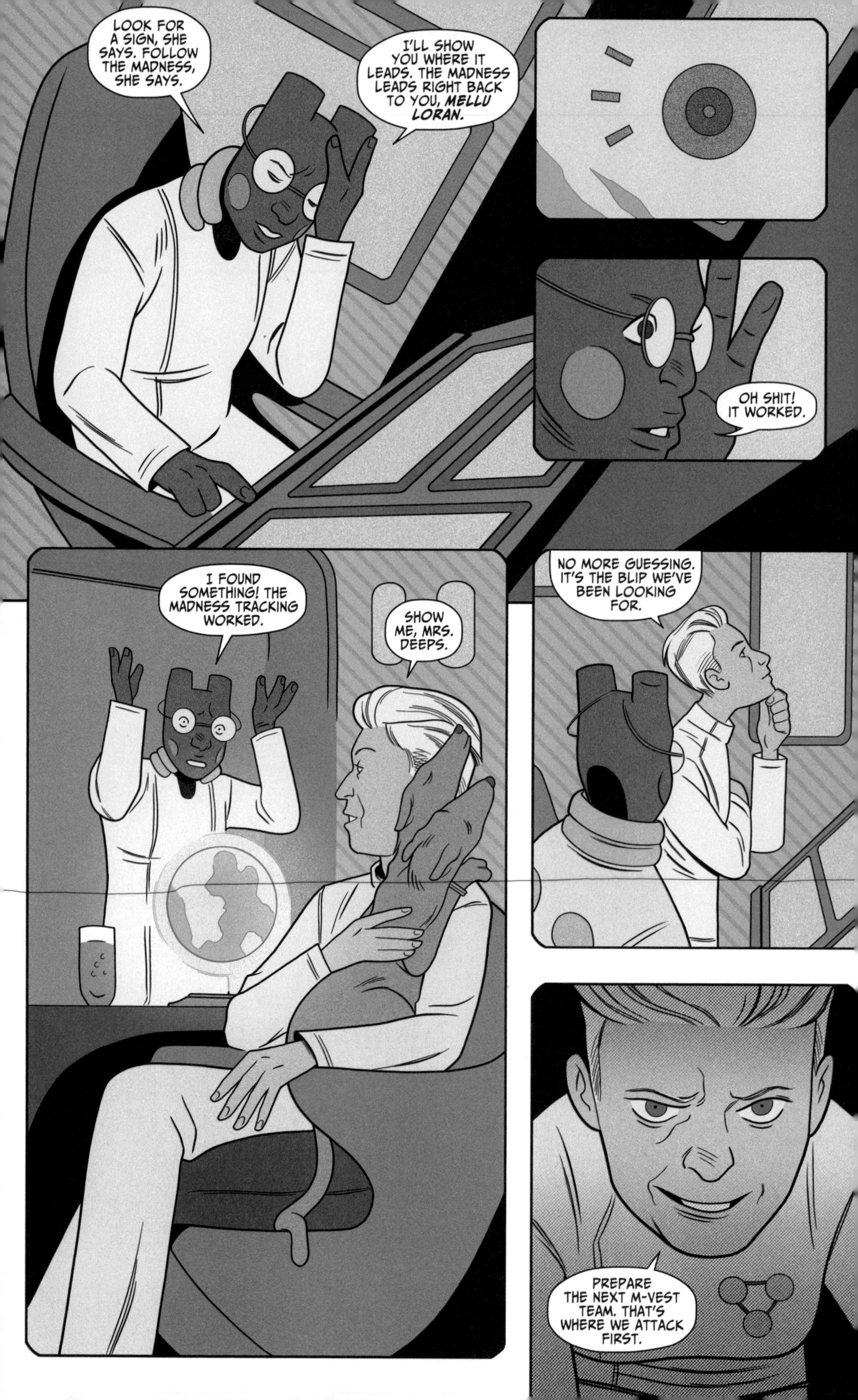
LOOK FOR A SIGN, SHE SAYS. FOLLOW THE MADNESS, SHE SAYS.
I'LL SHOW YOU WHERE IT LEADS. THE MADNESS LEADS RIGHT BACK TO YOU, *MELLU LORAN.*
OH SHIT! IT WORKED.
I FOUND SOMETHING! THE MADNESS TRACKING WORKED.
SHOW ME, MRS. DEEPS.
NO MORE GUESSING. IT'S THE BLIP WE'VE BEEN LOOKING FOR.
PREPARE THE NEXT M-VEST TEAM. THAT'S WHERE WE ATTACK FIRST.

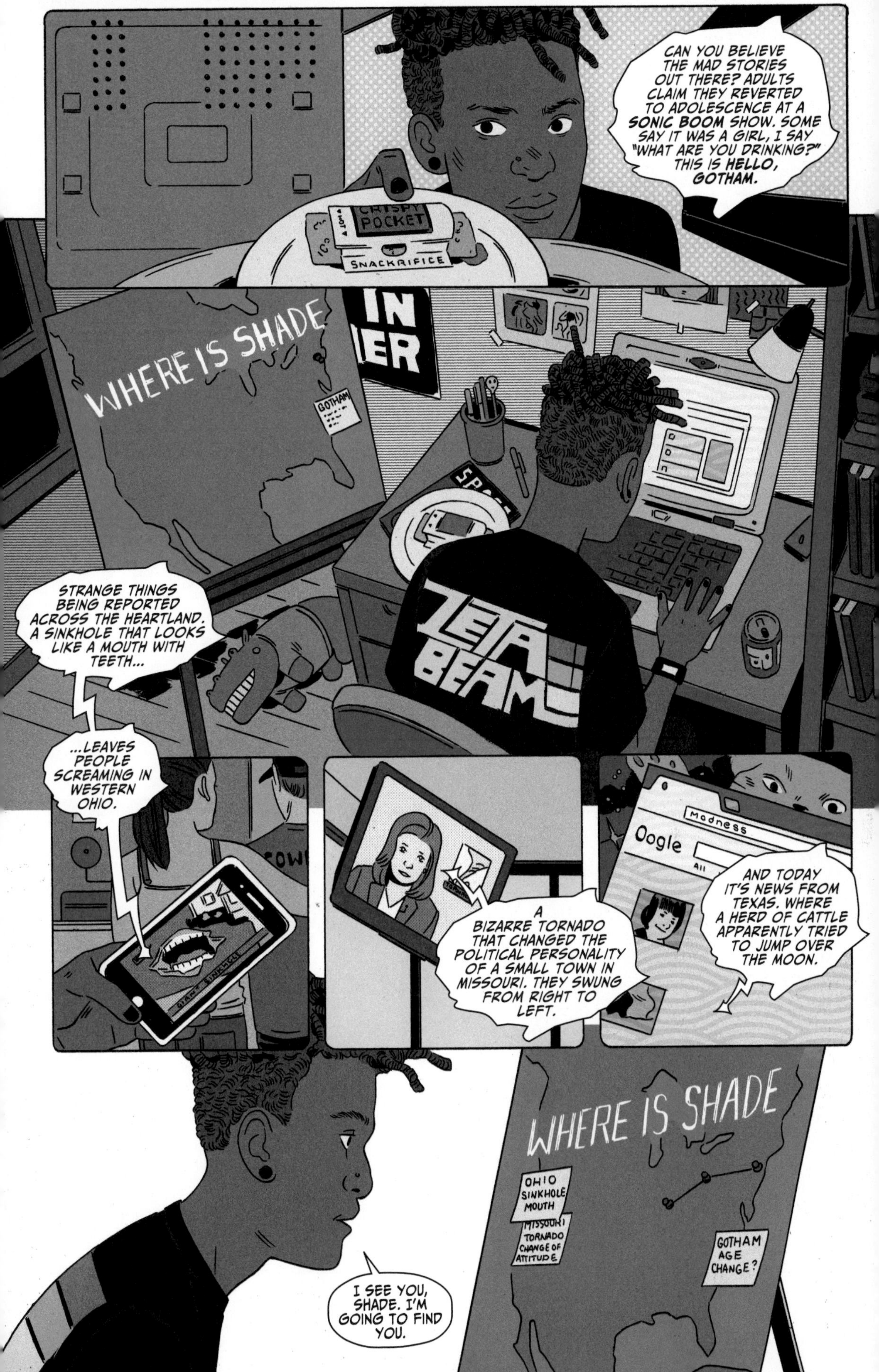
CAN YOU BELIEVE THE MAD STORIES OUT THERE? ADULTS CLAIM THEY REVERTED TO ADOLESCENCE AT A SONIC BOOM SHOW. SOME SAY IT WAS A GIRL, I SAY "WHAT ARE YOU DRINKING?" THIS IS HELLO, GOTHAM.
CRISPY POCKET
SNACKRIFICE
WHERE IS SHADE
GOTHAM
STRANGE THINGS BEING REPORTED ACROSS THE HEARTLAND. A SINKHOLE THAT LOOKS LIKE A MOUTH WITH TEETH...
ZETA BEAM
...LEAVES PEOPLE SCREAMING IN WESTERN OHIO.
A BIZARRE TORNADO THAT CHANGED THE POLITICAL PERSONALITY OF A SMALL TOWN IN MISSOURI. THEY SWUNG FROM RIGHT TO LEFT.
Madness
Oogle
AND TODAY IT'S NEWS FROM TEXAS. WHERE A HERD OF CATTLE APPARENTLY TRIED TO JUMP OVER THE MOON.
WHERE IS SHADE
OHIO SINKHOLE MOUTH
MISSOURI TORNADO CHANGE OF ATTITUDE
GOTHAM AGE CHANGE?
I SEE YOU, SHADE. I'M GOING TO FIND YOU.

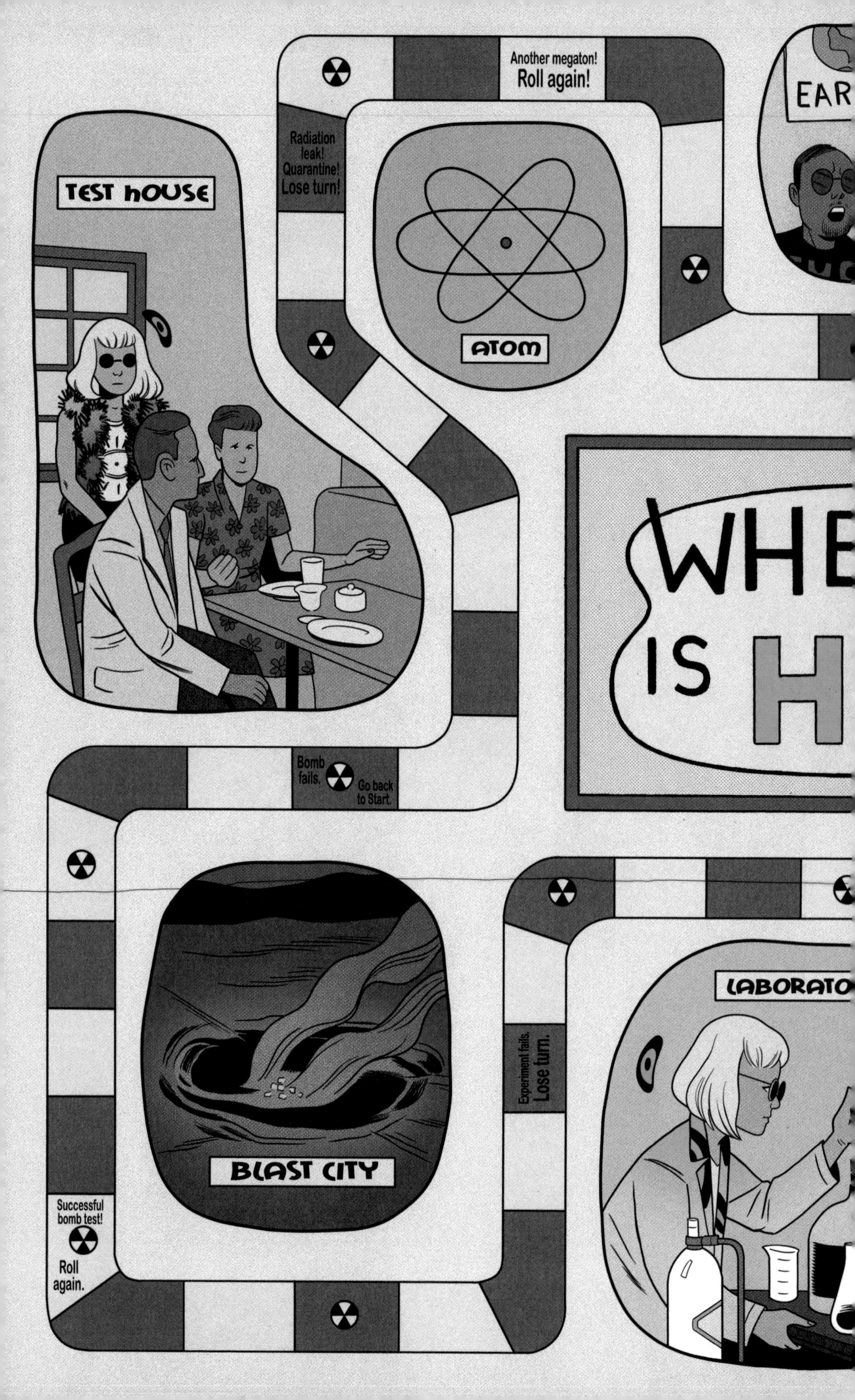

Another megaton! Roll again!
Radiation leak! Quarantine! Lose turn!
TEST hOUSE
ATOM
Bomb fails. Go back to Start.
BLAST CITY
Experiment fails. Lose turn.
Successful bomb test! Roll again.

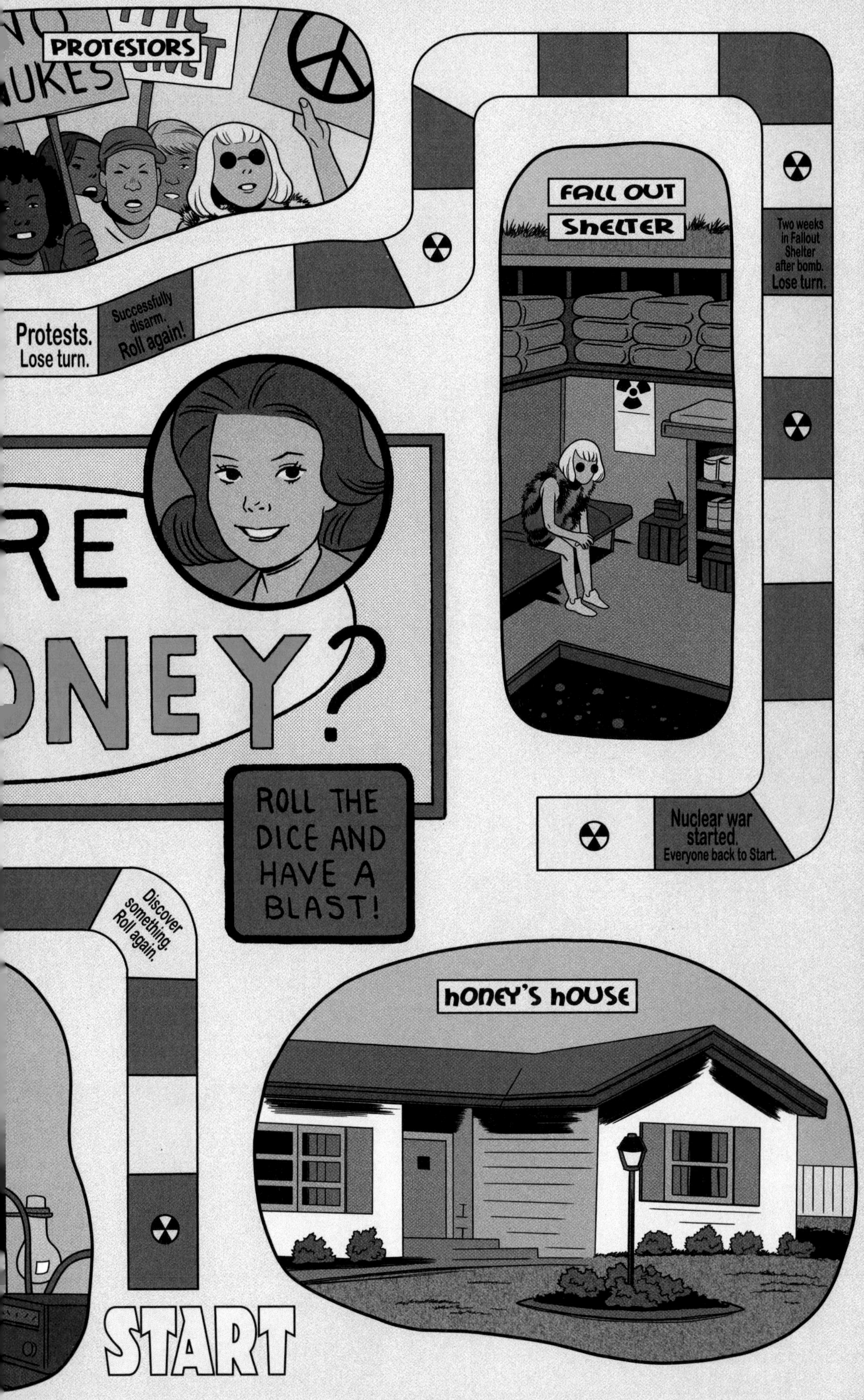
PROTESTORS
FALL OUT SHELTER
Two weeks in Fallout Shelter after bomb. Lose turn.
Successfully disarm. Roll again!
Protests. Lose turn.
RE
ONEY?
ROLL THE DICE AND HAVE A BLAST!
Nuclear war started. Everyone back to Start.
Discover something. Roll again.
HONEY'S HOUSE
START

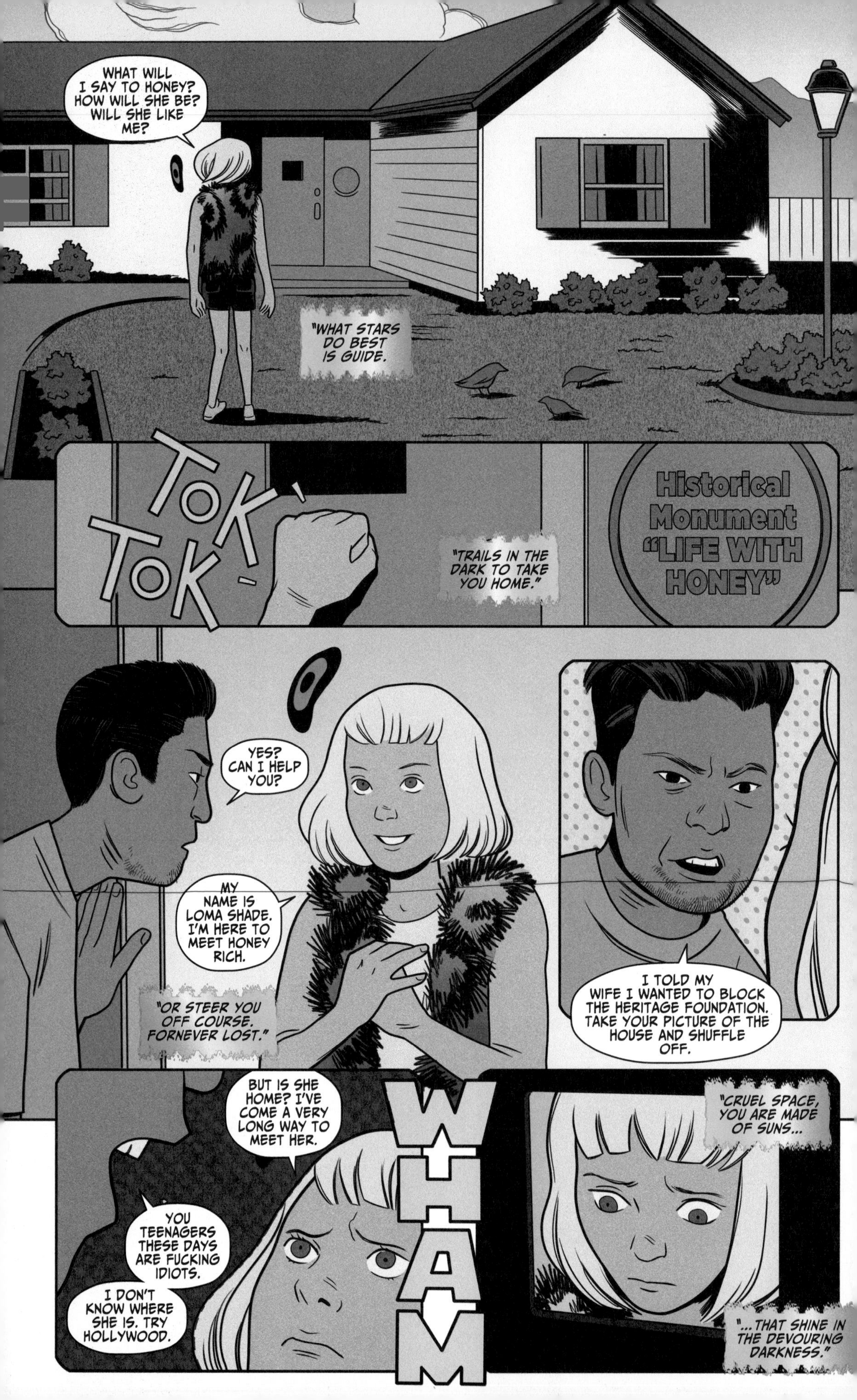
WHAT WILL I SAY TO HONEY? HOW WILL SHE BE? WILL SHE LIKE ME?
"WHAT STARS DO BEST IS GUIDE.
TOK TOK
"TRAILS IN THE DARK TO TAKE YOU HOME."
Historical Monument "LIFE WITH HONEY"
YES? CAN I HELP YOU?
MY NAME IS LOMA SHADE. I'M HERE TO MEET HONEY RICH.
"OR STEER YOU OFF COURSE. FORNEVER LOST."
I TOLD MY WIFE I WANTED TO BLOCK THE HERITAGE FOUNDATION. TAKE YOUR PICTURE OF THE HOUSE AND SHUFFLE OFF.
BUT IS SHE HOME? I'VE COME A VERY LONG WAY TO MEET HER.
YOU TEENAGERS THESE DAYS ARE FUCKING IDIOTS.
I DON'T KNOW WHERE SHE IS. TRY HOLLYWOOD.
WHAM
"CRUEL SPACE, YOU ARE MADE OF SUNS...
"...THAT SHINE IN THE DEVOURING DARKNESS."

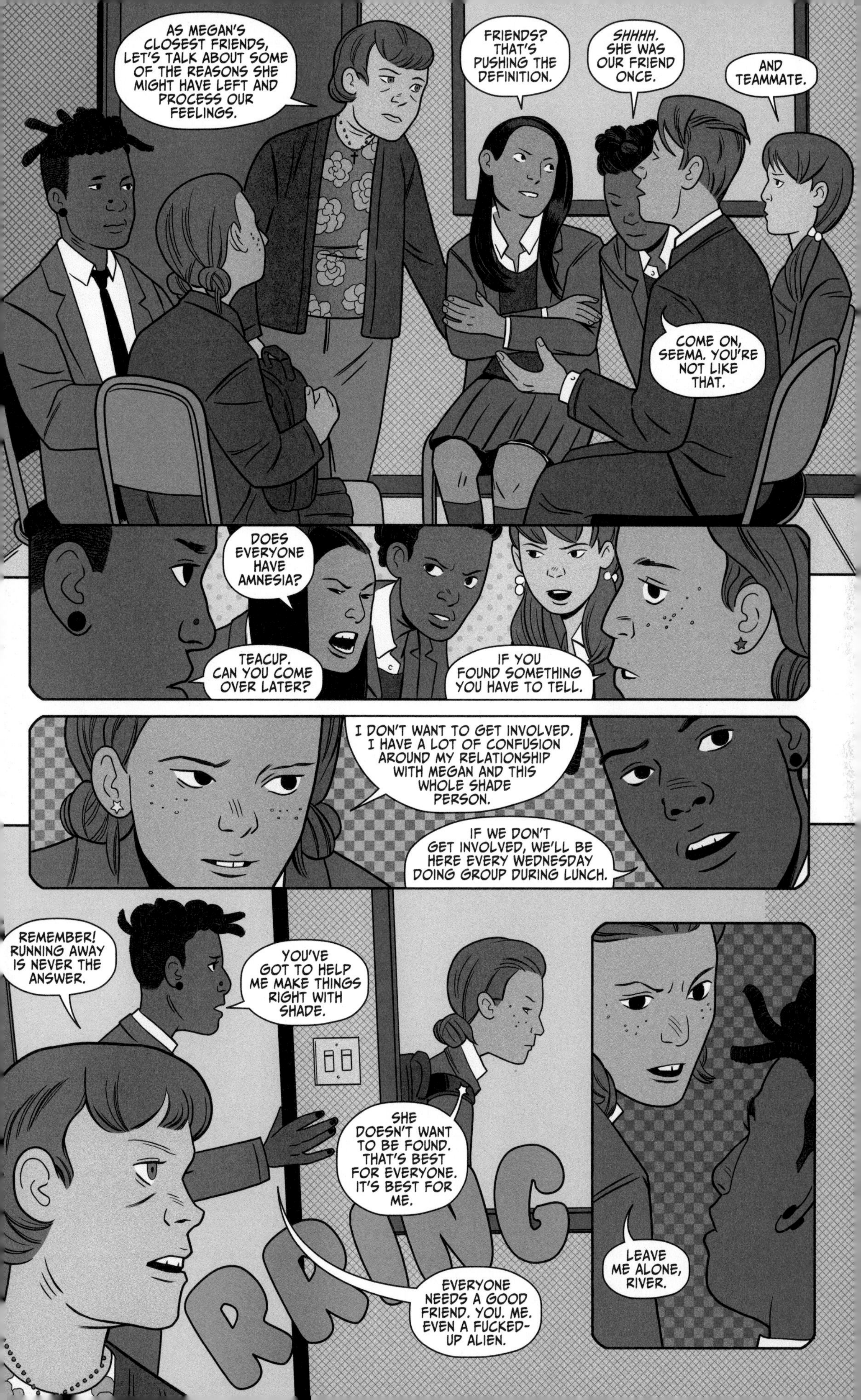
AS MEGAN'S CLOSEST FRIENDS, LET'S TALK ABOUT SOME OF THE REASONS SHE MIGHT HAVE LEFT AND PROCESS OUR FEELINGS.
FRIENDS? THAT'S PUSHING THE DEFINITION.
SHHHH. SHE WAS OUR FRIEND ONCE.
AND TEAMMATE.
COME ON, SEEMA. YOU'RE NOT LIKE THAT.
DOES EVERYONE HAVE AMNESIA?
TEACUP. CAN YOU COME OVER LATER?
IF YOU FOUND SOMETHING YOU HAVE TO TELL.
I DON'T WANT TO GET INVOLVED. I HAVE A LOT OF CONFUSION AROUND MY RELATIONSHIP WITH MEGAN AND THIS WHOLE SHADE PERSON.
IF WE DON'T GET INVOLVED, WE'LL BE HERE EVERY WEDNESDAY DOING GROUP DURING LUNCH.
REMEMBER! RUNNING AWAY IS NEVER THE ANSWER.
YOU'VE GOT TO HELP ME MAKE THINGS RIGHT WITH SHADE.
SHE DOESN'T WANT TO BE FOUND. THAT'S BEST FOR EVERYONE. IT'S BEST FOR ME.
RRRING
EVERYONE NEEDS A GOOD FRIEND. YOU. ME. EVEN A FUCKED-UP ALIEN.
LEAVE ME ALONE, RIVER.

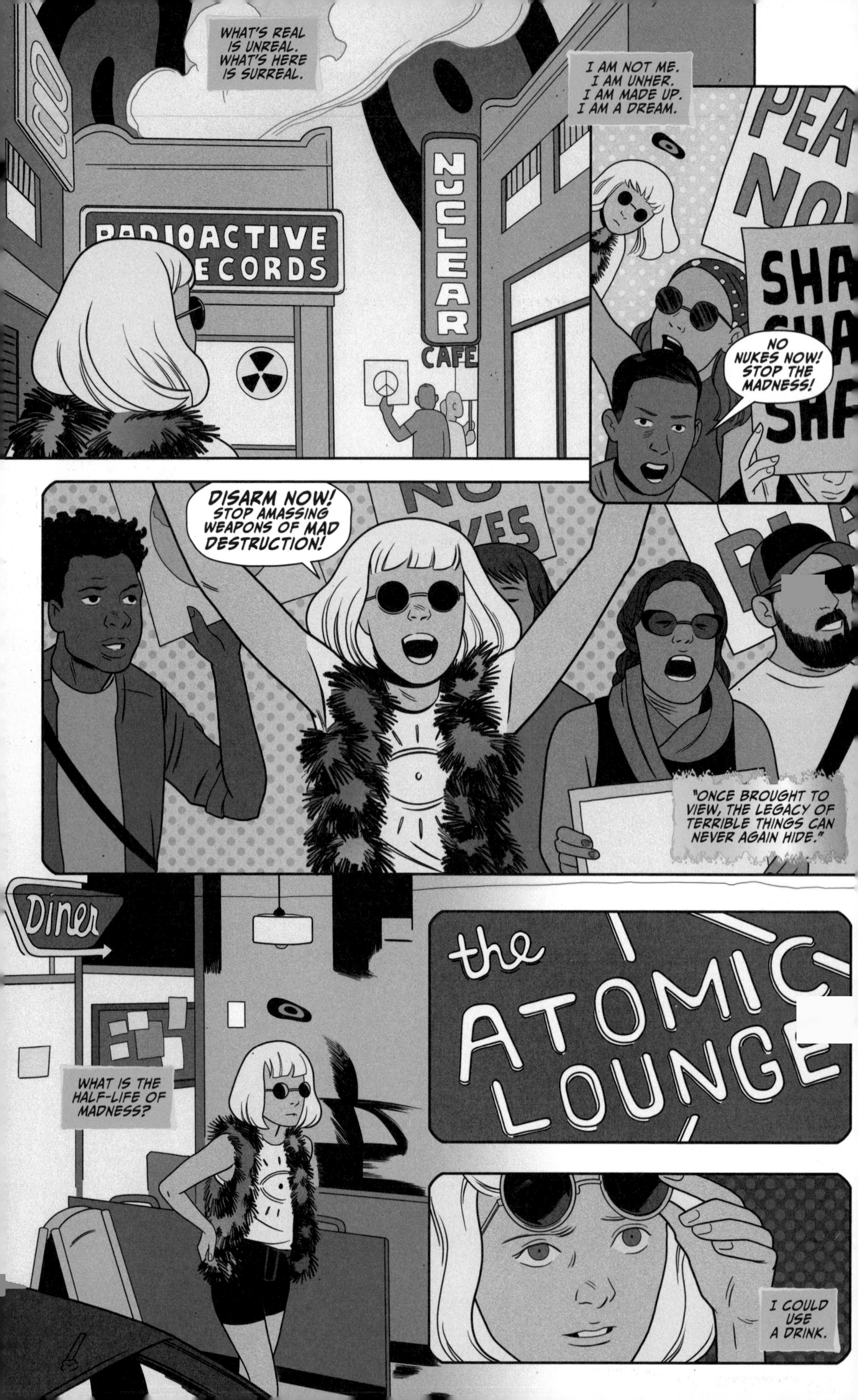
WHAT'S REAL IS UNREAL. WHAT'S HERE IS SURREAL.
RADIOACTIVE RECORDS
NUCLEAR CAFE
I AM NOT ME. I AM UNHER. I AM MADE UP. I AM A DREAM.
NO NUKES NOW! STOP THE MADNESS!
DISARM NOW! STOP AMASSING WEAPONS OF MAD DESTRUCTION!
"ONCE BROUGHT TO VIEW, THE LEGACY OF TERRIBLE THINGS CAN NEVER AGAIN HIDE."
Diner
the ATOMIC LOUNGE
WHAT IS THE HALF-LIFE OF MADNESS?
I COULD USE A DRINK.

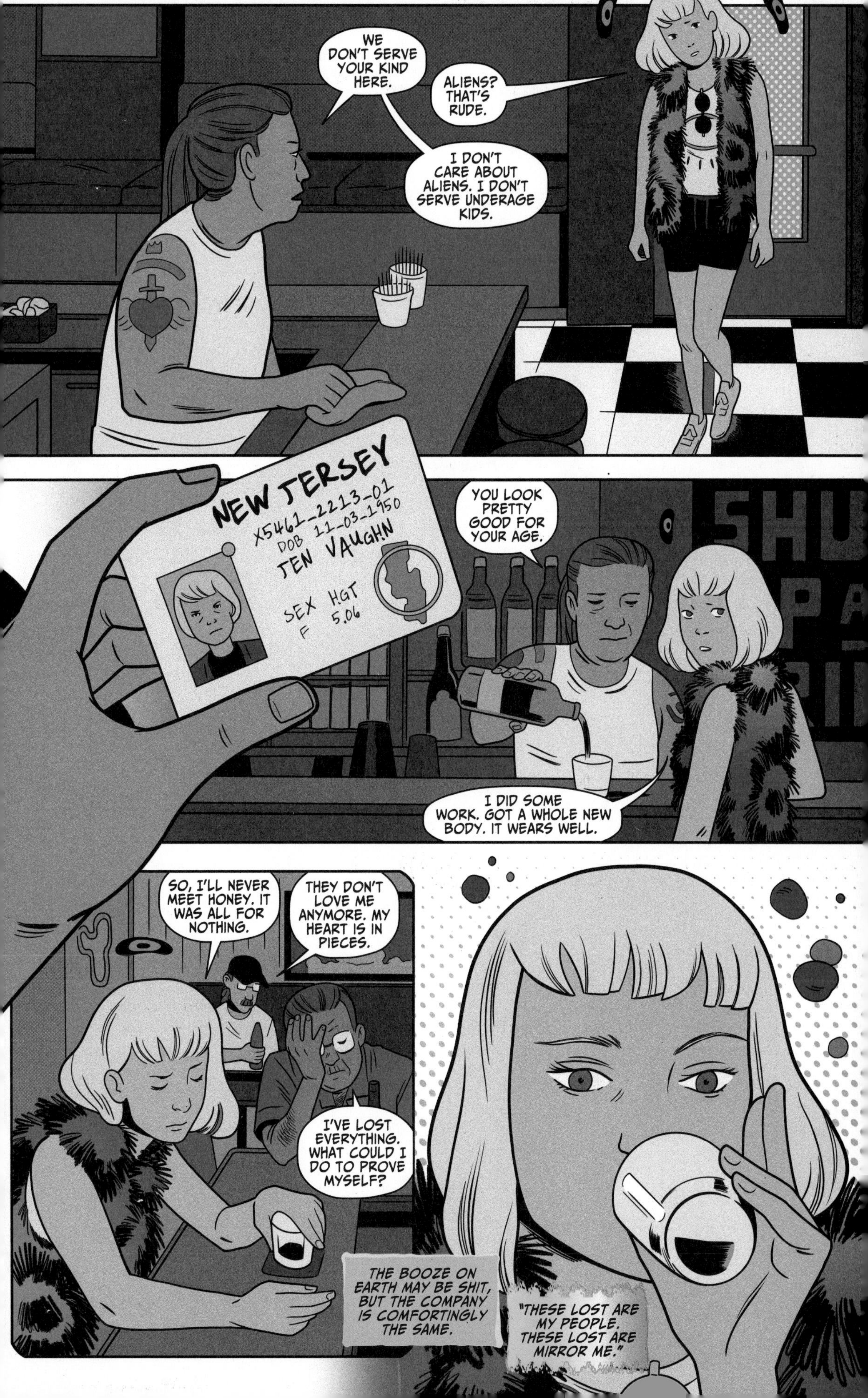
WE DON'T SERVE YOUR KIND HERE.
ALIENS? THAT'S RUDE.
I DON'T CARE ABOUT ALIENS. I DON'T SERVE UNDERAGE KIDS.
NEW JERSEY
X5461_2213_01
DOB 11-03-1950
JEN VAUGHN
SEX F
HGT 5.06
YOU LOOK PRETTY GOOD FOR YOUR AGE.
I DID SOME WORK. GOT A WHOLE NEW BODY. IT WEARS WELL.
SO, I'LL NEVER MEET HONEY. IT WAS ALL FOR NOTHING.
THEY DON'T LOVE ME ANYMORE. MY HEART IS IN PIECES.
I'VE LOST EVERYTHING. WHAT COULD I DO TO PROVE MYSELF?
THE BOOZE ON EARTH MAY BE SHIT, BUT THE COMPANY IS COMFORTINGLY THE SAME.
"THESE LOST ARE MY PEOPLE. THESE LOST ARE MIRROR ME."

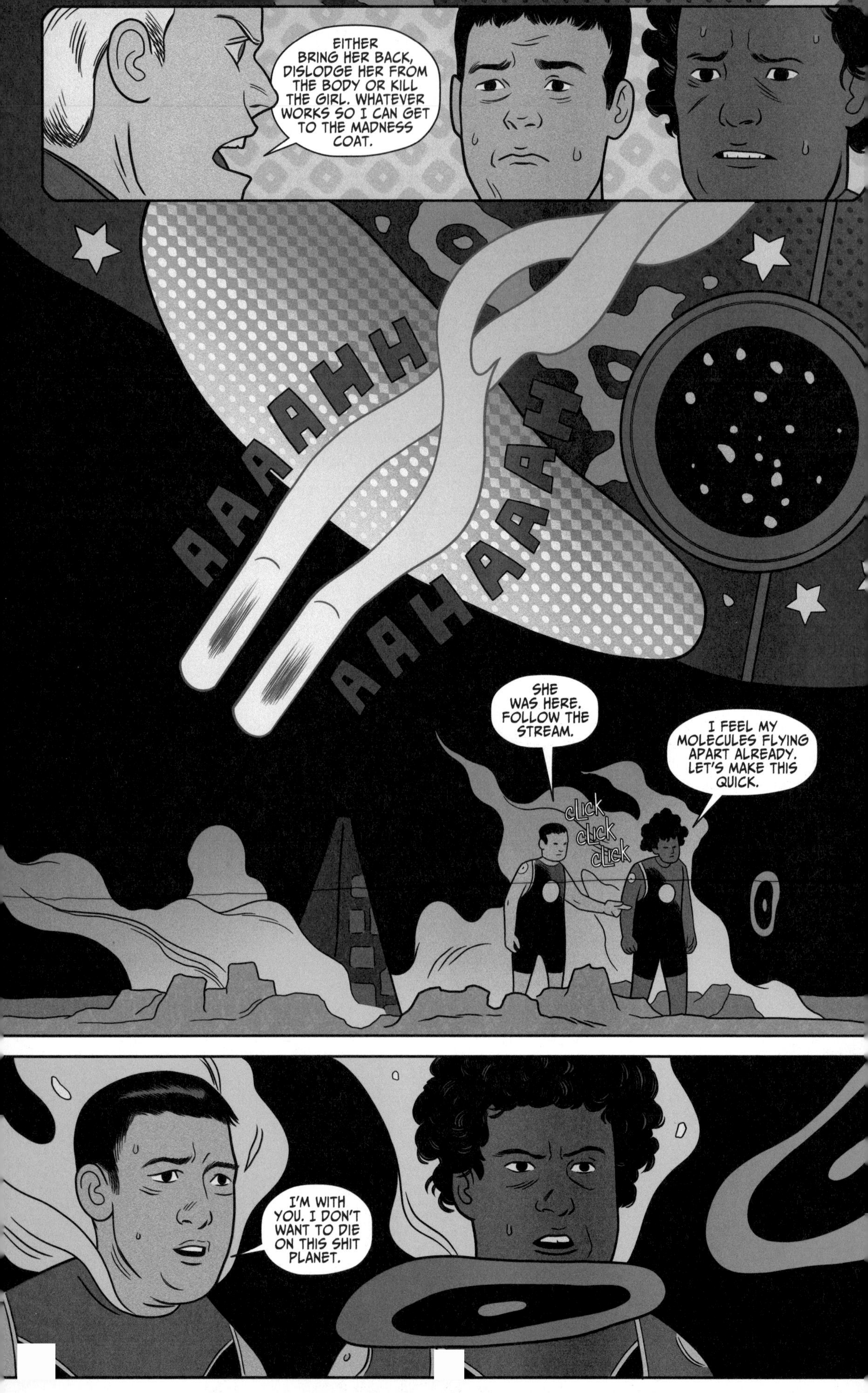
EITHER BRING HER BACK, DISLODGE HER FROM THE BODY OR KILL THE GIRL. WHATEVER WORKS SO I CAN GET TO THE MADNESS COAT.
AAAAHH
AAAAAAH
AAH
SHE WAS HERE. FOLLOW THE STREAM.
CLICK CLICK CLICK
I FEEL MY MOLECULES FLYING APART ALREADY. LET'S MAKE THIS QUICK.
I'M WITH YOU. I DON'T WANT TO DIE ON THIS SHIT PLANET.

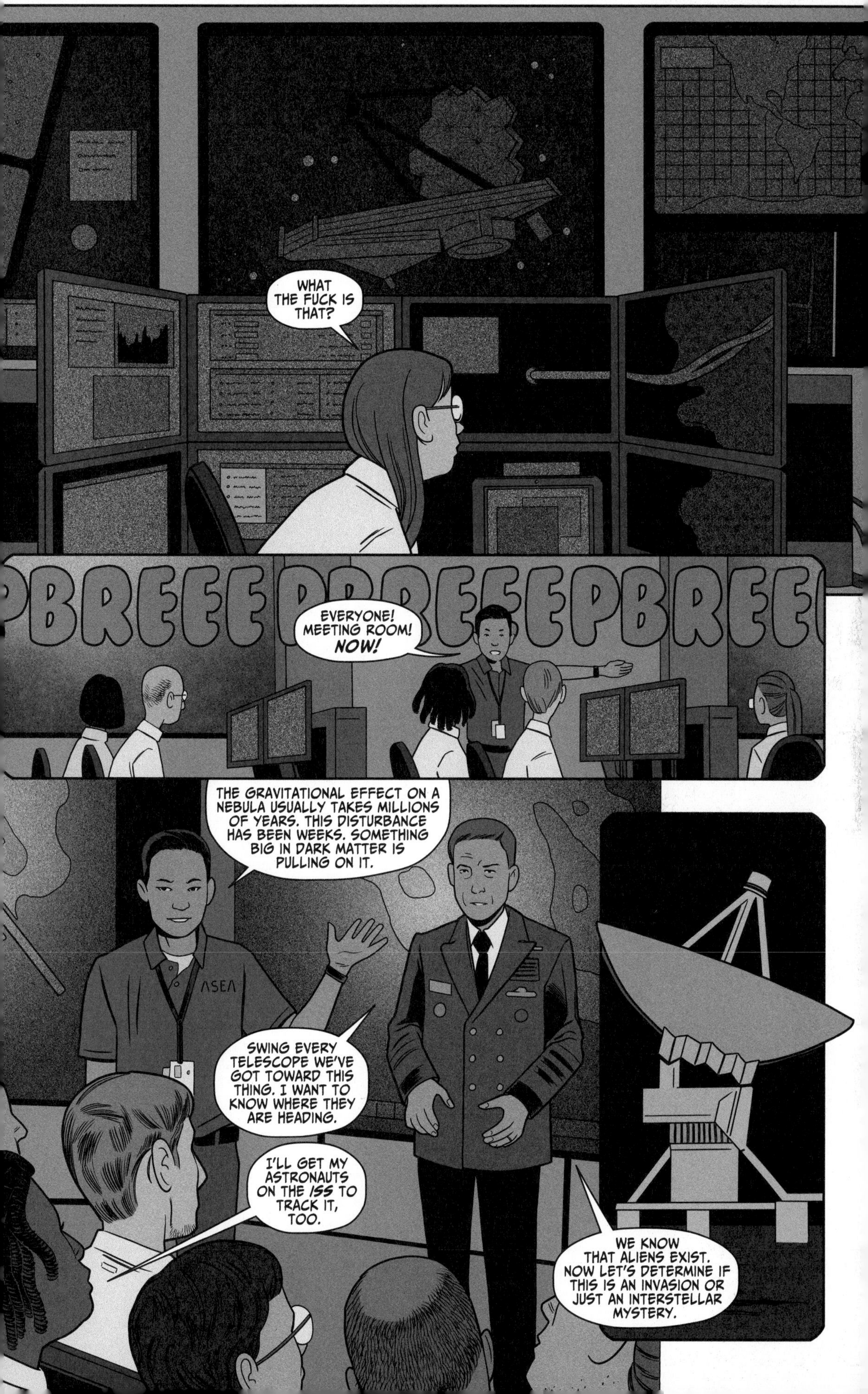
WHAT THE FUCK IS THAT?
PBREEEPBREEEPBREEEPBREE
EVERYONE! MEETING ROOM! NOW!
THE GRAVITATIONAL EFFECT ON A NEBULA USUALLY TAKES MILLIONS OF YEARS. THIS DISTURBANCE HAS BEEN WEEKS. SOMETHING BIG IN DARK MATTER IS PULLING ON IT.
ASEA
SWING EVERY TELESCOPE WE'VE GOT TOWARD THIS THING. I WANT TO KNOW WHERE THEY ARE HEADING.
I'LL GET MY ASTRONAUTS ON THE ISS TO TRACK IT, TOO.
WE KNOW THAT ALIENS EXIST. NOW LET'S DETERMINE IF THIS IS AN INVASION OR JUST AN INTERSTELLAR MYSTERY.

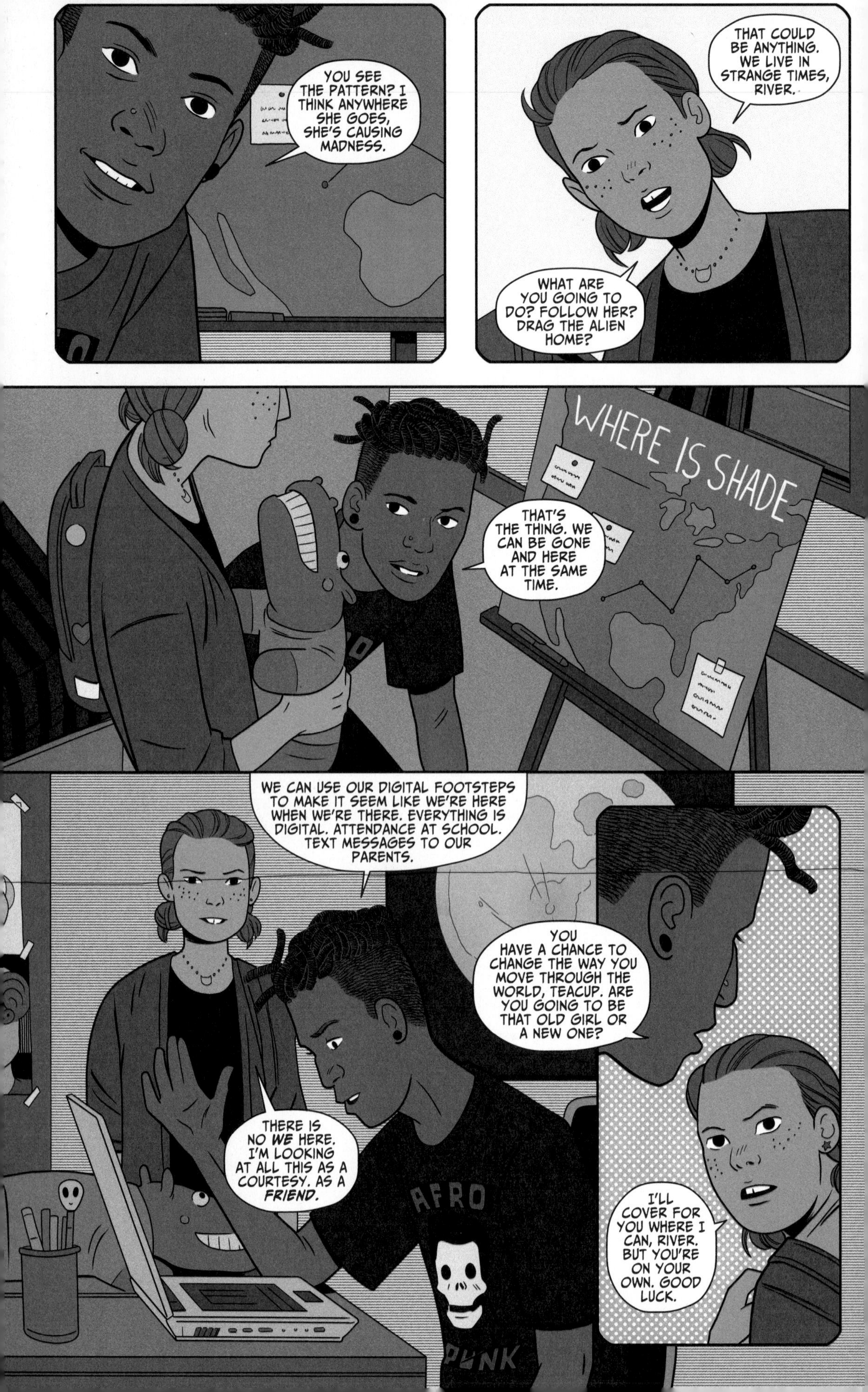
YOU SEE THE PATTERN? I THINK ANYWHERE SHE GOES, SHE'S CAUSING MADNESS.
THAT COULD BE ANYTHING. WE LIVE IN STRANGE TIMES, RIVER.
WHAT ARE YOU GOING TO DO? FOLLOW HER? DRAG THE ALIEN HOME?
WHERE IS SHADE
THAT'S THE THING. WE CAN BE GONE AND HERE AT THE SAME TIME.
WE CAN USE OUR DIGITAL FOOTSTEPS TO MAKE IT SEEM LIKE WE'RE HERE WHEN WE'RE THERE. EVERYTHING IS DIGITAL. ATTENDANCE AT SCHOOL. TEXT MESSAGES TO OUR PARENTS.
THERE IS NO *WE* HERE. I'M LOOKING AT ALL THIS AS A COURTESY. AS A *FRIEND*.
YOU HAVE A CHANCE TO CHANGE THE WAY YOU MOVE THROUGH THE WORLD, TEACUP. ARE YOU GOING TO BE THAT OLD GIRL OR A NEW ONE?
I'LL COVER FOR YOU WHERE I CAN, RIVER. BUT YOU'RE ON YOUR OWN. GOOD LUCK.
AFRO
PUNK

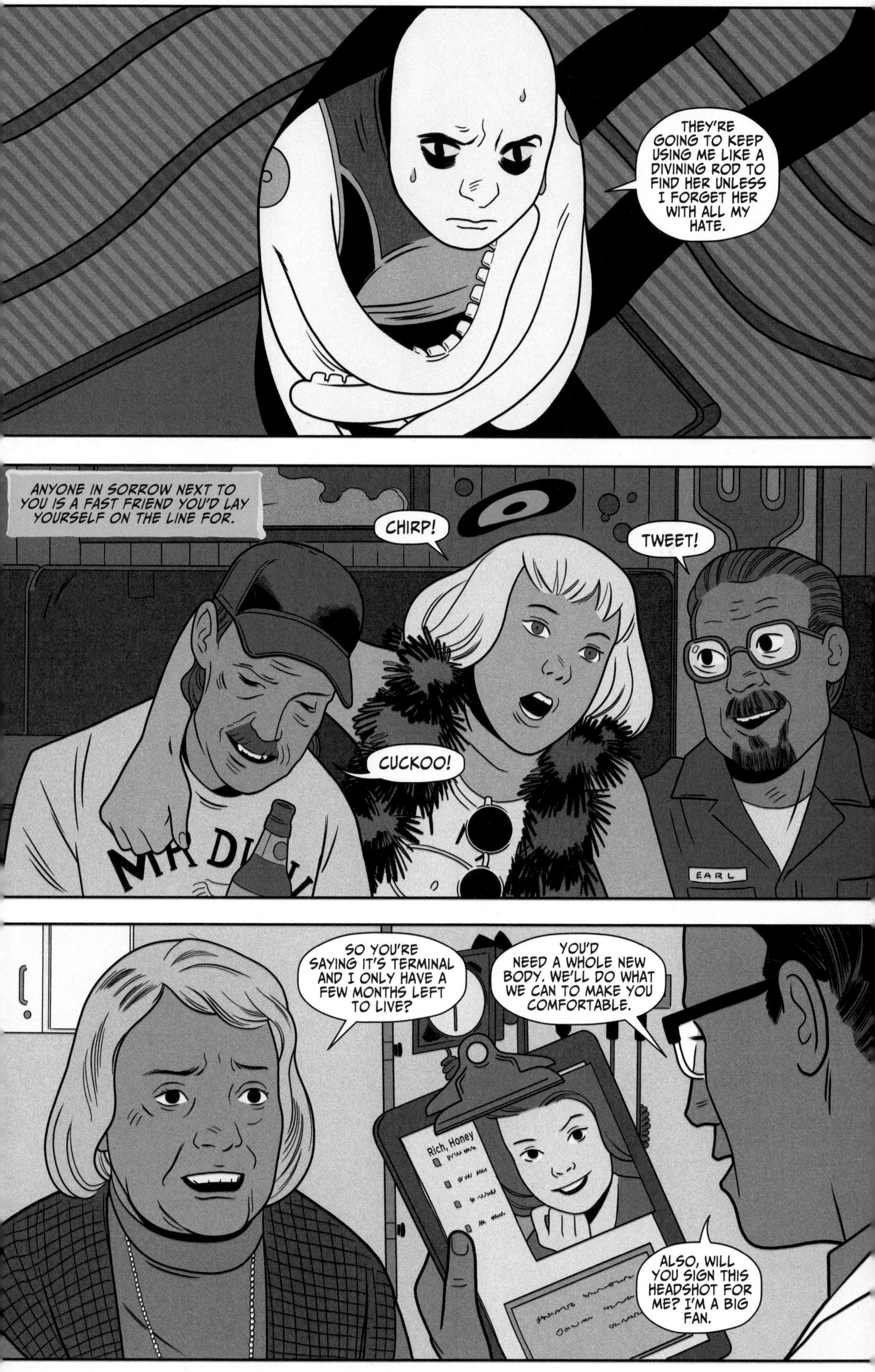
THEY'RE GOING TO KEEP USING ME LIKE A DIVINING ROD TO FIND HER UNLESS I FORGET HER WITH ALL MY HATE.
ANYONE IN SORROW NEXT TO YOU IS A FAST FRIEND YOU'D LAY YOURSELF ON THE LINE FOR.
CHIRP!
TWEET!
CUCKOO!
EARL
SO YOU'RE SAYING IT'S TERMINAL AND I ONLY HAVE A FEW MONTHS LEFT TO LIVE?
YOU'D NEED A WHOLE NEW BODY. WE'LL DO WHAT WE CAN TO MAKE YOU COMFORTABLE.
Rich, Honey
ALSO, WILL YOU SIGN THIS HEADSHOT FOR ME? I'M A BIG FAN.

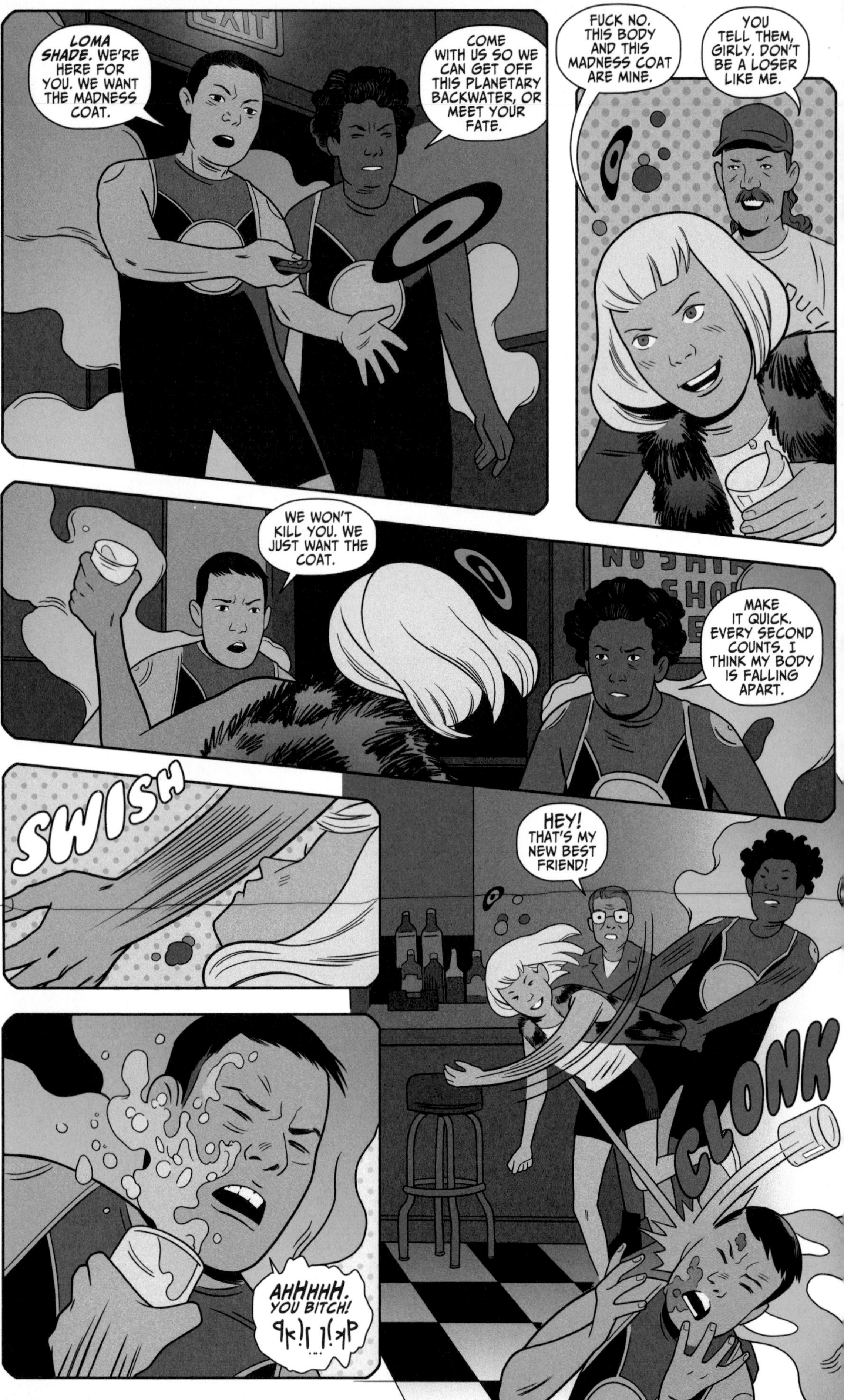
LOMA SHADE. WE'RE HERE FOR YOU. WE WANT THE MADNESS COAT.
COME WITH US SO WE CAN GET OFF THIS PLANETARY BACKWATER, OR MEET YOUR FATE.
FUCK NO. THIS BODY AND THIS MADNESS COAT ARE MINE.
YOU TELL THEM, GIRLY. DON'T BE A LOSER LIKE ME.
WE WON'T KILL YOU. WE JUST WANT THE COAT.
MAKE IT QUICK. EVERY SECOND COUNTS. I THINK MY BODY IS FALLING APART.
SWISH
HEY! THAT'S MY NEW BEST FRIEND!
CLONK
AHHHHH. YOU BITCH!

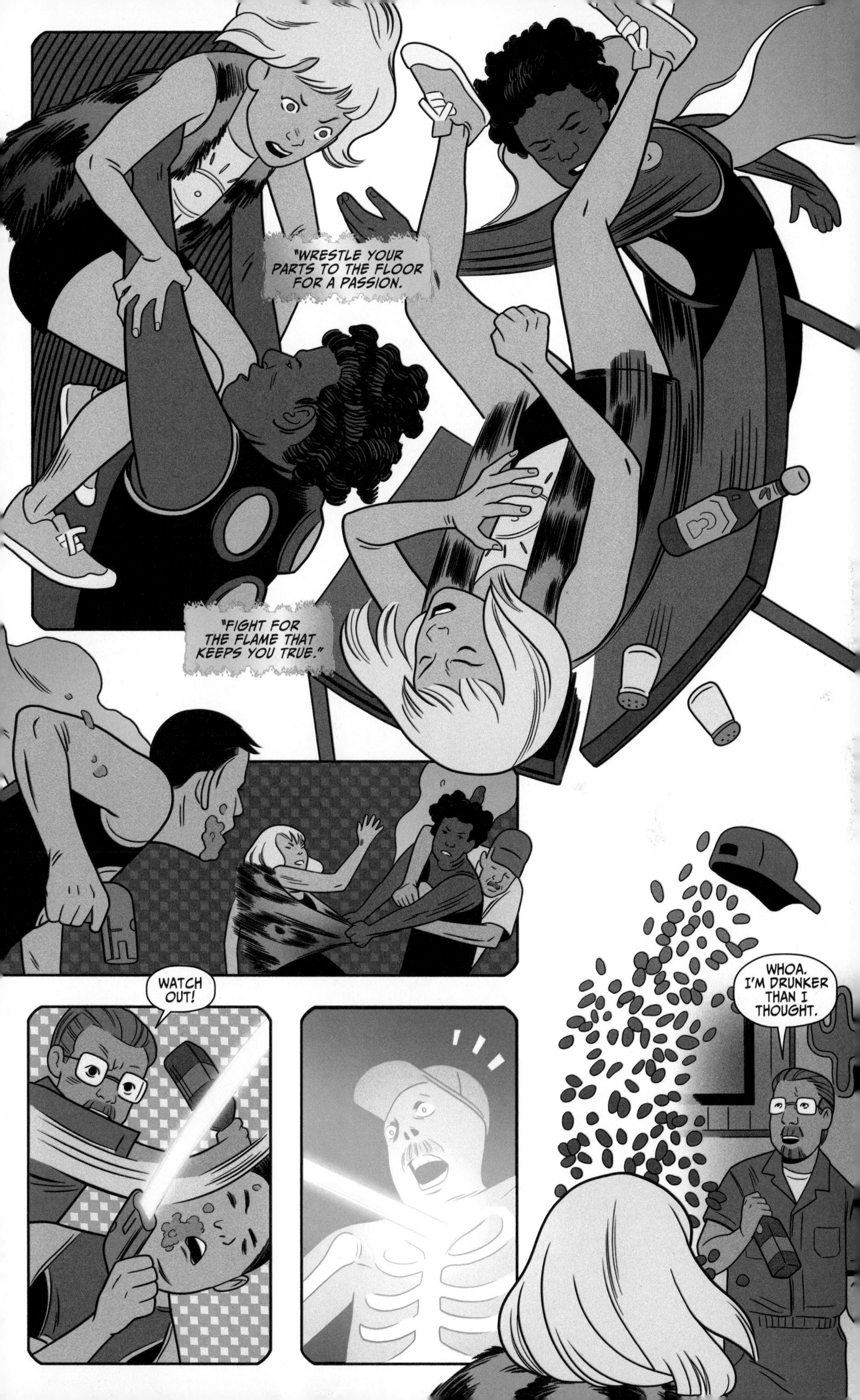
"WRESTLE YOUR PARTS TO THE FLOOR FOR A PASSION.
"FIGHT FOR THE FLAME THAT KEEPS YOU TRUE."
WATCH OUT!
WHOA. I'M DRUNKER THAN I THOUGHT.

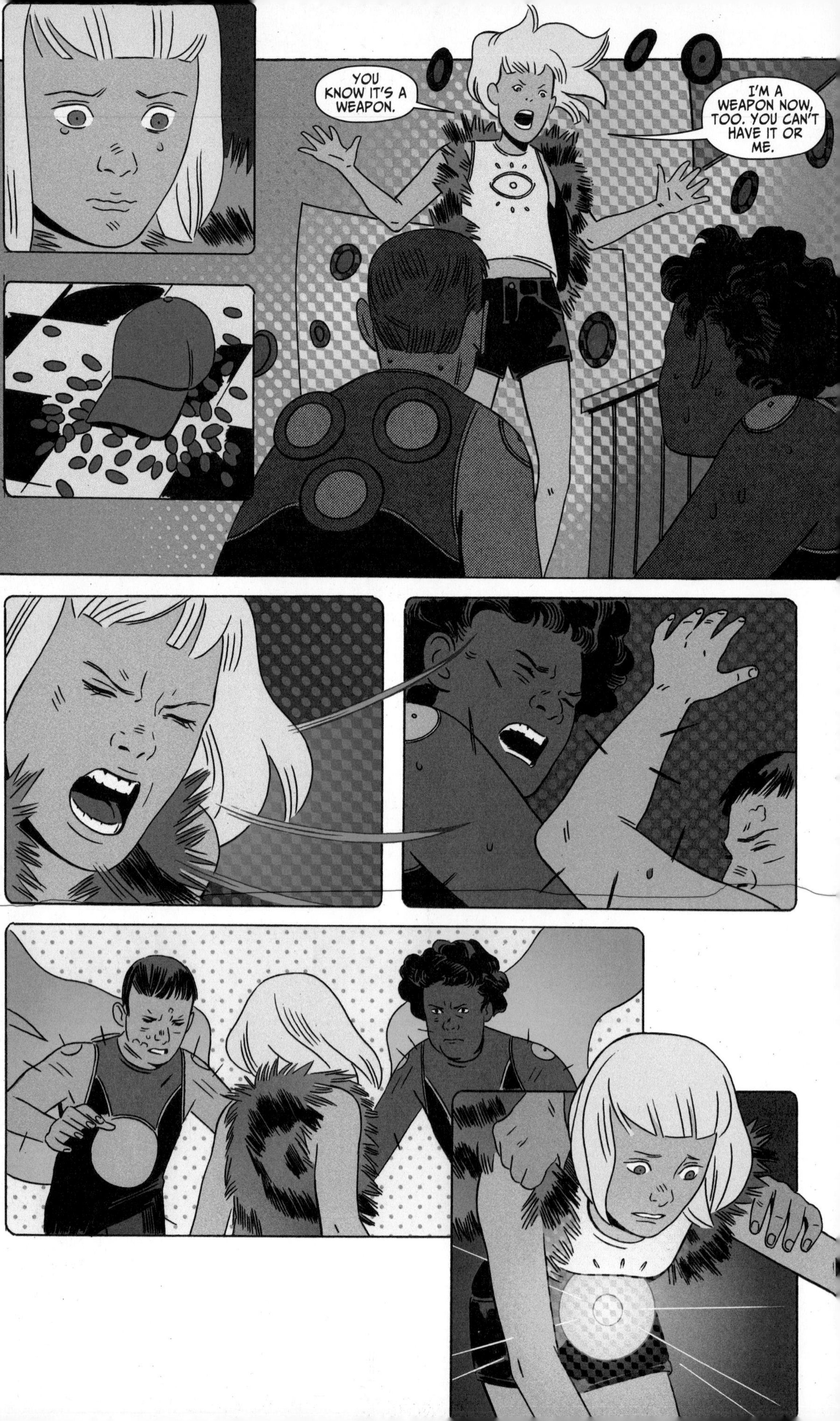
YOU KNOW IT'S A WEAPON.
I'M A WEAPON NOW, TOO. YOU CAN'T HAVE IT OR ME.

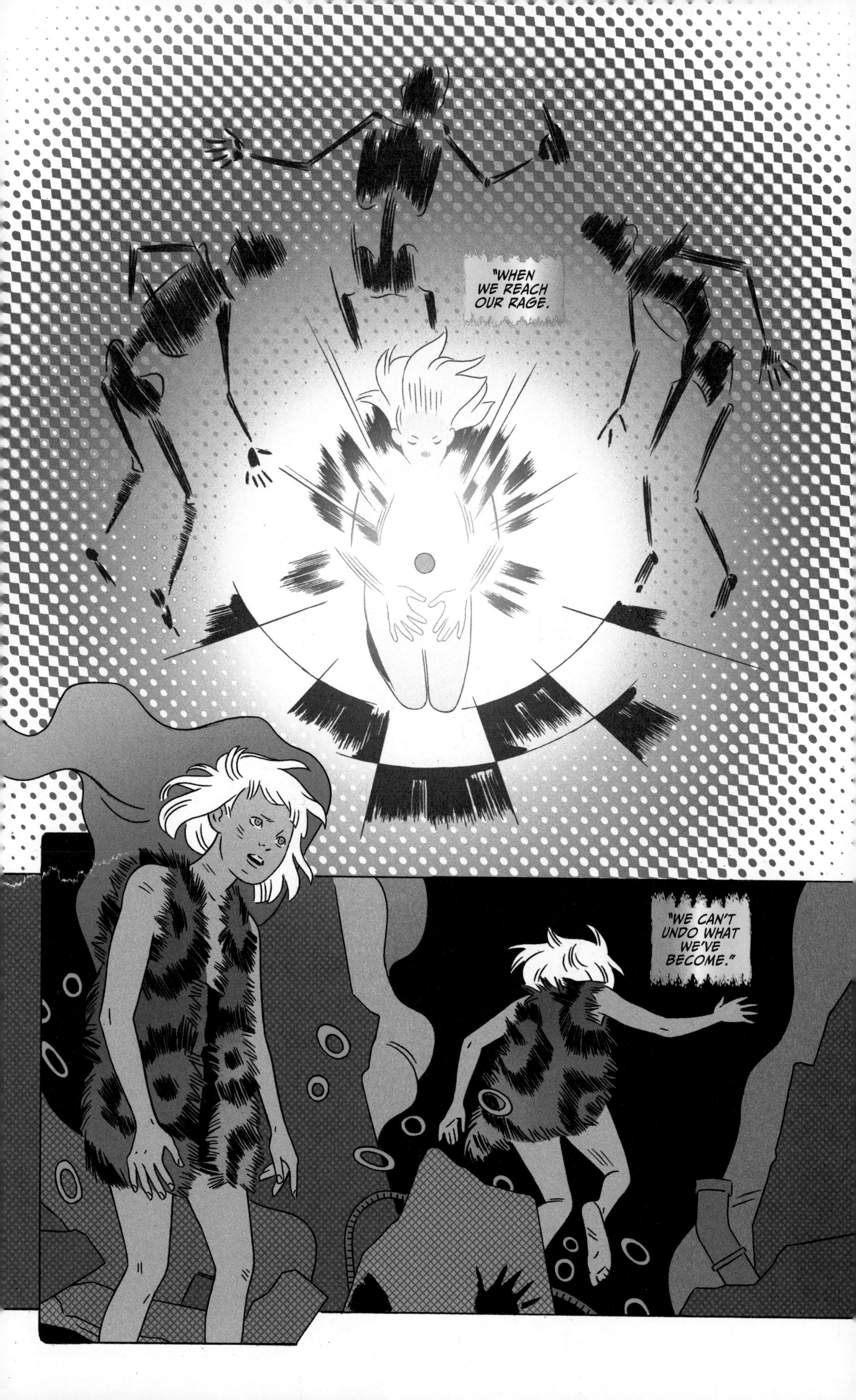
"WHEN WE REACH OUR RAGE.
"WE CAN'T UNDO WHAT WE'VE BECOME."

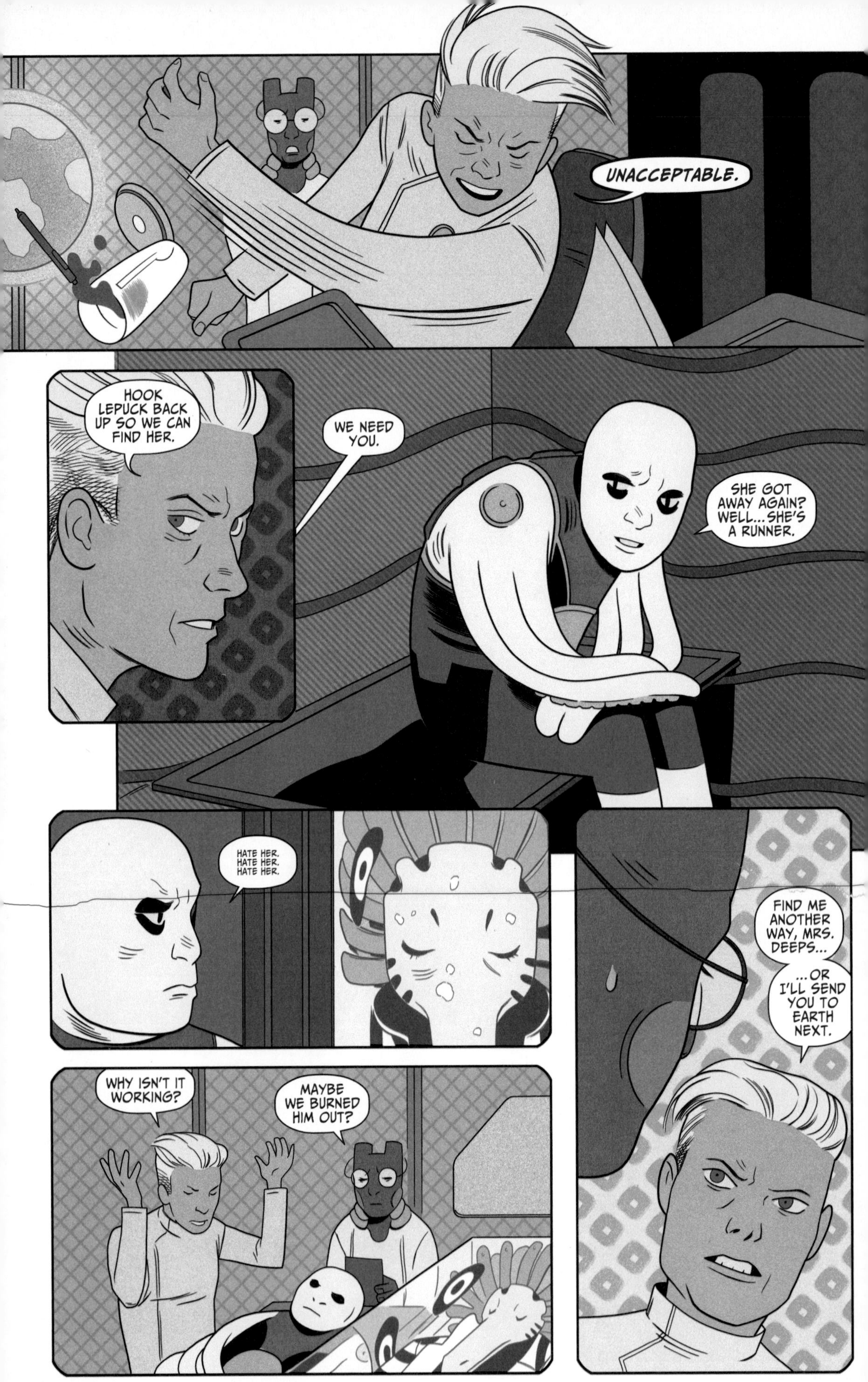
UNACCEPTABLE.
HOOK LEPUCK BACK UP SO WE CAN FIND HER.
WE NEED YOU.
SHE GOT AWAY AGAIN? WELL...SHE'S A RUNNER.
HATE HER. HATE HER. HATE HER.
FIND ME ANOTHER WAY, MRS. DEEPS...
...OR I'LL SEND YOU TO EARTH NEXT.
WHY ISN'T IT WORKING?
MAYBE WE BURNED HIM OUT?

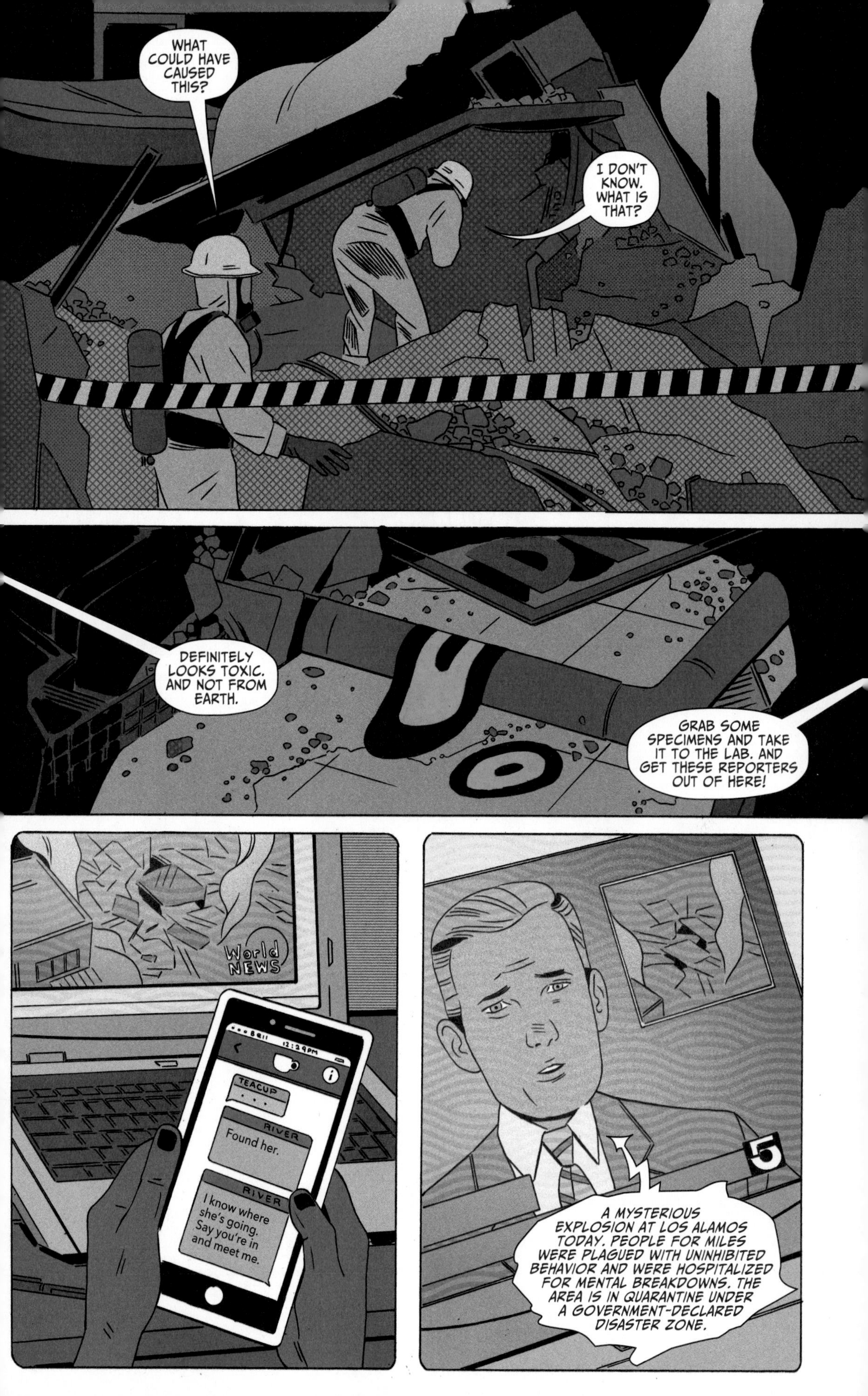
WHAT COULD HAVE CAUSED THIS?
I DON'T KNOW. WHAT IS THAT?
DEFINITELY LOOKS TOXIC. AND NOT FROM EARTH.
GRAB SOME SPECIMENS AND TAKE IT TO THE LAB. AND GET THESE REPORTERS OUT OF HERE!
World NEWS
TEACUP
RIVER
Found her.
RIVER
I know where she's going. Say you're in and meet me.
A MYSTERIOUS EXPLOSION AT LOS ALAMOS TODAY. PEOPLE FOR MILES WERE PLAGUED WITH UNINHIBITED BEHAVIOR AND WERE HOSPITALIZED FOR MENTAL BREAKDOWNS. THE AREA IS IN QUARANTINE UNDER A GOVERNMENT-DECLARED DISASTER ZONE.

"WILD WOMB WHAT WILL YOU BEAR? A DREAM? A LOVE? A DISAPPOINTMENT? A CARE?"

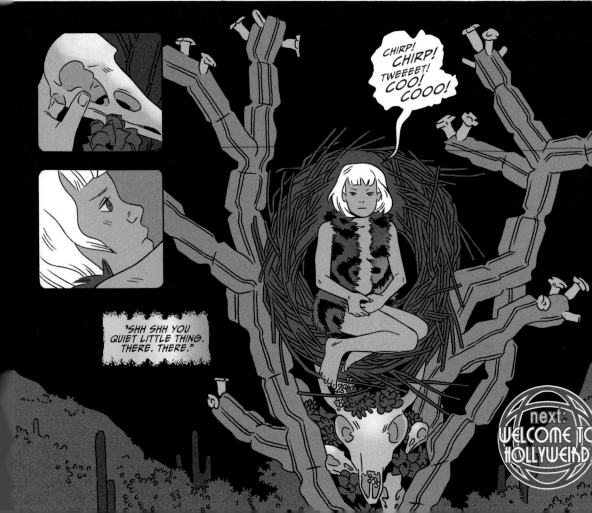

CHIRP! CHIRP! TWEEEET! COO! COOO!

"SHH SHH YOU QUIET LITTLE THING. THERE. THERE."

next: WELCOME TO HOLLYWEIRD

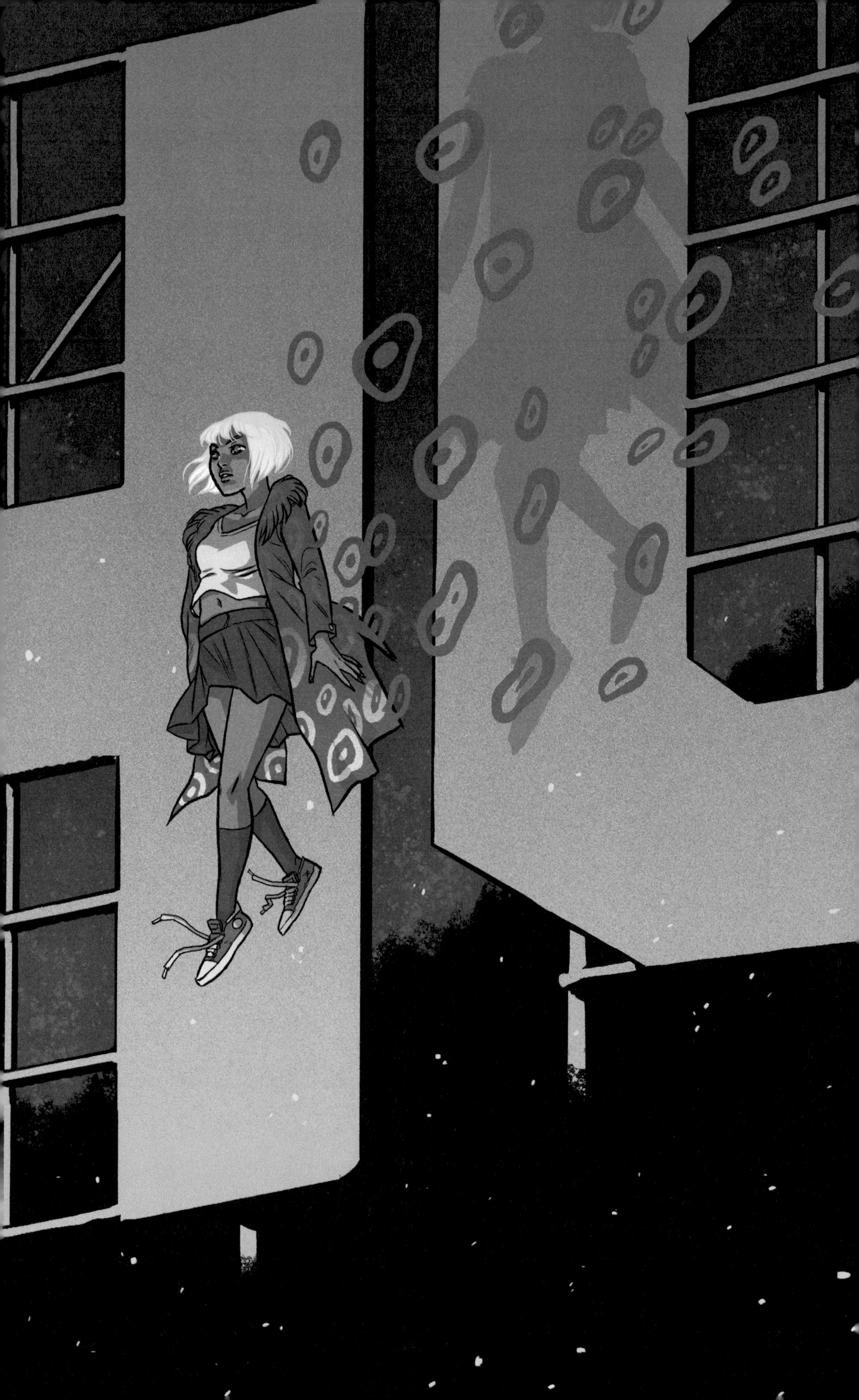

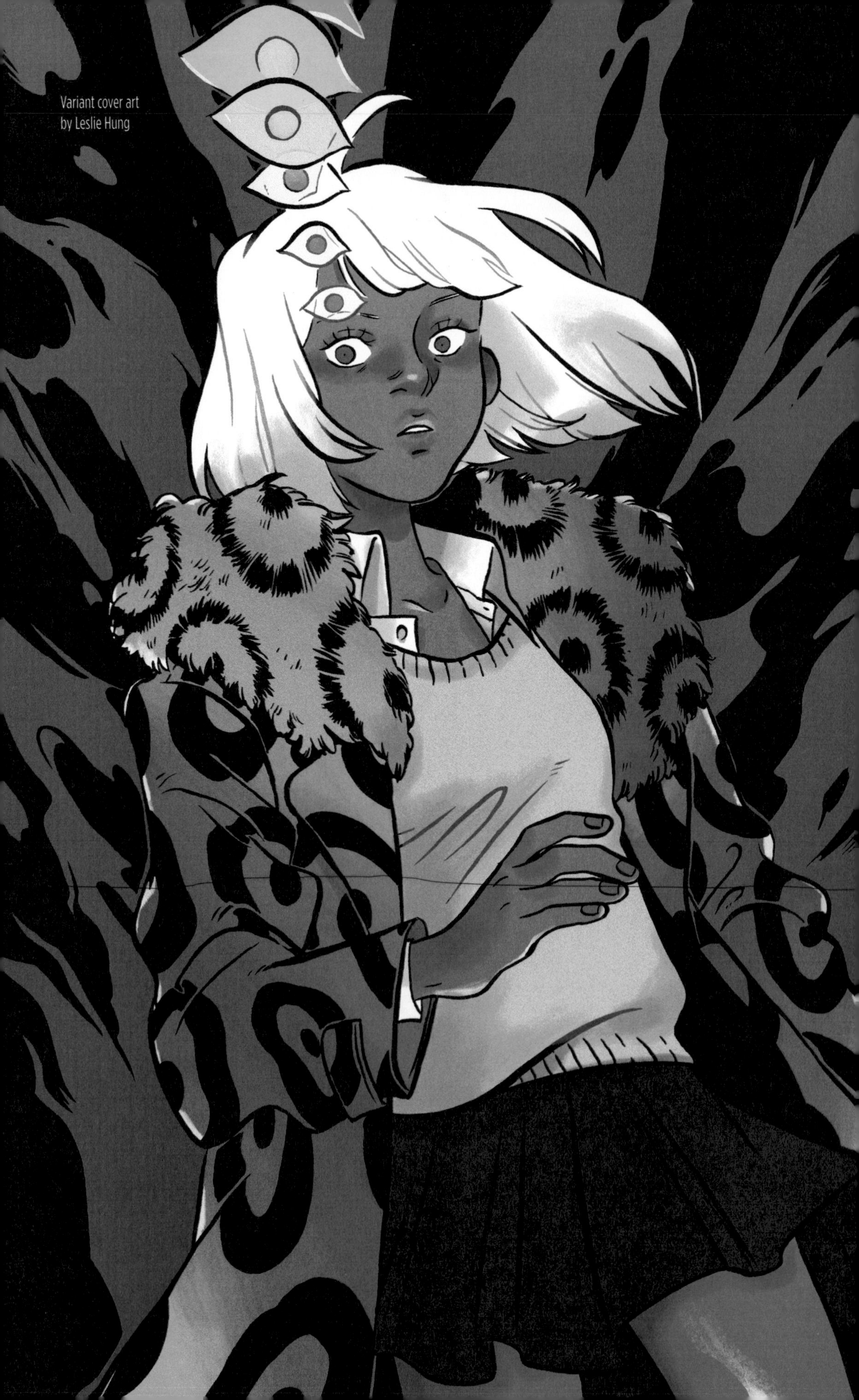

Variant cover art
by Leslie Hung

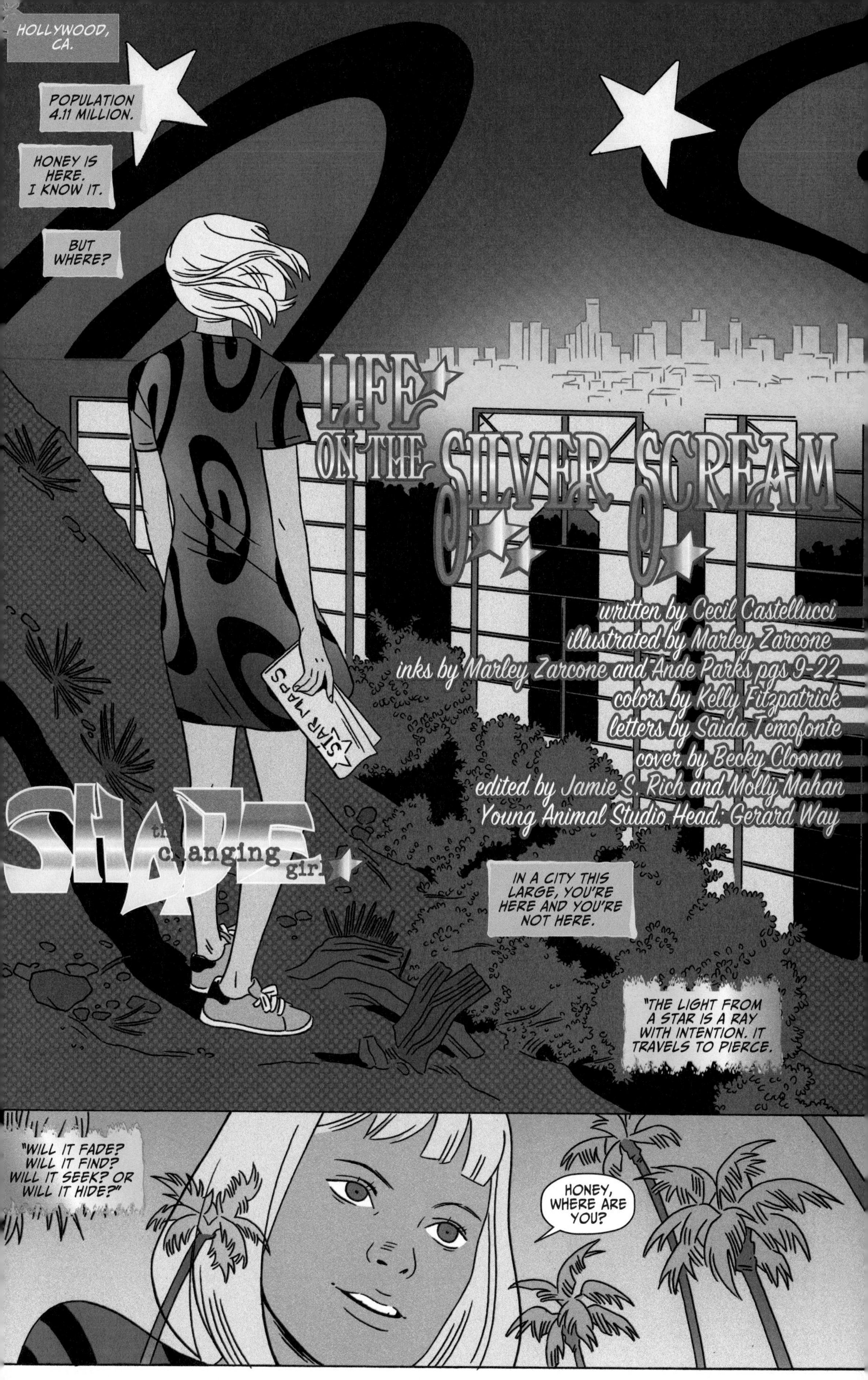

HOLLYWOOD, CA.
POPULATION 4.11 MILLION.
HONEY IS HERE. I KNOW IT.
BUT WHERE?
LIFE ON THE SILVER SCREAM
written by Cecil Castellucci
illustrated by Marley Zarcone
inks by Marley Zarcone and Ande Parks pgs 9-22
colors by Kelly Fitzpatrick
letters by Saida Temofonte
cover by Becky Cloonan
edited by Jamie S. Rich and Molly Mahan
Young Animal Studio Head: Gerard Way
SHADE the changing girl
STAR MAPS
IN A CITY THIS LARGE, YOU'RE HERE AND YOU'RE NOT HERE.
"THE LIGHT FROM A STAR IS A RAY WITH INTENTION. IT TRAVELS TO PIERCE.
"WILL IT FADE? WILL IT FIND? WILL IT SEEK? OR WILL IT HIDE?"
HONEY, WHERE ARE YOU?

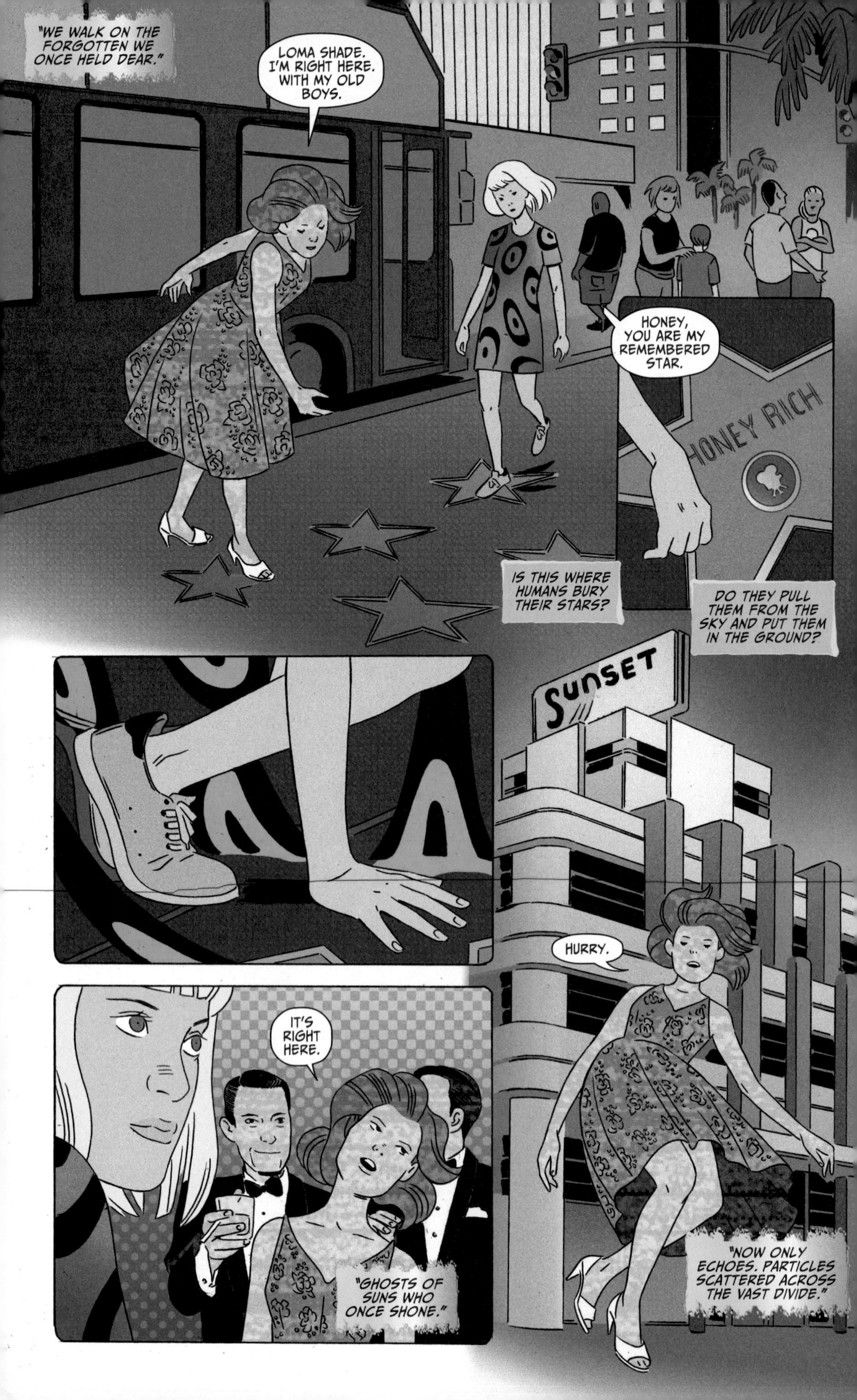
"WE WALK ON THE FORGOTTEN WE ONCE HELD DEAR."
LOMA SHADE. I'M RIGHT HERE. WITH MY OLD BOYS.
HONEY, YOU ARE MY REMEMBERED STAR.
HONEY RICH
IS THIS WHERE HUMANS BURY THEIR STARS?
DO THEY PULL THEM FROM THE SKY AND PUT THEM IN THE GROUND?
SUNSET
HURRY.
IT'S RIGHT HERE.
"GHOSTS OF SUNS WHO ONCE SHONE."
"NOW ONLY ECHOES. PARTICLES SCATTERED ACROSS THE VAST DIVIDE."

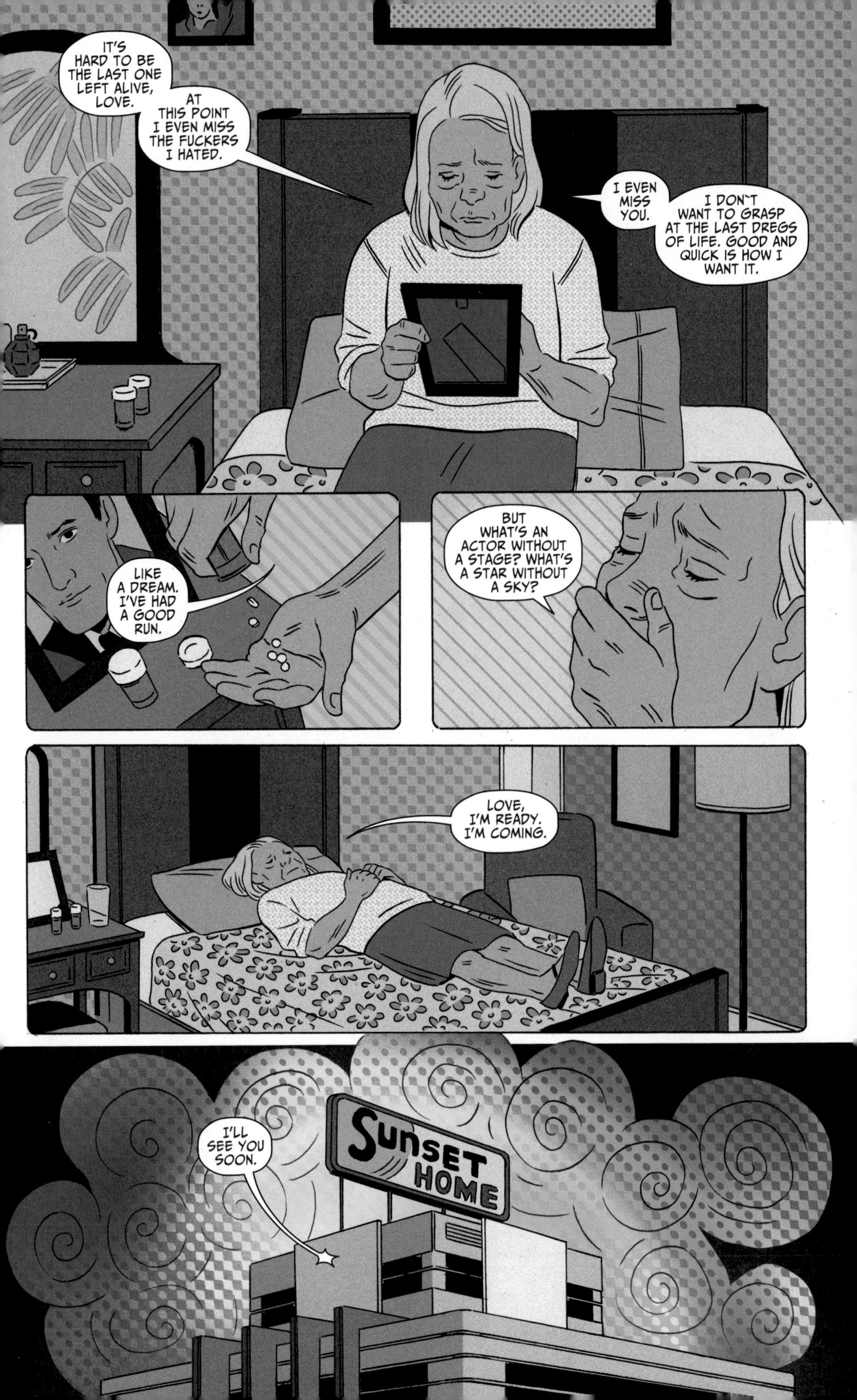
IT'S HARD TO BE THE LAST ONE LEFT ALIVE, LOVE.
AT THIS POINT I EVEN MISS THE FUCKERS I HATED.
I EVEN MISS YOU.
I DON'T WANT TO GRASP AT THE LAST DREGS OF LIFE. GOOD AND QUICK IS HOW I WANT IT.
LIKE A DREAM. I'VE HAD A GOOD RUN.
BUT WHAT'S AN ACTOR WITHOUT A STAGE? WHAT'S A STAR WITHOUT A SKY?
LOVE, I'M READY. I'M COMING.
I'LL SEE YOU SOON.
SUNSET HOME

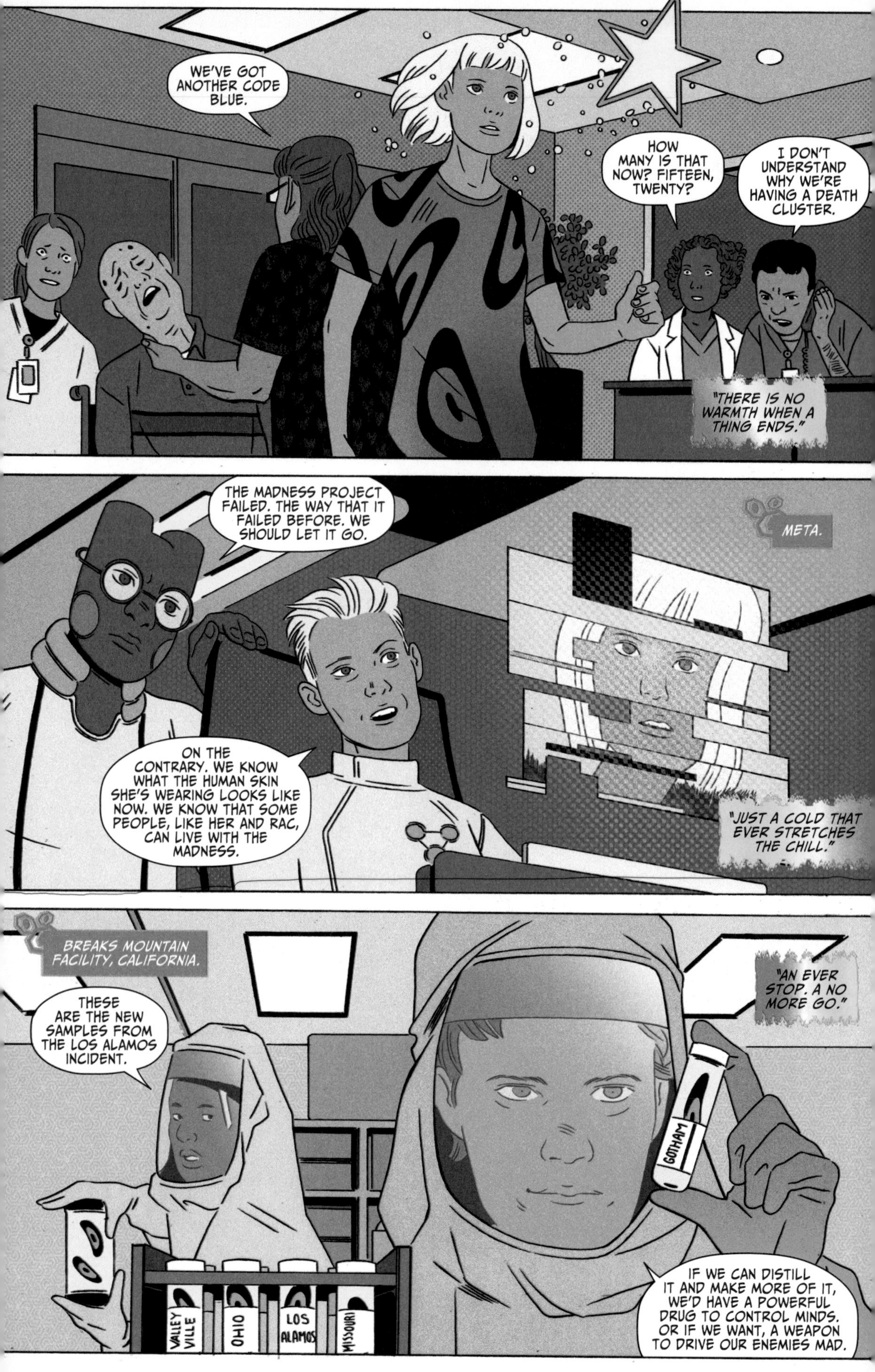
WE'VE GOT ANOTHER CODE BLUE.
HOW MANY IS THAT NOW? FIFTEEN, TWENTY?
I DON'T UNDERSTAND WHY WE'RE HAVING A DEATH CLUSTER.
"THERE IS NO WARMTH WHEN A THING ENDS."
META.
THE MADNESS PROJECT FAILED. THE WAY THAT IT FAILED BEFORE. WE SHOULD LET IT GO.
ON THE CONTRARY. WE KNOW WHAT THE HUMAN SKIN SHE'S WEARING LOOKS LIKE NOW. WE KNOW THAT SOME PEOPLE, LIKE HER AND RAC, CAN LIVE WITH THE MADNESS.
"JUST A COLD THAT EVER STRETCHES THE CHILL."
BREAKS MOUNTAIN FACILITY, CALIFORNIA.
"AN EVER STOP. A NO MORE GO."
THESE ARE THE NEW SAMPLES FROM THE LOS ALAMOS INCIDENT.
GOTHAM
VALLEY VILLE
OHIO
LOS ALAMOS
MISSOURI
IF WE CAN DISTILL IT AND MAKE MORE OF IT, WE'D HAVE A POWERFUL DRUG TO CONTROL MINDS. OR IF WE WANT, A WEAPON TO DRIVE OUR ENEMIES MAD.

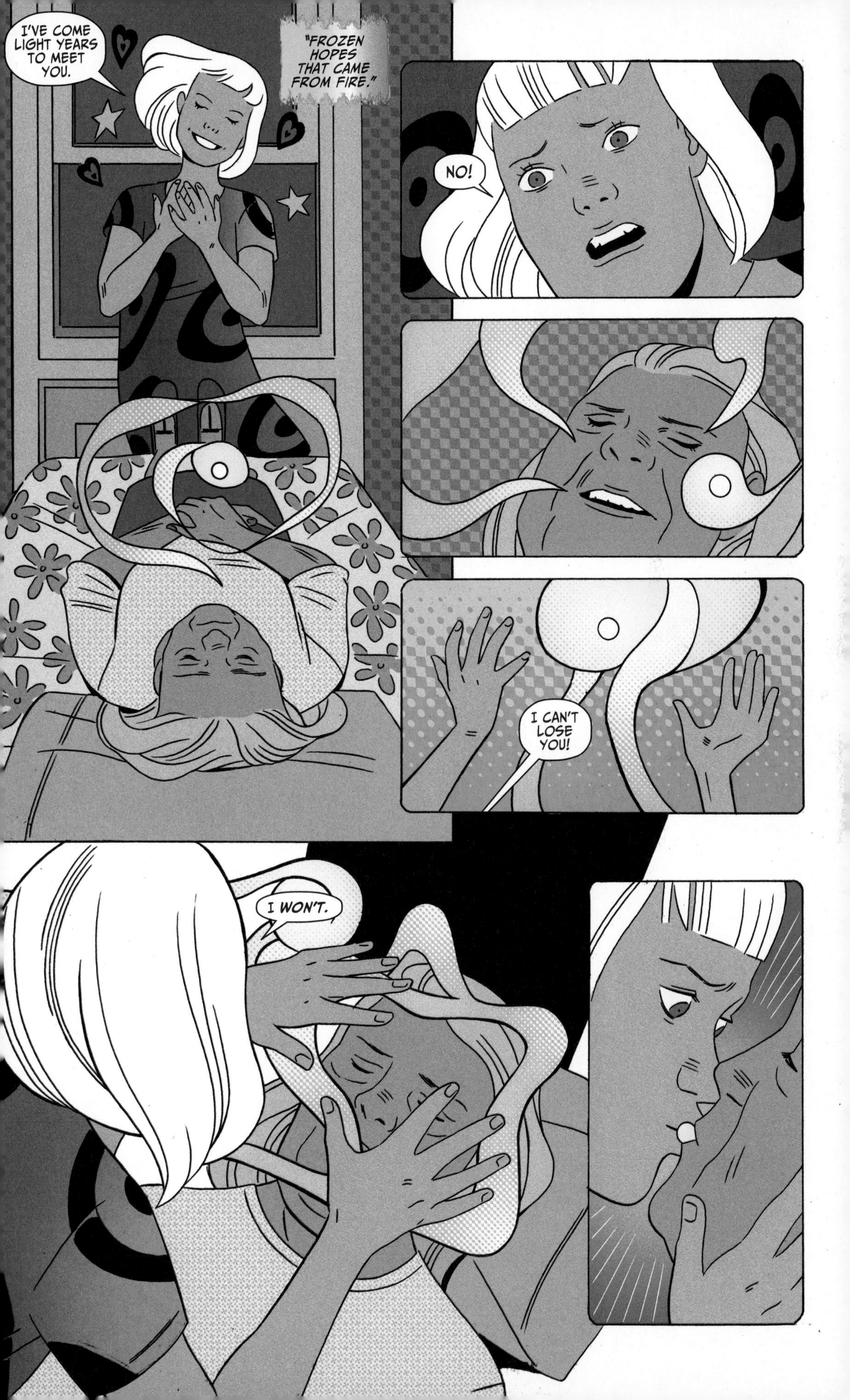
I'VE COME LIGHT YEARS TO MEET YOU.
"FROZEN HOPES THAT CAME FROM FIRE."
NO!
I CAN'T LOSE YOU!
I WON'T.

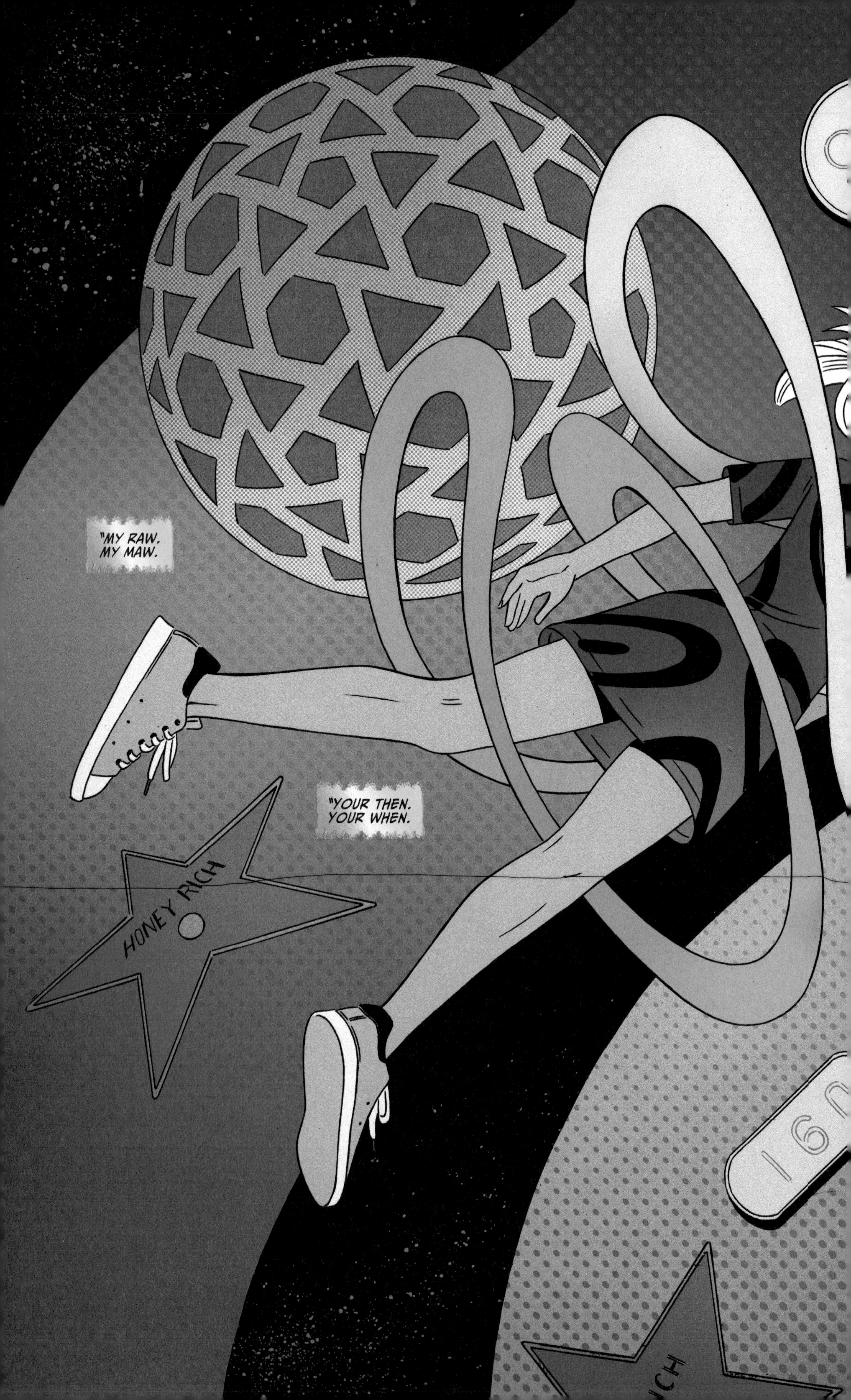
"MY RAW.
MY MAW.
"YOUR THEN.
YOUR WHEN.
HONEY RICH

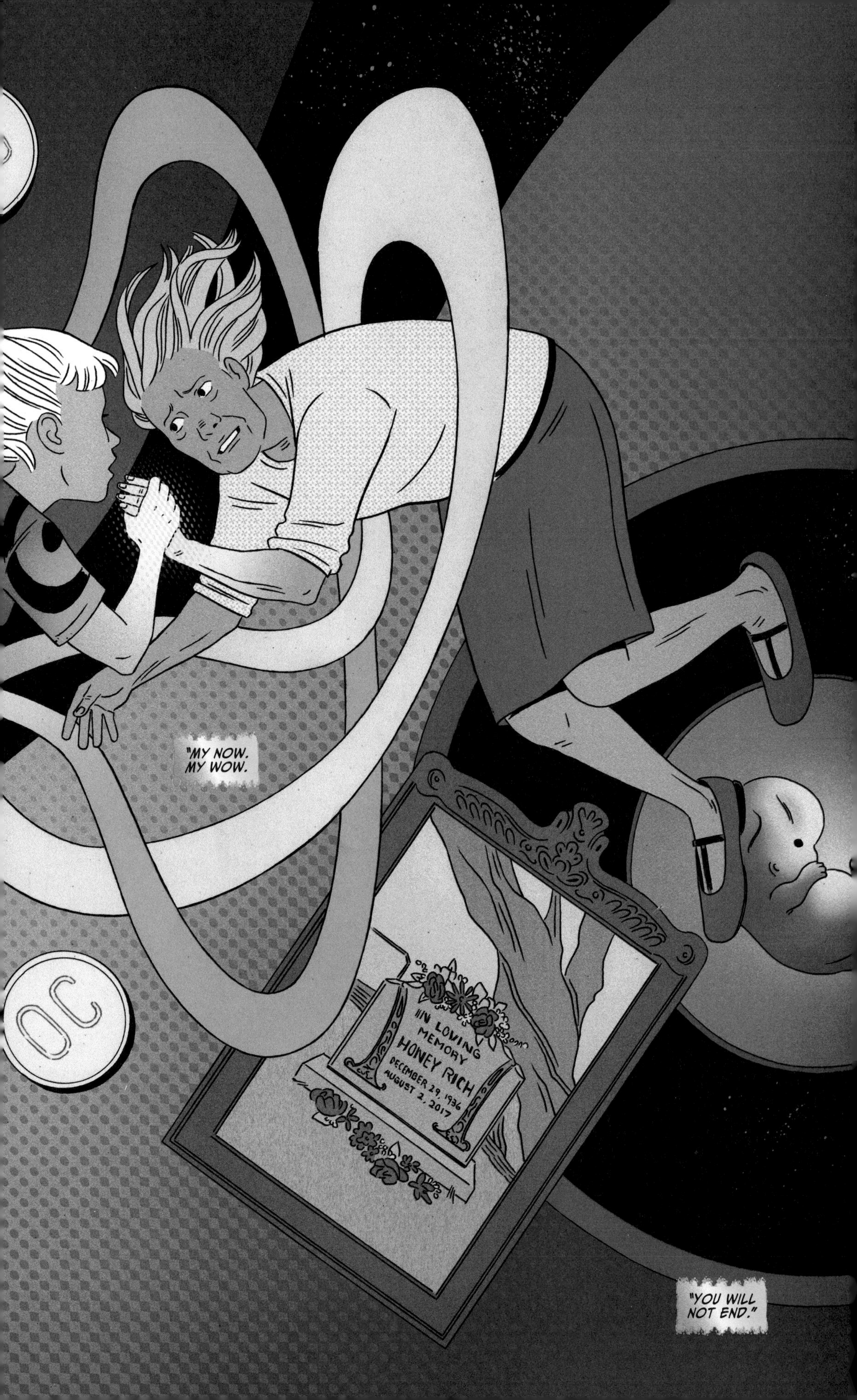
"MY NOW.
MY WOW.
IN LOVING
MEMORY
HONEY RICH
DECEMBER 29, 1936
AUGUST 2, 2017
"YOU WILL
NOT END."

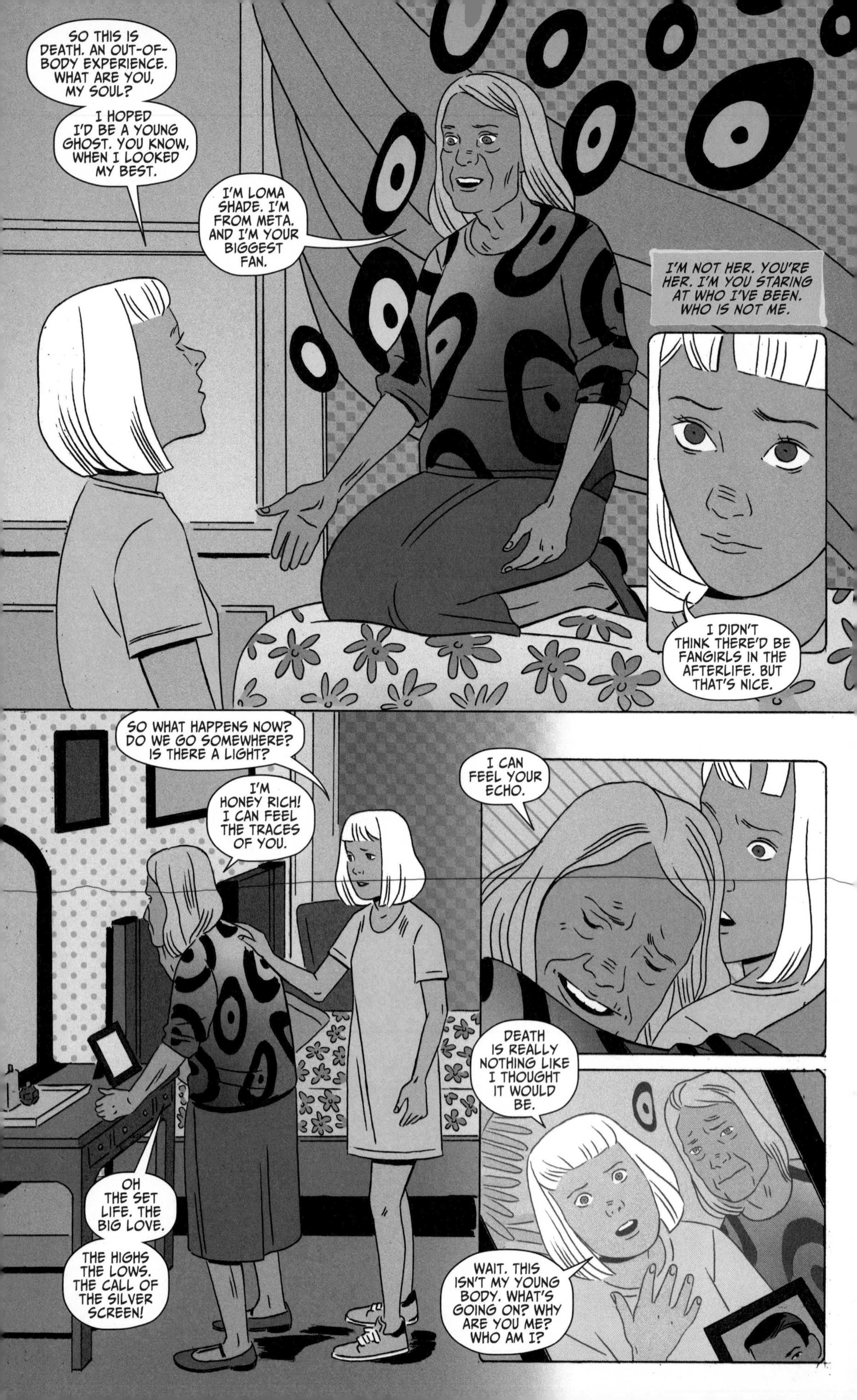
SO THIS IS DEATH. AN OUT-OF-BODY EXPERIENCE. WHAT ARE YOU, MY SOUL?
I HOPED I'D BE A YOUNG GHOST. YOU KNOW, WHEN I LOOKED MY BEST.
I'M LOMA SHADE. I'M FROM META. AND I'M YOUR BIGGEST FAN.
I'M NOT HER. YOU'RE HER. I'M YOU STARING AT WHO I'VE BEEN. WHO IS NOT ME.
I DIDN'T THINK THERE'D BE FANGIRLS IN THE AFTERLIFE. BUT THAT'S NICE.
SO WHAT HAPPENS NOW? DO WE GO SOMEWHERE? IS THERE A LIGHT?
I'M HONEY RICH! I CAN FEEL THE TRACES OF YOU.
OH THE SET LIFE. THE BIG LOVE.
THE HIGHS THE LOWS. THE CALL OF THE SILVER SCREEN!
I CAN FEEL YOUR ECHO.
DEATH IS REALLY NOTHING LIKE I THOUGHT IT WOULD BE.
WAIT. THIS ISN'T MY YOUNG BODY. WHAT'S GOING ON? WHY ARE YOU ME? WHO AM I?

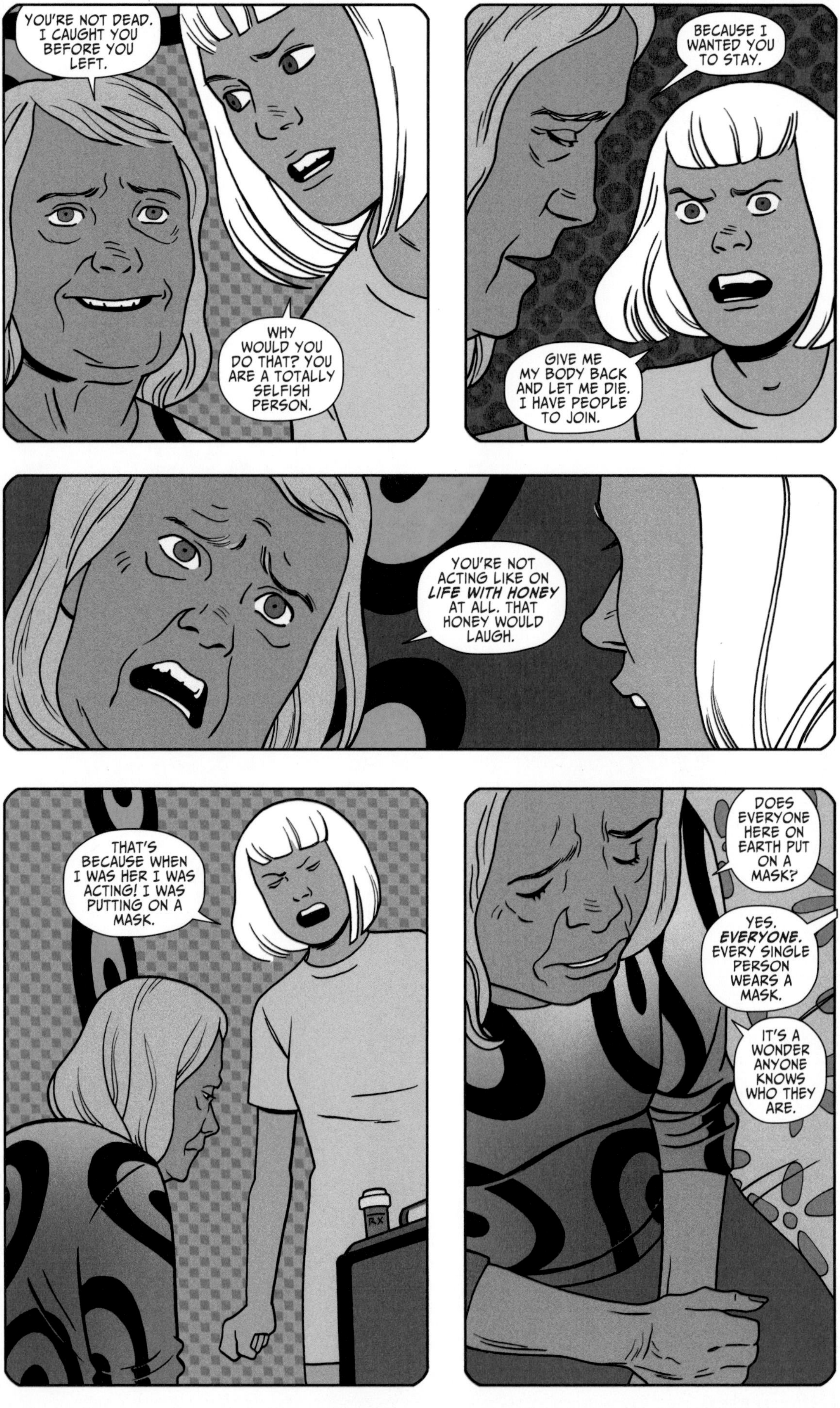
YOU'RE NOT DEAD. I CAUGHT YOU BEFORE YOU LEFT.
WHY WOULD YOU DO THAT? YOU ARE A TOTALLY SELFISH PERSON.
BECAUSE I WANTED YOU TO STAY.
GIVE ME MY BODY BACK AND LET ME DIE. I HAVE PEOPLE TO JOIN.
YOU'RE NOT ACTING LIKE ON *LIFE WITH HONEY* AT ALL. THAT HONEY WOULD LAUGH.
THAT'S BECAUSE WHEN I WAS HER I WAS ACTING! I WAS PUTTING ON A MASK.
RX
DOES EVERYONE HERE ON EARTH PUT ON A MASK?
YES. ***EVERYONE.*** EVERY SINGLE PERSON WEARS A MASK.
IT'S A WONDER ANYONE KNOWS WHO THEY ARE.

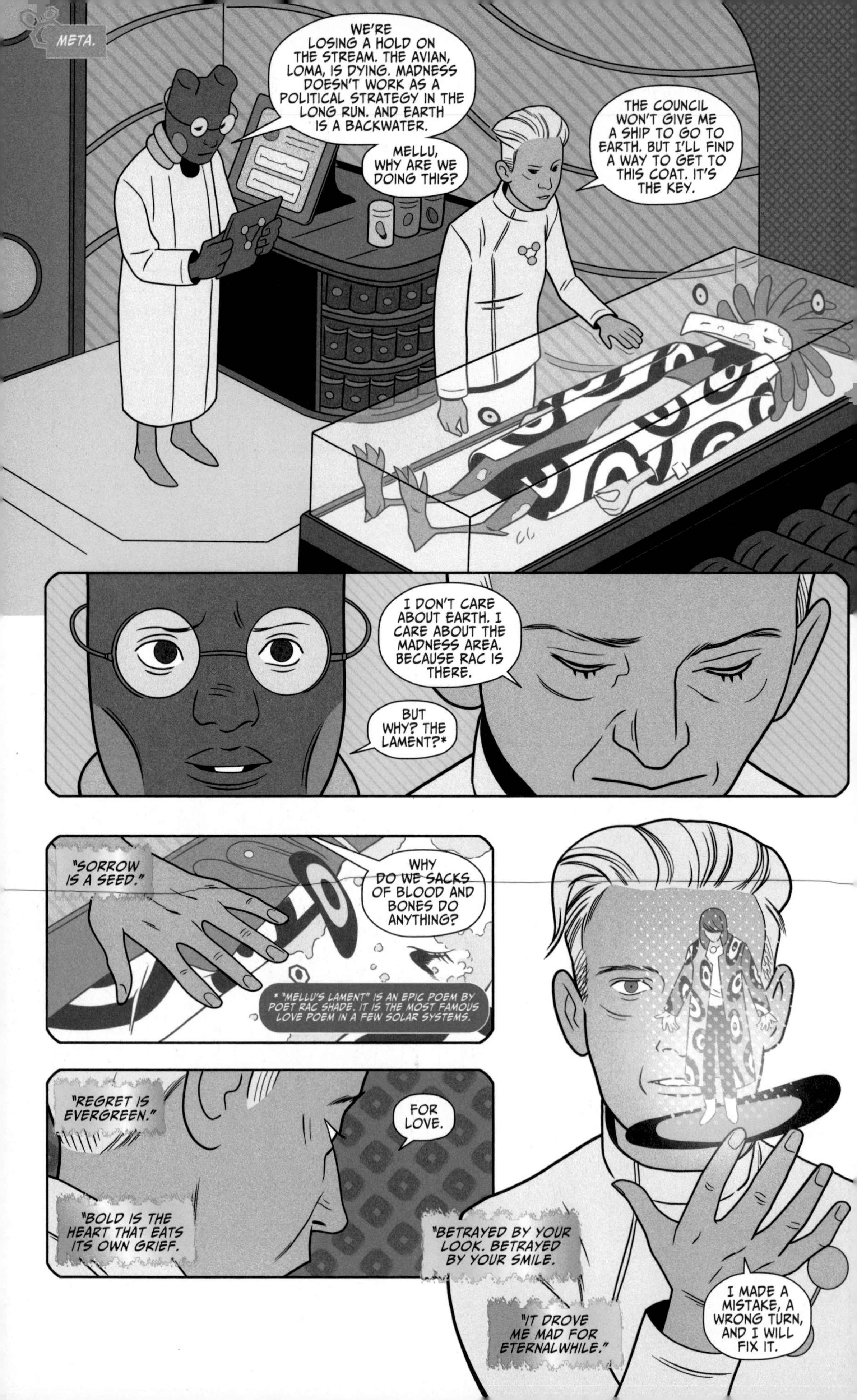
META.
WE'RE LOSING A HOLD ON THE STREAM. THE AVIAN, LOMA, IS DYING. MADNESS DOESN'T WORK AS A POLITICAL STRATEGY IN THE LONG RUN. AND EARTH IS A BACKWATER.
MELLU, WHY ARE WE DOING THIS?
THE COUNCIL WON'T GIVE ME A SHIP TO GO TO EARTH. BUT I'LL FIND A WAY TO GET TO THIS COAT. IT'S THE KEY.
I DON'T CARE ABOUT EARTH. I CARE ABOUT THE MADNESS AREA. BECAUSE RAC IS THERE.
BUT WHY? THE LAMENT?*
"SORROW IS A SEED."
WHY DO WE SACKS OF BLOOD AND BONES DO ANYTHING?
* "MELLU'S LAMENT" IS AN EPIC POEM BY POET RAC SHADE. IT IS THE MOST FAMOUS LOVE POEM IN A FEW SOLAR SYSTEMS.
"REGRET IS EVERGREEN."
FOR LOVE.
"BOLD IS THE HEART THAT EATS ITS OWN GRIEF.
"BETRAYED BY YOUR LOOK. BETRAYED BY YOUR SMILE.
"IT DROVE ME MAD FOR ETERNALWHILE."
I MADE A MISTAKE, A WRONG TURN, AND I WILL FIX IT.

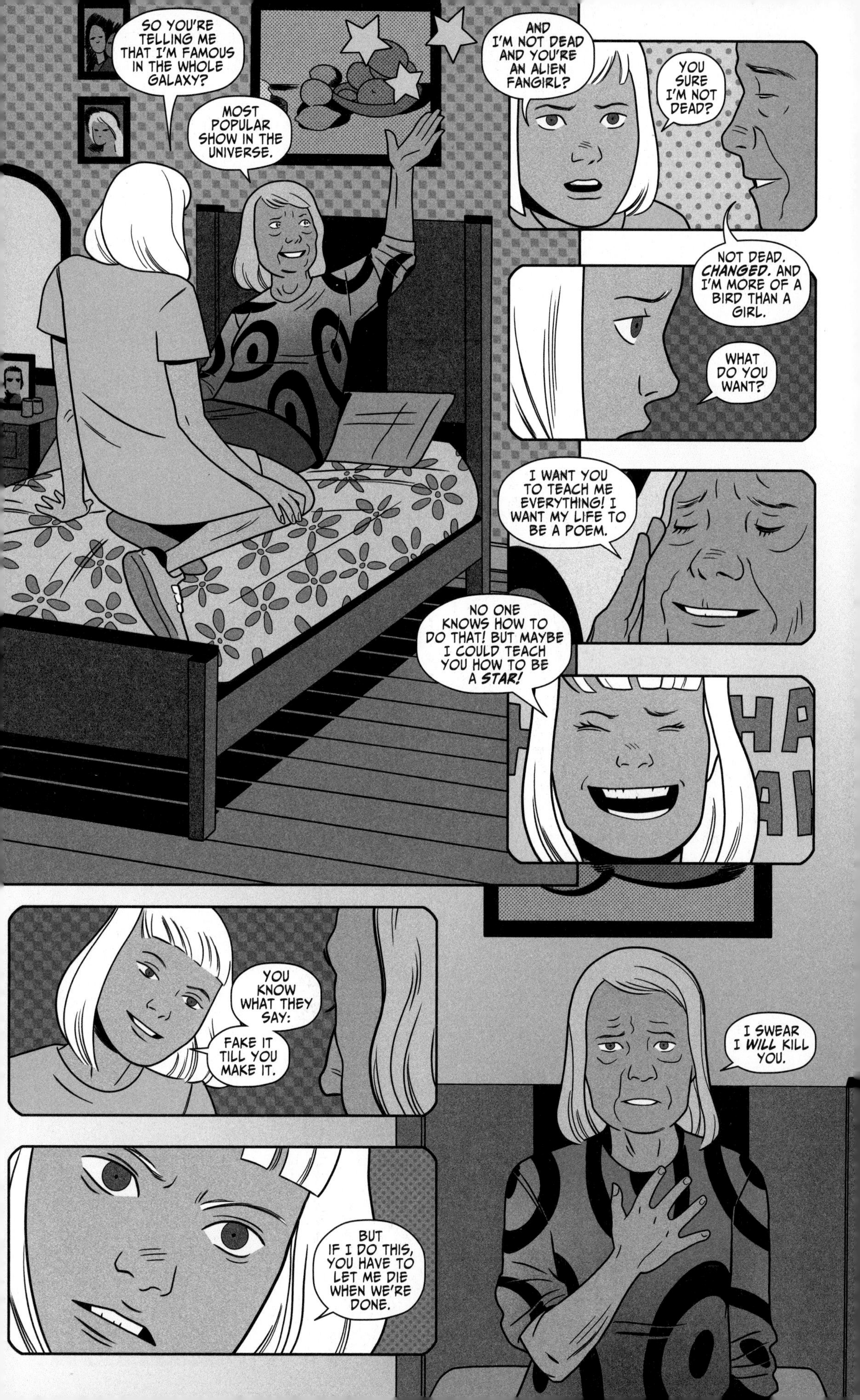
SO YOU'RE TELLING ME THAT I'M FAMOUS IN THE WHOLE GALAXY?
MOST POPULAR SHOW IN THE UNIVERSE.
AND I'M NOT DEAD AND YOU'RE AN ALIEN FANGIRL?
YOU SURE I'M NOT DEAD?
NOT DEAD. CHANGED. AND I'M MORE OF A BIRD THAN A GIRL.
WHAT DO YOU WANT?
I WANT YOU TO TEACH ME EVERYTHING! I WANT MY LIFE TO BE A POEM.
NO ONE KNOWS HOW TO DO THAT! BUT MAYBE I COULD TEACH YOU HOW TO BE A STAR!
YOU KNOW WHAT THEY SAY:
FAKE IT TILL YOU MAKE IT.
BUT IF I DO THIS, YOU HAVE TO LET ME DIE WHEN WE'RE DONE.
I SWEAR I WILL KILL YOU.

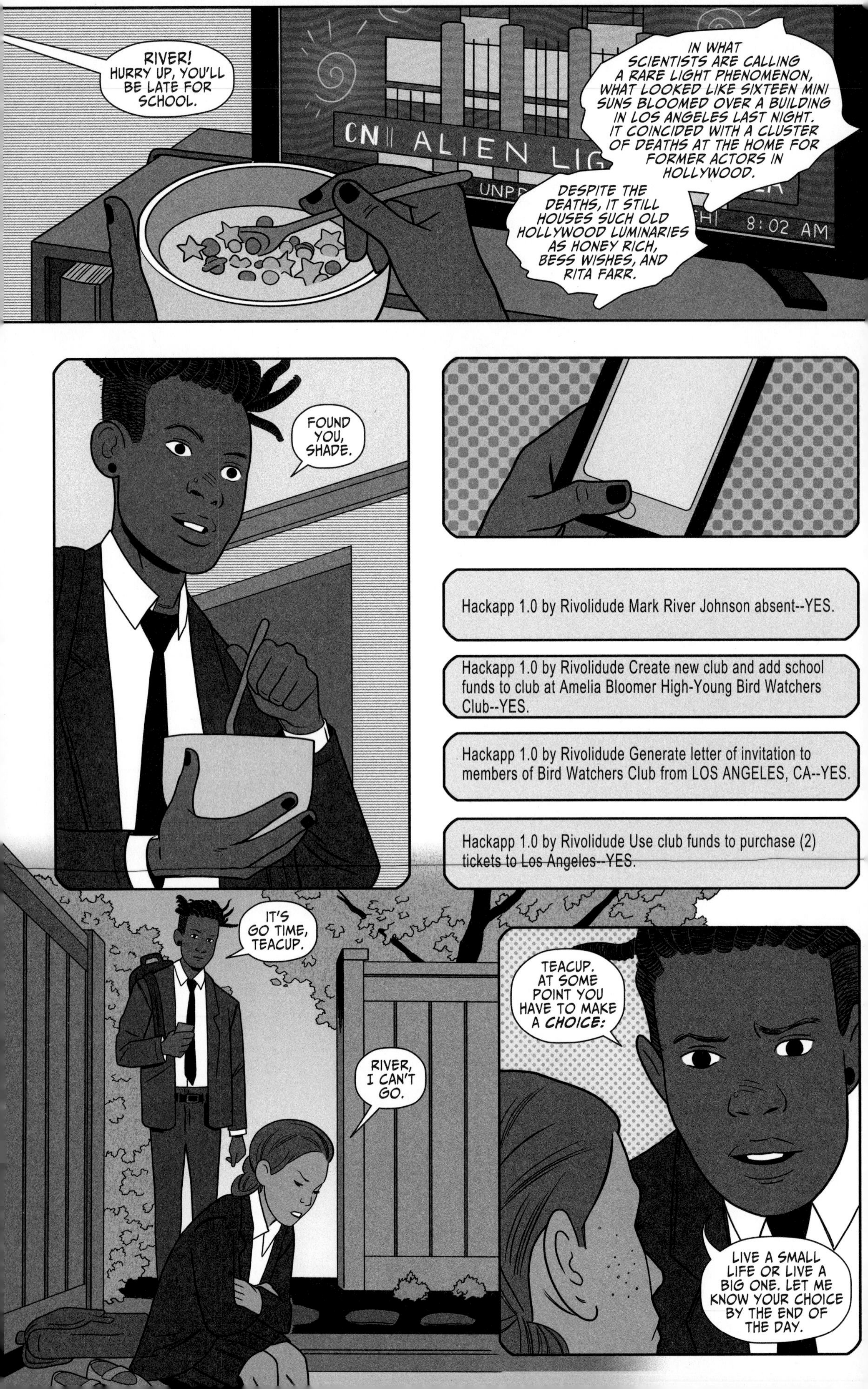
RIVER! HURRY UP, YOU'LL BE LATE FOR SCHOOL.
CN ALIEN LIG
UNPR
8:02 AM
IN WHAT SCIENTISTS ARE CALLING A RARE LIGHT PHENOMENON, WHAT LOOKED LIKE SIXTEEN MINI SUNS BLOOMED OVER A BUILDING IN LOS ANGELES LAST NIGHT. IT COINCIDED WITH A CLUSTER OF DEATHS AT THE HOME FOR FORMER ACTORS IN HOLLYWOOD.
DESPITE THE DEATHS, IT STILL HOUSES SUCH OLD HOLLYWOOD LUMINARIES AS HONEY RICH, BESS WISHES, AND RITA FARR.
FOUND YOU, SHADE.
Hackapp 1.0 by Rivolidude Mark River Johnson absent--YES.
Hackapp 1.0 by Rivolidude Create new club and add school funds to club at Amelia Bloomer High-Young Bird Watchers Club--YES.
Hackapp 1.0 by Rivolidude Generate letter of invitation to members of Bird Watchers Club from LOS ANGELES, CA--YES.
Hackapp 1.0 by Rivolidude Use club funds to purchase (2) tickets to Los Angeles--YES.
IT'S GO TIME, TEACUP.
RIVER, I CAN'T GO.
TEACUP. AT SOME POINT YOU HAVE TO MAKE A CHOICE:
LIVE A SMALL LIFE OR LIVE A BIG ONE. LET ME KNOW YOUR CHOICE BY THE END OF THE DAY.

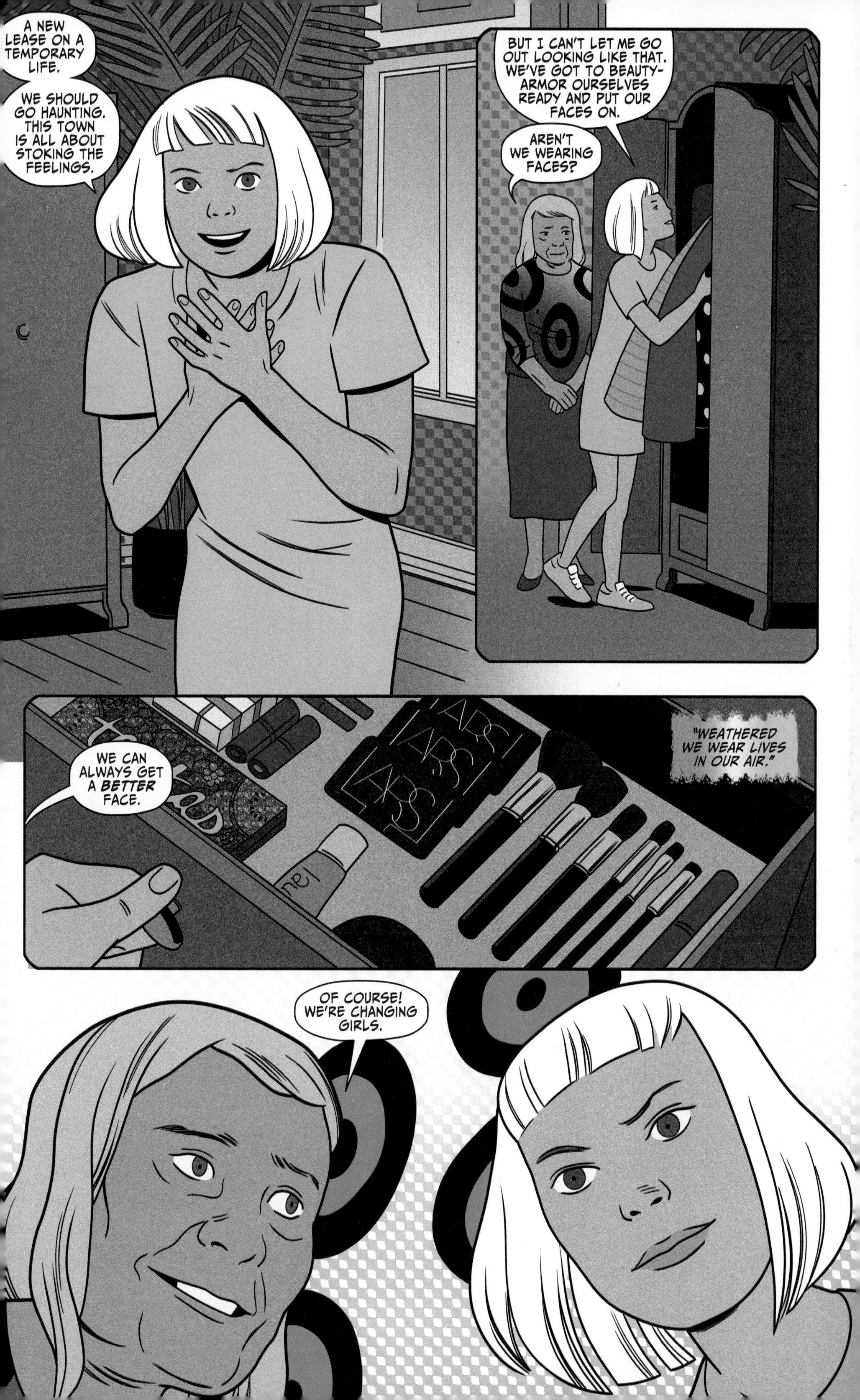
A NEW LEASE ON A TEMPORARY LIFE.
WE SHOULD GO HAUNTING. THIS TOWN IS ALL ABOUT STOKING THE FEELINGS.
BUT I CAN'T LET ME GO OUT LOOKING LIKE THAT. WE'VE GOT TO BEAUTY-ARMOR OURSELVES READY AND PUT OUR FACES ON.
AREN'T WE WEARING FACES?
WE CAN ALWAYS GET A *BETTER* FACE.
"WEATHERED WE WEAR LIVES IN OUR AIR."
OF COURSE! WE'RE CHANGING GIRLS.

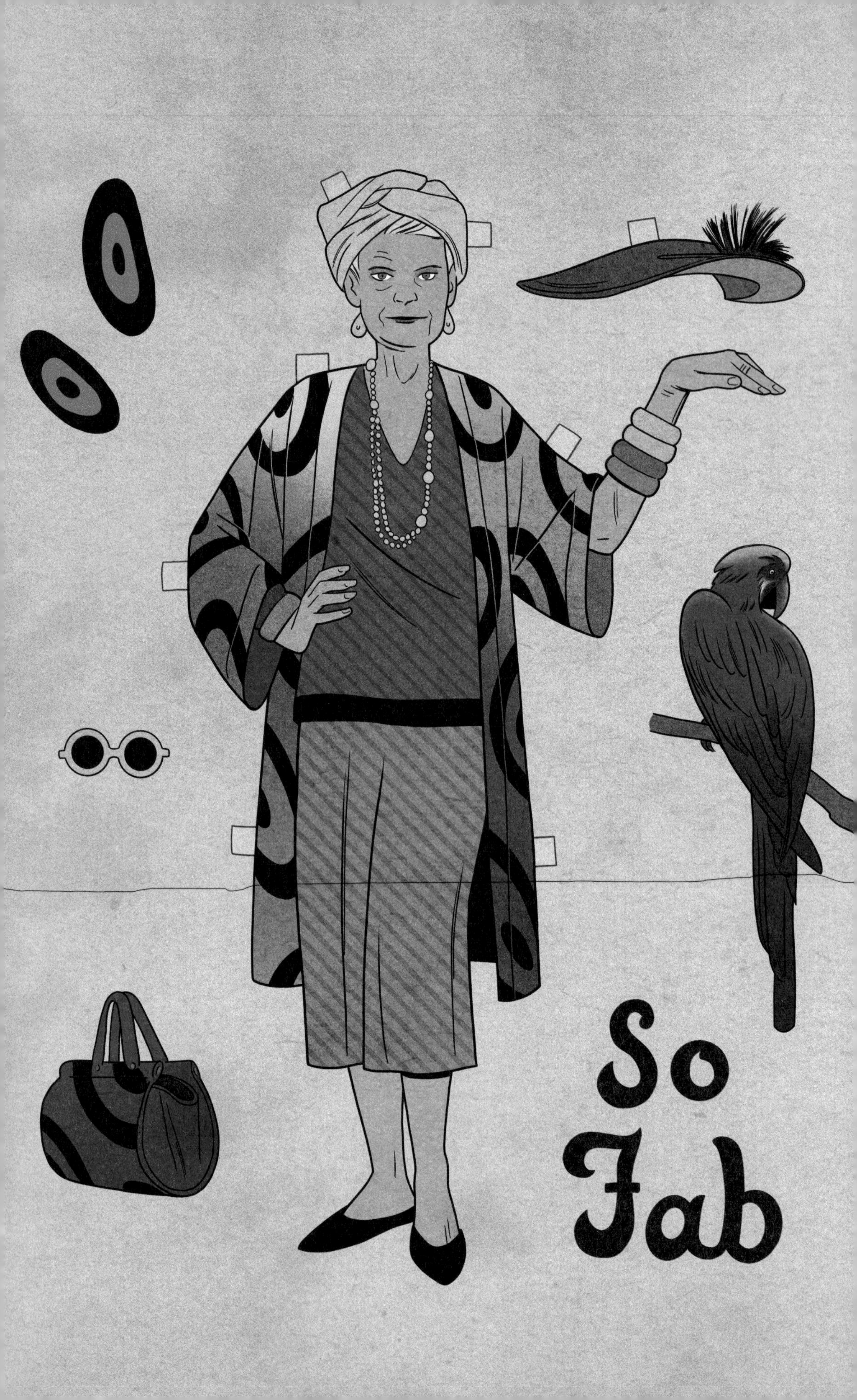
So
Fab

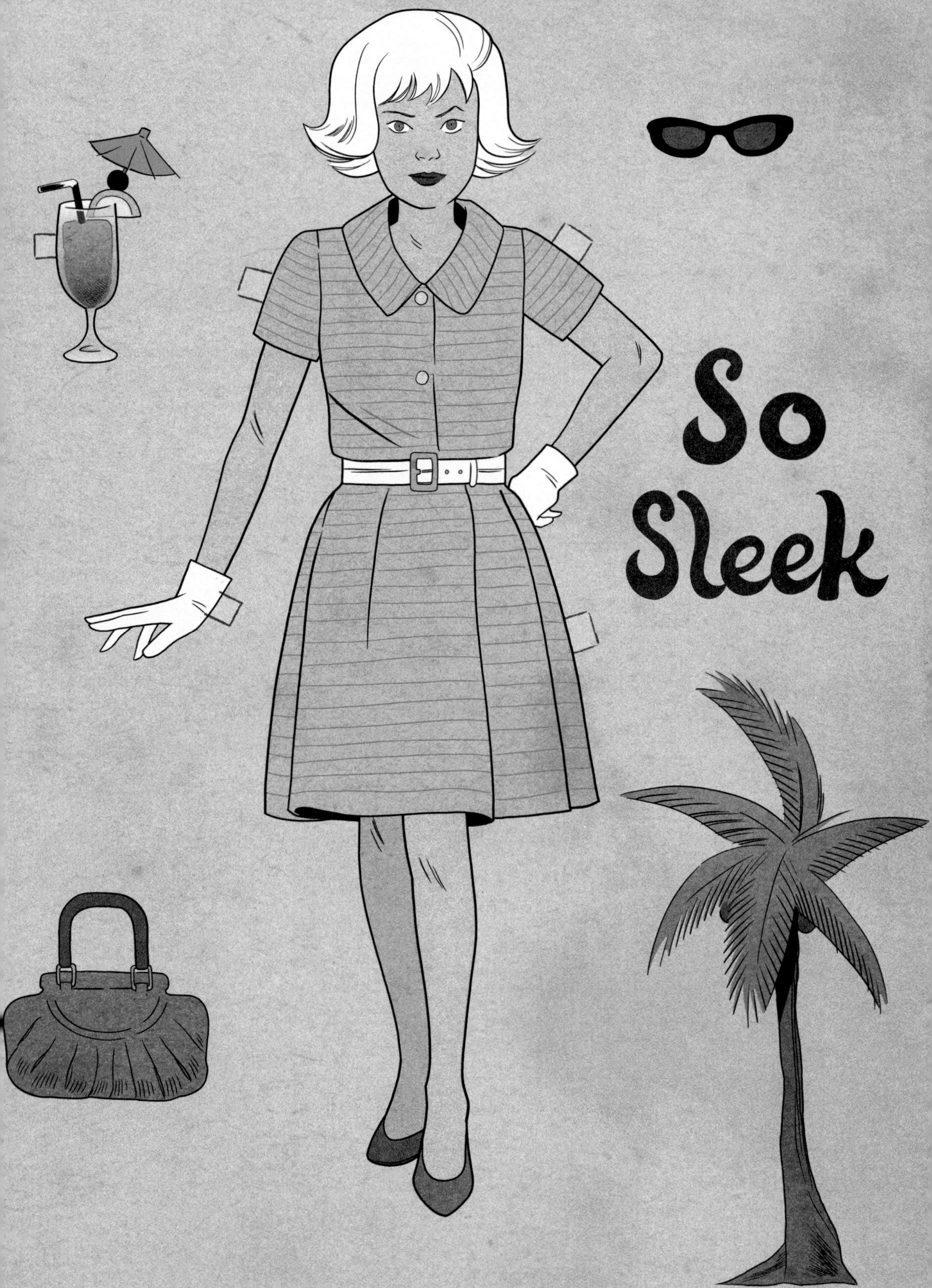
So Sleek

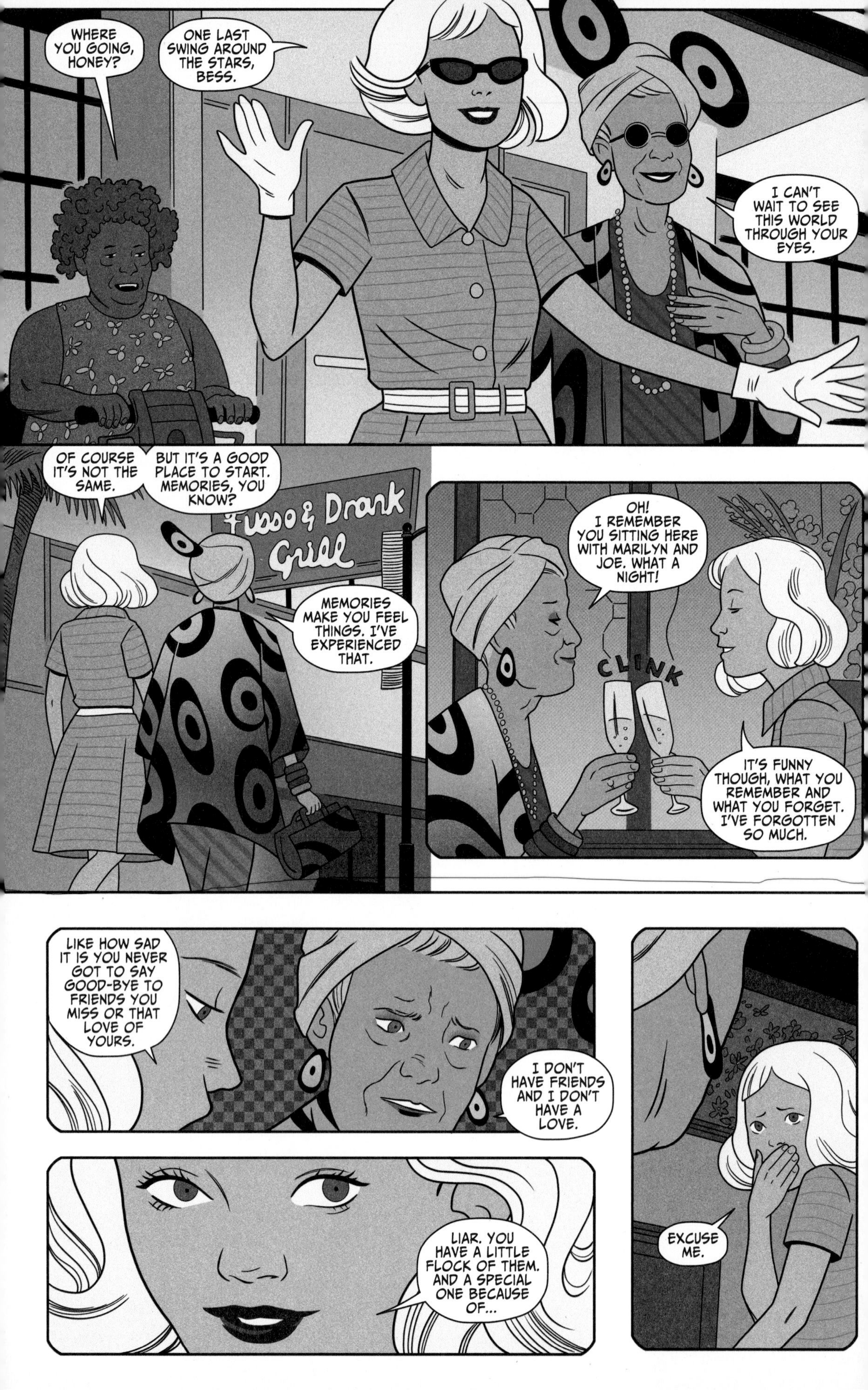
WHERE YOU GOING, HONEY?
ONE LAST SWING AROUND THE STARS, BESS.
I CAN'T WAIT TO SEE THIS WORLD THROUGH YOUR EYES.
OF COURSE IT'S NOT THE SAME.
BUT IT'S A GOOD PLACE TO START. MEMORIES, YOU KNOW?
Fusso & Drank Grill
MEMORIES MAKE YOU FEEL THINGS. I'VE EXPERIENCED THAT.
OH! I REMEMBER YOU SITTING HERE WITH MARILYN AND JOE. WHAT A NIGHT!
CLINK
IT'S FUNNY THOUGH, WHAT YOU REMEMBER AND WHAT YOU FORGET. I'VE FORGOTTEN SO MUCH.
LIKE HOW SAD IT IS YOU NEVER GOT TO SAY GOOD-BYE TO FRIENDS YOU MISS OR THAT LOVE OF YOURS.
I DON'T HAVE FRIENDS AND I DON'T HAVE A LOVE.
LIAR. YOU HAVE A LITTLE FLOCK OF THEM. AND A SPECIAL ONE BECAUSE OF...
EXCUSE ME.

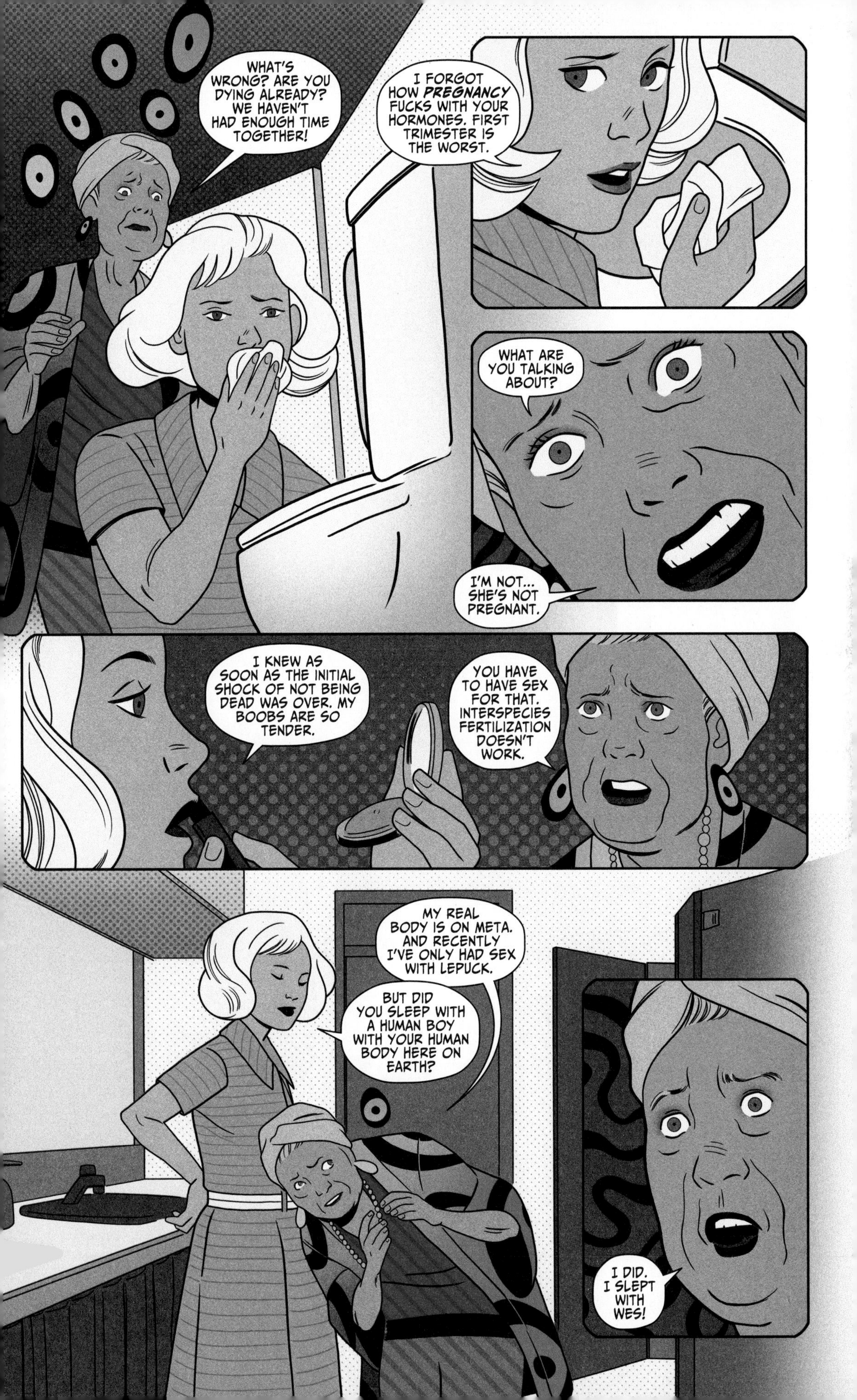
WHAT'S WRONG? ARE YOU DYING ALREADY? WE HAVEN'T HAD ENOUGH TIME TOGETHER!
I FORGOT HOW PREGNANCY FUCKS WITH YOUR HORMONES. FIRST TRIMESTER IS THE WORST.
WHAT ARE YOU TALKING ABOUT?
I'M NOT... SHE'S NOT PREGNANT.
I KNEW AS SOON AS THE INITIAL SHOCK OF NOT BEING DEAD WAS OVER. MY BOOBS ARE SO TENDER.
YOU HAVE TO HAVE SEX FOR THAT. INTERSPECIES FERTILIZATION DOESN'T WORK.
MY REAL BODY IS ON META. AND RECENTLY I'VE ONLY HAD SEX WITH LEPUCK.
BUT DID YOU SLEEP WITH A HUMAN BOY WITH YOUR HUMAN BODY HERE ON EARTH?
I DID. I SLEPT WITH WES!

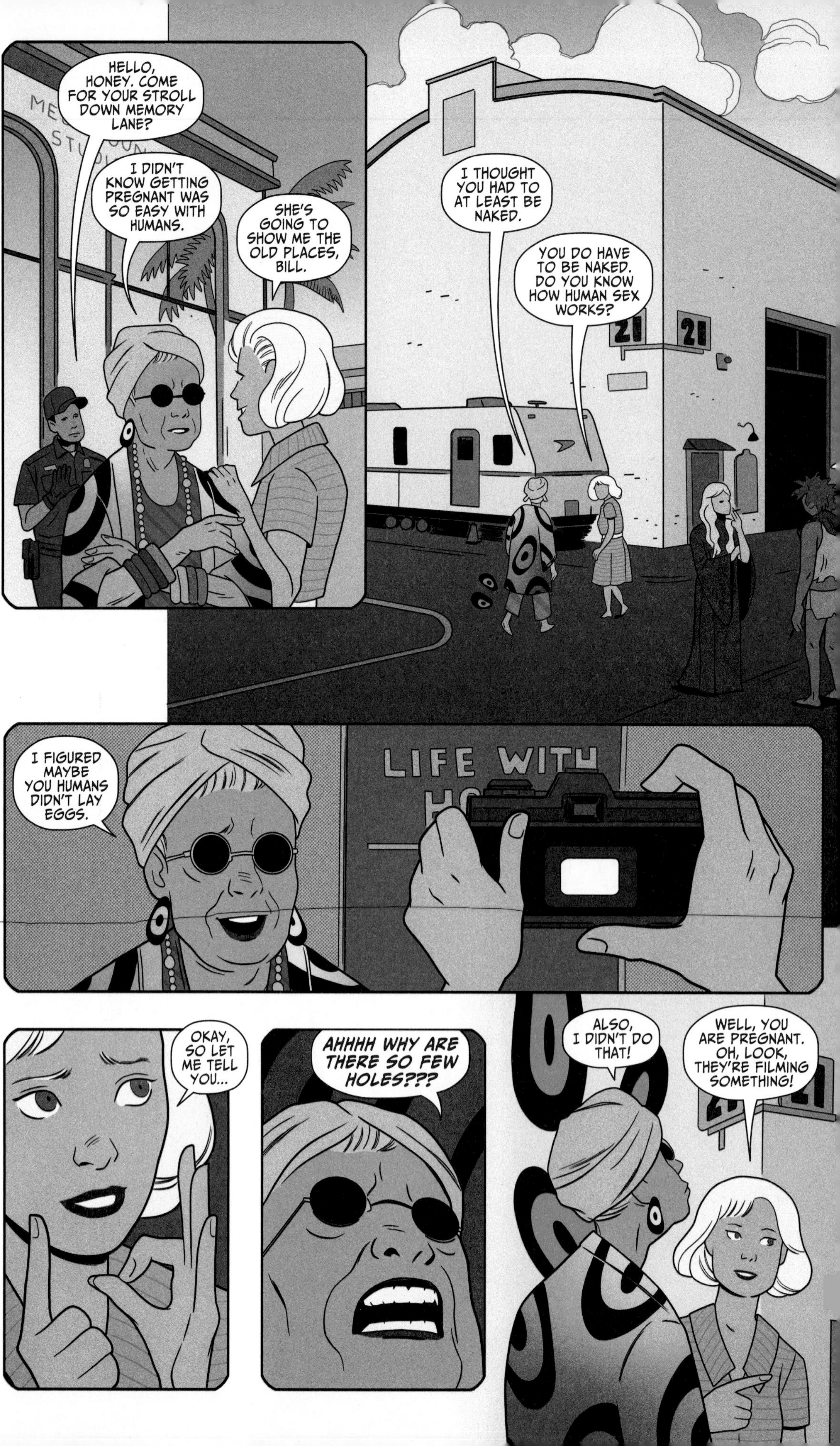
HELLO, HONEY. COME FOR YOUR STROLL DOWN MEMORY LANE?
I DIDN'T KNOW GETTING PREGNANT WAS SO EASY WITH HUMANS.
SHE'S GOING TO SHOW ME THE OLD PLACES, BILL.
I THOUGHT YOU HAD TO AT LEAST BE NAKED.
YOU DO HAVE TO BE NAKED. DO YOU KNOW HOW HUMAN SEX WORKS?
21
21
I FIGURED MAYBE YOU HUMANS DIDN'T LAY EGGS.
LIFE WITH
OKAY, SO LET ME TELL YOU...
AHHHH WHY ARE THERE SO FEW HOLES???
ALSO, I DIDN'T DO THAT!
WELL, YOU ARE PREGNANT. OH, LOOK, THEY'RE FILMING SOMETHING!

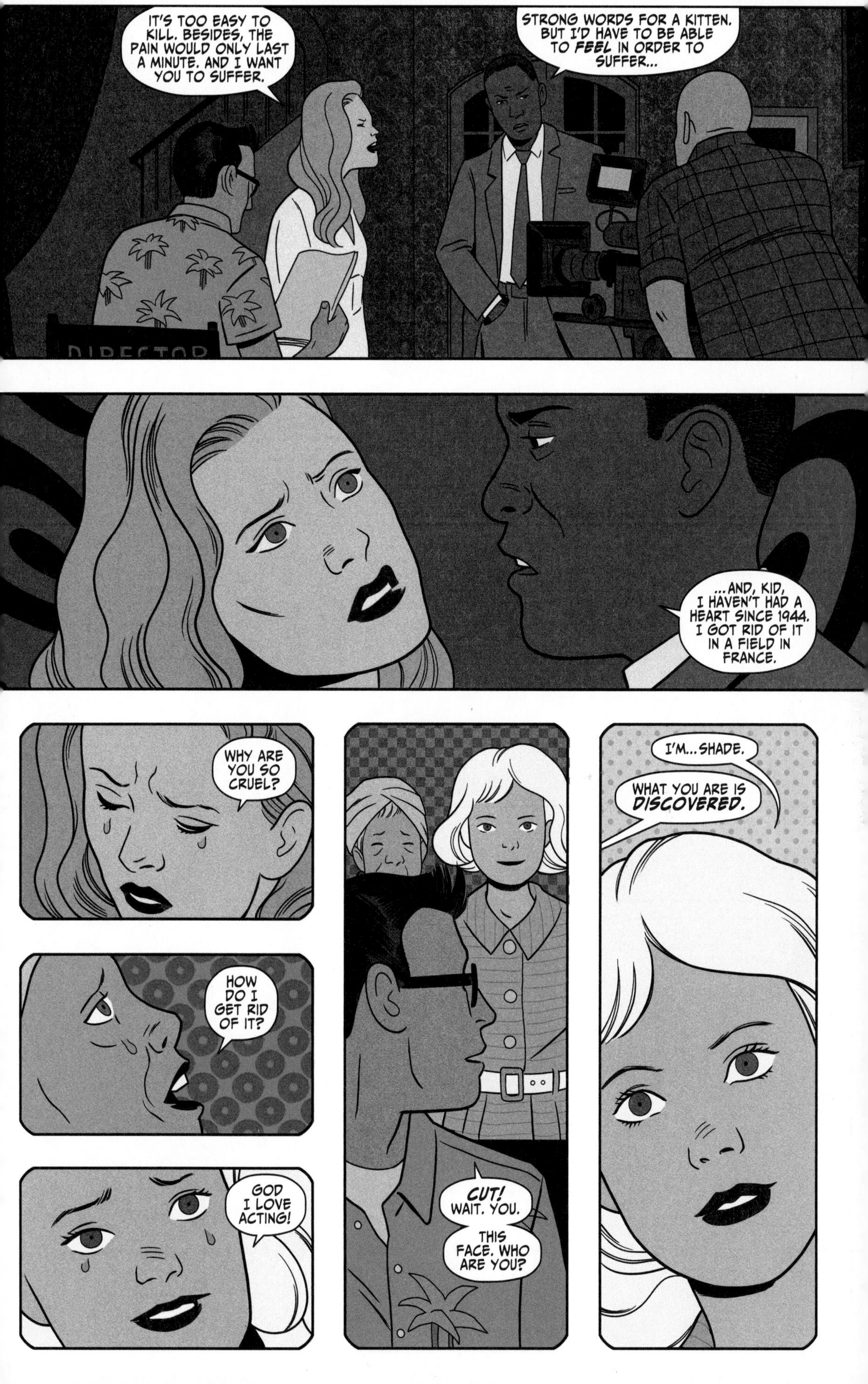
IT'S TOO EASY TO KILL. BESIDES, THE PAIN WOULD ONLY LAST A MINUTE. AND I WANT YOU TO SUFFER.
STRONG WORDS FOR A KITTEN. BUT I'D HAVE TO BE ABLE TO ***FEEL*** IN ORDER TO SUFFER...
...AND, KID, I HAVEN'T HAD A HEART SINCE 1944. I GOT RID OF IT IN A FIELD IN FRANCE.
WHY ARE YOU SO CRUEL?
HOW DO I GET RID OF IT?
GOD I LOVE ACTING!
CUT! WAIT. YOU.
THIS FACE. WHO ARE YOU?
I'M...SHADE.
WHAT YOU ARE IS ***DISCOVERED.***

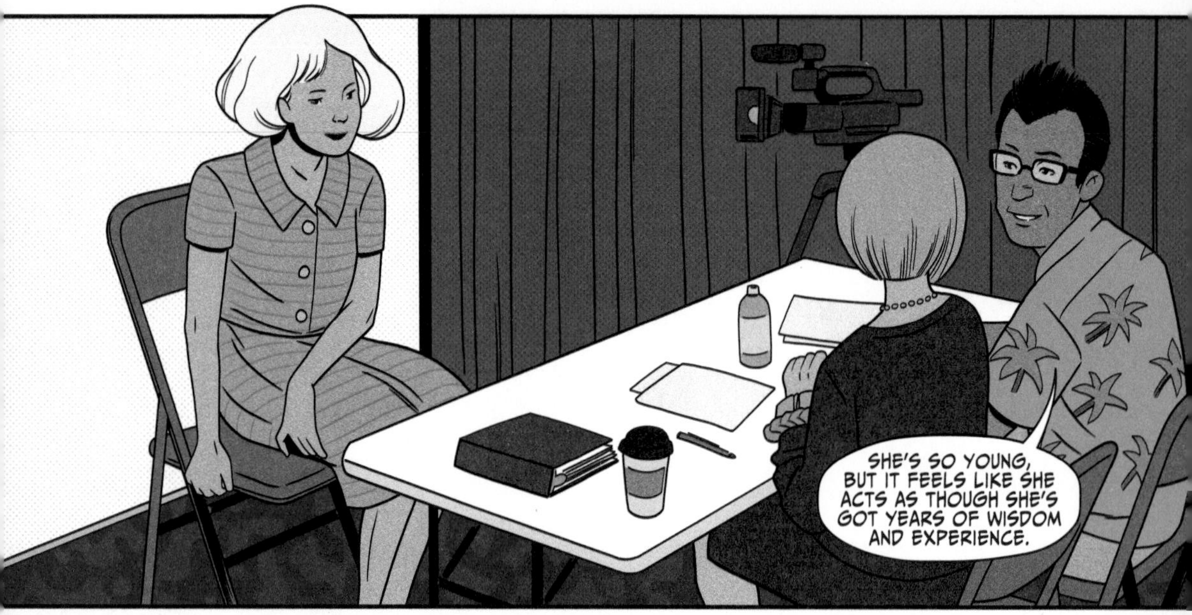
SHE'S SO YOUNG, BUT IT FEELS LIKE SHE ACTS AS THOUGH SHE'S GOT YEARS OF WISDOM AND EXPERIENCE.

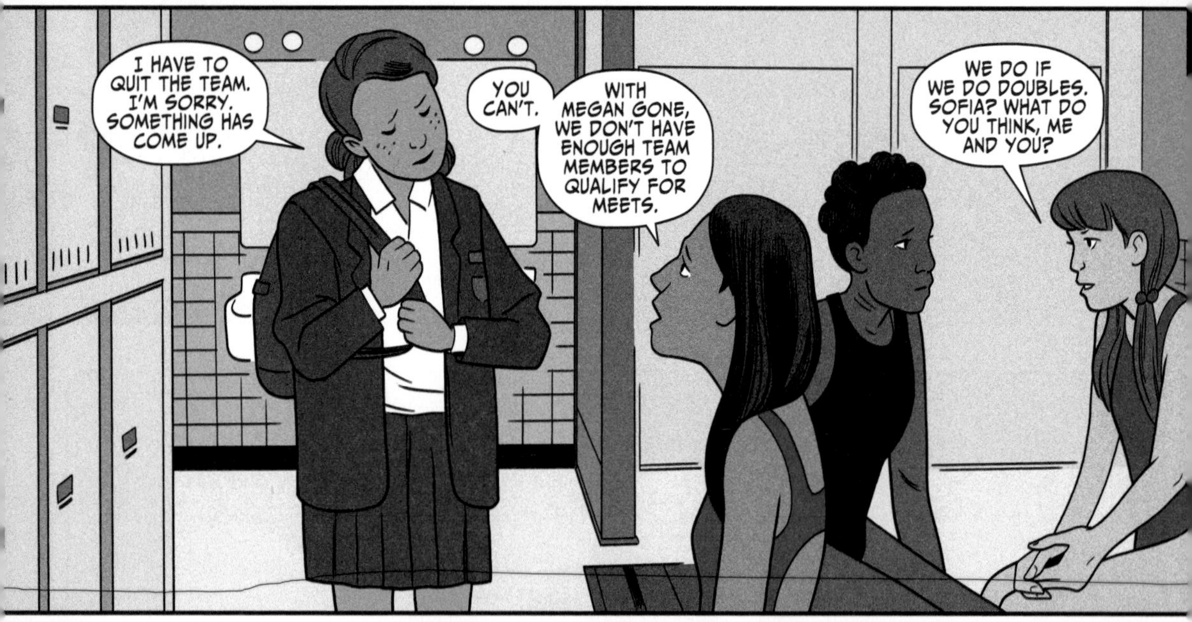
I HAVE TO QUIT THE TEAM. I'M SORRY. SOMETHING HAS COME UP.
YOU CAN'T.
WITH MEGAN GONE, WE DON'T HAVE ENOUGH TEAM MEMBERS TO QUALIFY FOR MEETS.
WE DO IF WE DO DOUBLES. SOFIA? WHAT DO YOU THINK, ME AND YOU?

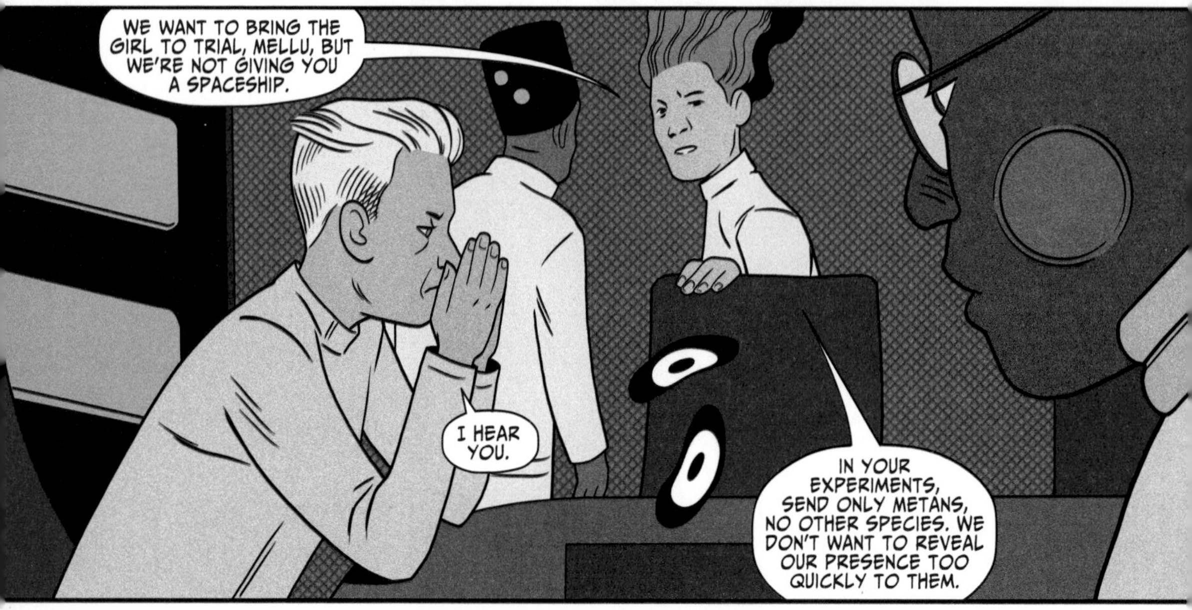
WE WANT TO BRING THE GIRL TO TRIAL, MELLU, BUT WE'RE NOT GIVING YOU A SPACESHIP.
I HEAR YOU.
IN YOUR EXPERIMENTS, SEND ONLY METANS, NO OTHER SPECIES. WE DON'T WANT TO REVEAL OUR PRESENCE TOO QUICKLY TO THEM.

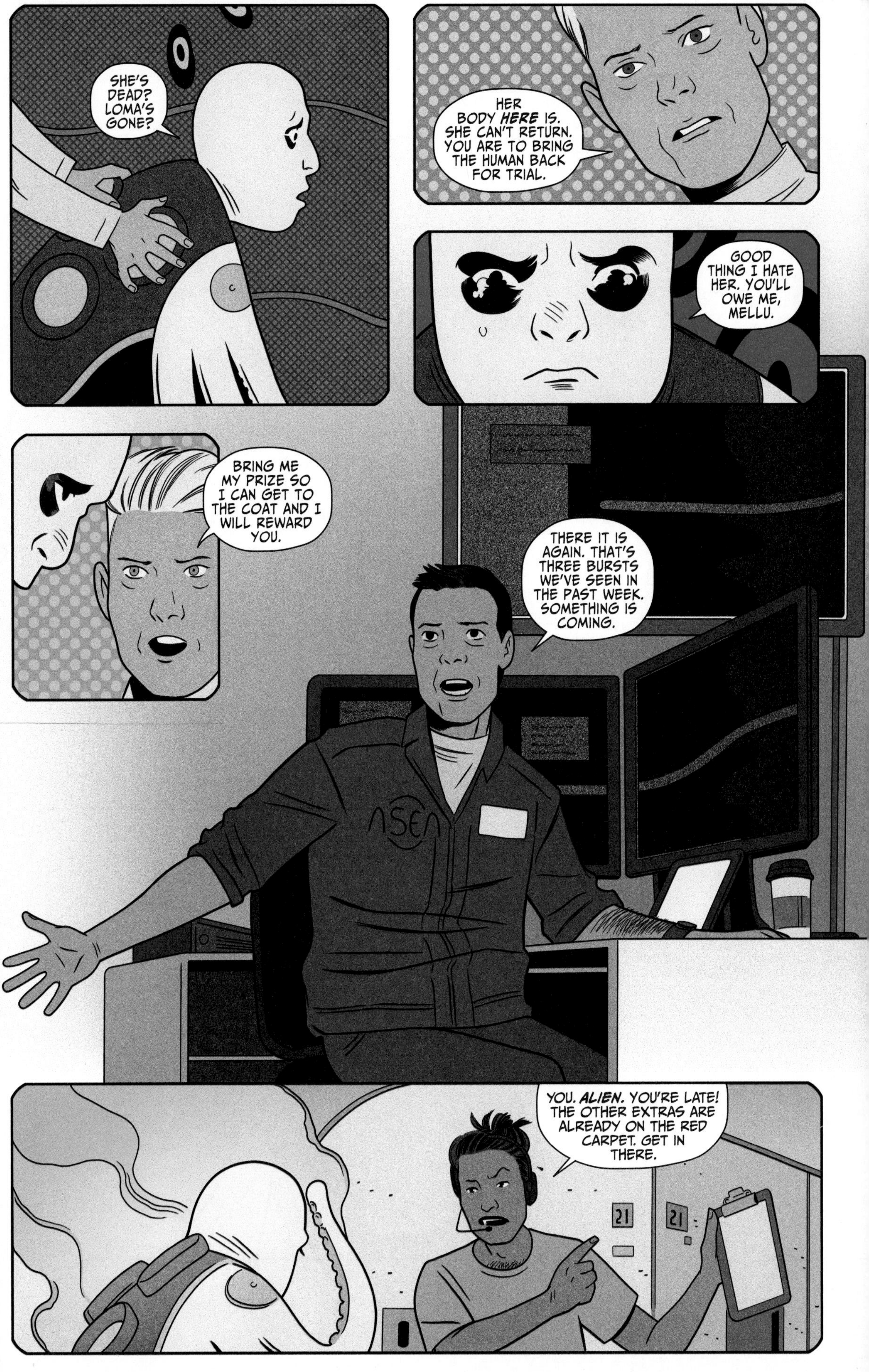
SHE'S DEAD? LOMA'S GONE?
HER BODY HERE IS. SHE CAN'T RETURN. YOU ARE TO BRING THE HUMAN BACK FOR TRIAL.
GOOD THING I HATE HER. YOU'LL OWE ME, MELLU.
BRING ME MY PRIZE SO I CAN GET TO THE COAT AND I WILL REWARD YOU.
THERE IT IS AGAIN. THAT'S THREE BURSTS WE'VE SEEN IN THE PAST WEEK. SOMETHING IS COMING.
YOU. ALIEN. YOU'RE LATE! THE OTHER EXTRAS ARE ALREADY ON THE RED CARPET. GET IN THERE.
21
21

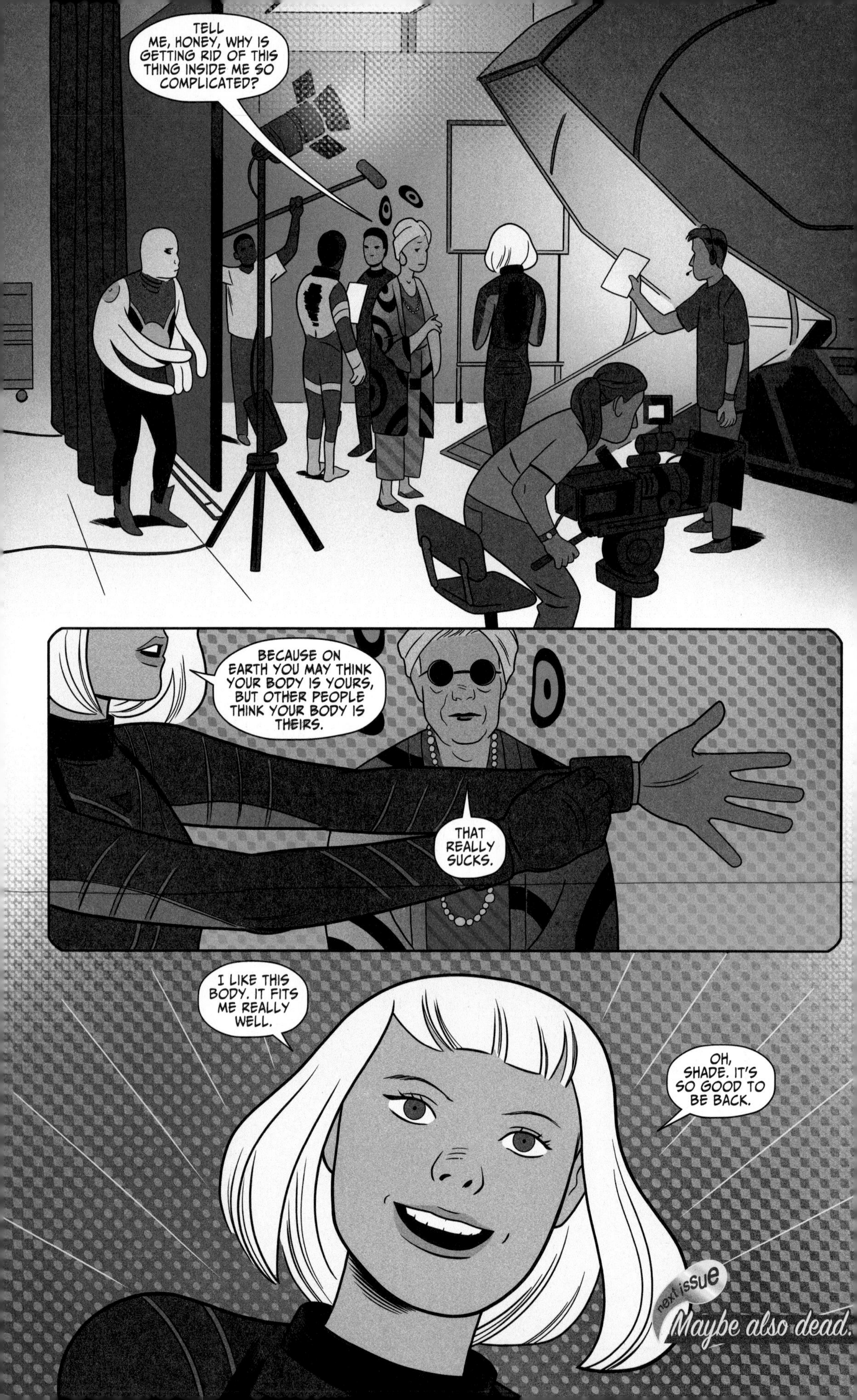
TELL ME, HONEY, WHY IS GETTING RID OF THIS THING INSIDE ME SO COMPLICATED?
BECAUSE ON EARTH YOU MAY THINK YOUR BODY IS YOURS, BUT OTHER PEOPLE THINK YOUR BODY IS THEIRS.
THAT REALLY SUCKS.
I LIKE THIS BODY. IT FITS ME REALLY WELL.
OH, SHADE. IT'S SO GOOD TO BE BACK.
next issue
Maybe also dead.

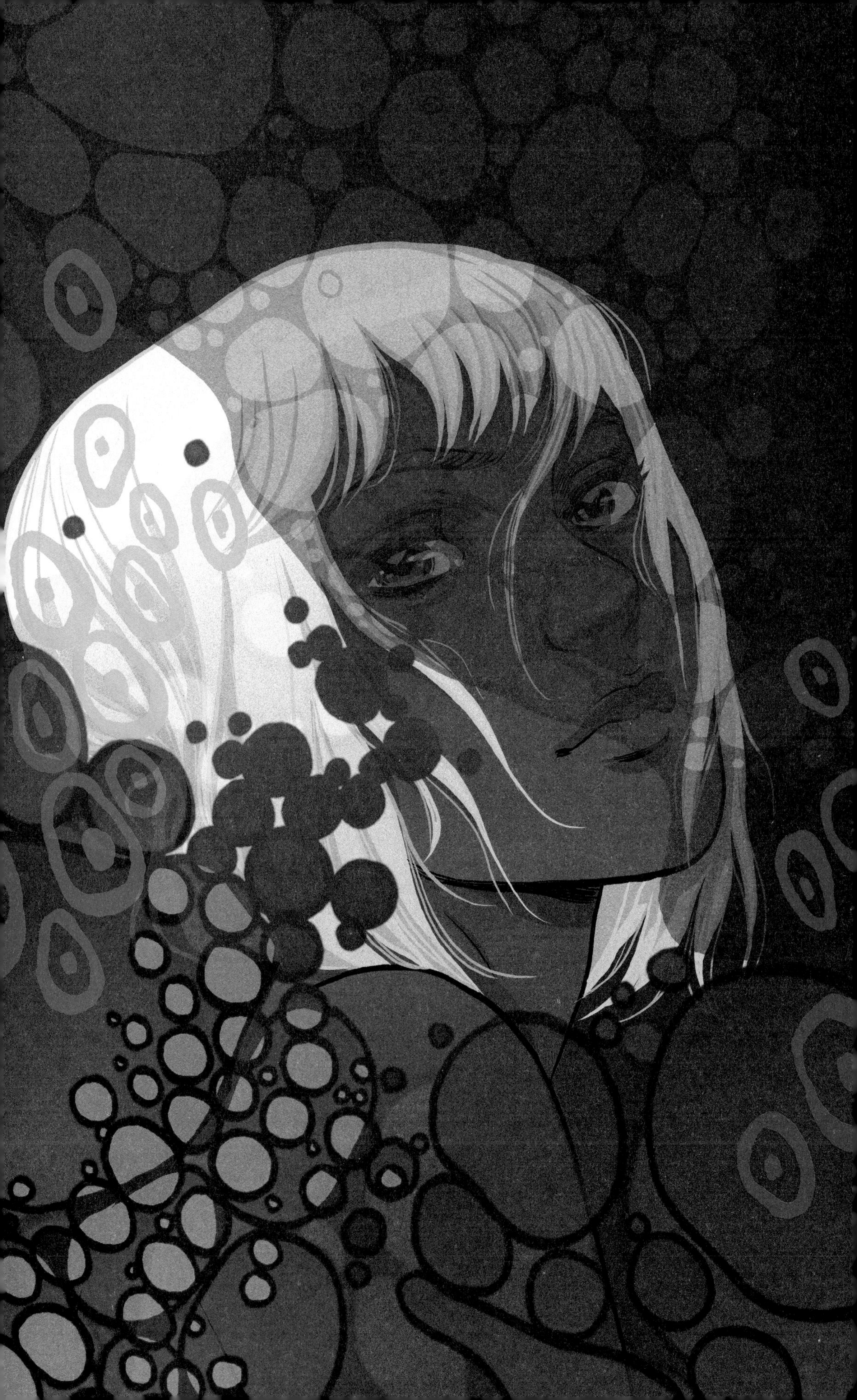

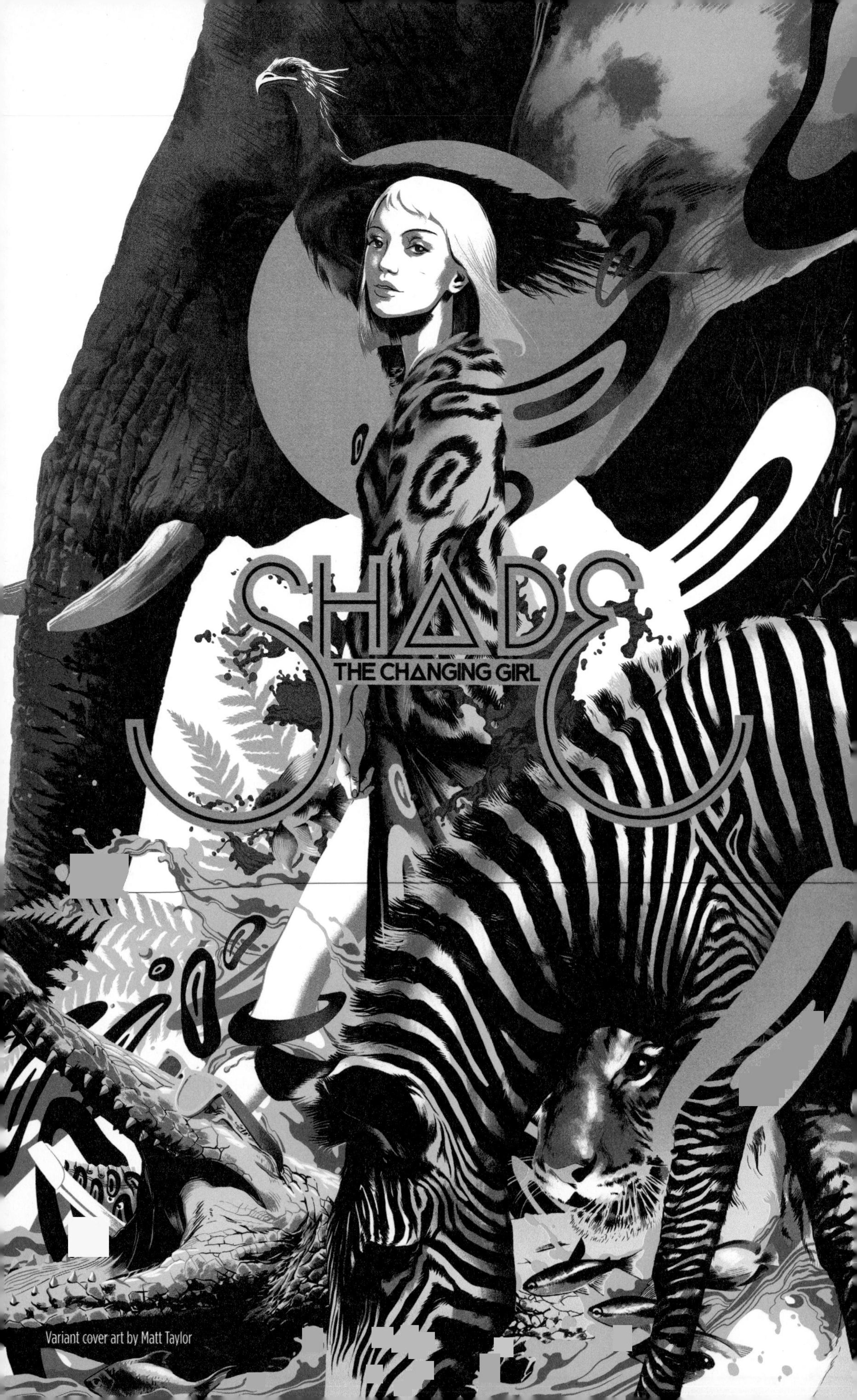
SHADE
THE CHANGING GIRL

Variant cover art by Matt Taylor

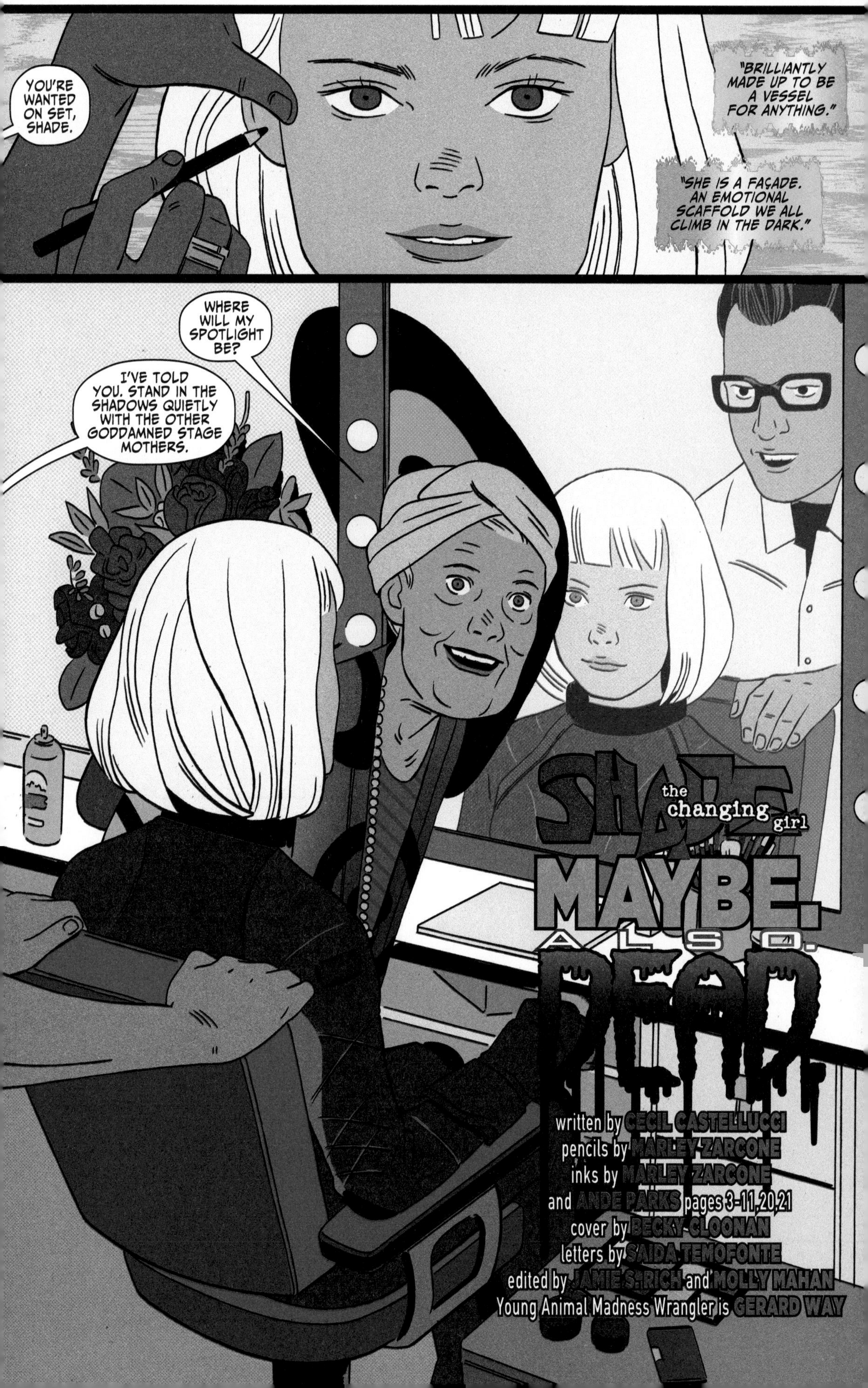
YOU'RE WANTED ON SET, SHADE.
"BRILLIANTLY MADE UP TO BE A VESSEL FOR ANYTHING."
"SHE IS A FAÇADE. AN EMOTIONAL SCAFFOLD WE ALL CLIMB IN THE DARK."
WHERE WILL MY SPOTLIGHT BE?
I'VE TOLD YOU. STAND IN THE SHADOWS QUIETLY WITH THE OTHER GODDAMNED STAGE MOTHERS.
SHADE the changing girl
MAYBE. ALSO. DEAD.
written by CECIL CASTELLUCCI
pencils by MARLEY ZARCONE
inks by MARLEY ZARCONE
and ANDE PARKS pages 3-11,20,21
cover by BECKY CLOONAN
letters by SAIDA TEMOFONTE
edited by JAMIE S. RICH and MOLLY MAHAN
Young Animal Madness Wrangler is GERARD WAY

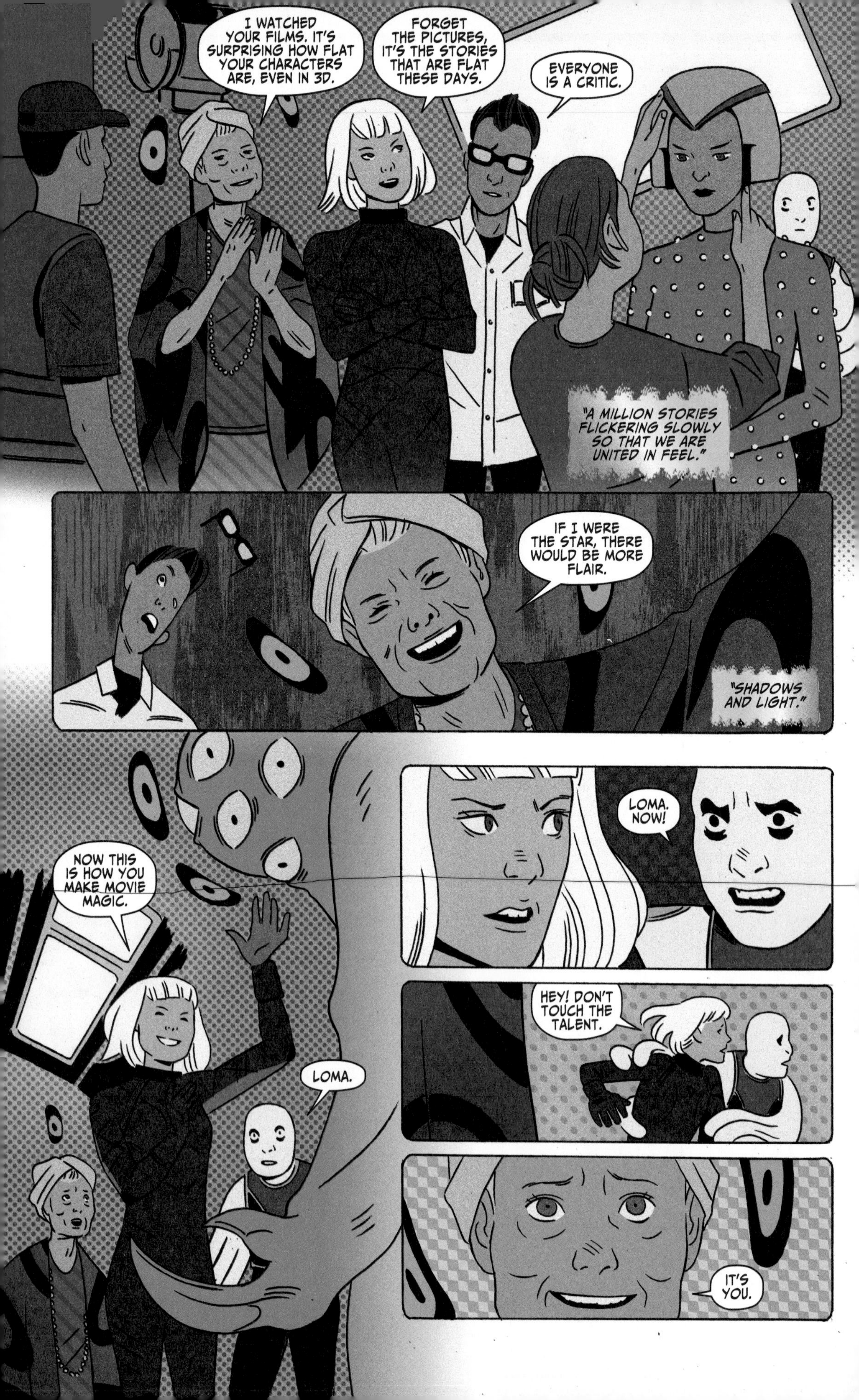
I WATCHED YOUR FILMS. IT'S SURPRISING HOW FLAT YOUR CHARACTERS ARE, EVEN IN 3D.
FORGET THE PICTURES, IT'S THE STORIES THAT ARE FLAT THESE DAYS.
EVERYONE IS A CRITIC.
"A MILLION STORIES FLICKERING SLOWLY SO THAT WE ARE UNITED IN FEEL."
IF I WERE THE STAR, THERE WOULD BE MORE FLAIR.
"SHADOWS AND LIGHT."
NOW THIS IS HOW YOU MAKE MOVIE MAGIC.
LOMA.
LOMA. NOW!
HEY! DON'T TOUCH THE TALENT.
IT'S YOU.

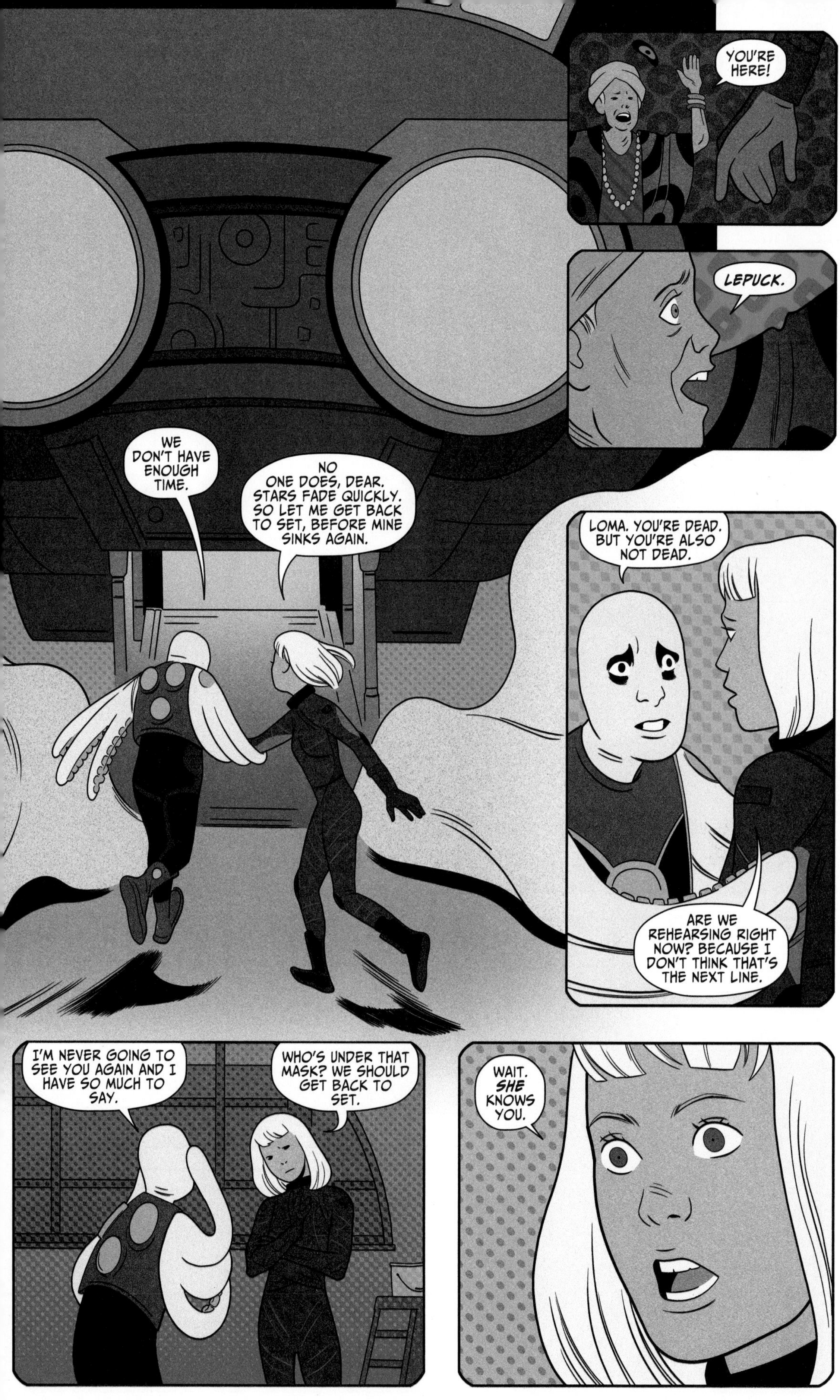
YOU'RE HERE!
LEPUCK.
WE DON'T HAVE ENOUGH TIME.
NO ONE DOES, DEAR. STARS FADE QUICKLY. SO LET ME GET BACK TO SET, BEFORE MINE SINKS AGAIN.
LOMA. YOU'RE DEAD. BUT YOU'RE ALSO NOT DEAD.
ARE WE REHEARSING RIGHT NOW? BECAUSE I DON'T THINK THAT'S THE NEXT LINE.
I'M NEVER GOING TO SEE YOU AGAIN AND I HAVE SO MUCH TO SAY.
WHO'S UNDER THAT MASK? WE SHOULD GET BACK TO SET.
WAIT. SHE KNOWS YOU.

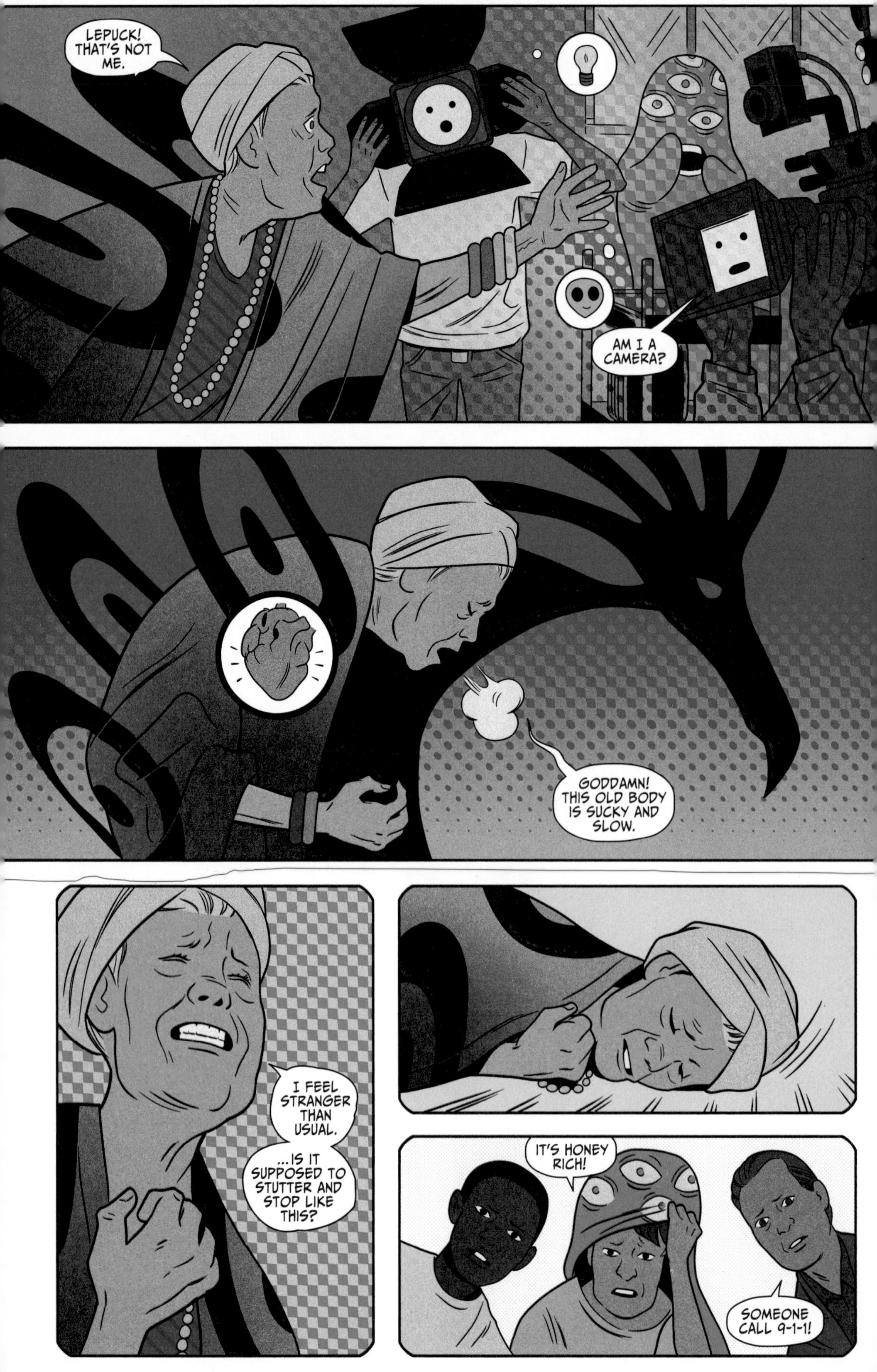
LEPUCK! THAT'S NOT ME.
AM I A CAMERA?
GODDAMN! THIS OLD BODY IS SUCKY AND SLOW.
I FEEL STRANGER THAN USUAL.
...IS IT SUPPOSED TO STUTTER AND STOP LIKE THIS?
IT'S HONEY RICH!
SOMEONE CALL 9-1-1!

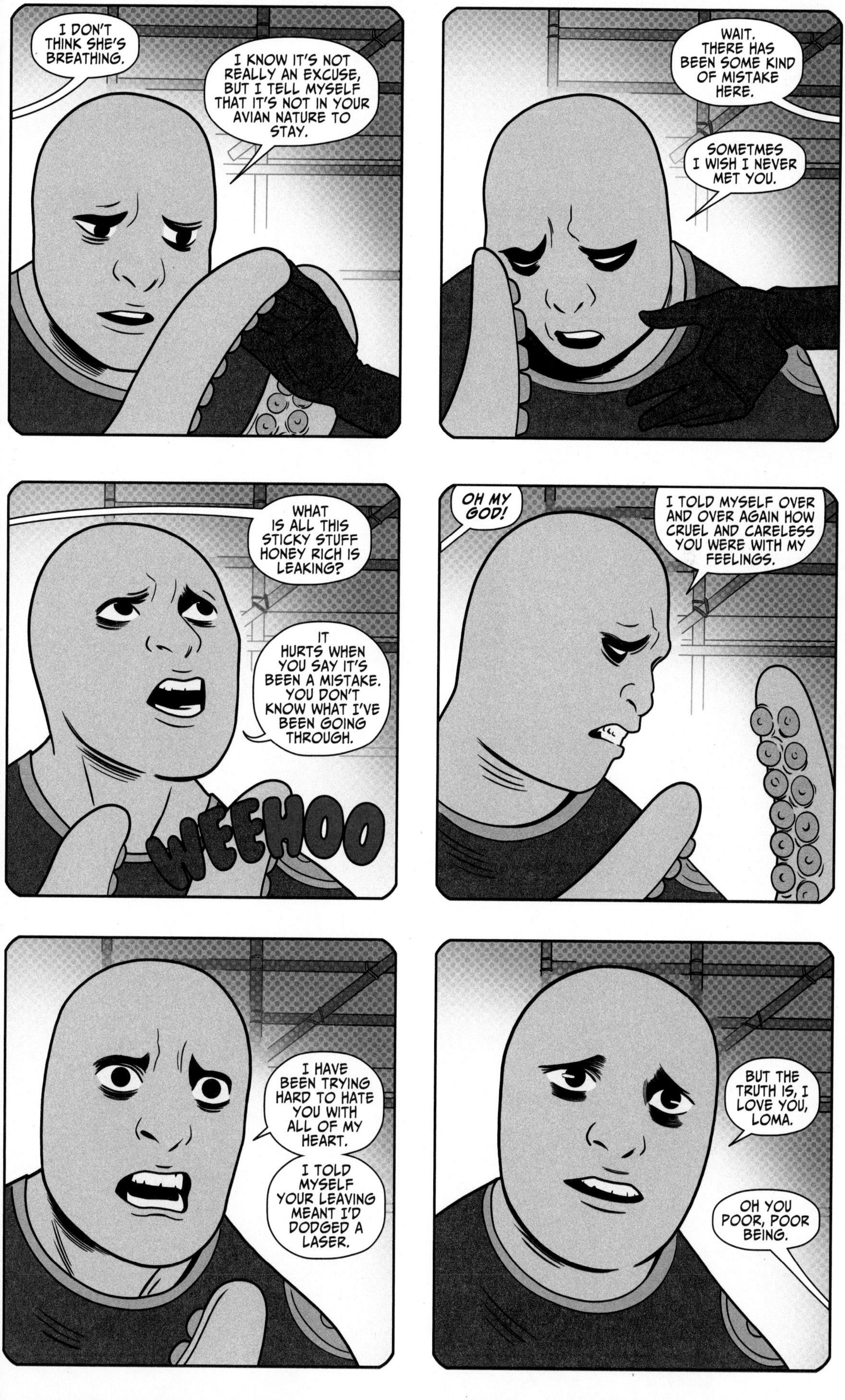
I DON'T THINK SHE'S BREATHING.
I KNOW IT'S NOT REALLY AN EXCUSE, BUT I TELL MYSELF THAT IT'S NOT IN YOUR AVIAN NATURE TO STAY.
WAIT. THERE HAS BEEN SOME KIND OF MISTAKE HERE.
SOMETMES I WISH I NEVER MET YOU.
WHAT IS ALL THIS STICKY STUFF HONEY RICH IS LEAKING?
IT HURTS WHEN YOU SAY IT'S BEEN A MISTAKE. YOU DON'T KNOW WHAT I'VE BEEN GOING THROUGH.
WEEHOO
OH MY GOD!
I TOLD MYSELF OVER AND OVER AGAIN HOW CRUEL AND CARELESS YOU WERE WITH MY FEELINGS.
I HAVE BEEN TRYING HARD TO HATE YOU WITH ALL OF MY HEART.
I TOLD MYSELF YOUR LEAVING MEANT I'D DODGED A LASER.
BUT THE TRUTH IS, I LOVE YOU, LOMA.
OH YOU POOR, POOR BEING.

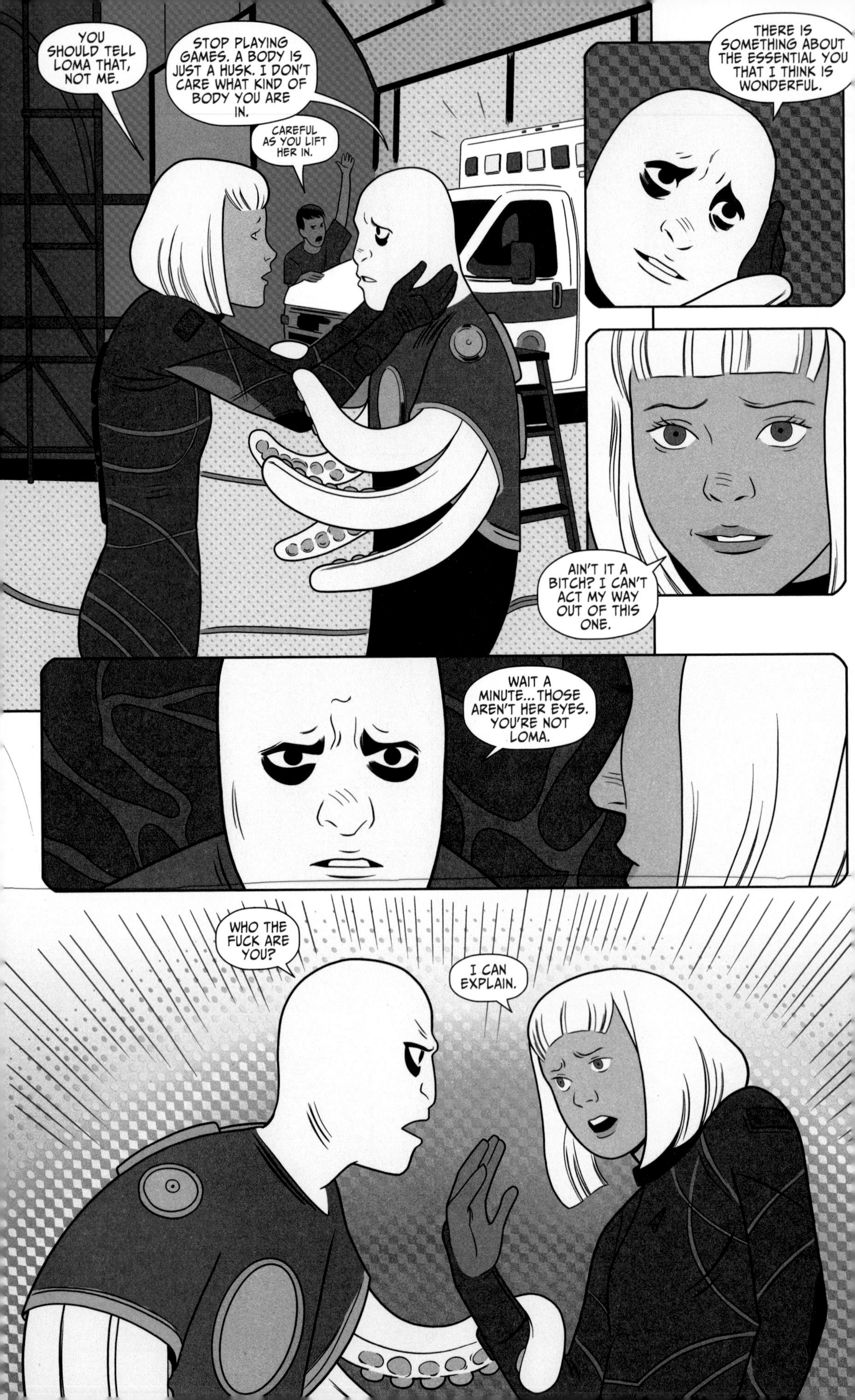
YOU SHOULD TELL LOMA THAT, NOT ME.
STOP PLAYING GAMES. A BODY IS JUST A HUSK. I DON'T CARE WHAT KIND OF BODY YOU ARE IN.
CAREFUL AS YOU LIFT HER IN.
THERE IS SOMETHING ABOUT THE ESSENTIAL YOU THAT I THINK IS WONDERFUL.
AIN'T IT A BITCH? I CAN'T ACT MY WAY OUT OF THIS ONE.
WAIT A MINUTE... THOSE AREN'T HER EYES. YOU'RE NOT LOMA.
WHO THE FUCK ARE YOU?
I CAN EXPLAIN.

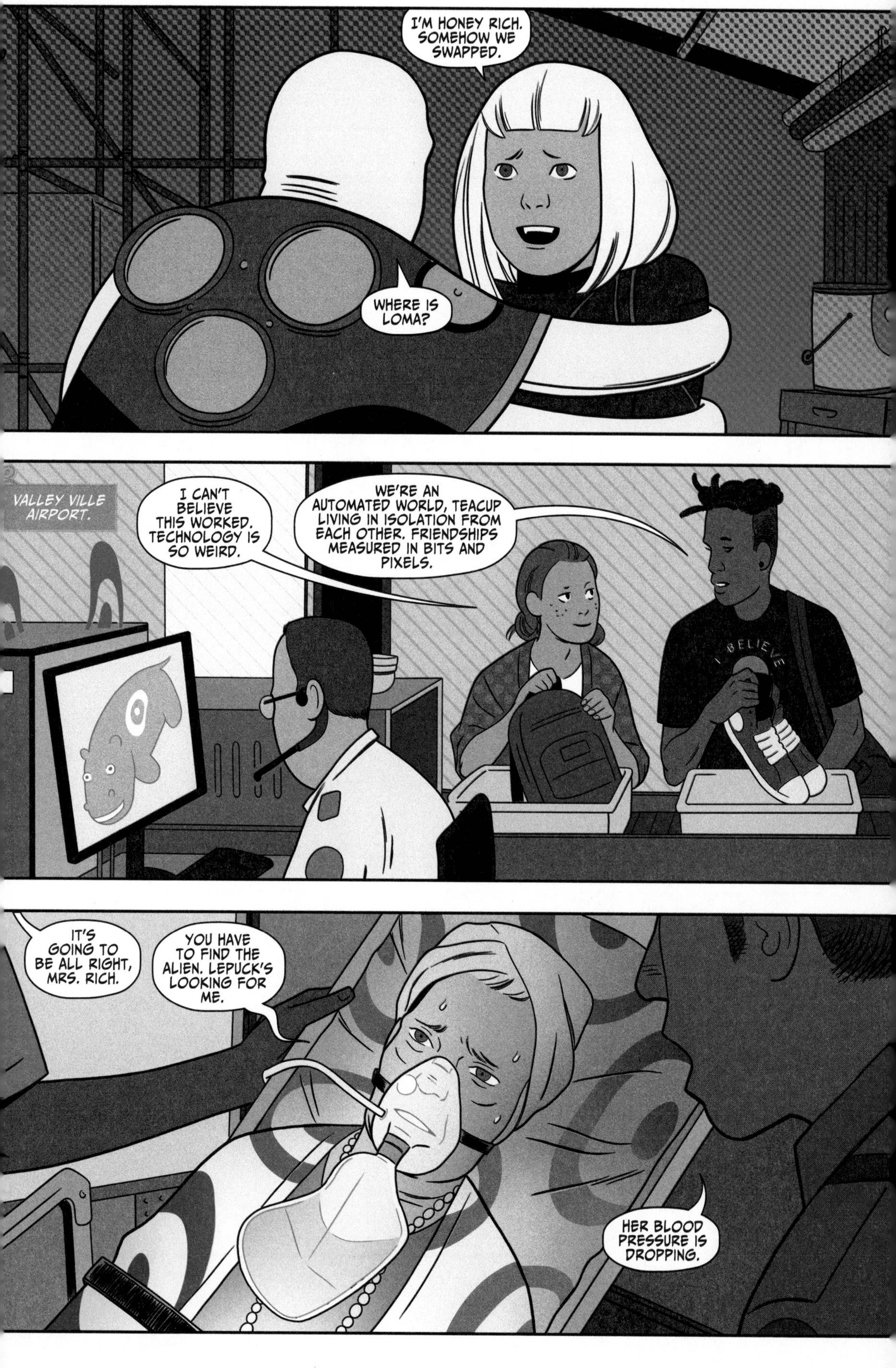
I'M HONEY RICH. SOMEHOW WE SWAPPED.
WHERE IS LOMA?
VALLEY VILLE AIRPORT.
I CAN'T BELIEVE THIS WORKED. TECHNOLOGY IS SO WEIRD.
WE'RE AN AUTOMATED WORLD, TEACUP LIVING IN ISOLATION FROM EACH OTHER. FRIENDSHIPS MEASURED IN BITS AND PIXELS.
I BELIEVE
IT'S GOING TO BE ALL RIGHT, MRS. RICH.
YOU HAVE TO FIND THE ALIEN. LEPUCK'S LOOKING FOR ME.
HER BLOOD PRESSURE IS DROPPING.

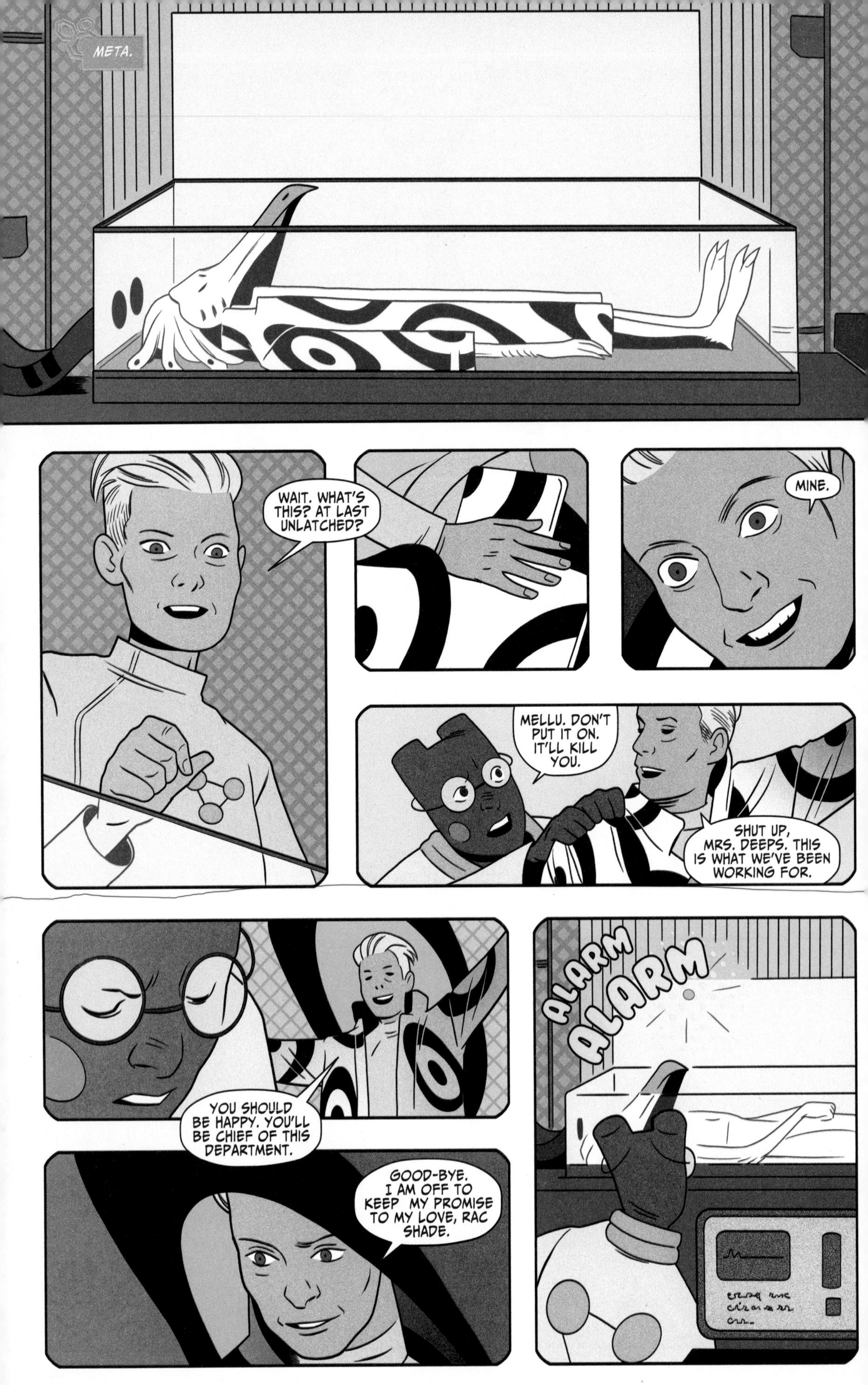
META.
WAIT. WHAT'S THIS? AT LAST UNLATCHED?
MINE.
MELLU. DON'T PUT IT ON. IT'LL KILL YOU.
SHUT UP, MRS. DEEPS. THIS IS WHAT WE'VE BEEN WORKING FOR.
YOU SHOULD BE HAPPY. YOU'LL BE CHIEF OF THIS DEPARTMENT.
GOOD-BYE. I AM OFF TO KEEP MY PROMISE TO MY LOVE, RAC SHADE.
ALARM
ALARM

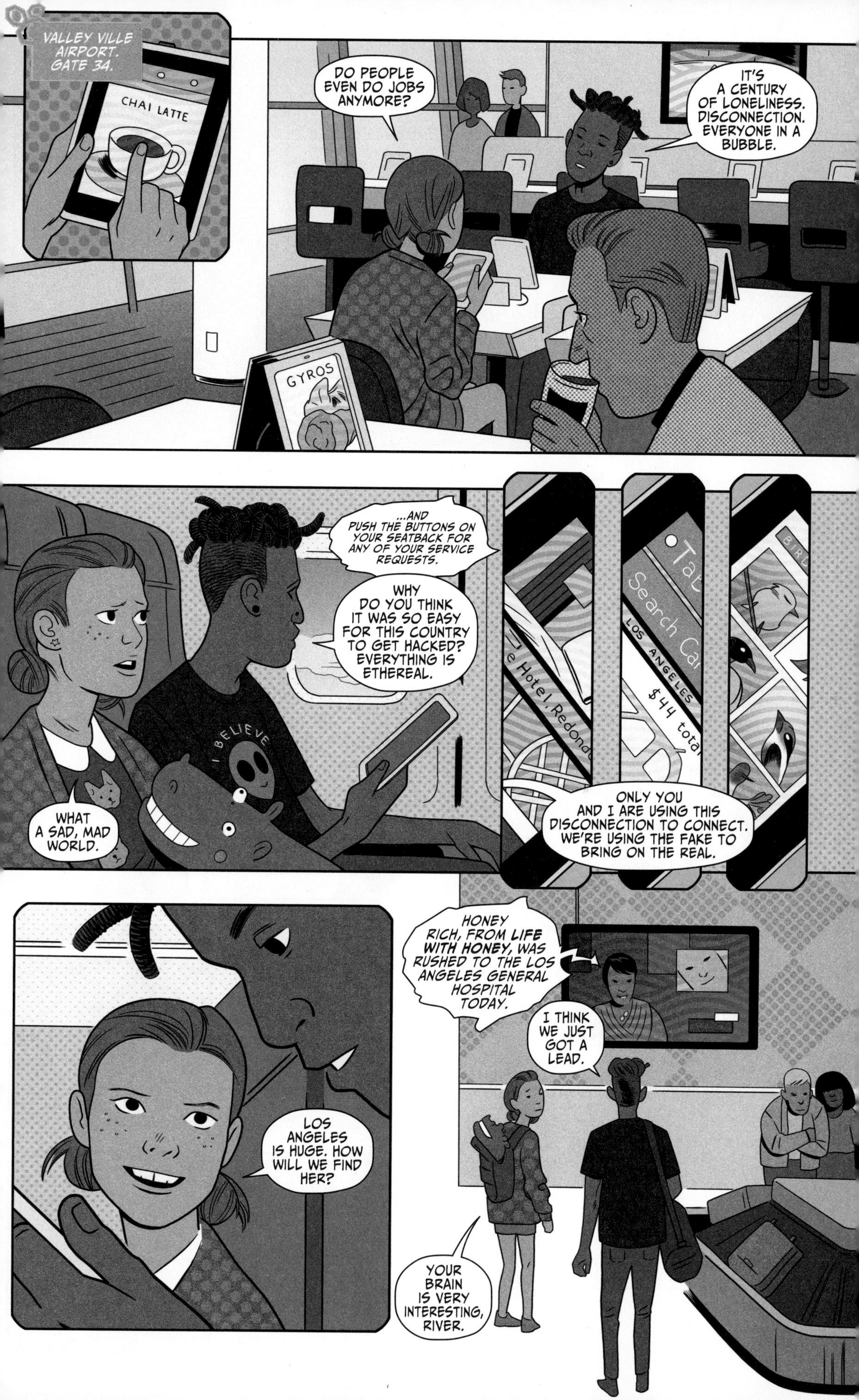
VALLEY VILLE AIRPORT. GATE 34.
CHAI LATTE
DO PEOPLE EVEN DO JOBS ANYMORE?
IT'S A CENTURY OF LONELINESS. DISCONNECTION. EVERYONE IN A BUBBLE.
GYROS
...AND PUSH THE BUTTONS ON YOUR SEATBACK FOR ANY OF YOUR SERVICE REQUESTS.
WHY DO YOU THINK IT WAS SO EASY FOR THIS COUNTRY TO GET HACKED? EVERYTHING IS ETHEREAL.
I BELIEVE
WHAT A SAD, MAD WORLD.
e Hotel, Redondo
Search Ca
LOS ANGELES
$44 total
ONLY YOU AND I ARE USING THIS DISCONNECTION TO CONNECT. WE'RE USING THE FAKE TO BRING ON THE REAL.
LOS ANGELES IS HUGE. HOW WILL WE FIND HER?
HONEY RICH, FROM LIFE WITH HONEY, WAS RUSHED TO THE LOS ANGELES GENERAL HOSPITAL TODAY.
I THINK WE JUST GOT A LEAD.
YOUR BRAIN IS VERY INTERESTING, RIVER.

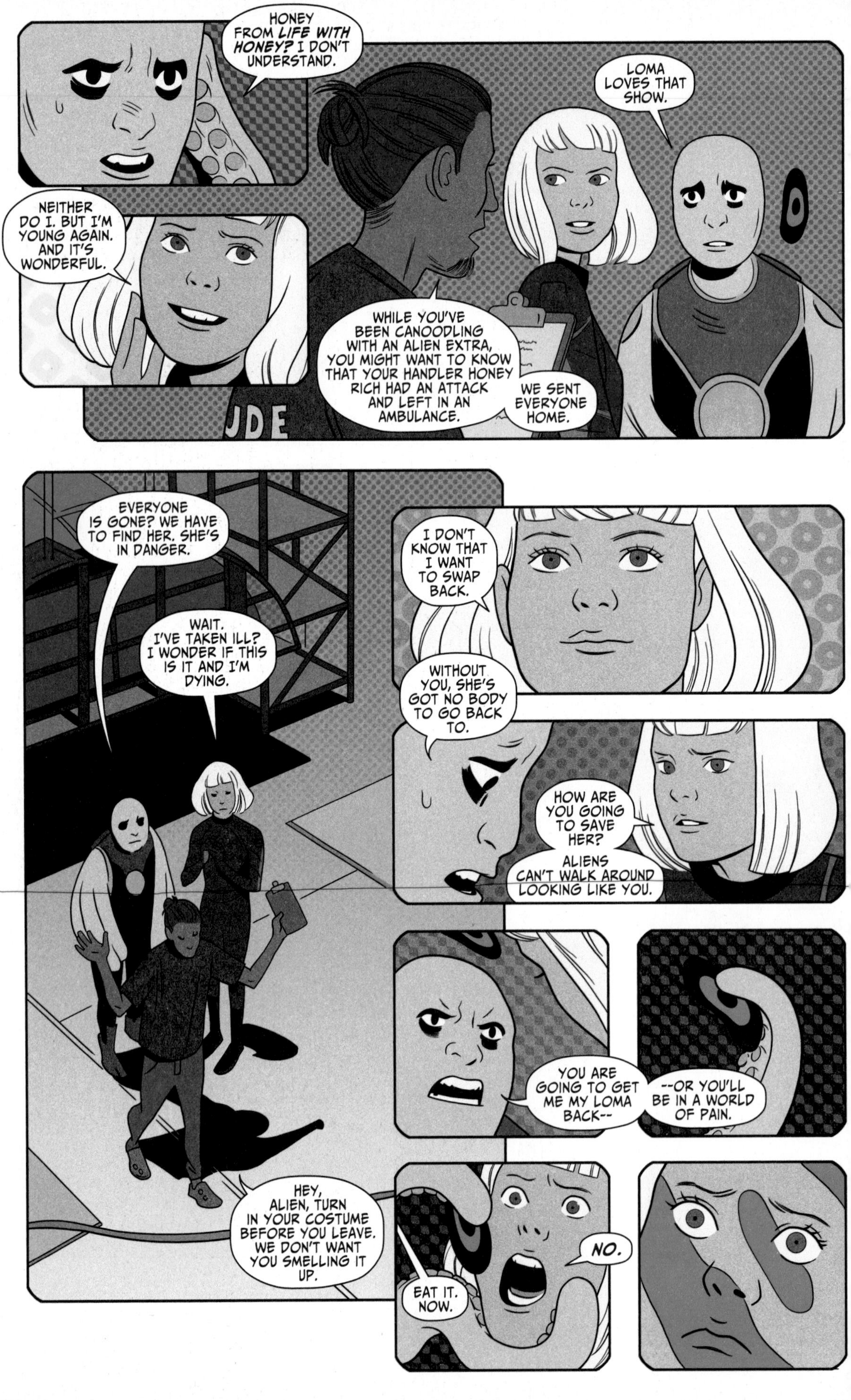
HONEY FROM LIFE WITH HONEY? I DON'T UNDERSTAND.
NEITHER DO I. BUT I'M YOUNG AGAIN. AND IT'S WONDERFUL.
LOMA LOVES THAT SHOW.
WHILE YOU'VE BEEN CANOODLING WITH AN ALIEN EXTRA, YOU MIGHT WANT TO KNOW THAT YOUR HANDLER HONEY RICH HAD AN ATTACK AND LEFT IN AN AMBULANCE.
WE SENT EVERYONE HOME.
JDE
EVERYONE IS GONE? WE HAVE TO FIND HER. SHE'S IN DANGER.
WAIT. I'VE TAKEN ILL? I WONDER IF THIS IS IT AND I'M DYING.
HEY, ALIEN, TURN IN YOUR COSTUME BEFORE YOU LEAVE. WE DON'T WANT YOU SMELLING IT UP.
I DON'T KNOW THAT I WANT TO SWAP BACK.
WITHOUT YOU, SHE'S GOT NO BODY TO GO BACK TO.
HOW ARE YOU GOING TO SAVE HER?
ALIENS CAN'T WALK AROUND LOOKING LIKE YOU.
YOU ARE GOING TO GET ME MY LOMA BACK--
--OR YOU'LL BE IN A WORLD OF PAIN.
EAT IT. NOW.
NO.

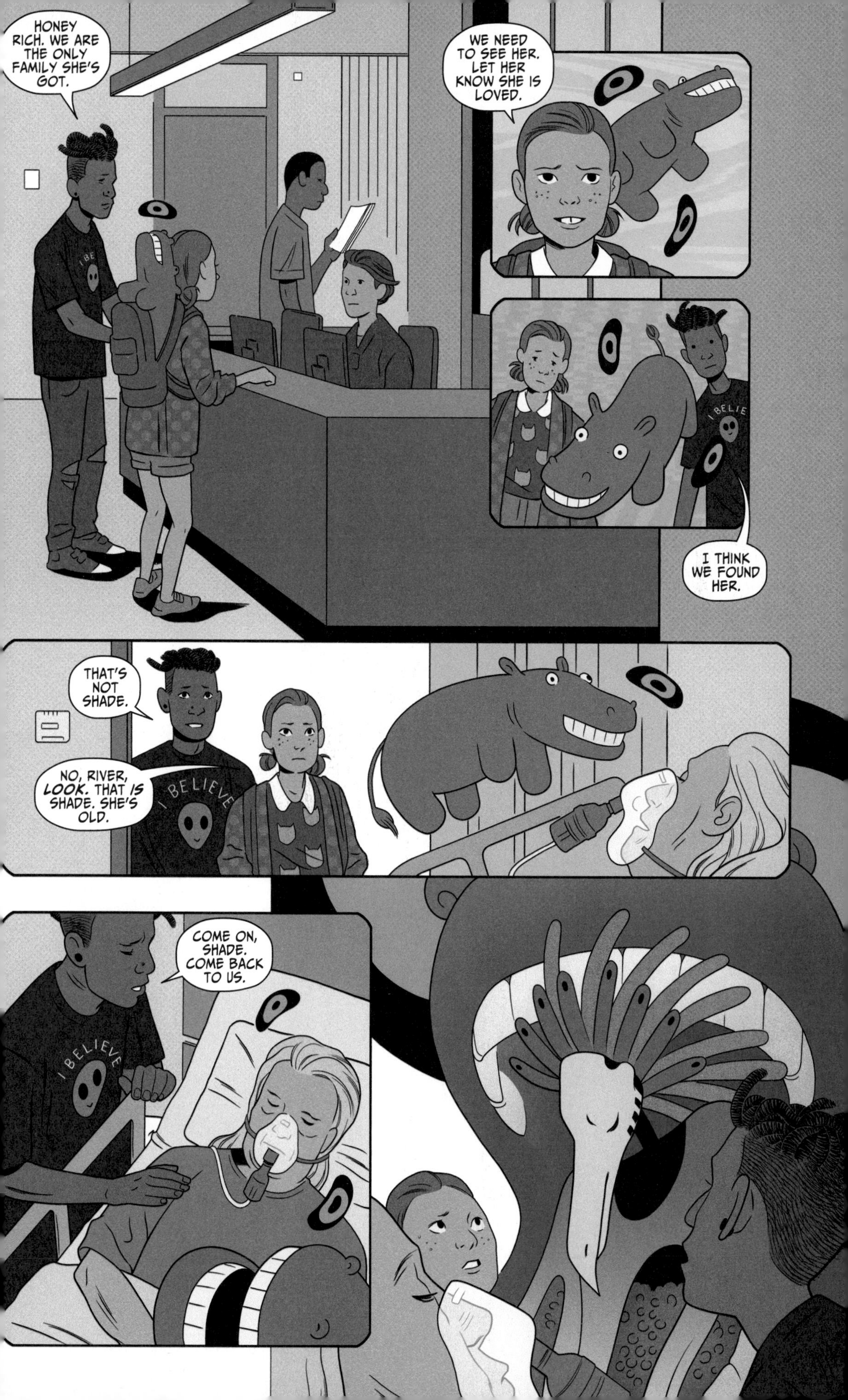
HONEY RICH. WE ARE THE ONLY FAMILY SHE'S GOT.
WE NEED TO SEE HER. LET HER KNOW SHE IS LOVED.
I BELIEVE
I THINK WE FOUND HER.
THAT'S NOT SHADE.
NO, RIVER, *LOOK.* THAT *IS* SHADE. SHE'S OLD.
I BELIEVE
COME ON, SHADE. COME BACK TO US.
I BELIEVE

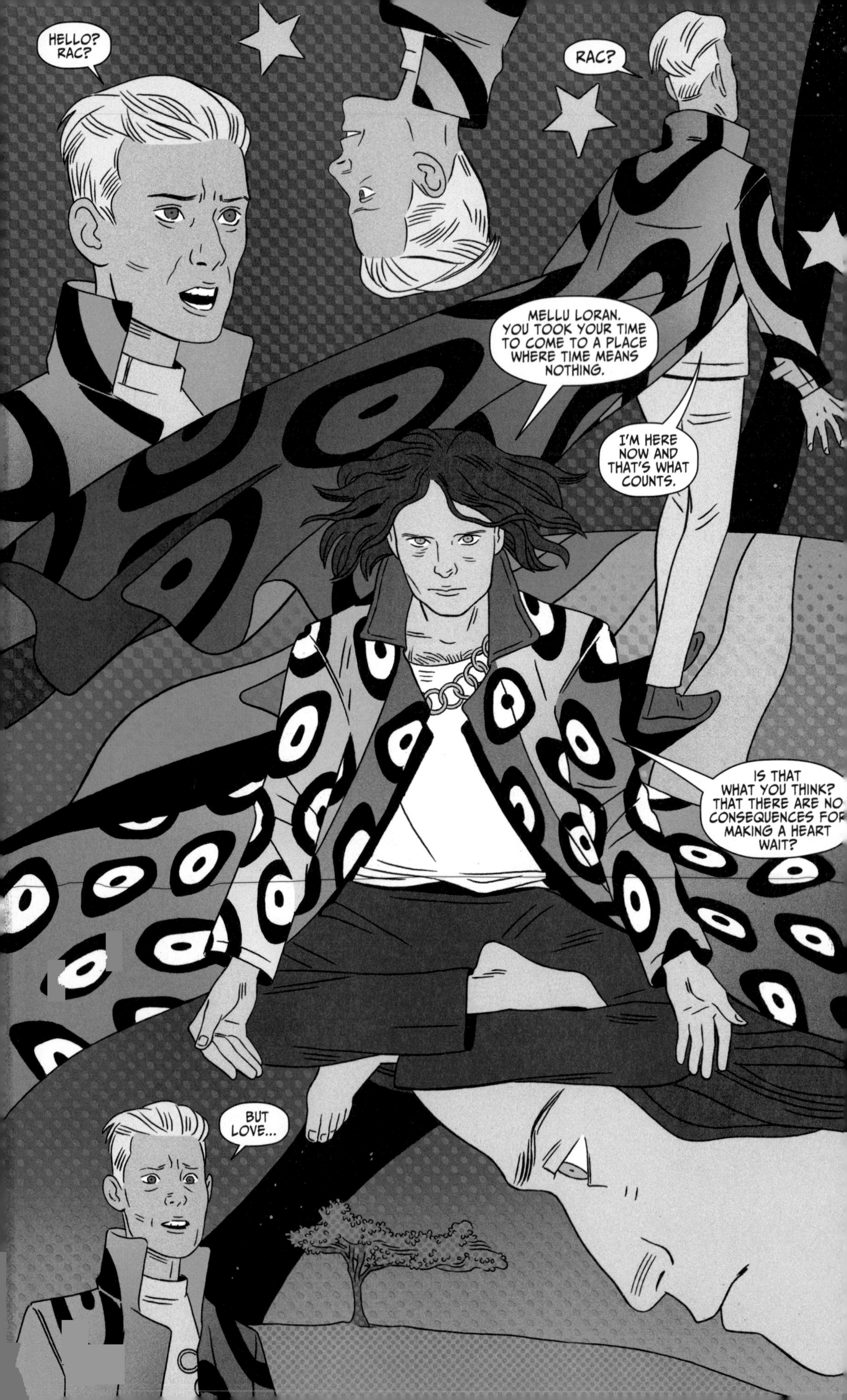
HELLO? RAC?
RAC?
MELLU LORAN. YOU TOOK YOUR TIME TO COME TO A PLACE WHERE TIME MEANS NOTHING.
I'M HERE NOW AND THAT'S WHAT COUNTS.
IS THAT WHAT YOU THINK? THAT THERE ARE NO CONSEQUENCES FOR MAKING A HEART WAIT?
BUT LOVE...

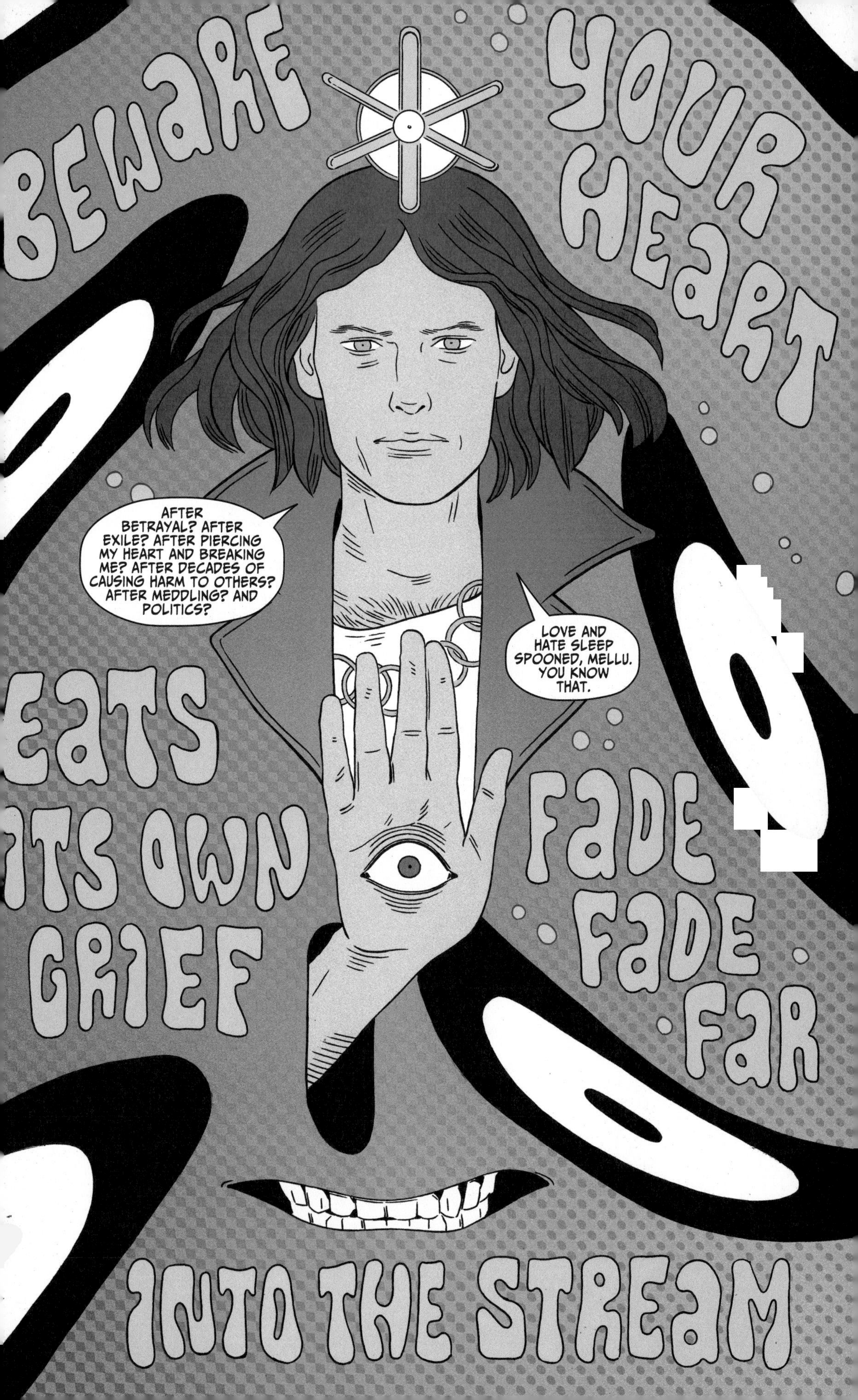
BEWARE
YOUR HEART
AFTER BETRAYAL? AFTER EXILE? AFTER PIERCING MY HEART AND BREAKING ME? AFTER DECADES OF CAUSING HARM TO OTHERS? AFTER MEDDLING? AND POLITICS?
LOVE AND HATE SLEEP SPOONED, MELLU. YOU KNOW THAT.
EATS ITS OWN GRIEF
FADE FADE FAR
INTO THE STREAM

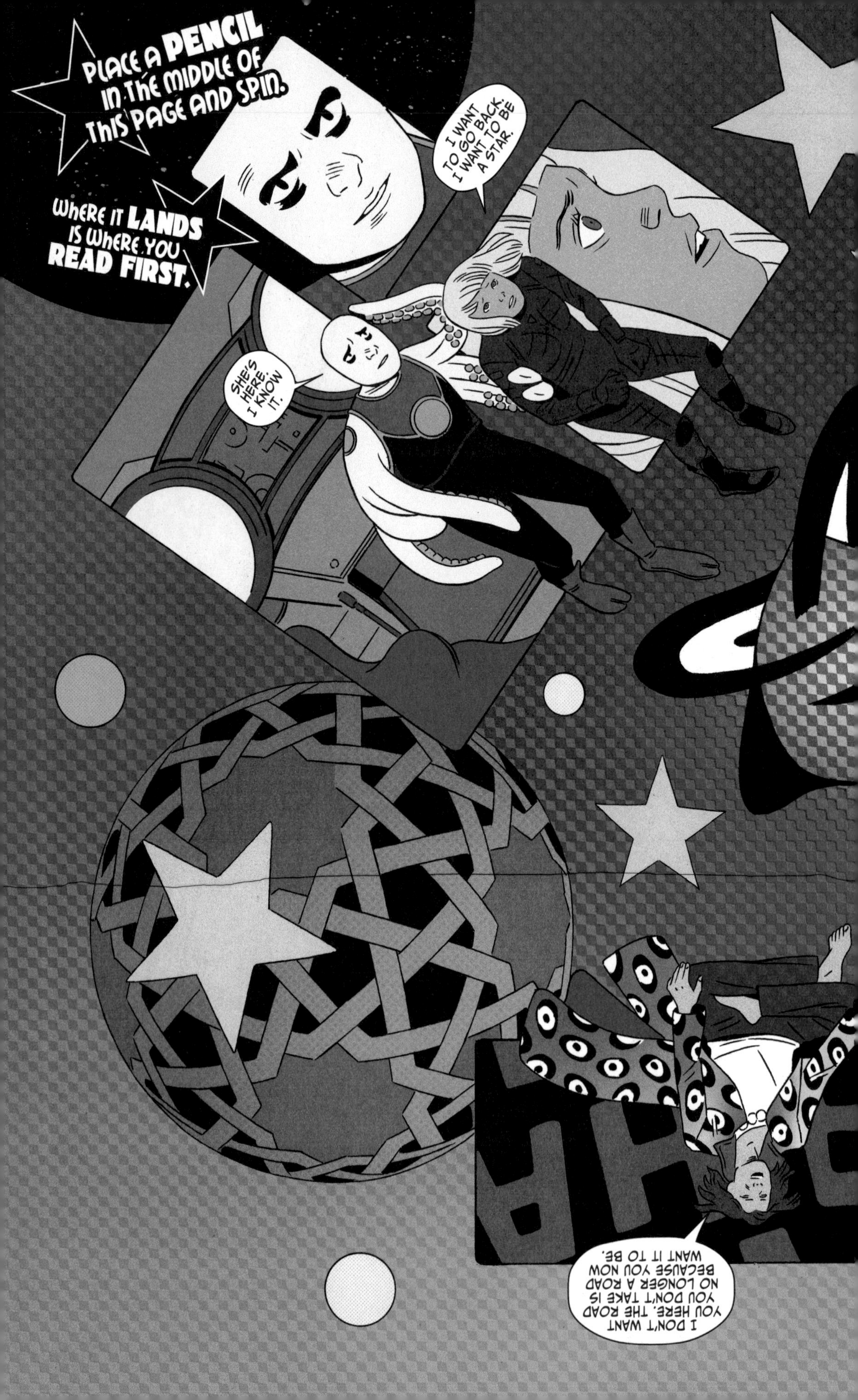
PLACE A PENCIL IN THE MIDDLE OF THIS PAGE AND SPIN.
WHERE IT LANDS IS WHERE YOU READ FIRST.
I WANT TO GO BACK. I WANT TO BE A STAR.
SHE'S HERE. I KNOW IT.
I DON'T WANT YOU HERE. THE ROAD YOU DON'T TAKE IS NO LONGER A ROAD BECAUSE YOU NOW WANT IT TO BE.

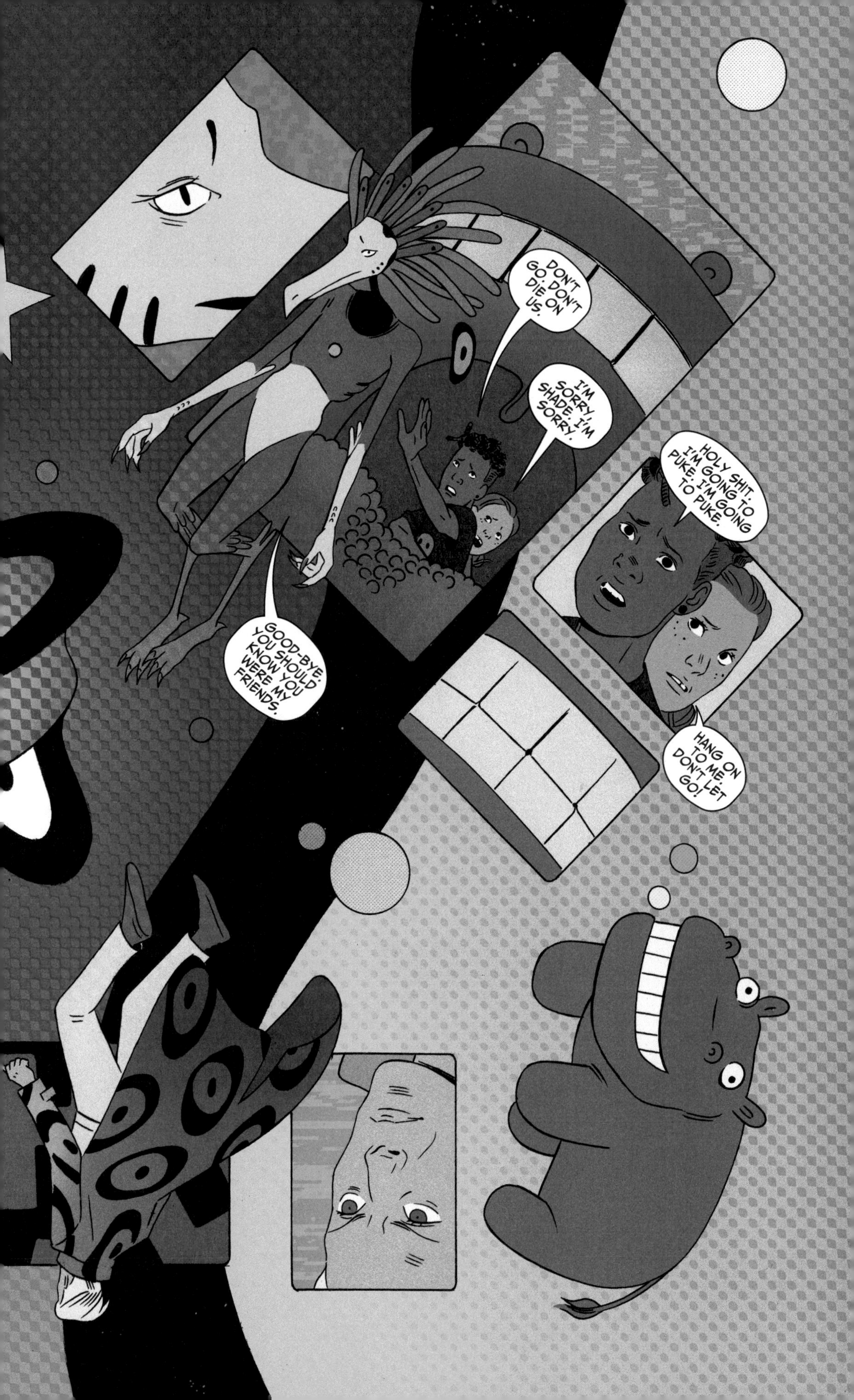
DON'T GO. DON'T DIE ON US.
I'M SORRY, SHADE. I'M SORRY.
HOLY SHIT. I'M GOING TO PUKE. I'M GOING TO PUKE.
HANG ON TO ME. DON'T LET GO!
GOOD-BYE. YOU SHOULD KNOW YOU WERE MY FRIENDS.

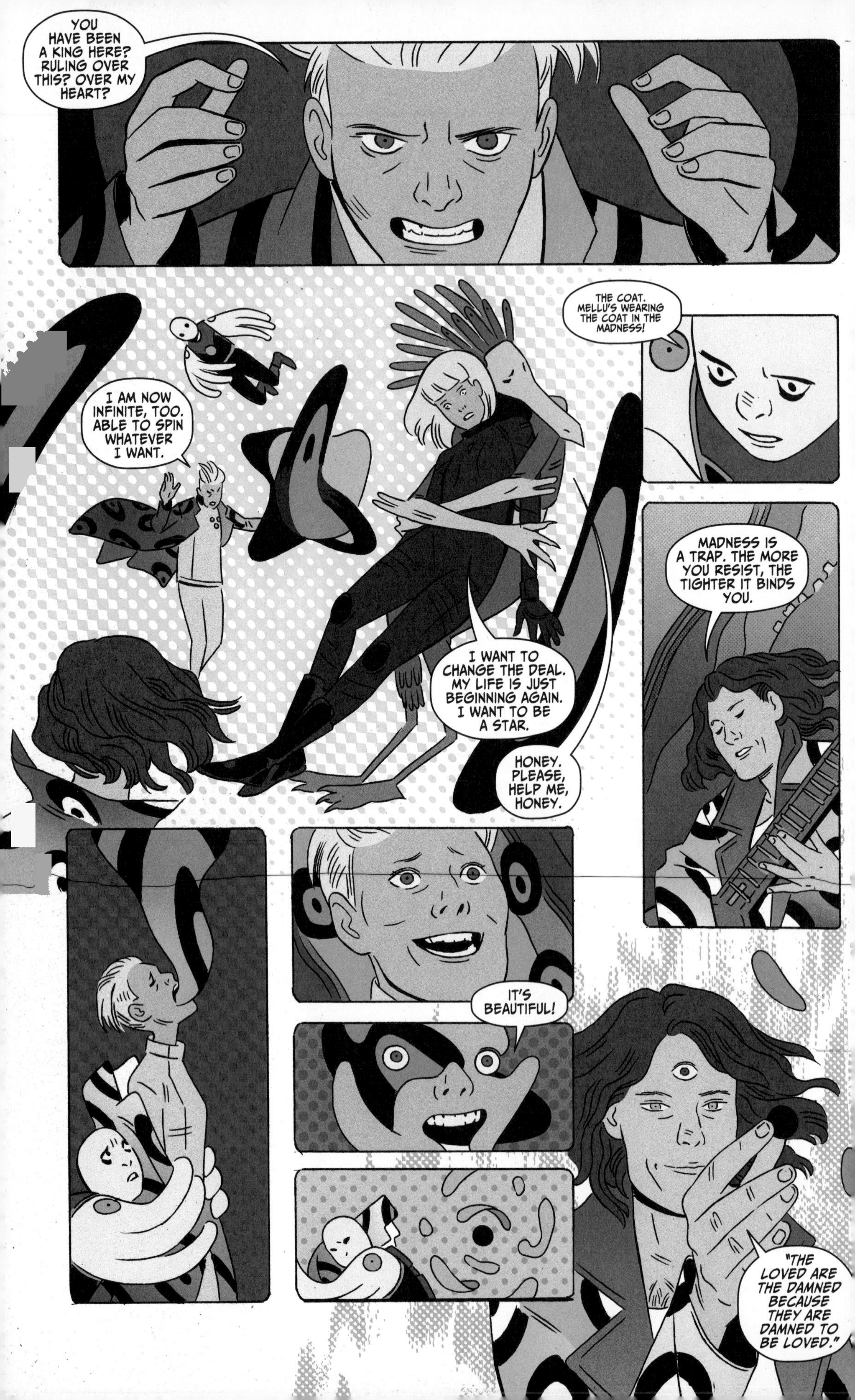
YOU HAVE BEEN A KING HERE? RULING OVER THIS? OVER MY HEART?
I AM NOW INFINITE, TOO. ABLE TO SPIN WHATEVER I WANT.
THE COAT. MELLU'S WEARING THE COAT IN THE MADNESS!
I WANT TO CHANGE THE DEAL. MY LIFE IS JUST BEGINNING AGAIN. I WANT TO BE A STAR.
HONEY. PLEASE, HELP ME, HONEY.
MADNESS IS A TRAP. THE MORE YOU RESIST, THE TIGHTER IT BINDS YOU.
IT'S BEAUTIFUL!
"THE LOVED ARE THE DAMNED BECAUSE THEY ARE DAMNED TO BE LOVED."

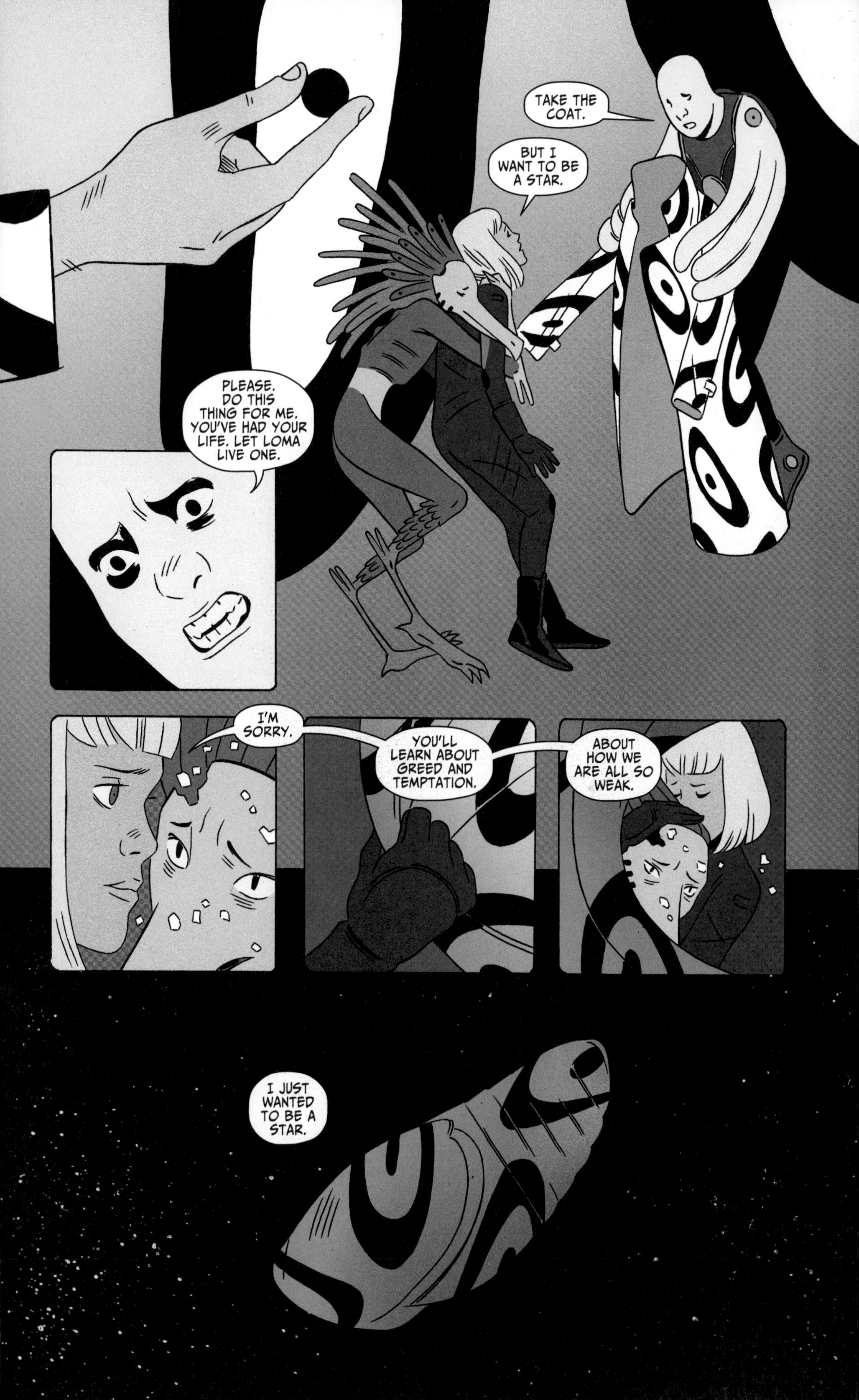
TAKE THE COAT.
BUT I WANT TO BE A STAR.
PLEASE. DO THIS THING FOR ME. YOU'VE HAD YOUR LIFE. LET LOMA LIVE ONE.
I'M SORRY.
YOU'LL LEARN ABOUT GREED AND TEMPTATION.
ABOUT HOW WE ARE ALL SO WEAK.
I JUST WANTED TO BE A STAR.

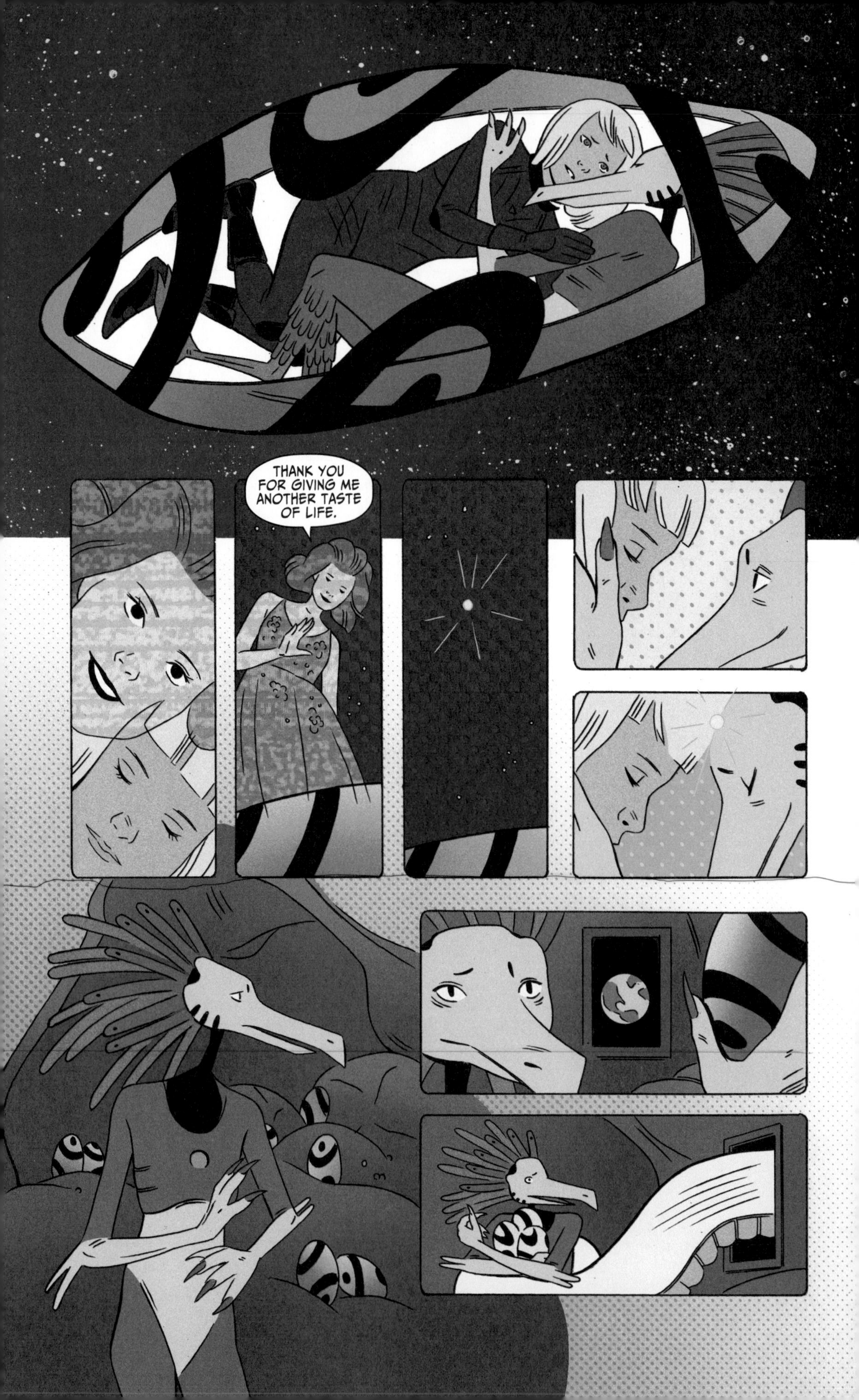
THANK YOU FOR GIVING ME ANOTHER TASTE OF LIFE.

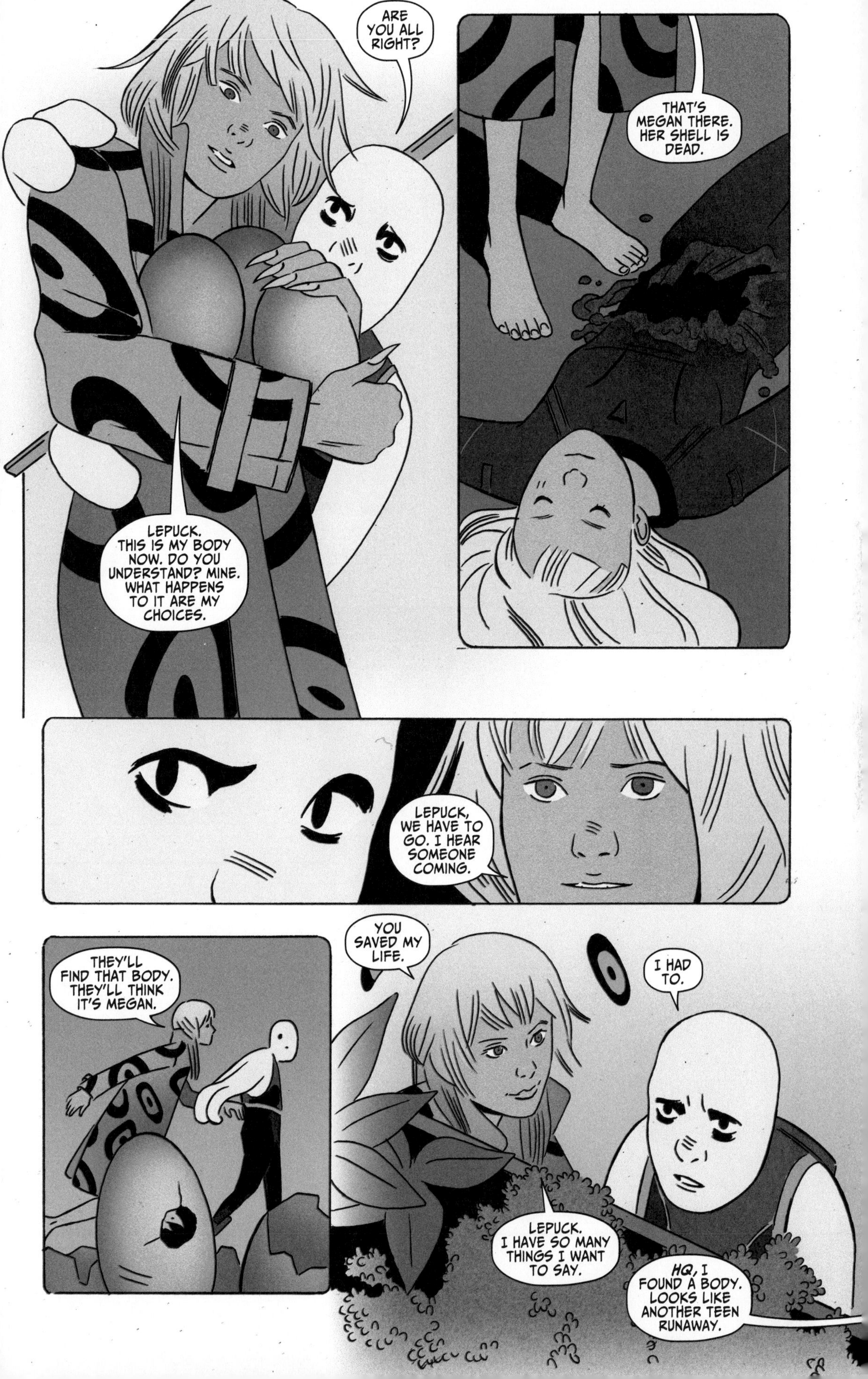
ARE YOU ALL RIGHT?
THAT'S MEGAN THERE. HER SHELL IS DEAD.
LEPUCK. THIS IS MY BODY NOW. DO YOU UNDERSTAND? MINE. WHAT HAPPENS TO IT ARE MY CHOICES.
LEPUCK, WE HAVE TO GO. I HEAR SOMEONE COMING.
THEY'LL FIND THAT BODY. THEY'LL THINK IT'S MEGAN.
YOU SAVED MY LIFE.
I HAD TO.
LEPUCK. I HAVE SO MANY THINGS I WANT TO SAY.
HQ, I FOUND A BODY. LOOKS LIKE ANOTHER TEEN RUNAWAY.

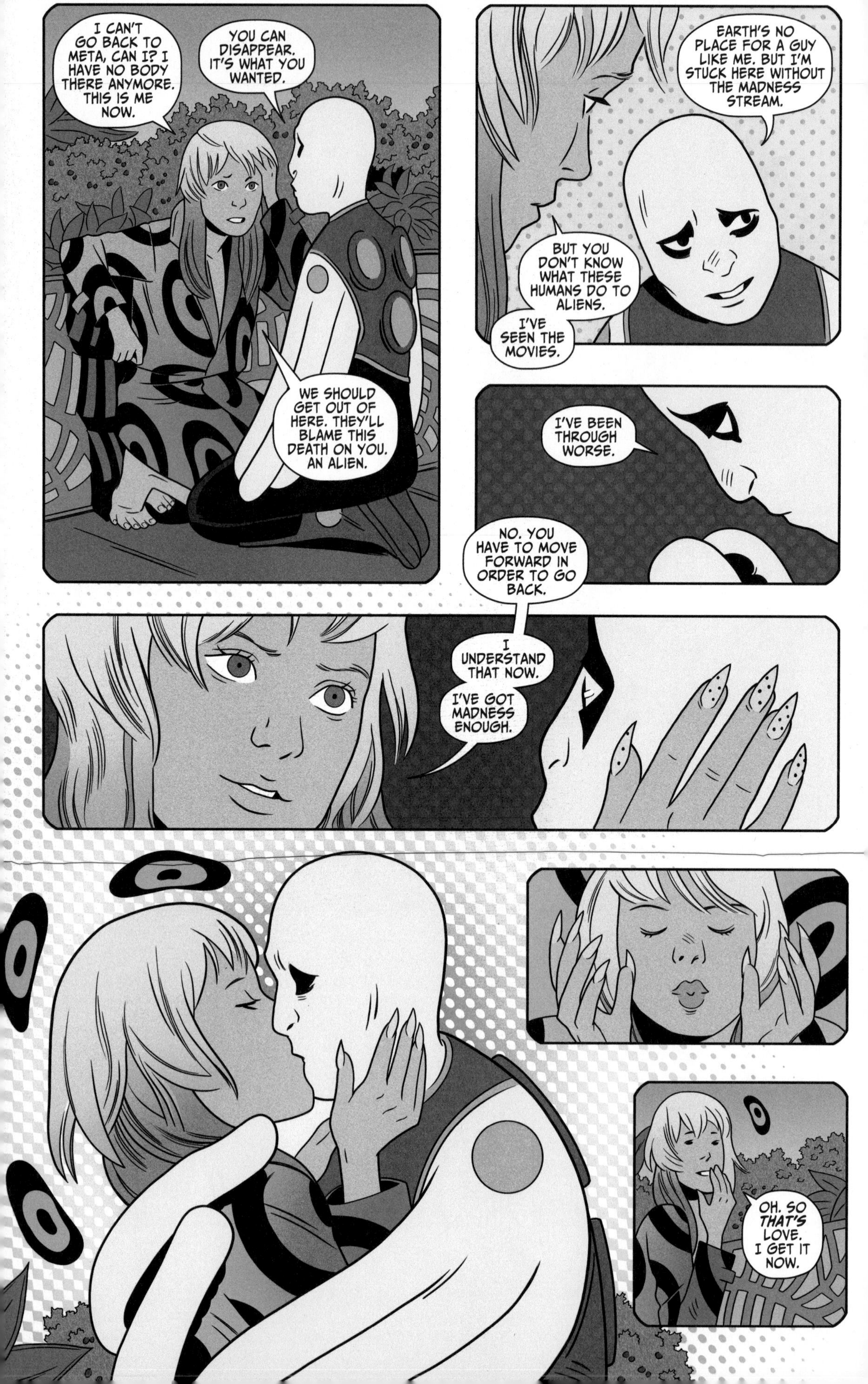
I CAN'T GO BACK TO META, CAN I? I HAVE NO BODY THERE ANYMORE. THIS IS ME NOW.
YOU CAN DISAPPEAR. IT'S WHAT YOU WANTED.
WE SHOULD GET OUT OF HERE. THEY'LL BLAME THIS DEATH ON YOU. AN ALIEN.
EARTH'S NO PLACE FOR A GUY LIKE ME. BUT I'M STUCK HERE WITHOUT THE MADNESS STREAM.
BUT YOU DON'T KNOW WHAT THESE HUMANS DO TO ALIENS.
I'VE SEEN THE MOVIES.
I'VE BEEN THROUGH WORSE.
NO. YOU HAVE TO MOVE FORWARD IN ORDER TO GO BACK.
I UNDERSTAND THAT NOW.
I'VE GOT MADNESS ENOUGH.
OH. SO *THAT'S* LOVE. I GET IT NOW.

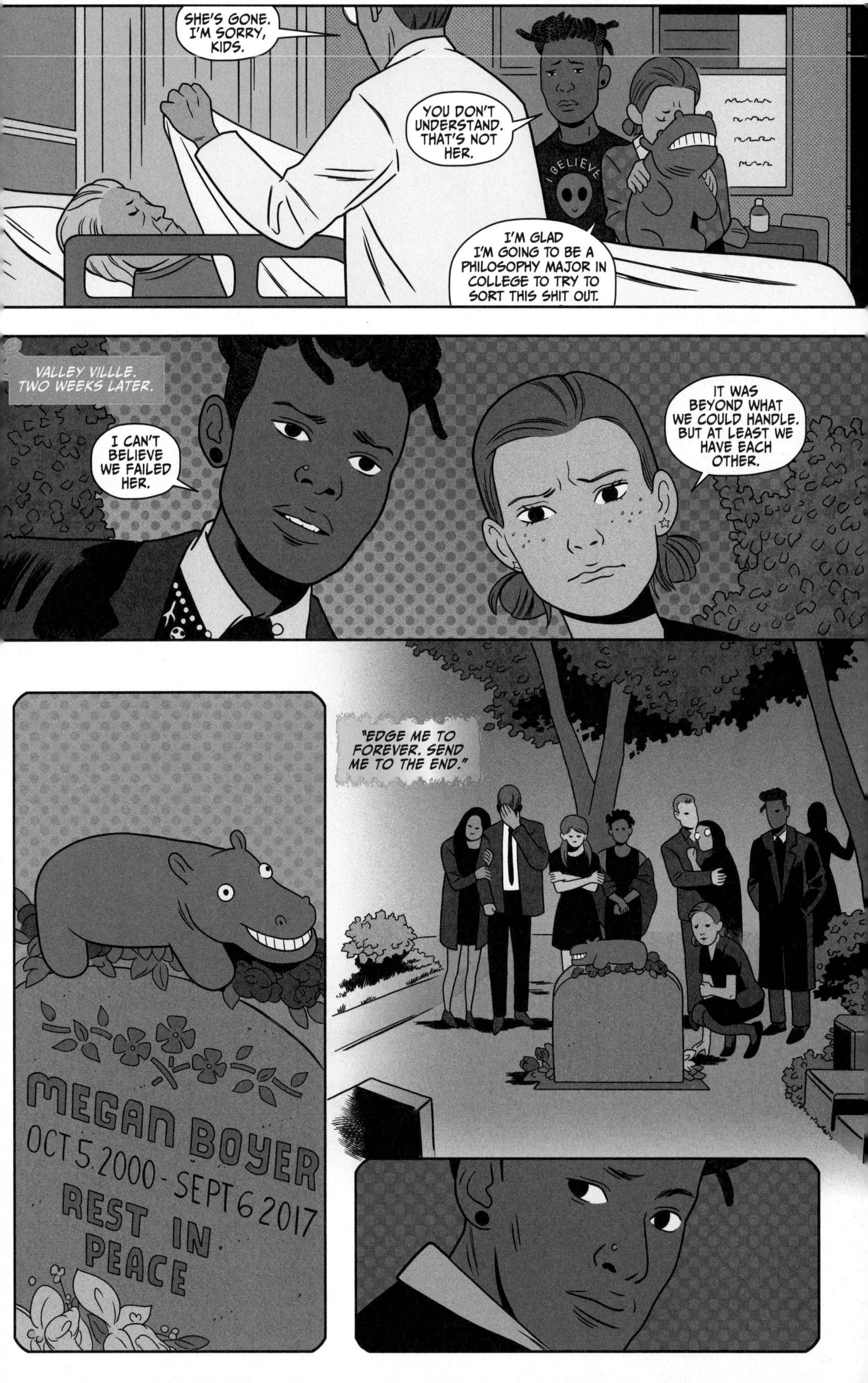
SHE'S GONE. I'M SORRY, KIDS.
YOU DON'T UNDERSTAND. THAT'S NOT HER.
I BELIEVE
I'M GLAD I'M GOING TO BE A PHILOSOPHY MAJOR IN COLLEGE TO TRY TO SORT THIS SHIT OUT.
VALLEY VILLLE. TWO WEEKS LATER.
I CAN'T BELIEVE WE FAILED HER.
IT WAS BEYOND WHAT WE COULD HANDLE. BUT AT LEAST WE HAVE EACH OTHER.
"EDGE ME TO FOREVER. SEND ME TO THE END."
MEGAN BOYER
OCT 5. 2000 - SEPT 6 2017
REST IN PEACE

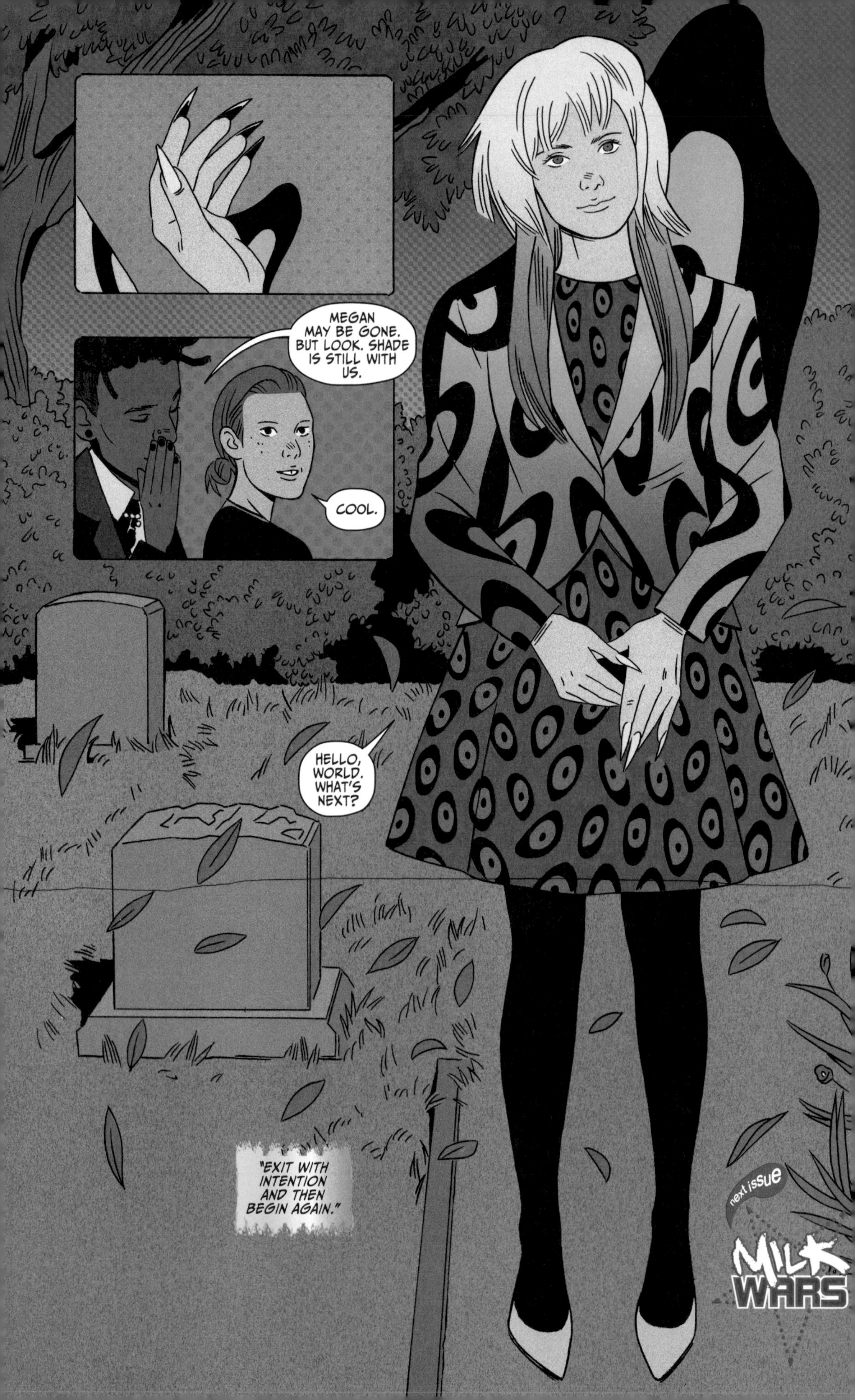
MEGAN MAY BE GONE. BUT LOOK. SHADE IS STILL WITH US.
COOL.
HELLO, WORLD. WHAT'S NEXT?
"EXIT WITH INTENTION AND THEN BEGIN AGAIN."
next issue
MILK WARS

Who's Who

DC's Young Animal

PERSONAL DATA

Name: Becky Cloonan
Occupation: Cover Artist
First Appearance: SHADE, THE CHANGING GIRL #1

HISTORY

My secret origins have been declassified, so I suppose it's safe to share.

I grew up in a small town in New Hampshire, and as soon as I discovered comic books, I knew that's what I would dedicate my life to (much to the dismay of my parents, I'm sure). I was pretty singular in this goal, but the '90s were rough. After a treacherous journey through high school, I decided to go to college for animation instead, at the School of Visual Arts in NYC. It was a good time. I expanded my horizons and met people I still count among my friends. My time at SVA only lasted a few years, however; I dropped out and ended up making comics anyway. Nothing I could do—it was pre-ordained. It wasn't an easy path—there were new challenges every day. But here I am, and I wouldn't change it for anything! ♥

THE PROCESS OF MAKING A SHADE COVER

Let's talk about two very different SHADE covers. She keeps getting more and more fun to draw! Usually I'll do a few sketches, like we can see with SHADE #7. Since issue #6 was so crazy, I wanted something fun for issue #7. The prom issue. We all agreed Shade in a fancy dress made of feathers would do nicely.

If I don't have a clear vision for how the cover should look, I'll do a couple of sketches and send them over. My thumbnails are a little hard to read, but if you squint and tilt your head you might see that the first sketch is a close-up of Shade, dress billowing out around her. The second is Shade sitting again, but a bit more elegant, more refined. The third is Shade sitting on a trapeze, and the fourth… (squints) (tilts head) we used the second one, so the fourth is not important.

I work digitally for the SHADE covers, so my process is a little lost here, I'm sorry to say. I did a few sketches of dress ideas, but after that I went straight to final, trying to give her a mid-'60s look, with the shapes and madness and colors. This cover was a lot of fun and pretty, in the end, but it doesn't tell as much of a story as the next issue…

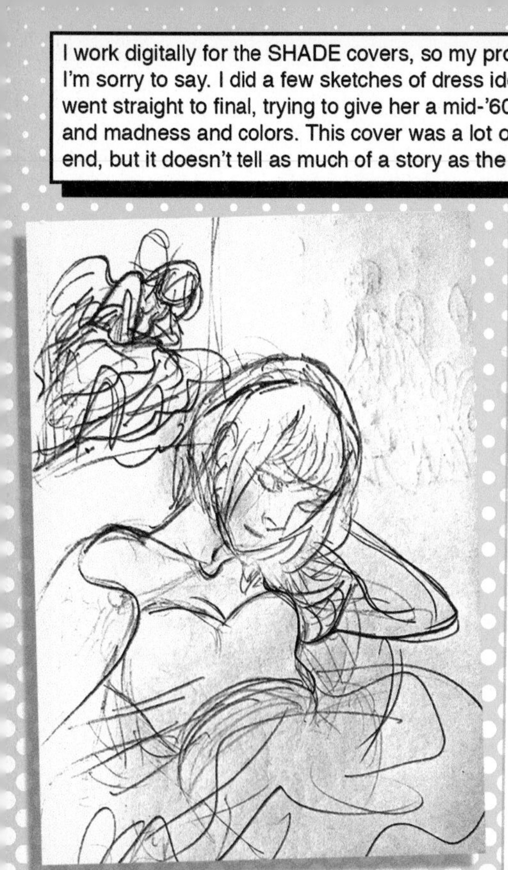

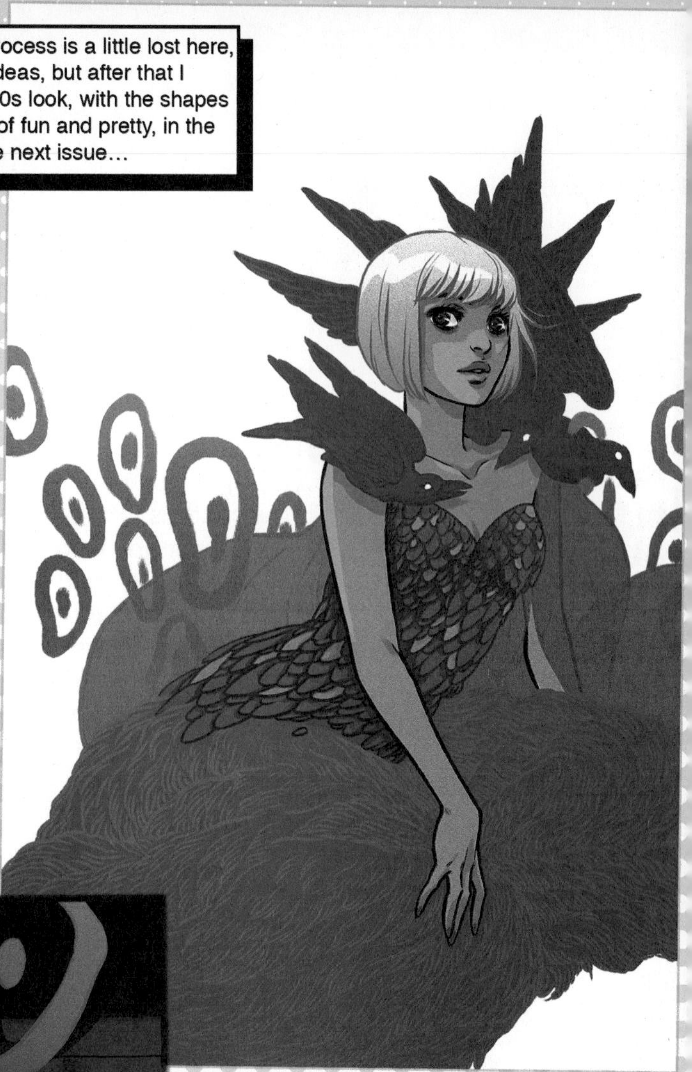

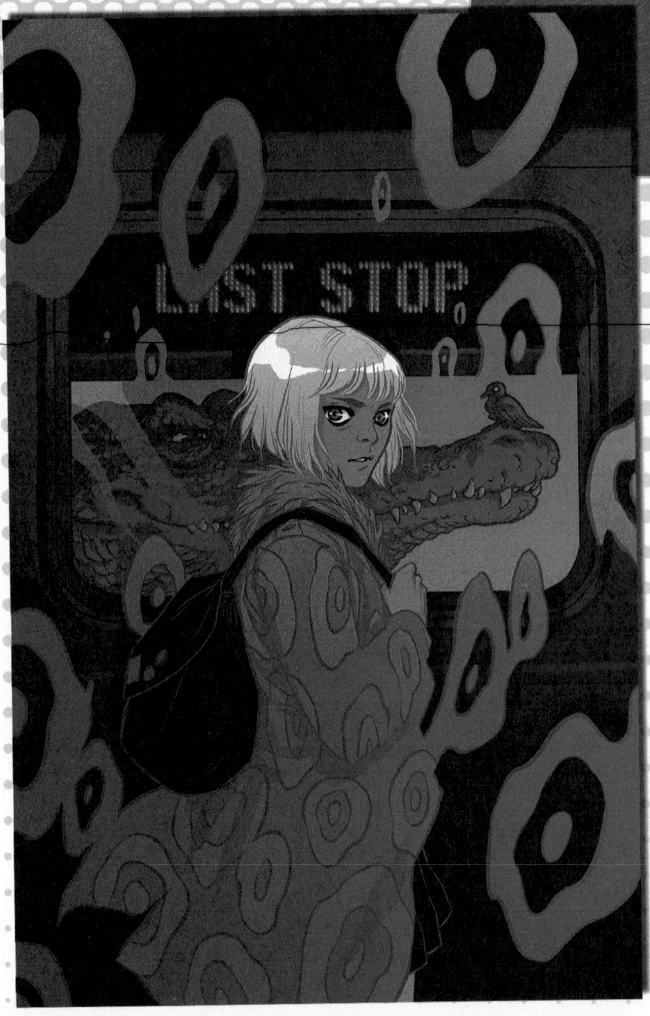
LAST STOP

ISSUE #8! I had an idea in my head for this cover the second I heard what it was about. Shade in the City! Of course it had to be on the subway. My rough here was more for me to double-check that the composition that I saw in my head would work on paper. Shade standing in front of some subway doors. A quick doodle of her expression, and voilà!

A few changes to the final: mostly instead of standing by the door she is against a window. I love how the bright pinks and purples play against the gray of the subway car. Working with these colors is one of the most fun things about doing these. I'm constantly trying to find new ways to use the color, and often surprise myself along the way. I also get inspired by the way Marley draws—I want to keep the cover art faithful to the spirit of the comic, and help tell the story—from the second you see the book on the shelf to the turn of the last page. I'm so proud to be a part of Team Shade!

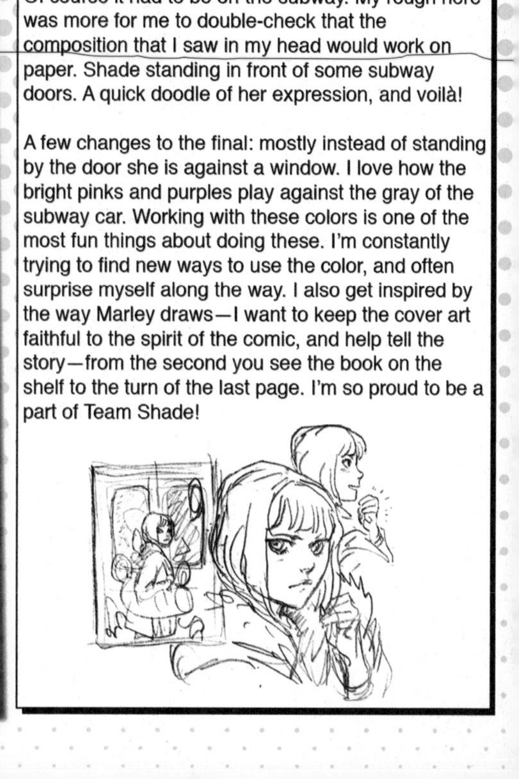

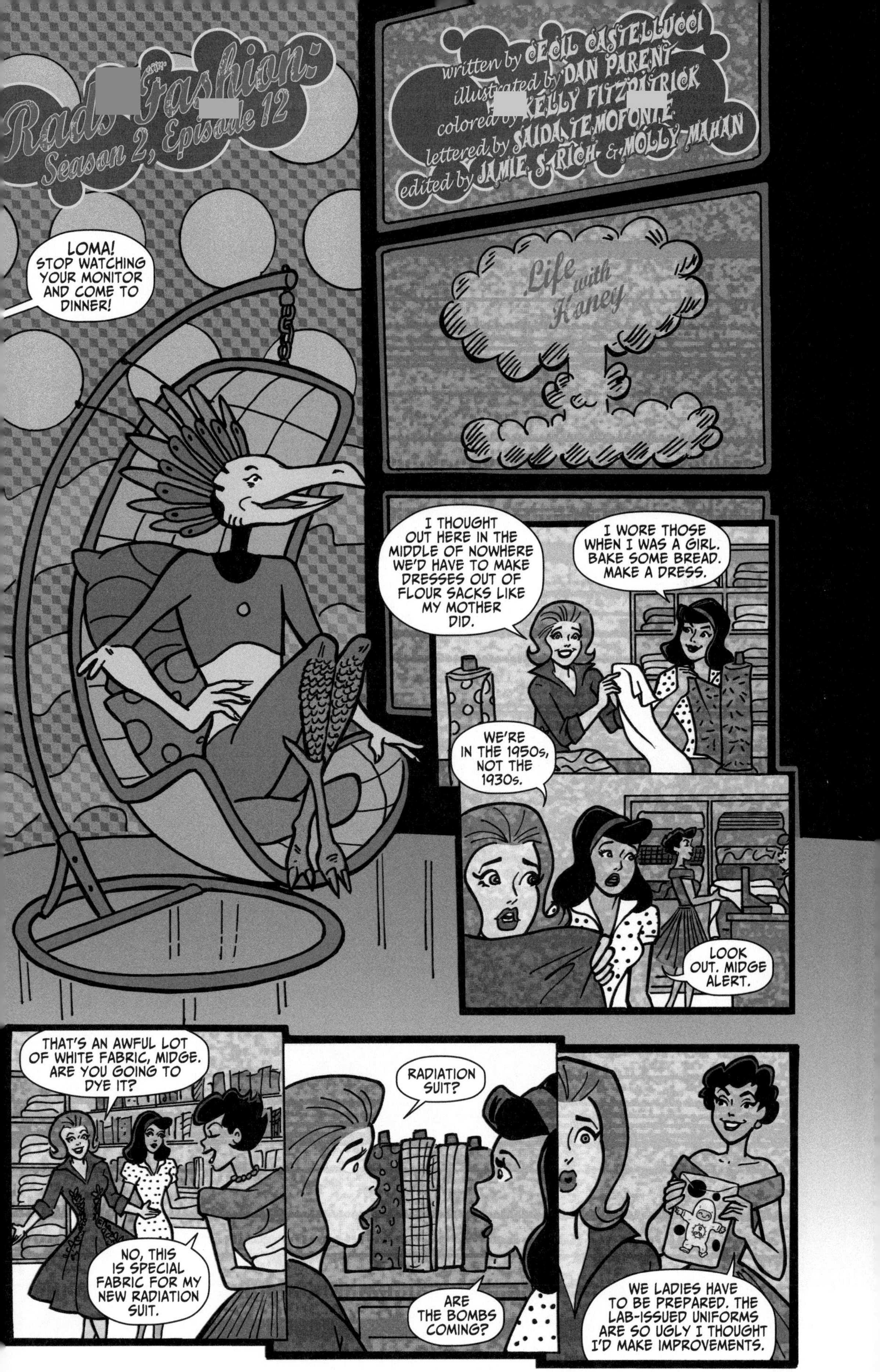
Rads [redacted] Fashion: Season 2, Episode 12
written by CECIL CASTELLUCCI
illustrated by DAN PARENT
colored by [redacted] KELLY FITZ[redacted]RICK
lettered by SAIDA TEMOFONTE
edited by JAMIE S. RICH & MOLLY MAHAN
LOMA! STOP WATCHING YOUR MONITOR AND COME TO DINNER!
Life with Kaney
I THOUGHT OUT HERE IN THE MIDDLE OF NOWHERE WE'D HAVE TO MAKE DRESSES OUT OF FLOUR SACKS LIKE MY MOTHER DID.
I WORE THOSE WHEN I WAS A GIRL. BAKE SOME BREAD. MAKE A DRESS.
WE'RE IN THE 1950s, NOT THE 1930s.
LOOK OUT. MIDGE ALERT.
THAT'S AN AWFUL LOT OF WHITE FABRIC, MIDGE. ARE YOU GOING TO DYE IT?
NO, THIS IS SPECIAL FABRIC FOR MY NEW RADIATION SUIT.
RADIATION SUIT?
ARE THE BOMBS COMING?
WE LADIES HAVE TO BE PREPARED. THE LAB-ISSUED UNIFORMS ARE SO UGLY I THOUGHT I'D MAKE IMPROVEMENTS.

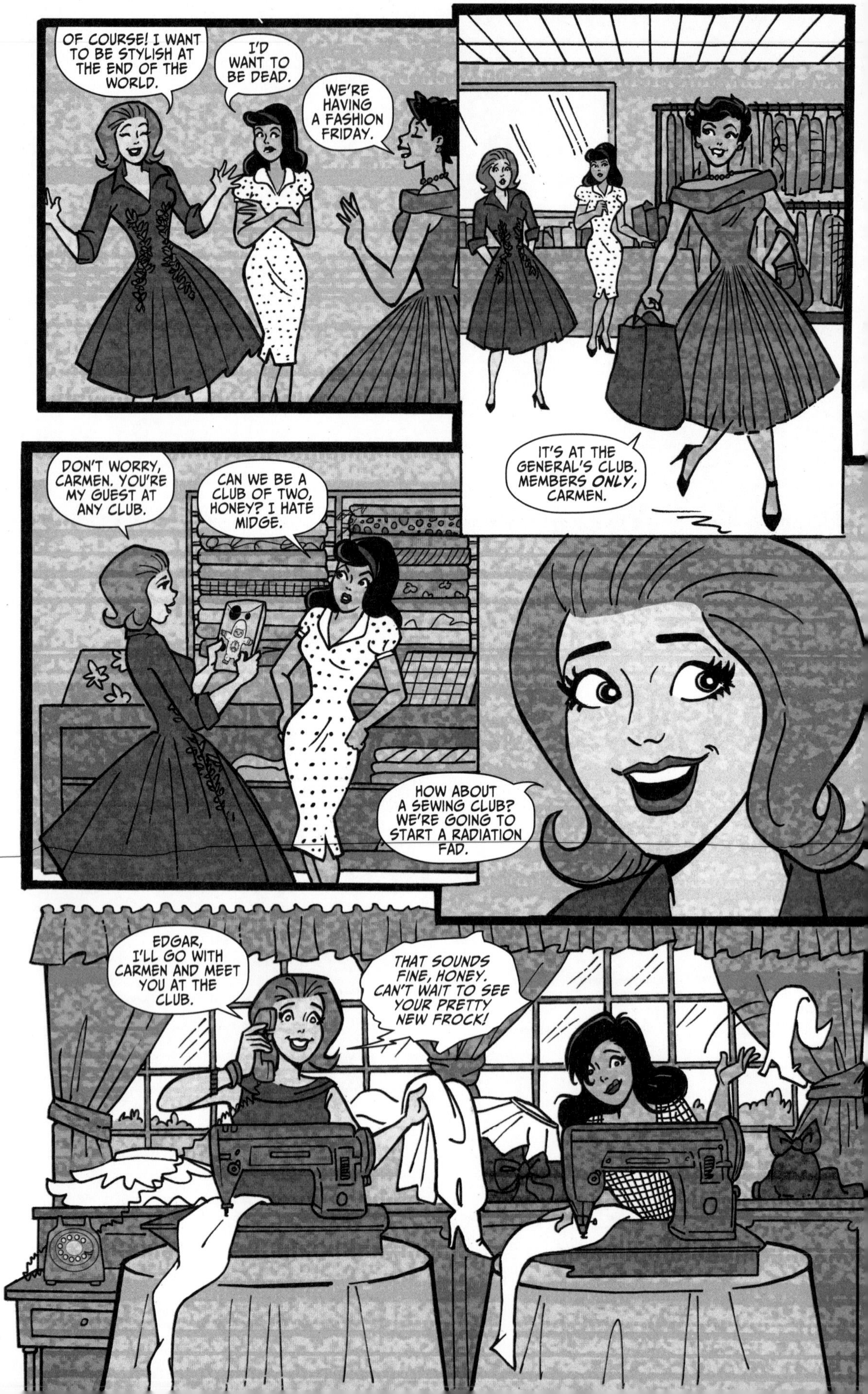
OF COURSE! I WANT TO BE STYLISH AT THE END OF THE WORLD.
I'D WANT TO BE DEAD.
WE'RE HAVING A FASHION FRIDAY.
IT'S AT THE GENERAL'S CLUB. MEMBERS ONLY, CARMEN.
DON'T WORRY, CARMEN. YOU'RE MY GUEST AT ANY CLUB.
CAN WE BE A CLUB OF TWO, HONEY? I HATE MIDGE.
HOW ABOUT A SEWING CLUB? WE'RE GOING TO START A RADIATION FAD.
EDGAR, I'LL GO WITH CARMEN AND MEET YOU AT THE CLUB.
THAT SOUNDS FINE, HONEY. CAN'T WAIT TO SEE YOUR PRETTY NEW FROCK!

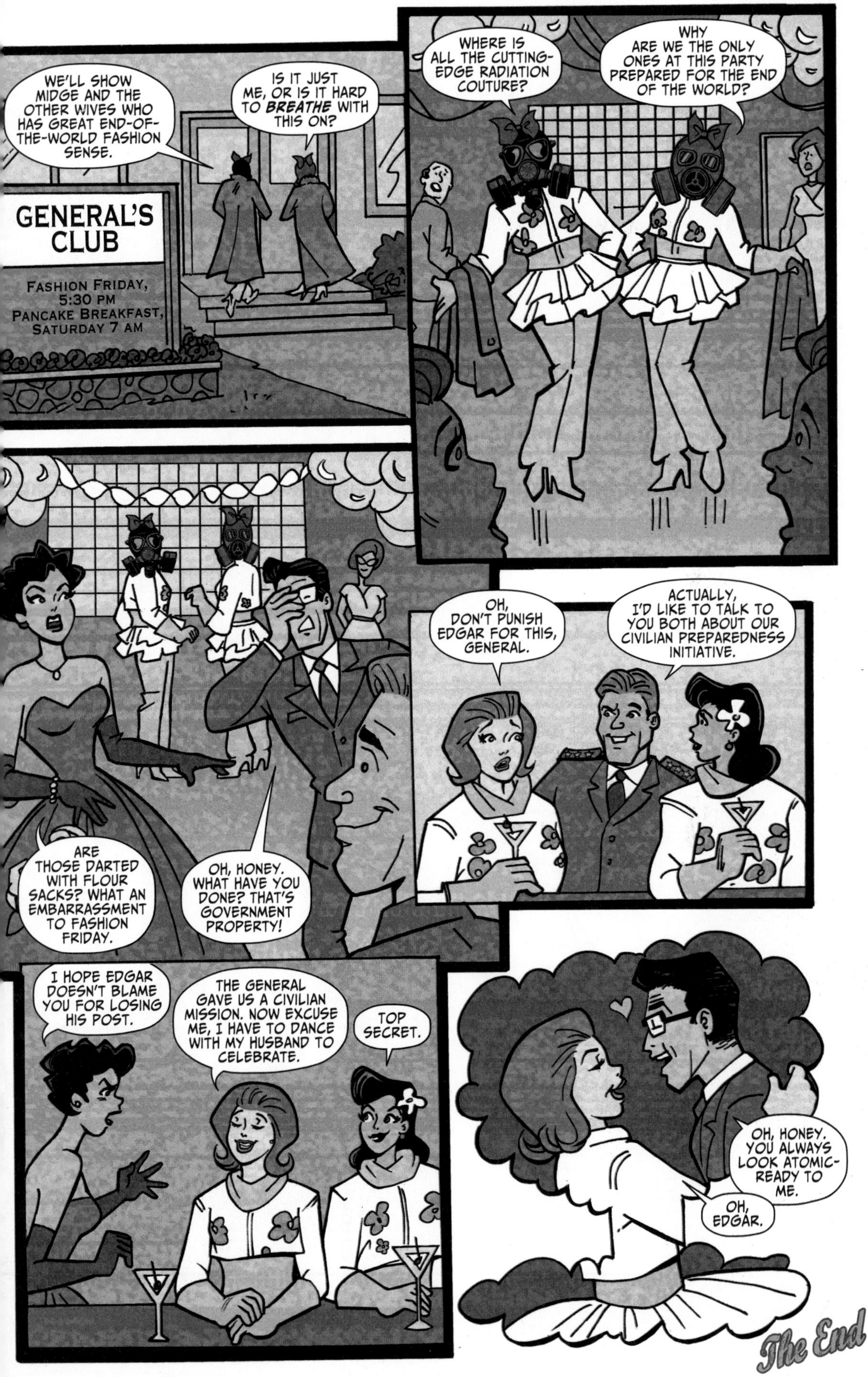
WE'LL SHOW MIDGE AND THE OTHER WIVES WHO HAS GREAT END-OF-THE-WORLD FASHION SENSE.
IS IT JUST ME, OR IS IT HARD TO BREATHE WITH THIS ON?
GENERAL'S CLUB
FASHION FRIDAY, 5:30 PM
PANCAKE BREAKFAST, SATURDAY 7 AM
WHERE IS ALL THE CUTTING-EDGE RADIATION COUTURE?
WHY ARE WE THE ONLY ONES AT THIS PARTY PREPARED FOR THE END OF THE WORLD?
ARE THOSE DARTED WITH FLOUR SACKS? WHAT AN EMBARRASSMENT TO FASHION FRIDAY.
OH, HONEY. WHAT HAVE YOU DONE? THAT'S GOVERNMENT PROPERTY!
OH, DON'T PUNISH EDGAR FOR THIS, GENERAL.
ACTUALLY, I'D LIKE TO TALK TO YOU BOTH ABOUT OUR CIVILIAN PREPAREDNESS INITIATIVE.
I HOPE EDGAR DOESN'T BLAME YOU FOR LOSING HIS POST.
THE GENERAL GAVE US A CIVILIAN MISSION. NOW EXCUSE ME, I HAVE TO DANCE WITH MY HUSBAND TO CELEBRATE.
TOP SECRET.
OH, HONEY. YOU ALWAYS LOOK ATOMIC-READY TO ME.
OH, EDGAR.
The End

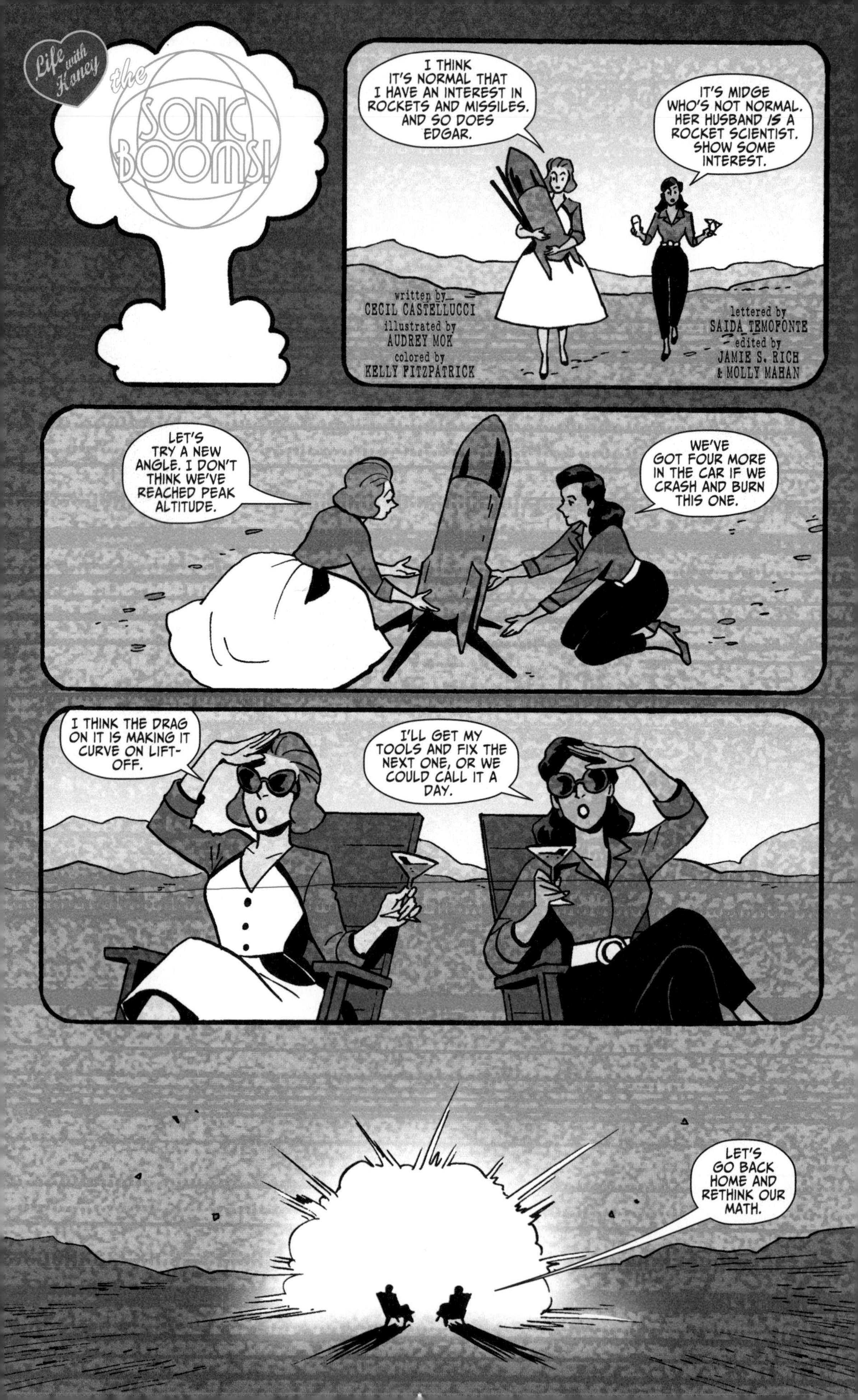
Life with Honey
the SONIC BOOMS!
I THINK IT'S NORMAL THAT I HAVE AN INTEREST IN ROCKETS AND MISSILES. AND SO DOES EDGAR.
IT'S MIDGE WHO'S NOT NORMAL. HER HUSBAND IS A ROCKET SCIENTIST. SHOW SOME INTEREST.
written by CECIL CASTELLUCCI
illustrated by AUDREY MOK
colored by KELLY FITZPATRICK
lettered by SAIDA TEMOFONTE
edited by JAMIE S. RICH & MOLLY MAHAN
LET'S TRY A NEW ANGLE. I DON'T THINK WE'VE REACHED PEAK ALTITUDE.
WE'VE GOT FOUR MORE IN THE CAR IF WE CRASH AND BURN THIS ONE.
I THINK THE DRAG ON IT IS MAKING IT CURVE ON LIFT-OFF.
I'LL GET MY TOOLS AND FIX THE NEXT ONE, OR WE COULD CALL IT A DAY.
LET'S GO BACK HOME AND RETHINK OUR MATH.

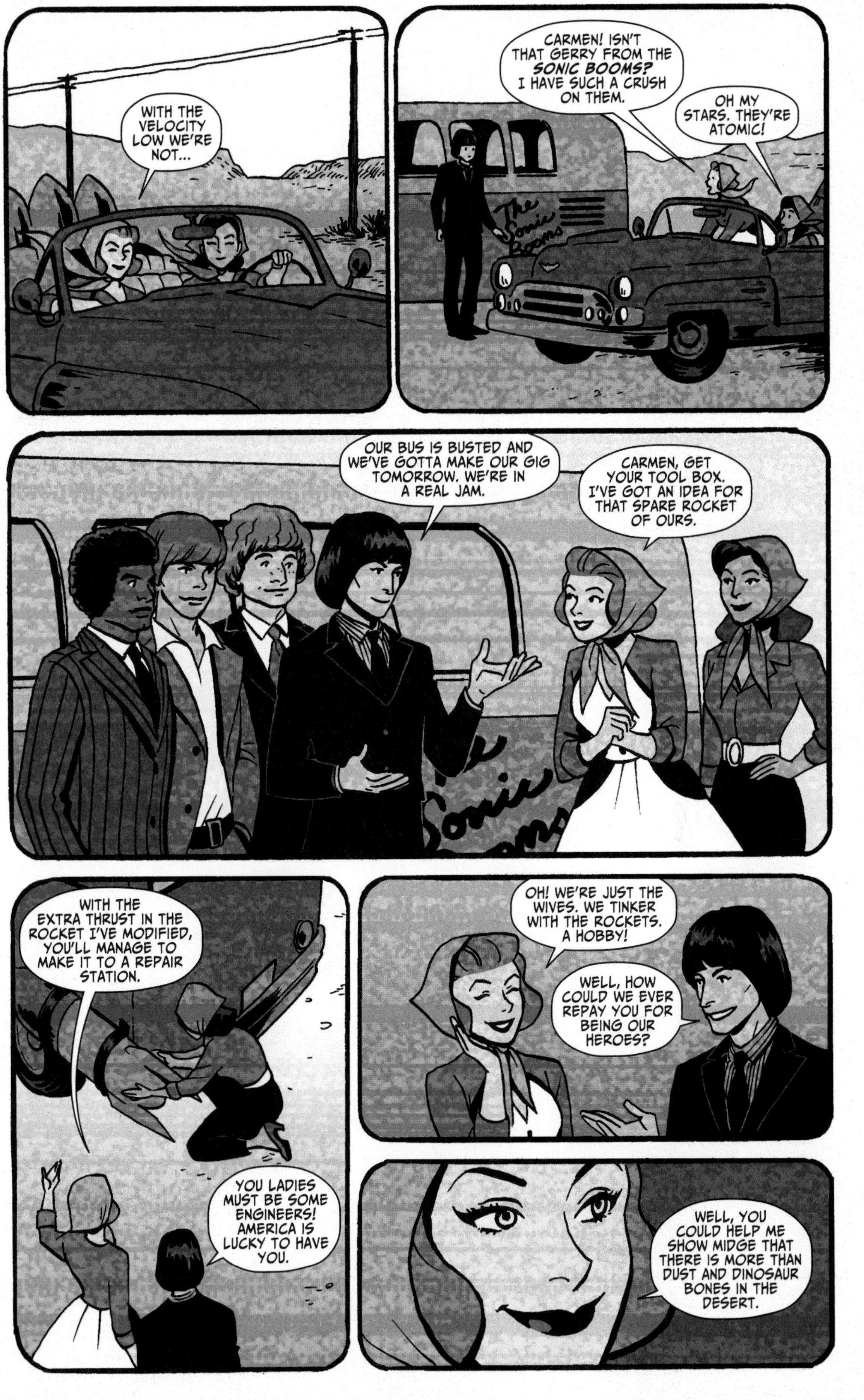
WITH THE VELOCITY LOW WE'RE NOT...
CARMEN! ISN'T THAT GERRY FROM THE SONIC BOOMS? I HAVE SUCH A CRUSH ON THEM.
OH MY STARS. THEY'RE ATOMIC!
The Sonic Booms
OUR BUS IS BUSTED AND WE'VE GOTTA MAKE OUR GIG TOMORROW. WE'RE IN A REAL JAM.
CARMEN, GET YOUR TOOL BOX. I'VE GOT AN IDEA FOR THAT SPARE ROCKET OF OURS.
WITH THE EXTRA THRUST IN THE ROCKET I'VE MODIFIED, YOU'LL MANAGE TO MAKE IT TO A REPAIR STATION.
YOU LADIES MUST BE SOME ENGINEERS! AMERICA IS LUCKY TO HAVE YOU.
OH! WE'RE JUST THE WIVES. WE TINKER WITH THE ROCKETS. A HOBBY!
WELL, HOW COULD WE EVER REPAY YOU FOR BEING OUR HEROES?
WELL, YOU COULD HELP ME SHOW MIDGE THAT THERE IS MORE THAN DUST AND DINOSAUR BONES IN THE DESERT.

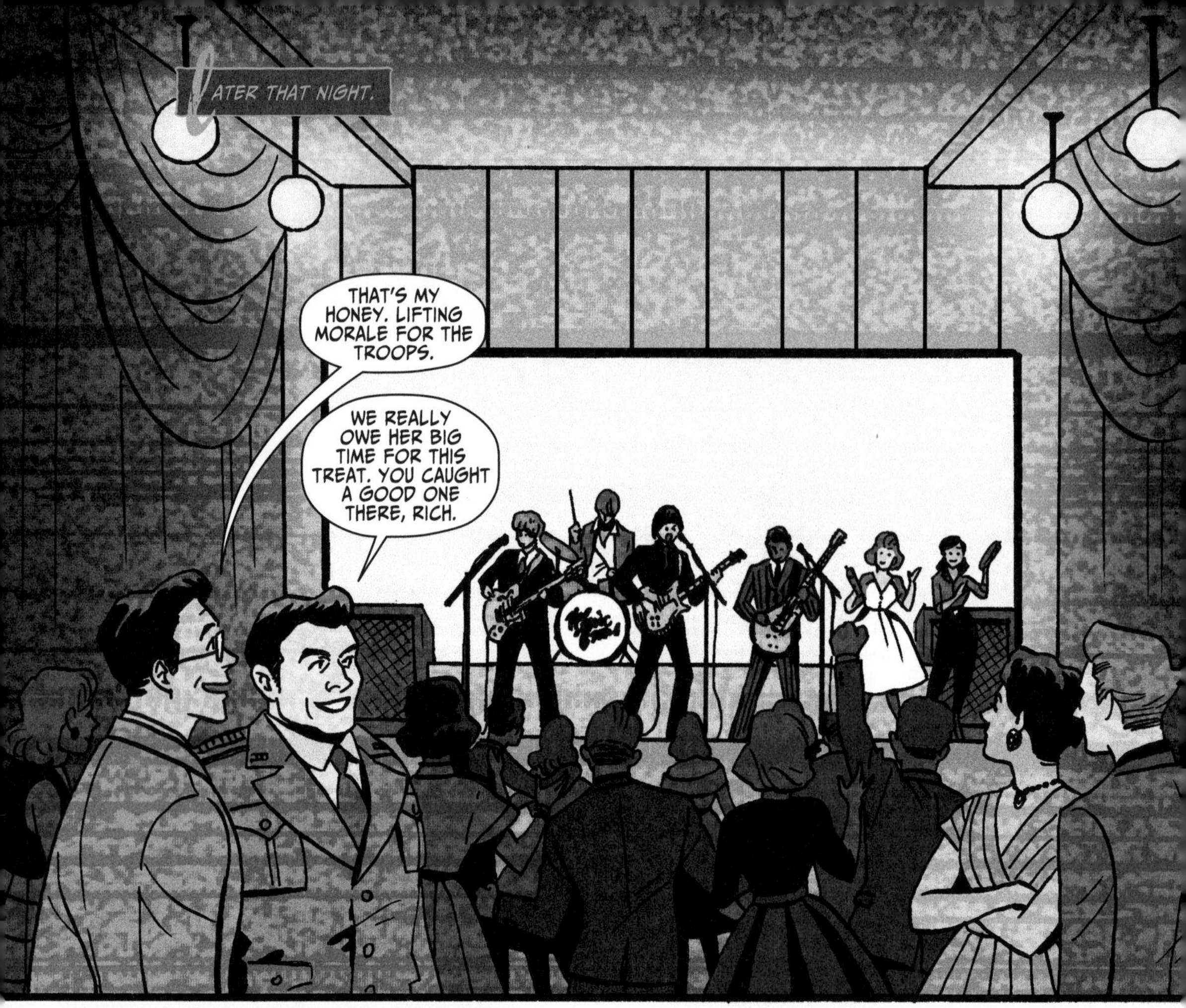
LATER THAT NIGHT.
THAT'S MY HONEY. LIFTING MORALE FOR THE TROOPS.
WE REALLY OWE HER BIG TIME FOR THIS TREAT. YOU CAUGHT A GOOD ONE THERE, RICH.

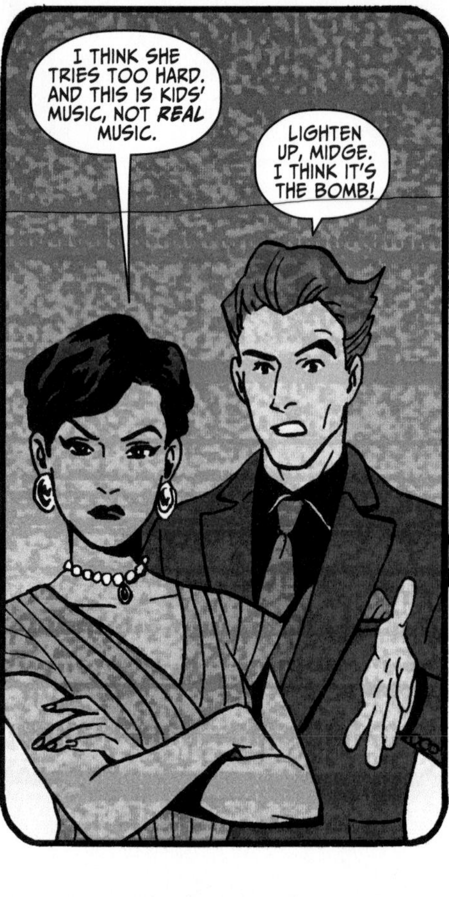
I THINK SHE TRIES TOO HARD. AND THIS IS KIDS' MUSIC, NOT REAL MUSIC.
LIGHTEN UP, MIDGE. I THINK IT'S THE BOMB!

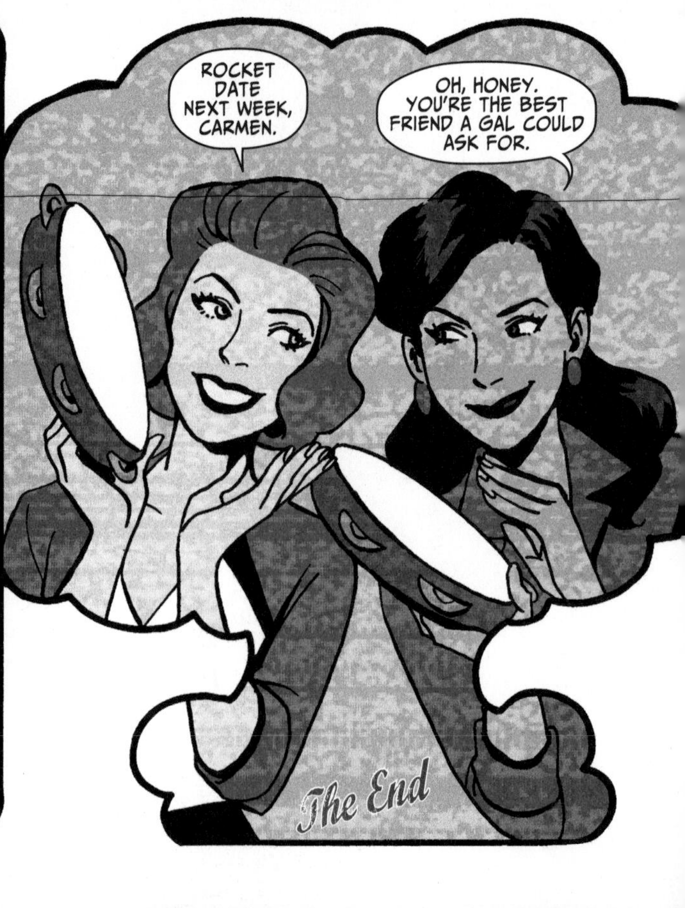
ROCKET DATE NEXT WEEK, CARMEN.
OH, HONEY. YOU'RE THE BEST FRIEND A GAL COULD ASK FOR.
The End

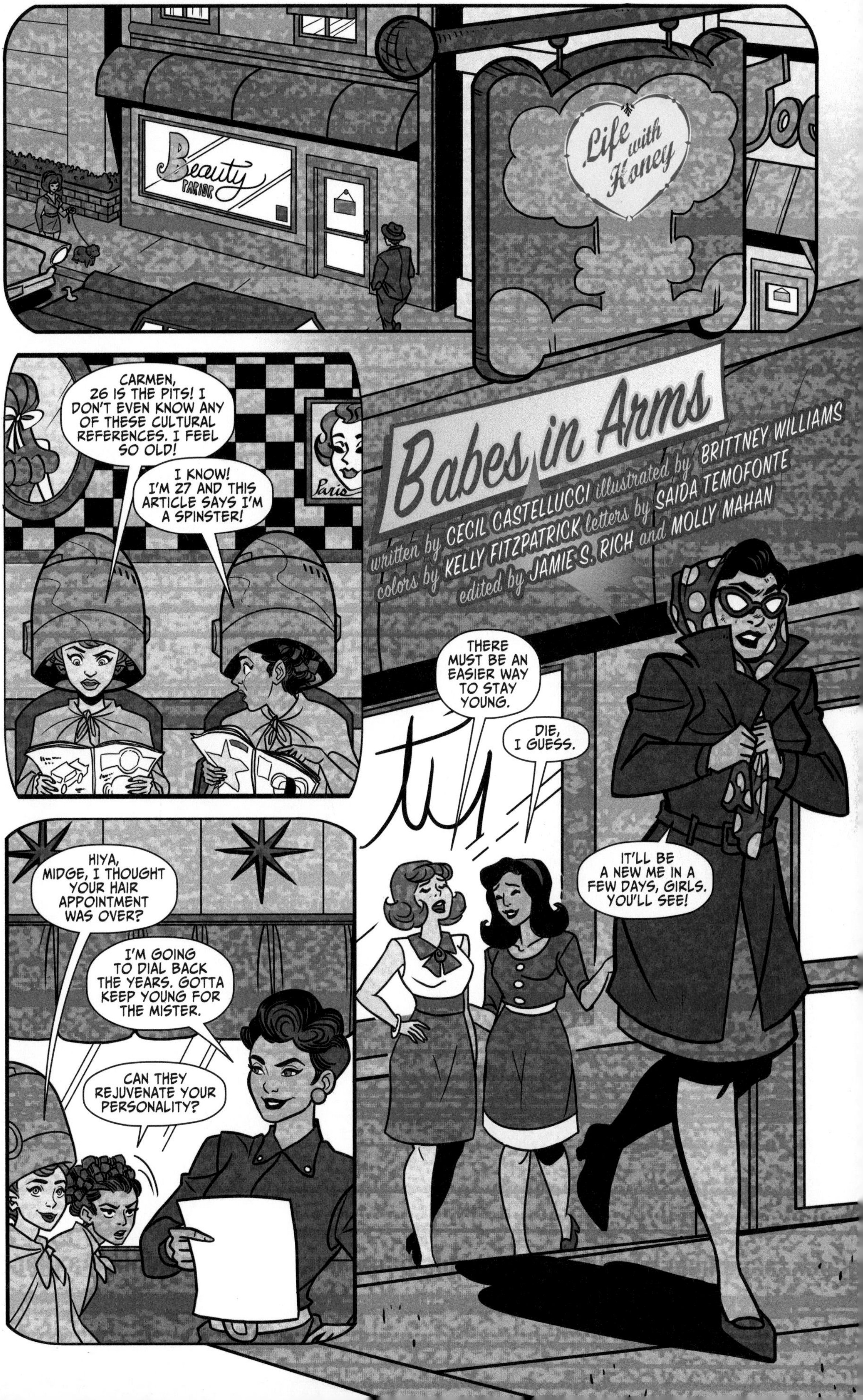
Beauty PARLOR
Life with Honey
CARMEN, 26 IS THE PITS! I DON'T EVEN KNOW ANY OF THESE CULTURAL REFERENCES. I FEEL SO OLD!
I KNOW! I'M 27 AND THIS ARTICLE SAYS I'M A SPINSTER!
Paris
Babes in Arms
written by CECIL CASTELLUCCI illustrated by BRITTNEY WILLIAMS
colors by KELLY FITZPATRICK letters by SAIDA TEMOFONTE
edited by JAMIE S. RICH and MOLLY MAHAN
HIYA, MIDGE, I THOUGHT YOUR HAIR APPOINTMENT WAS OVER?
I'M GOING TO DIAL BACK THE YEARS. GOTTA KEEP YOUNG FOR THE MISTER.
CAN THEY REJUVENATE YOUR PERSONALITY?
THERE MUST BE AN EASIER WAY TO STAY YOUNG.
DIE, I GUESS.
IT'LL BE A NEW ME IN A FEW DAYS, GIRLS. YOU'LL SEE!

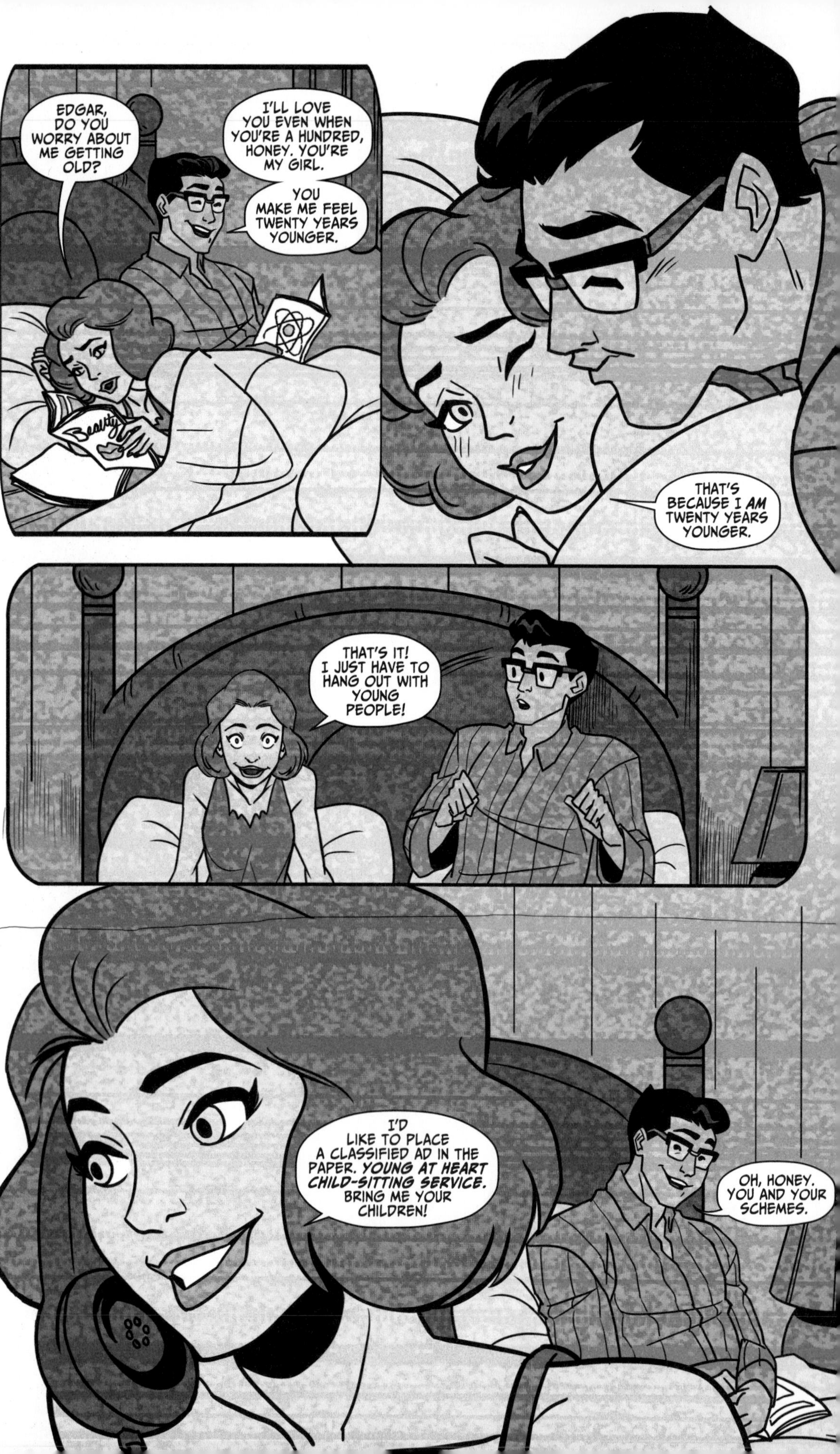
EDGAR, DO YOU WORRY ABOUT ME GETTING OLD?
I'LL LOVE YOU EVEN WHEN YOU'RE A HUNDRED, HONEY. YOU'RE MY GIRL.
YOU MAKE ME FEEL TWENTY YEARS YOUNGER.
Beauty
THAT'S BECAUSE I *AM* TWENTY YEARS YOUNGER.
THAT'S IT! I JUST HAVE TO HANG OUT WITH YOUNG PEOPLE!
I'D LIKE TO PLACE A CLASSIFIED AD IN THE PAPER. ***YOUNG AT HEART CHILD-SITTING SERVICE.*** BRING ME YOUR CHILDREN!
OH, HONEY. YOU AND YOUR SCHEMES.

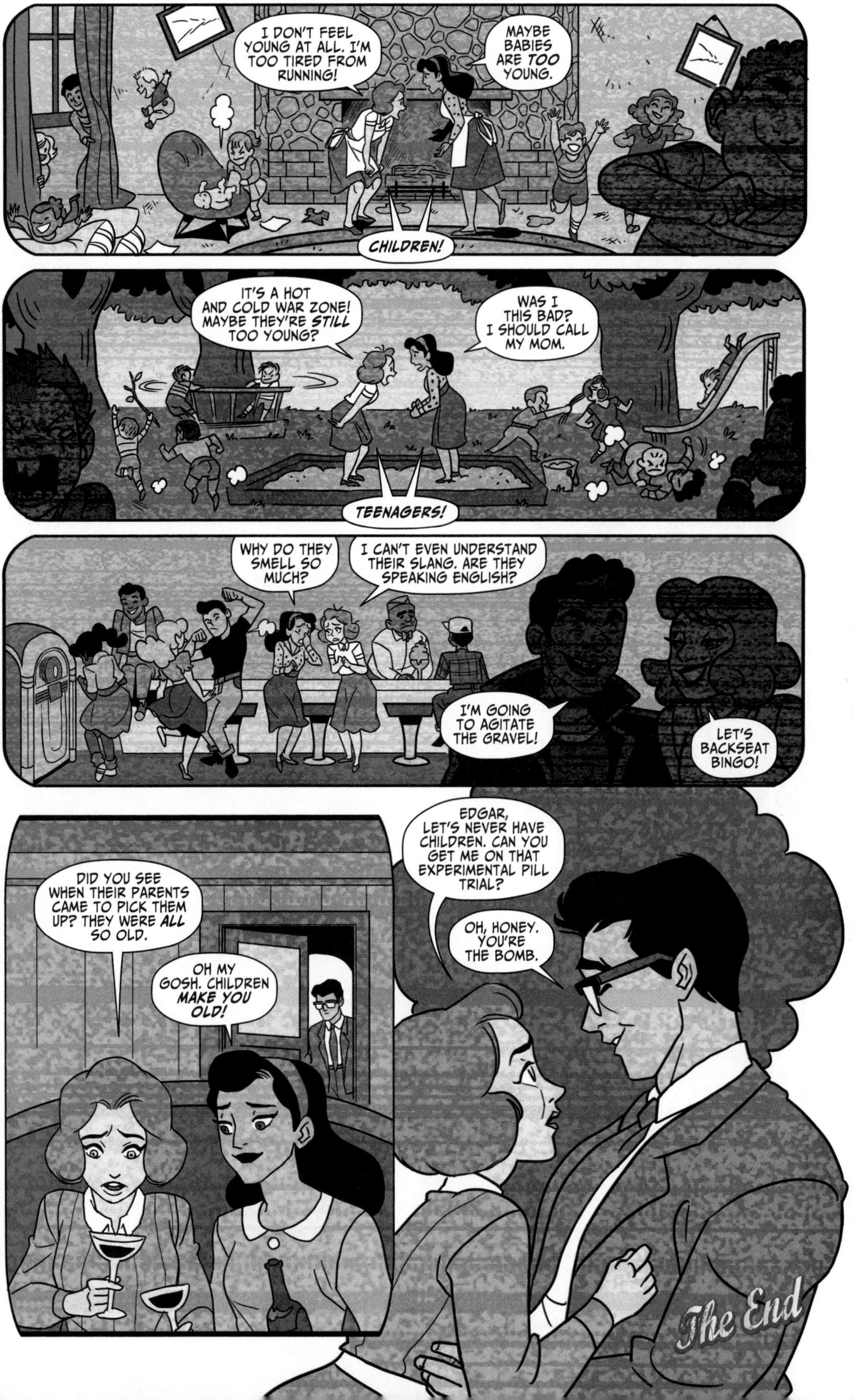
I DON'T FEEL YOUNG AT ALL. I'M TOO TIRED FROM RUNNING!
MAYBE BABIES ARE *TOO* YOUNG.
CHILDREN!
IT'S A HOT AND COLD WAR ZONE! MAYBE THEY'RE *STILL* TOO YOUNG?
WAS I THIS BAD? I SHOULD CALL MY MOM.
TEENAGERS!
WHY DO THEY SMELL SO MUCH?
I CAN'T EVEN UNDERSTAND THEIR SLANG. ARE THEY SPEAKING ENGLISH?
I'M GOING TO AGITATE THE GRAVEL!
LET'S BACKSEAT BINGO!
DID YOU SEE WHEN THEIR PARENTS CAME TO PICK THEM UP? THEY WERE *ALL* SO OLD.
OH MY GOSH. CHILDREN *MAKE YOU OLD!*
EDGAR, LET'S NEVER HAVE CHILDREN. CAN YOU GET ME ON THAT EXPERIMENTAL PILL TRIAL?
OH, HONEY. YOU'RE THE BOMB.
The End

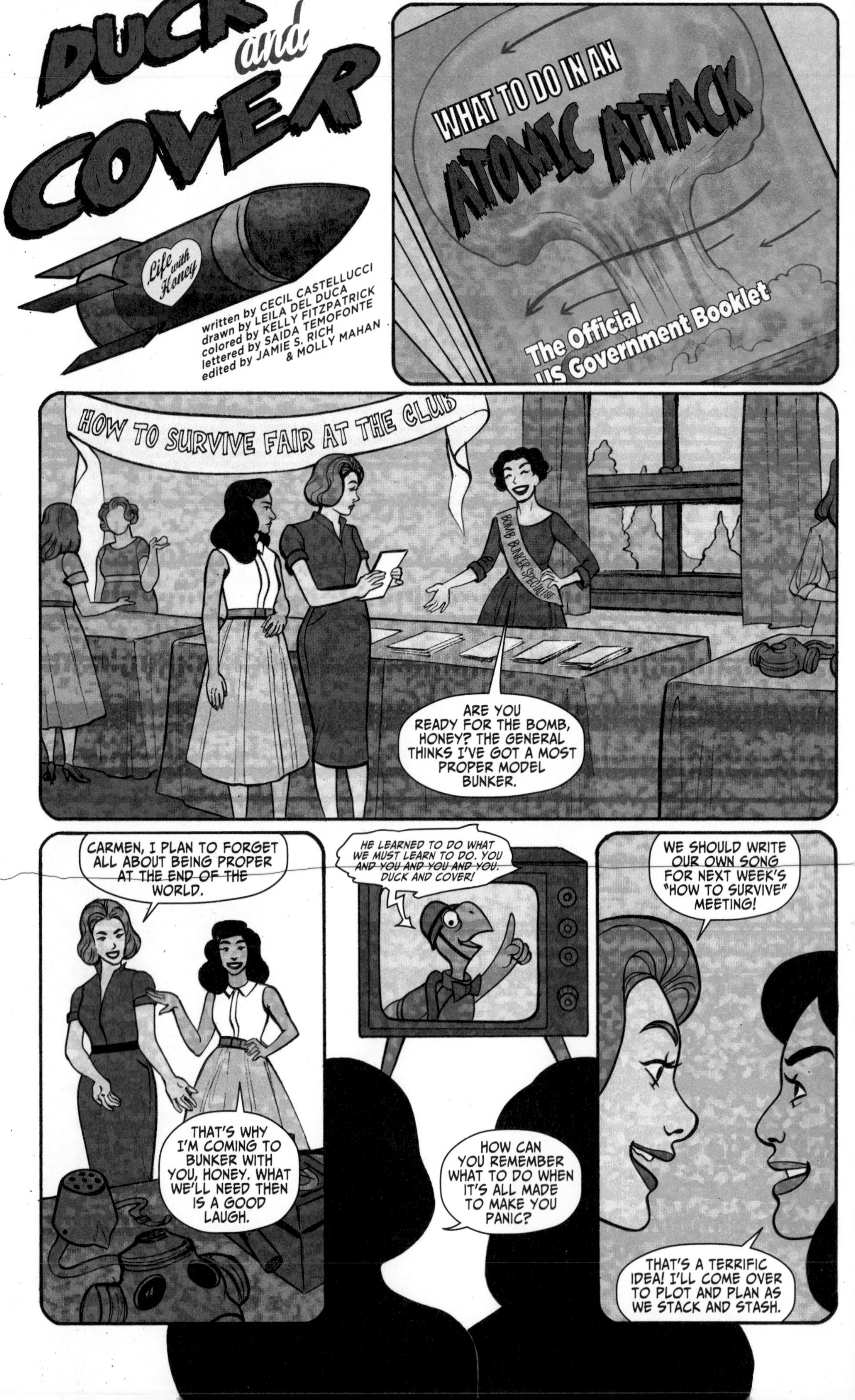
DUCK and COVER
Life with Honey
written by CECIL CASTELLUCCI
drawn by LEILA DEL DUCA
colored by KELLY FITZPATRICK
lettered by SAIDA TEMOFONTE
edited by JAMIE S. RICH & MOLLY MAHAN
WHAT TO DO IN AN ATOMIC ATTACK
The Official US Government Booklet
HOW TO SURVIVE FAIR AT THE CLUB
BOMB BUNKER SPECIALIST
ARE YOU READY FOR THE BOMB, HONEY? THE GENERAL THINKS I'VE GOT A MOST PROPER MODEL BUNKER.
CARMEN, I PLAN TO FORGET ALL ABOUT BEING PROPER AT THE END OF THE WORLD.
THAT'S WHY I'M COMING TO BUNKER WITH YOU, HONEY. WHAT WE'LL NEED THEN IS A GOOD LAUGH.
HE LEARNED TO DO WHAT WE MUST LEARN TO DO. YOU AND YOU AND YOU AND YOU. DUCK AND COVER!
HOW CAN YOU REMEMBER WHAT TO DO WHEN IT'S ALL MADE TO MAKE YOU PANIC?
WE SHOULD WRITE OUR OWN SONG FOR NEXT WEEK'S "HOW TO SURVIVE" MEETING!
THAT'S A TERRIFIC IDEA! I'LL COME OVER TO PLOT AND PLAN AS WE STACK AND STASH.

SO WE CAN'T SAY ANYTHING THAT IS A SECRET, ONLY THE INFORMATION A LADY NEEDS TO KNOW.
DO YOU KNOW ATOMIC SECRETS, HONEY?
WELL, SOMETIMES EDGAR MUMBLES IN HIS SLEEP. OR I SEE SOME EQUATIONS OPEN ON HIS DESK.
WOW. IF YOU WERE CAUGHT BY THE SOVIETS, YOU WOULDN'T EVEN KNOW WHAT YOU KNOW.
THE ONLY THING I KNOW BESIDES COMPLICATED MATH ARE THE STEPS TO OUR SONG AND TO OUR DANCE.
YOU DON'T THINK THEY'LL REALLY DROP THE BOMB, DO YOU?
NO, THAT WOULD BE JUST MADNESS, WOULDN'T IT?
HONEY'S BUNKER

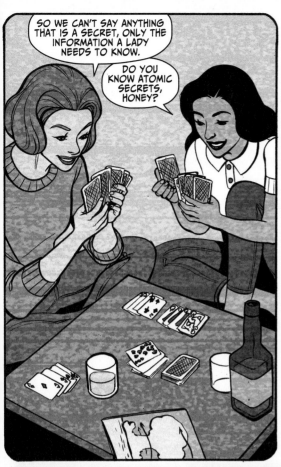

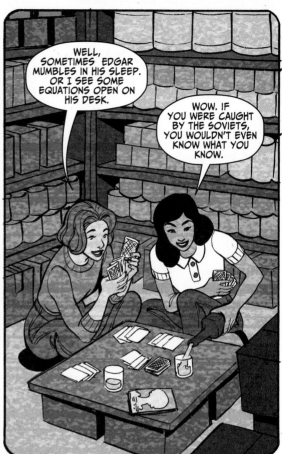

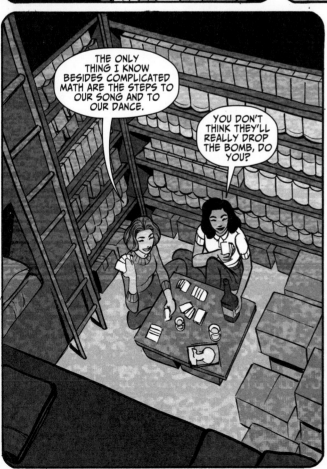

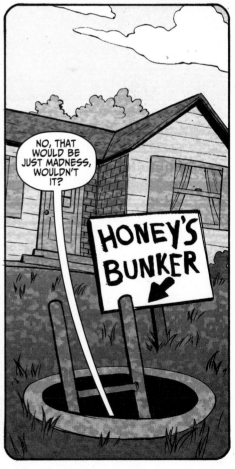

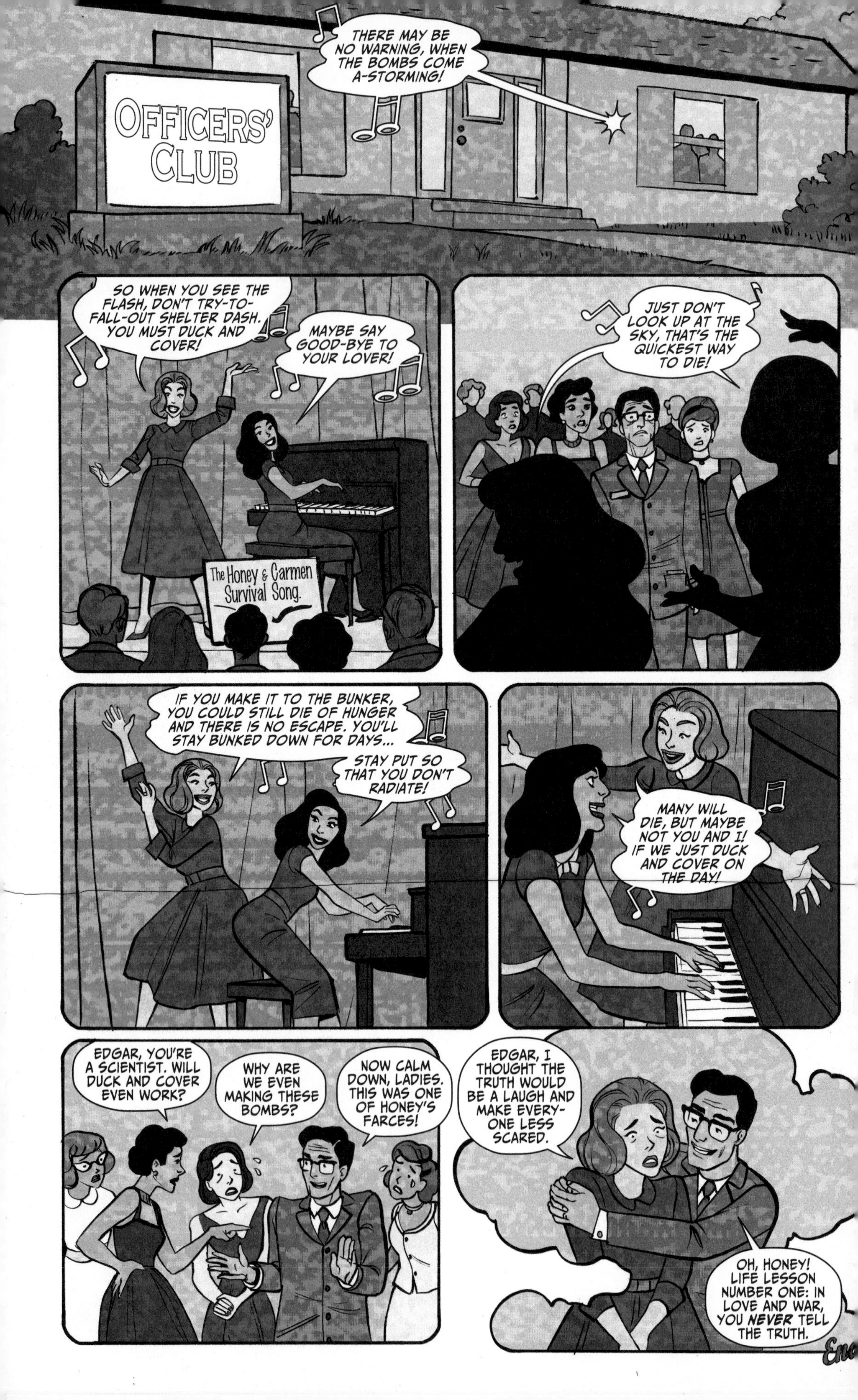
OFFICERS' CLUB
THERE MAY BE NO WARNING, WHEN THE BOMBS COME A-STORMING!
SO WHEN YOU SEE THE FLASH, DON'T TRY-TO-FALL-OUT SHELTER DASH. YOU MUST DUCK AND COVER!
MAYBE SAY GOOD-BYE TO YOUR LOVER!
The Honey & Carmen Survival Song.
JUST DON'T LOOK UP AT THE SKY, THAT'S THE QUICKEST WAY TO DIE!
IF YOU MAKE IT TO THE BUNKER, YOU COULD STILL DIE OF HUNGER AND THERE IS NO ESCAPE. YOU'LL STAY BUNKED DOWN FOR DAYS...
STAY PUT SO THAT YOU DON'T RADIATE!
MANY WILL DIE, BUT MAYBE NOT YOU AND I! IF WE JUST DUCK AND COVER ON THE DAY!
EDGAR, YOU'RE A SCIENTIST. WILL DUCK AND COVER EVEN WORK?
WHY ARE WE EVEN MAKING THESE BOMBS?
NOW CALM DOWN, LADIES. THIS WAS ONE OF HONEY'S FARCES!
EDGAR, I THOUGHT THE TRUTH WOULD BE A LAUGH AND MAKE EVERY-ONE LESS SCARED.
OH, HONEY! LIFE LESSON NUMBER ONE: IN LOVE AND WAR, YOU NEVER TELL THE TRUTH.

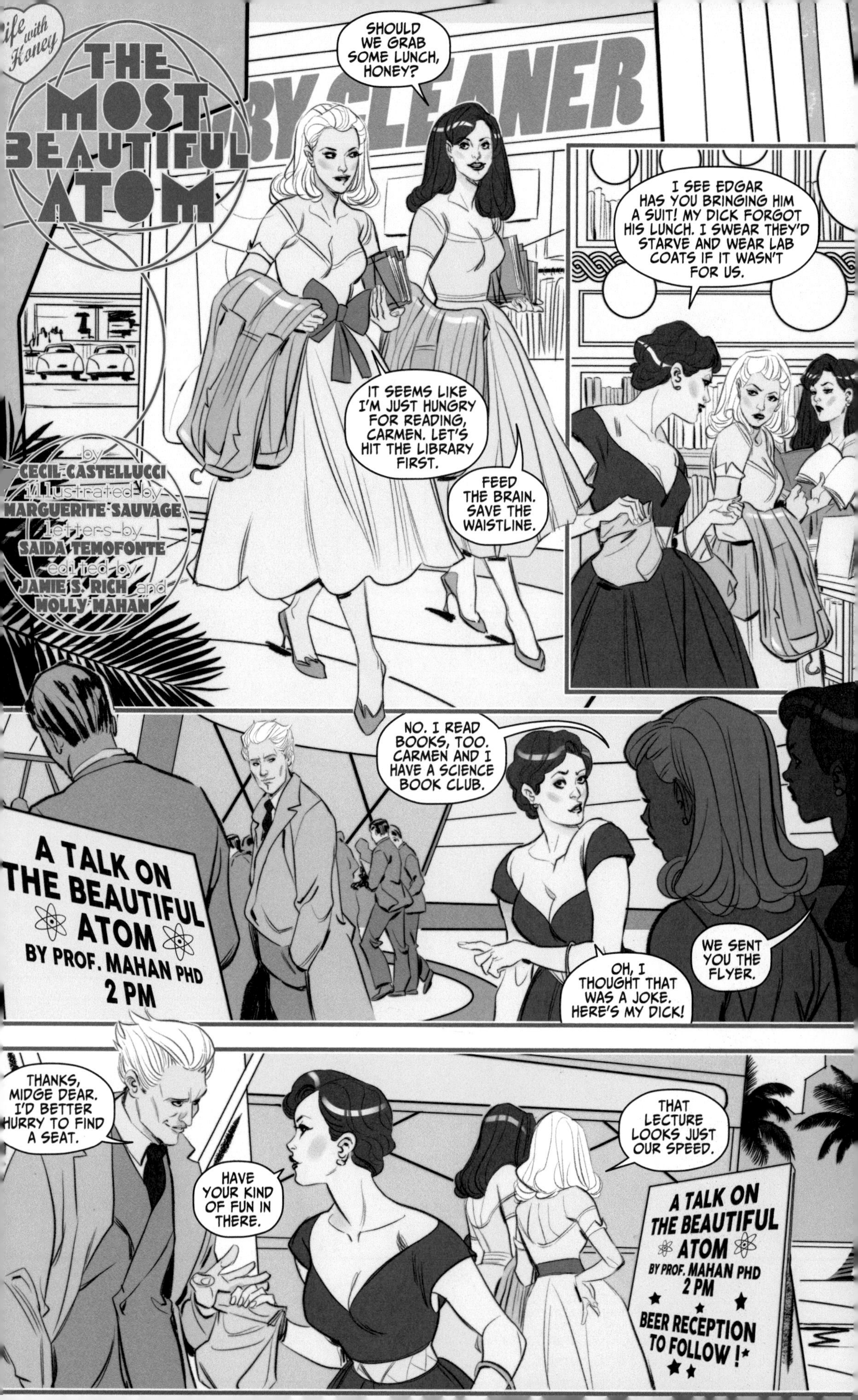
Life with Honey
THE MOST BEAUTIFUL ATOM
SHOULD WE GRAB SOME LUNCH, HONEY?
BY CLEANER
I SEE EDGAR HAS YOU BRINGING HIM A SUIT! MY DICK FORGOT HIS LUNCH. I SWEAR THEY'D STARVE AND WEAR LAB COATS IF IT WASN'T FOR US.
IT SEEMS LIKE I'M JUST HUNGRY FOR READING, CARMEN. LET'S HIT THE LIBRARY FIRST.
FEED THE BRAIN. SAVE THE WAISTLINE.
by CECIL CASTELLUCCI illustrated by MARGUERITE SAUVAGE letters by SAIDA TEMOFONTE edited by JAMIE S. RICH and MOLLY MAHAN
A TALK ON THE BEAUTIFUL ATOM BY PROF. MAHAN PHD 2 PM
NO. I READ BOOKS, TOO. CARMEN AND I HAVE A SCIENCE BOOK CLUB.
OH, I THOUGHT THAT WAS A JOKE. HERE'S MY DICK!
WE SENT YOU THE FLYER.
THANKS, MIDGE DEAR. I'D BETTER HURRY TO FIND A SEAT.
HAVE YOUR KIND OF FUN IN THERE.
THAT LECTURE LOOKS JUST OUR SPEED.
A TALK ON THE BEAUTIFUL ATOM BY PROF. MAHAN PHD 2 PM
BEER RECEPTION TO FOLLOW!

Panel 1:
WE'RE HERE, WE SHOULD GO.

THINKING GIVES YOU WRINKLES, HONEY. I CAN'T AFFORD THAT.

YOU GIVE ME WRINKLES.

Panel 2:
BESIDES, WE CAN'T ATTEND. WE'RE NOT SCIENTISTS, WE'RE WOMEN!

SO WHAT? WE CAN LEARN ANYTHING A MAN CAN.

MORE THAN THEM, I'D WAGER.

Panel 3:
SORRY, LADIES, THIS IS FOR PhDs ONLY. YOU HAVE TO BE A SCIENTIST.

BUT I AM A SCIENTIST OF THE HUMAN CONDITION. IT'S NOT FAIR.

WHAT SHE SAID.

Panel 4:
GOOD-BYE, LADIES. THE ONLY THING I DO WITH MY HEAD IS WASH MY HAIR.

IF THEY'RE SUPPOSED TO BE THE SMART ONES, WHY DO MEN ACT SO STUPID?

A MYSTERY FOR YEARS.

CARMEN! DO YOU HAVE YOUR MAKEUP BAG WITH YOU? I HAVE AN IDEA.

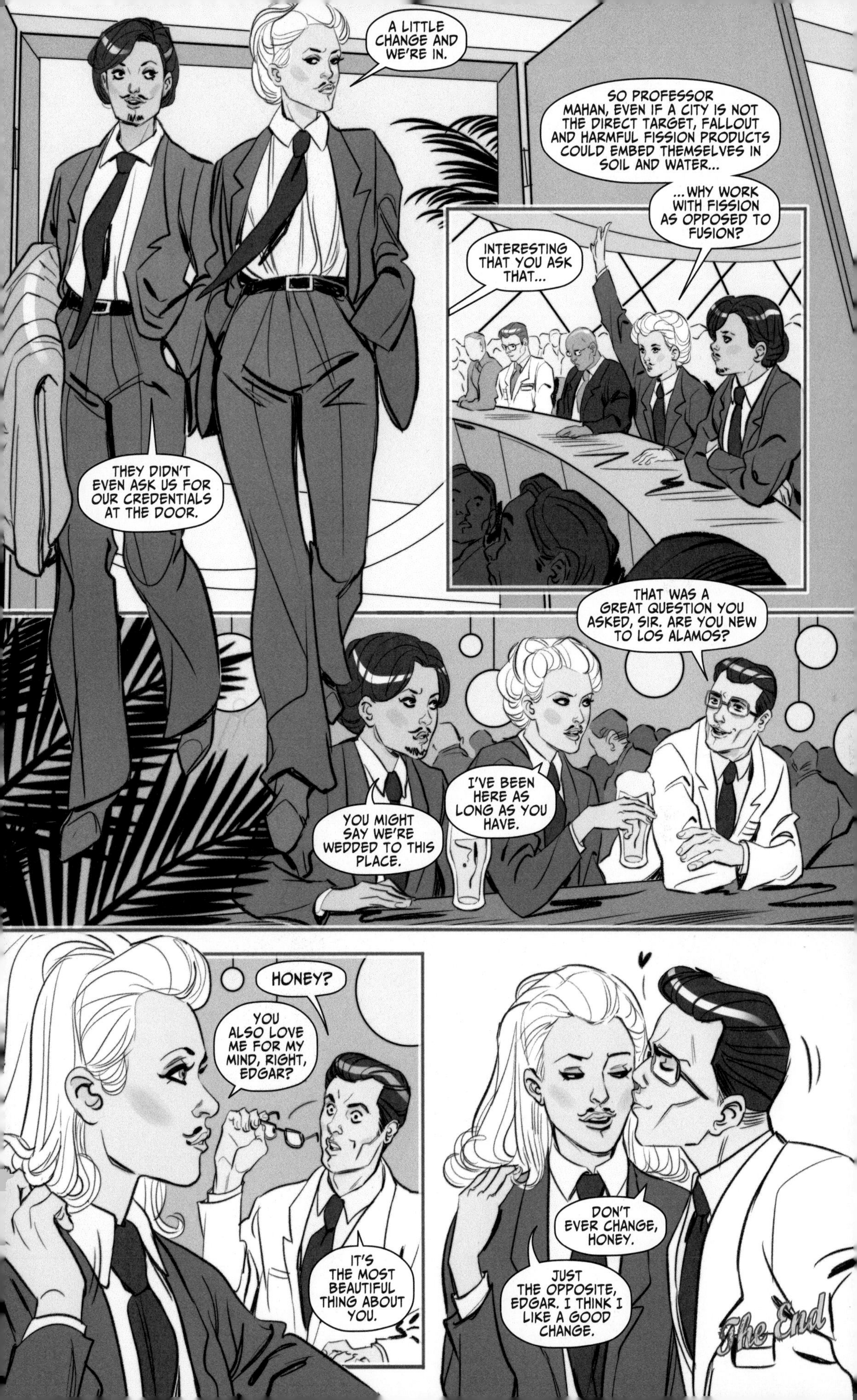
A LITTLE CHANGE AND WE'RE IN.
THEY DIDN'T EVEN ASK US FOR OUR CREDENTIALS AT THE DOOR.
SO PROFESSOR MAHAN, EVEN IF A CITY IS NOT THE DIRECT TARGET, FALLOUT AND HARMFUL FISSION PRODUCTS COULD EMBED THEMSELVES IN SOIL AND WATER...
...WHY WORK WITH FISSION AS OPPOSED TO FUSION?
INTERESTING THAT YOU ASK THAT...
THAT WAS A GREAT QUESTION YOU ASKED, SIR. ARE YOU NEW TO LOS ALAMOS?
I'VE BEEN HERE AS LONG AS YOU HAVE.
YOU MIGHT SAY WE'RE WEDDED TO THIS PLACE.
HONEY?
YOU ALSO LOVE ME FOR MY MIND, RIGHT, EDGAR?
IT'S THE MOST BEAUTIFUL THING ABOUT YOU.
DON'T EVER CHANGE, HONEY.
JUST THE OPPOSITE, EDGAR. I THINK I LIKE A GOOD CHANGE.
The End

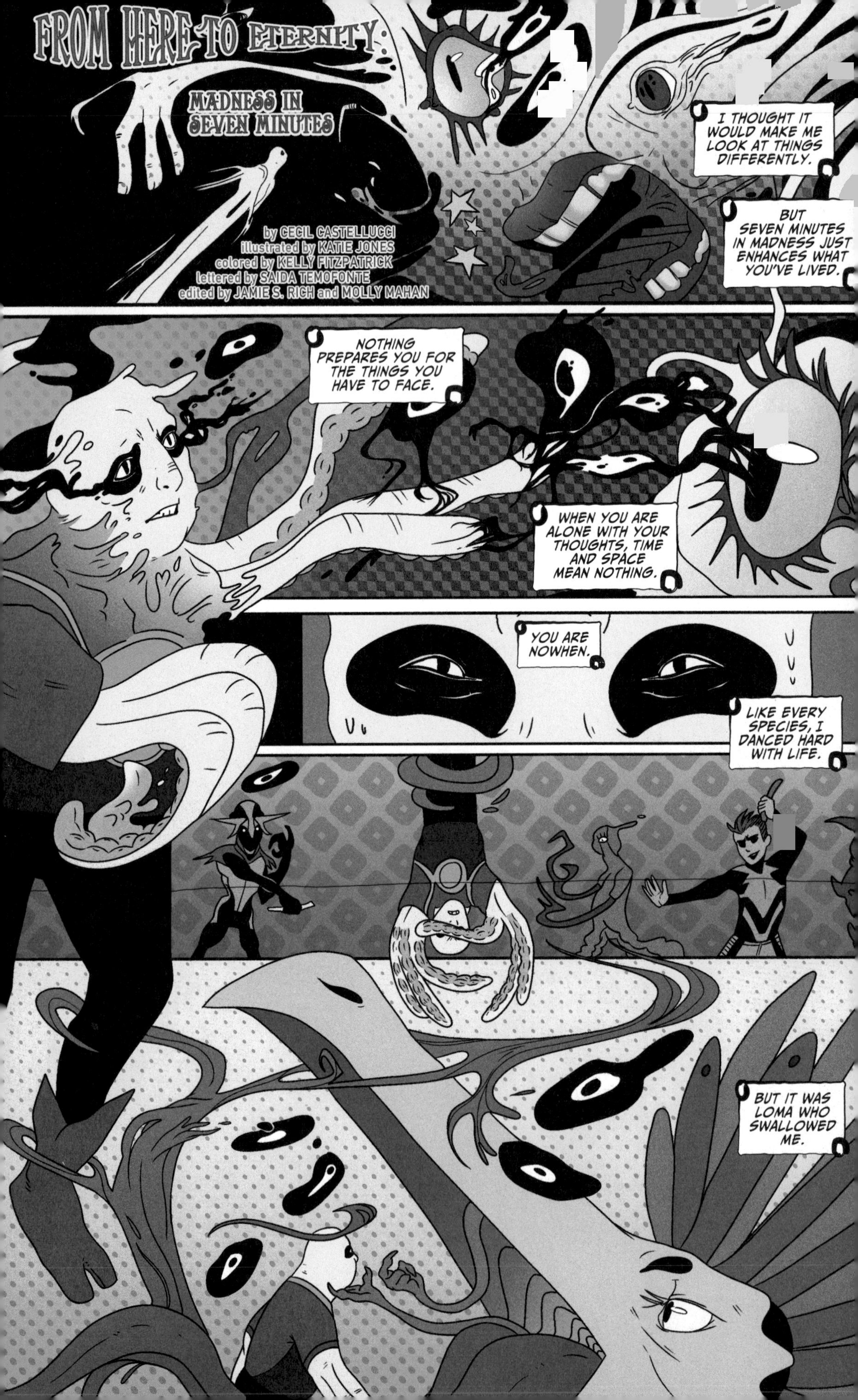
FROM HERE TO ETERNITY:
MADNESS IN SEVEN MINUTES
by CECIL CASTELLUCCI
illustrated by KATIE JONES
colored by KELLY FITZPATRICK
lettered by SAIDA TEMOFONTE
edited by JAMIE S. RICH and MOLLY MAHAN
I THOUGHT IT WOULD MAKE ME LOOK AT THINGS DIFFERENTLY.
BUT SEVEN MINUTES IN MADNESS JUST ENHANCES WHAT YOU'VE LIVED.
NOTHING PREPARES YOU FOR THE THINGS YOU HAVE TO FACE.
WHEN YOU ARE ALONE WITH YOUR THOUGHTS, TIME AND SPACE MEAN NOTHING.
YOU ARE NOWHEN.
LIKE EVERY SPECIES, I DANCED HARD WITH LIFE.
BUT IT WAS LOMA WHO SWALLOWED ME.

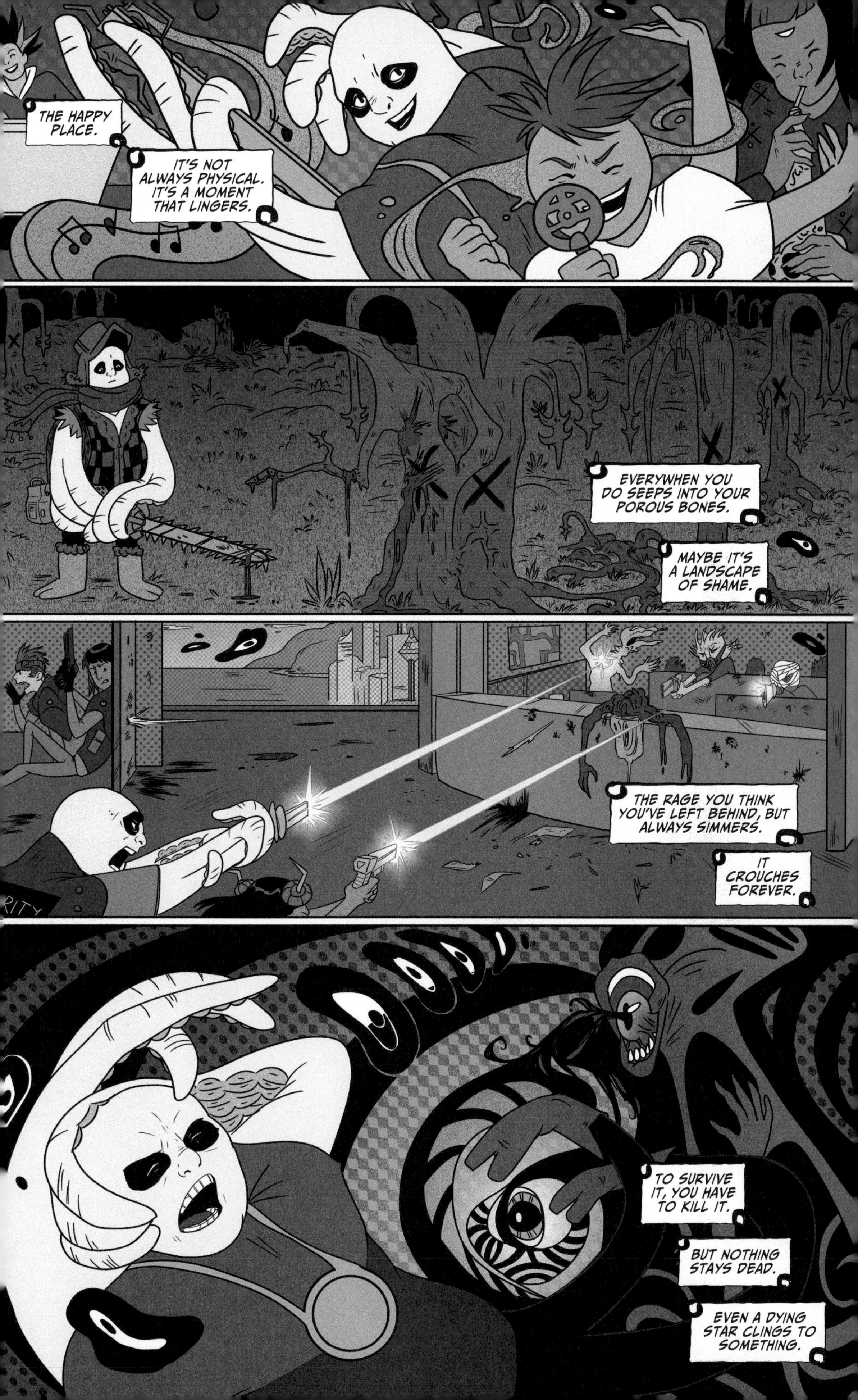
THE HAPPY PLACE.
IT'S NOT ALWAYS PHYSICAL. IT'S A MOMENT THAT LINGERS.
EVERYWHEN YOU DO SEEPS INTO YOUR POROUS BONES.
MAYBE IT'S A LANDSCAPE OF SHAME.
THE RAGE YOU THINK YOU'VE LEFT BEHIND, BUT ALWAYS SIMMERS.
IT CROUCHES FOREVER.
TO SURVIVE IT, YOU HAVE TO KILL IT.
BUT NOTHING STAYS DEAD.
EVEN A DYING STAR CLINGS TO SOMETHING.

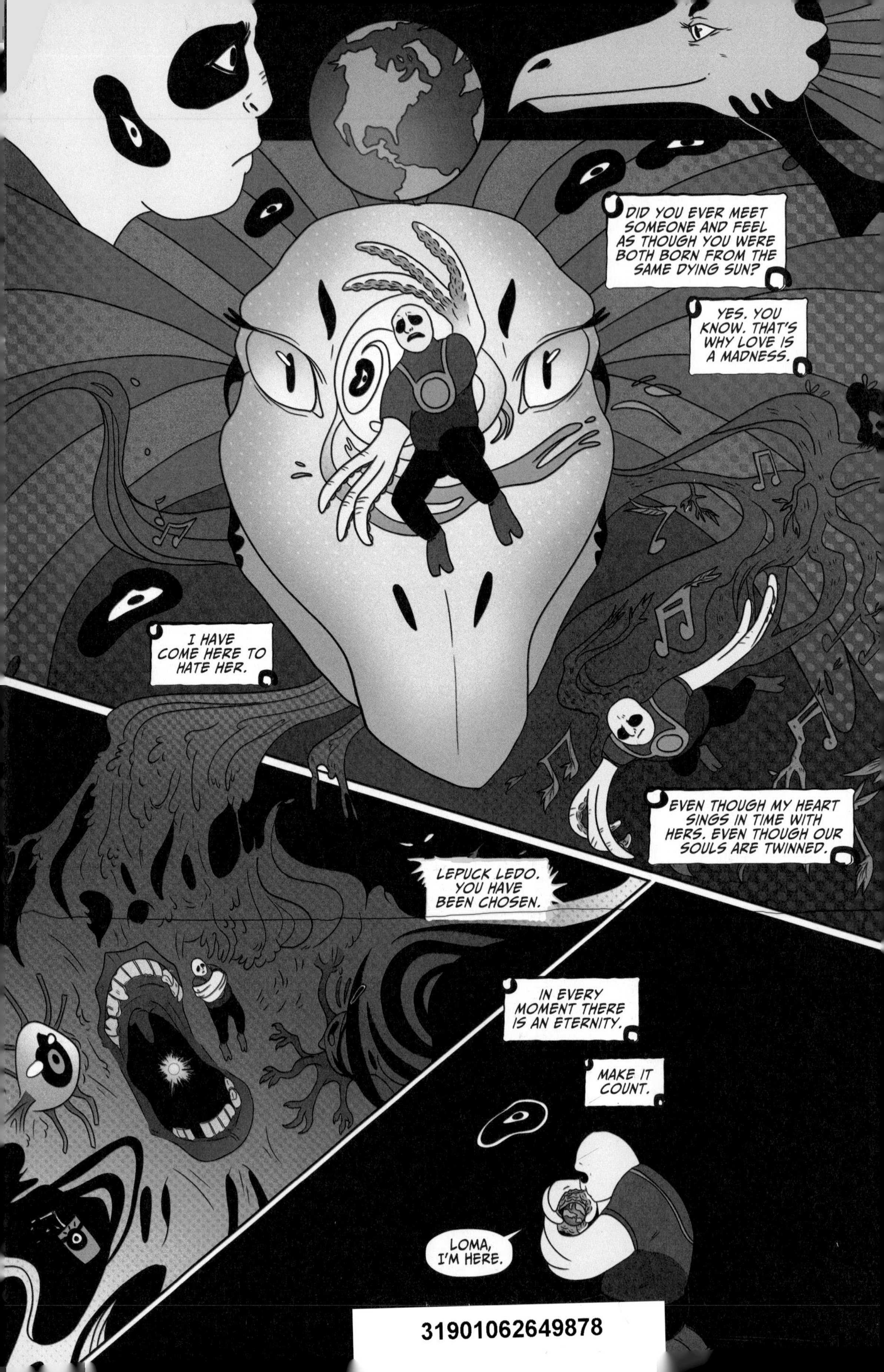
DID YOU EVER MEET SOMEONE AND FEEL AS THOUGH YOU WERE BOTH BORN FROM THE SAME DYING SUN?
YES. YOU KNOW. THAT'S WHY LOVE IS A MADNESS.
I HAVE COME HERE TO HATE HER.
EVEN THOUGH MY HEART SINGS IN TIME WITH HERS. EVEN THOUGH OUR SOULS ARE TWINNED.
LEPUCK LEDO. YOU HAVE BEEN CHOSEN.
IN EVERY MOMENT THERE IS AN ETERNITY.
MAKE IT COUNT.
LOMA, I'M HERE.